A View from the Hover

I owe five people a big thank you for their help with this book:

My wife Adèle for her computing expertise in turning my sketches into the diagrams I wanted and her patience as I nit-picked the results of her labours.

My proof reader Val for her never ending enthusiasm about correcting my grammar and the skill she brought to that job.

Ian and Martin at Seager Publishing for never once complaining over the time I took to write it and Ollie for his help with preparing this edition.

A View from the Hover

A View from the Hover

My Life in Aviation

John Farley

Originally published by Seager Publishing Ltd in 2008
This second edition published in 2010
9 Riverside Court, Lower Bristol Road, Bath BA2 3DZ

www.aviewfromthehover.com

Cover photograph: BAE SYSTEMS
Back cover photograph: Jamie Hunter/Aviacom

ISBN 978 0 95327 52 0 5 (Hardback)

Printed and bound in the UK by Cambrian Printers

Chapter 1

Start here

One day in 1982 I found myself thinking about the people I worked with at Kingston and Dunsfold. At the time I was flying Harrier engine development trials at the USAF Flight Test Centre at Edwards Air Force Base in California. We were there because 'Edwards', as it is known, had several huge dry lakebed runways which made it easy to carry out a glide landing should the engine misbehave. Because of the sheer space available, Edwards was also the landing site of choice in the early days of the NASA Space Shuttle. In a wonderful PR spectacular NASA arranged for the Shuttle to return from orbit and land at Edwards on Independence Day 1982 and for the crew to be welcomed by President Reagan. Naturally such an event on a major public holiday attracted enormous numbers of people and their cars, SUVs and camper vans to the perimeter of the highly guarded lakebed test site.

The McDonnell Douglas hangar that we were using had a control room at the top with a prime view of the lakebed. Come mid-morning on the 4th July this was full of some 50 VIP guests eagerly awaiting the arrival of the Shuttle. Jack Jackson, a McDonnell Douglas test pilot colleague of mine, was standing at the big observation window hosting the visitors and commenting on the unfolding events. To anyone in the test flying business watching the Shuttle appear miles up as a mere dot streaming a contrail and seeing it decelerate from many times the speed of sound, dropping a double sonic boom in the process, followed by a glide round in a big circuit to a perfect touchdown was the ultimate demonstration of technology and capability. I for one was certainly very impressed. Naturally Jack's VIPs were in full cheering mode as the President and the marching bands moved off below to greet the returning astronauts. Jack then announced completely off the cuff and because he was like that, "There is a Brit at the back of the room. Let's ask him what he thinks of what we have just seen". Every head turned round and looked at me. It is not easy for a lone Brit to keep his end up in those circumstances then I thought about all the unsung workers at home who had contributed to the Harrier standing on the pan below. So I waved my arm generally in the Harrier's direction, shrugged my shoulders and said, "Pity it didn't land vertically".

Despite starting with that story, this book is not an autobiography about my test flying days as I did not keep a diary and without one I cannot remember enough names from the past.

It is an obvious point to make but with companies that manufacture single-seat military aircraft the test pilots are the only employees who are able to experience the product that their company sells. In my view this places on them a duty to communicate at all levels from the main board to the shop floor.

Working at Dunsfold convinced me of the important contributions made by many unsung members of the organisation. Indeed, without meaning to be dramatic, a test pilot's safety can depend on the quality of work carried out by some of the most junior people in the company, such as those who install a new engine or spot a fault before the aircraft is wheeled out to fly. Then there are the flight test engineers who brief us in detail on the tests and others who help us strap in and double check the seat connections. The list of people who directly support test pilots is a long one. With no diary how can I do justice to so many people?

All of which begs the question what is this book about and why am I writing it? Quite simply I have been helped in my understanding of aeroplanes and the flying of them by some very special people and I have learned much which would have been useful to know when I started in aviation. Therefore this is a book that I hope may be of interest to other pilots, especially those who fly as a hobby. I would also like to think that some chapters are helpful when it comes to documenting what the UK has achieved in the field of jet VSTOL.

From Chapter 10 onwards the book changes to something that readers, especially private pilots, can dip into on a subject by subject basis should they like to know my views or perhaps benefit from my experiences and mistakes. In putting together some of these chapters I have revisited articles that I wrote for *FLYER* magazine over several years, expanding some topics beyond the confines governing a monthly column while combining others to better cover a particular subject. There is no significance to the order of these chapters and each one is intended to stand alone. However, in order to avoid repetition, Chapters 11 and 12 do need the reader to have read Chapter 10.

The chapters vary in length and I am sure some of the longer ones will not be for everybody but this book is not meant to be read from front to back but by chapter and topic according to the reader's interests. Some chapters have Annexes as repositories for specialist or detailed information likely to be of interest to only a few people.

Finally, because our views are always the result of our own experiences, the next chapter describes how I came to be interested in aviation and the start of my early career which may help you appreciate why I write what I do later on.

To be able to work and play in the aviation business in one capacity or another for over 50 years has been a real privilege.

Chapter 2

My early background

While I have no idea what I was doing last month, my first serious aviation-related memory is permanently etched on my mind. It was Sunday 3rd September 1939, just after 11am and I was a six-and-a-half year old lad playing in the back garden of my parents' shop that formed part of the main terrace of shops in the village of Ore on the northern outskirts of Hastings. My mother was leaning out of an upstairs window shouting at me to come in at once over the noise of the air-raid siren that was wailing from the top of the church tower just down the road. The noise of the siren was strangely frightening. A few weeks earlier when looking out of our attic window I had seen a Graf Zeppelin going by low and slow on a westerly heading. My parents had scared me at the time by saying that I should not be up there when "those things were about".

The penny gradually dropped after that Sunday in the garden and I realised all the adults around me were very worried about being attacked from the air. The first bombs fell on Hastings on the 26th July 1940 and I remember two quite well. One dug a groove in the pavement outside our shop, skipped down the road and blew in the church windows. The other knocked a corner off my school. It was only 7.15 in the morning so we kids were still at home but a teacher was killed.

Then a maiden aunt gave me a book on aircraft recognition for my tenth birthday. I don't know what gave her that idea but the book turned out to be everything to me. At that age one has a memory like a sponge and in went every dot, comma and three view aircraft silhouette. It was destined to be the first of many wartime books on the subject of aircraft recognition which I acquired. Such books were not intended to enthral youngsters but to help adults decide whether to shoot or wave. When you saw an aeroplane flying low up the street in those days there was only one question that mattered – was it one of ours or one of theirs? Years later as Manager of Dunsfold Aerodrome I sometimes had to deal with irate neighbours and their noise complaints. Where possible I used to visit them and if they looked as old as me or older, I used to put on a very serious expression, apologise and explain that we had a job to do. Then I would ask if they remembered "the times when all that mattered was whether it was one of ours". This usually produced the teapot and a sensible chat.

I was 12 when the war ended and like many young lads of that era I spent a lot of time making model aeroplanes. Initially they were of the sort that flew because you threw them and later because you wound up their rubber band motor. I don't know why but even then I had not the slightest interest in making flying scale models of real aircraft only pure model aeroplanes that were designed to fly as well as possible. Performance was all that mattered. I must have done something right because after I joined the local aeromodelling club I had some success in competitions even in the adult category. My first flight was also from our model flying field when a Miles Messenger dropped in there in 1949 and offered trips for five shillings. The chap was kind enough to find and orbit our shop. I can clearly remember thinking our street looked very strange from above.

With this background and the end of school on the horizon I naturally wanted to become an RAF pilot. It was 1949 and that summer an RAF recruiting trailer set up shop on Hastings pier so naturally I was there like a shot. Among the leaflets I took home was one that listed the medical requirements for aircrew and just like I can remember that first air-raid siren, I can still remember the feeling in the pit of my stomach as I read 'No deformity to the hands or feet' because by then I was down to eight toes and nine and a half fingers. In those days if you were an only child of Victorian parents you did not expect to discuss life choices with them and careers advice at school had simply not been invented. As a result I brooded and the outcome was that I decided (please don't laugh) that if I learned how to design aeroplanes, the RAF would be so pleased to have an aircraft designer who wanted to be a pilot that they would not worry about my fingers and toes.

Having asked around, it appeared that the three year aircraft engineering course at the de Havilland Technical School at Hatfield was the best in the UK. However the fees were £3,000. Goodness knows what sort of money that would be today, although I suspect it would make current tuition fees seem pretty reasonable. Clearly there was no way I could go there. Then I learned about the five year Ministry of Supply civil service engineering apprenticeships at various research establishments, including the Royal Aircraft Establishment at Farnborough. These were not only free, they actually paid you thirty shillings a week so that you could share a room with another apprentice in a YMCA hostel. Problem solved. The only snag was that you had to pass a competitive civil service entrance exam the syllabus for which included topics not even taught at my school. I went off to the headmaster to ask his permission for me to spend the next four months on my own in the 'spare' classroom with a bunch of 'Teach Yourself' books. He agreed. It really was a different world in those days.

When the results of the exams were published only 302 of over 700 applicants were called forward for interview to compete for the 30 places at Farnborough and I was virtually at the bottom of this list with 631 marks out of a possible 900 from the written subjects. This is not altogether surprising when you think of my DIY preparation. The interview went better and I got 280 out of 300 with only one chap getting a better score of 290. The combination was enough to get me up to eighth overall and a place at the RAE Technical College as a student engineering apprentice.

Once on the course it was clear I was way behind all the others academically and I was bottom of the heap at the end of the first term. I failed three of the five exams and was sent home for Christmas 1950 with a report for my father to sign that said, "Must exert more effort, both in the classroom and in the training shop. Ability below average". My Dad, bless him, took one look at it and said that I must have been given somebody else's report. I explained that I had no doubt there was no mix-up and I needed time to catch up. At the end of the five years I had managed to get up to second in my year and was offered a further two year Diploma Course at the new College of Aeronautics at Cranfield.

Fortunately I had the sense to realise that I had been working much harder than my mates in order to compensate for my limited ability in maths and thus it was silly to contemplate a career as a professional engineer. Putting in a special effort for a few years was one thing, to do it for the rest of your life was quite another. Accordingly I told the college principal, Mr R D Peggs, that I did not want to go to Cranfield but had decided to join the RAF and become a test pilot. He lost his temper and had a major rant about wasting all my education, the efforts of his staff and so on but I am glad to say I was mature enough to recognise my limitations and stick to my plan. I really did have a plan and the RAF test pilot stuff was not a simple throw-away wannabe line although with hindsight Mr Peggs may have seen it as such. He was too cross to ask me to elaborate and therefore I saw no point in volunteering an explanation.

In those days the RAE offered its student apprentices what was known as a sandwich course. The year was divided into three terms and, apart from the first term which was spent full time in the college classrooms and training workshop, our time was split between college and one of the RAE departments. Naturally many of the departments were flight testing the ideas of their boffins using one of the many aircraft that were at RAE between 1950 and 1955. Many of these were multi-crew and needed flight test observers to help out with operation of cameras, instrumentation and the like. Student apprentices were allowed to volunteer for flight test observer duties and I did just that. This meant that I flew with and got to know, in a master/servant way, several of the RAE test pilots of that period. As a result I no longer wanted to join the RAF as a pilot but I wanted to do research flying, preferably on the Aerodynamics Research Flight where (in my view) the most interesting flying was being carried out.

Because of this developing ambition I made a nuisance of myself in the final year of my course until I found one of the senior departmental heads who had social connections with the Commandant of the Empire Test Pilots' School and asked him for an introduction. As a result I received this note from Mr W G Bushell.

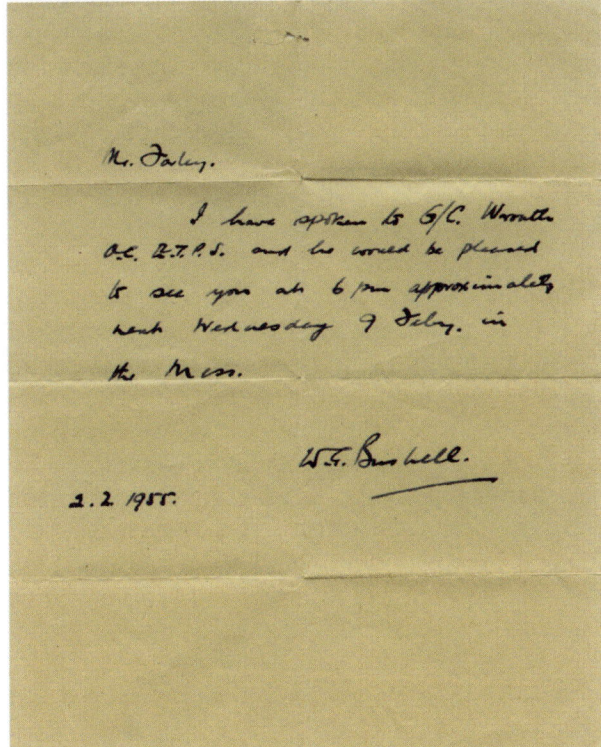

"I have spoken to G/C Wroath O.C. E.T.P.S, and he would be pleased to see you at 6pm approximately next Wednesday 9 Feb in the Mess."

The great man invited me into his office and after I had sat down said simply, "Why do you want to be a test pilot?" Although I was too young to realise it at the time, I had just been asked the best question anyone can ask any interviewee because the answer can be extremely revealing about what thought they have given to the matter. As background to my reply you should know that by chance the room I shared in the YMCA hostel was directly across a narrow road from the main entrance to the ETPS officers' mess. Therefore each Saturday night I had a splendid view of the high-heeled young ladies getting out of various MG sports cars and going in to the floodlit mess on the arms of test pilots. In the immediate foreground was my sit up and beg push-bike leaning up against the hostel hedge. To my mind it was clear that I belonged across the road.

Young and naive as I was I realised it was no good saying that I wanted to be a test pilot because they had more money and a better social life so I tried, "I am fascinated by aeroplanes and want to learn all I can about them. It seems to me test pilots have more chance to do that than most people." That got me to question two and a 45 minute discussion that included what technical qualifications I would have at the end of my apprenticeship. He then escorted me to the door of the mess, explained that I seemed to be just the sort of youngster they liked to have come on the course, put a hand on my shoulder and said, "But you will have to go away and learn to fly first". He did not say that in any sarcastic way but almost as an aside. I walked back towards the hostel with all the arrogance of youth thinking to myself, "Right, the RAF can teach me to do that".

However, there was still the fingers and toes thing to be sorted. Fortunately in those days you could ask the RAF for pre-assessment which meant you did the medical and flying aptitude tests and they told you whether you qualified for pilot training. During this medical I found myself standing in a line of stark naked applicants while a Wing Commander doctor in a white coat walked slowly along looking intently at each of us in turn. When he got to my feet and saw that a toe had been removed from both he said, "That was a neat job. I wonder who did that?" Without waiting for any reply he moved on. The only person in the RAF ever to comment about my bent and distorted little finger (which had been broken in a couple of places by a diesel engined model aeroplane propeller, how else?) was a drill sergeant at our officer cadet training camp who did not like the way it stuck out when I saluted and thought I was taking the mick.

Clearly I might have been successful had I applied for pilot training straight from school but in that case I would not have gone to RAE and would have been much less likely to enjoy a career in test flying without such a background. Sometimes things work out for the best.

My RAF flying training started in December 1955 at No 2 FTS Hullavington on the Piston Provost. My instructor was Master Pilot Jimmy Hindson. Master pilot was the most senior non-commissioned aircrew rank of those days making him a warrant officer. Although I was an acting pilot officer, he made it very clear that I was to address him as 'Sir'. He got no argument from me. At some stage of the war he had lost the thumb on his right hand so he held the stick by the simple expedient of planting his hand on the top of it. He spoke with an upper-class accent that you could cut with a knife and he could fly like an angel. Hard and strict though he was, I never felt I had other than the right instructor for me and what more can any student ask for?

After Hullavington we went to No 8 FTS at Swinderby where we flew the two-seat Vampire T11s and the single-seat Vampire 5s plus one Vampire 9 (a 5 fitted with the new-fangled pressurisation). The T11s had ejection seats but the 5s and the 9 did not. My new instructor, Flight Lieutenant Dickie Lord, was the archetypal fighter pilot type with bent down sides to his SD cap and top button undone even on parade. We all wanted to be just like him when we grew up. As with Jimmy Hindson, I again felt I had just the right instructor for me. Two events will illustrate Dickie Lord's style. We had just taken off in a T11 and I was doing the after takeoff checks when I noticed the fuel gauge showed zero. "Sir," I said and pointed at the gauge. He seemed totally unfazed and remarked, "Well Farley, we either have a gauge failure or a massive fuel leak. We shall know which quite soon." Some 40 minutes later he remarked, "Take us back, Farley. We will do a few minutes less than usual to be on the safe side." On another day he walked out to join me as I was finishing the outside checks. I said the aircraft was fine except that there were no screws holding the acorn fairing between the fin and tailplane on the port side. My first thoughts were that the screws had been taken out at his request to test how well I did my checks. His remarks before he shot off towards the hangar made me realise this was not the case!

Then on the 4th April 1957, a few weeks before our wings parade due in June, the Minister of Defence, Duncan Sandys, produced his infamous White Paper announcing that the RAF would have no more manned fighters as they would be replaced by surface-to-air missiles. This caused

11

more concern among the instructors than the students because we had other more pressing things to worry about, like passing the course. Naturally Sandys was wrong. There would be manned fighters and we were determined to fly them. Accordingly we pressed on. It was only after our wings parade that we got our first clue that the post-Sandys RAF was not sure what to do with us. Although expecting to go at once to start a Hunter conversion course we were actually sent home on extended leave.

Wings parade Swinderby
14th June 1957.

Getting started in aviation
was a very serious business!

A month later we got posting notices to 7 FTS Valley which had become a holding unit for new pilots. Like Swinderby, Valley had Vampire 5s, 9s and T11s but with fewer students joining they had spare aircraft available to keep any newly-winged wonders in practice. Unlike Swinderby, none of us was killed at Valley although I don't know why. At this stage, with only about 100 hours solo to our names, flying together in two-seat Vampire T11s, the how fast, how high, how low, temptations were countless.

On one sortie I was accompanied by Barrie Tonkinson, who later tested Harriers for HSA. At 40,000 ft he spotted a Valley instructor leading a pair of students (not real pilots like us, you understand) as they popped up through the cloud tops at 15,000 ft. To a pair of fighter pilots in waiting they were just asking to be bounced. The dive, plus the flash past underneath and the pull up in front of them, doubtless achieved the aim of startling the formation but it also overstressed our aircraft, broke an engine bearing and left the poor DH Goblin with no alternative but to shake and seize. Being above total cloud cover, over the Welsh mountains, with limited standby instruments and no means of navigation in a gliding jet might have bothered an experienced crew. Not us though. We just did as we had been trained to do which was to get some steers towards base, establish ourselves in the overhead, spiral down with a stack of knots, break cloud somewhere in the circuit, use the excess speed to adjust the circuit shape, turn finals and, when sure of getting in one third of the way down the runway, bring the touchdown point forward by use of the flaps. I got to sort this out since I had signed for the aircraft while Barrie got on with the more skilled and untrained task of trying to remove the lock on the resetting knob on the g meter. This involved much use of his dinghy knife as a screwdriver, many slits in his flying gloves and some blood being spilt. We kept our speed up on the runway, cleared at the end on to the taxiway and got out to await a lift. We were very mindful that in those days it was a cardinal sin at any jet airfield to block the runway because so many people came back without much fuel. Given the way things turned out it is clear there was a Being of greater ability than Duncan Sandys looking after the future of RAF pilots. Not altogether surprising when you think about it.

After a short wait the Wing Commander Flying drove up in his Land Rover. He asked what the trouble was and we replied, "The engine, Sir." He did not say a word, got a broom out of the back of his Land Rover and pushed the handle into the air intake. When he found the engine would not turn, he remarked, "Well done chaps" and without further words gave us a lift back to the squadron offices. Later the "Well done chaps" was retracted when the instructor we had bounced returned in quite an unpleasant frame of mind. However, after four months at Valley some of us did eventually make the Hunter conversion course at Chivenor. We went straight on to the Mk 4 version as there were no two-seat Hunters in those days. It seemed like a spaceship to us after the Vampire. With hindsight it was akin to passing your driving test and then being given a Formula 1 racing car to play with. Three months later six of us were told we had passed the course.

Then things *really* went wrong.

It was now nine months after the Sandys White Paper and the RAF had decided that only permanent commission (PC) pilots would be posted to the 'dying' fighter squadrons. There were two PC chaps among our six so off they went to Hunters, while the remaining four of us on short service commissions were posted to a ground job. I cannot begin to describe what a blow that ground posting was to us. For two years we had struggled, against seemingly impossible odds, to satisfy our instructors only to be grounded by a politician. We had studied, we had marched and we had flown. We had done everything asked of us. That even included walking through a village knocking on doors and getting permission to enter people's gardens in order to pick up pieces of wrecked Vampire after one of us was killed on a solo sortie. We did not deserve a ground tour. We had been good enough and determined enough for anything the RAF asked of us. We deserved to fly.

Our posting was to the Royal Radar Establishment (RRE) at Malvern. In those days Fighter Command, to which we now belonged, was struggling with the problem of how to defend the UK with subsonic Hunters from Russian bombers that had a supersonic dash capability.

One idea was to fly a Hunter towards an incoming bomber but on a parallel track offset by a few miles to the side of the threat. Then, when the bomber was still some miles away, turn the fighter in towards its track and hopefully get a shot at it as it momentarily crossed in front. For such a manoeuvre to succeed the fighter had to be displaced to the side by just the right amount and turn in at just the right moment, along a very precise curved path. Only then would the target pass across the fighter's nose within range of its guns, say between 100 and 500 yards. Furthermore, the interception pattern depended on the bomber's speed and altitude. In order to see if this would work, a trials unit was set up at Malvern using an experimental ground controlled interception station called Z block.

In one room was the fighter controller with his radar display and lots of transparent sheets (called overlays) on which were drawn various combinations of bomber and fighter tracks for different speed and height cases. In another room was a technician able to 'fly' a simulated bomber blip across the controller's screen. When the controller saw an incoming 'raid' he had to select and alert a UK fighter base so that a fighter, 'flown' from that location by another technician in another room, could be scrambled. When after a suitable delay the fighter blip appeared on his radar, the controller had to choose the best overlay, slap it on his screen and talk the blip along the path shown. When the interception was a success that was fine but when it failed the RRE boffins needed to know why. Had the controller chosen the wrong overlay? Scrambled the fighter too soon or too late? Issued the wrong instructions to the fighter? Perhaps the fighter pilot had not 'flown' accurately enough? Did the bomber pilot stick to his brief? These questions were left for an observer to answer.

After watching a few interceptions it was easy to spot what had gone wrong and any junior NCO could have done the task. The trouble was Fighter Command had none of those to spare but it did have plenty of new pilot officers without a job including Ken Cooper, Maurice Harvey, Mac McLaughlan and me.

We all lived in a local hotel, the Hornyold Arms. Because the trial had a high priority we worked shifts, involving weekends, evenings and nights, which meant we often had time off during the day and in the middle of the week. None of this luxury lifestyle was the slightest compensation for not flying though, not the slightest. Then one day Mac had to go to Barnstaple Magistrates Court in order to sort out a little matter involving his Austin Healey 2000 car when we were at Chivenor. After his court business was done he paid a visit to our old instructors. He found the station had 84 Hunters and very few students and he was advised that all the flying one could wish for awaited anybody posted to Chivenor.

When Mac got back we talked long into the night about how such a posting might be arranged. I can't remember who first mooted the idea that our salvation lay in the offices of Fighter Command Headquarters at Bentley Priory. The more we considered this, the more certain we all became that this was in fact the case. It was time to plan. We needed to nose around Headquarters but having no invitation, what would be the best time? Wednesday afternoons on RAF stations in the 1950s were traditionally taken up with sport (a perversion so far as real aviators were concerned) and so the number of people minding the shop was greatly reduced. Wednesday afternoon *had* to maximise our chances.

The next Wednesday Mac and I set off for Bentley Priory in his Austin Healey. As we drove I don't think either of us had a clear idea of what we were looking for. What we found was an office that contained two flight lieutenants, one responsible for day-fighter postings, the other for night-fighters. From there on it was all down hill. While the day-fighter guy was busy getting an early lunch before playing sport (ha!) we listened sympathetically to the night-fighter man explaining about his awful ground job and how he had to spend his hours filling in terrible posting forms – like these – when really he should have been flying. When he left for lunch we bade him farewell in the car park.

After his car disappeared round the corner it took only a moment to pop back to his empty office, put four names on the appropriate day-fighter paperwork and leave. The following week our boss at Malvern came to see us. He was very cross. He would never understand the RAF. We had been posted. Just as he had he got us trained and doing a useful job. Posted. It was ridiculous. We pulled long faces, and muttered, "Oh no, not really, Sir!" and added how much we loved working for him on such an important job, to say nothing of living in the Hornyold Arms. The 1957 batch of students at RADA could have done no better.

Ten days later we were airborne at Chivenor. Three weeks after that the Wing Commander Flying stood up at the end of Met Briefing, read out our four names and said, "Together in the Station Commander's Office at nine o'clock and don't take your caps off." What followed was just like a scene from a 'B' movie. Having been marched in by the Station Adjutant we stood in line, at attention, while the Station Commander continued to work, head down, with papers on his desk. He gave no indication that he even knew we were in the room. Eventually, after what seemed an age, he looked us up and down and slowly read out our names from a piece of paper. We stood in silence as he stared at us while our nether regions went sixpence, half a crown and dustbin lid.

"Well is that *you*?"

We each just managed a "Yes, Sir".

He then intoned that he had reason to believe we had interfered with Her Majesty's posting process and finished by barking, "Have you got anything to say for yourselves?"

"No, Sir" came out four times, followed by more silence and more staring on his part.

Finally he spoke. "Well I have. It's the best thing I've heard of since the war. Would you like to go to Hunter Squadrons?"

We all owe that man. It happened for us because Group Captain Pleasance was a WWII commander and a man who understood that what matters above all else with a fighting service is the motivation of its

16

troops. We were certainly motivated. The rest as they say is history. Mac finished up training British Airways 747 captains and Maurice went on to become the one star in charge of the whole RAF air traffic control system. Ken did his time on Hunters and went back to Holyhead to be reunited with his collection of old MG cars while eventually I got to write this book.

I arrived as the new junior pilot on No IV (AC) Squadron at RAF Jever in north Germany in May 1958. It was Cold War time and IV Squadron had just converted from Hunter 4s to Hunter 6s. The boss at the time was a bachelor and only two of the 18 pilots were married because in those days an RAF officer was not allowed even to request *permission* to marry until he was 25. Anyone who then got married had additionally to request permission to 'live out' and not in the mess.

Rather naturally the culture of the squadron was very much centred round flying and the mess bar. Having joined the RAF to be a test pilot not a fighter pilot, I had to make a conscious effort to 'conform' to their (as I saw it then) rather immature approach to aviation. I was totally wrong of course and the prevailing culture was the right one when operating such limited equipment. After all we navigated the Hunters using only a hand held map, a compass and a watch and our weapons were forward facing guns. No different in principle from the Spitfires or Hurricanes used in the Battle of Britain (or indeed the SE5s and Camels of WWI) except our Hunter 6s went a bit faster and higher and our controllers had better radar than their forebears in 1940. The results obtained from such a limited system were always going to be very dependent on the fighting skills of the pilots, hence the obsession of many to show they were the better than everybody else at pulling g, filling the gunnery flag target with holes or drinking beer. I was not by nature good at those things so retreated into the engineering side of our aircraft where it was easier for me to feel superior. I remember putting up posters round the squadron offices that showed the different mod states of our various aircraft and their ejection seats. The 'fighter pilots' seemed agog with indifference.

Alongside all this serious stuff, I was of course extremely excited by the ride offered by the Hunter 6. I was also incredibly proud to be on a fighter squadron and it was a challenge to learn the trade of operating them in the pretty poor weather that often existed in that part of the north German plain. I took the decision to apply to go to ETPS towards the end of this tour, despite being short of the 750 flying hours minimum specified by the school and was backed by my then commanding officer, Sqn Ldr R J Spiers, himself an ETPS graduate. Following the selection procedure, I was told I had insufficient flying experience and that I should go away, build up some hours and re-apply when I could expect to be accepted.

Accordingly I volunteered to go to the RAF Central Flying School (CFS) to learn how to be an instructor – something no fighter pilot worth talking to was ever prepared to consider. My posting from CFS was to the RAF College at Cranwell as an ab-initio instructor on the Jet Provost 3 and 4 aircraft. I finally got what I wanted half way through this tour when I received a posting notice to report to ETPS as a student on No 22 Fixed Wing course. The year was 1963 and, like everyone else, I remember what I was doing when I heard the news that John Kennedy had been shot. Since you also remember what you were up to that day, it follows that you can remember what you were doing when I was at ETPS!

I am going to stop this mini autobiography now because what I did over the next 30 plus years is reflected in the remaining chapters. Eventually I had to give up test flying in single-seat aircraft when the CAA pulled my medical certificate following a wobble on my ECG back in 1995. After that I was still able to do a bit more in multi-crew aeroplanes for a while and my last Harrier test flight was in 1999 in the VAAC research aircraft on a programme that rightly has a chapter all to itself in this book.

Chapter 3

RAE Farnborough

When I started my apprenticeship at the Royal Aircraft Establishment in 1950 its reputation was close to its peak. Indeed the same could probably be said of the UK aircraft industry as a whole.

During the 1950s the UK was able to design and put into RAF service three different V-bombers and the various engines that powered them. It was the time when the UK set about developing the first successful vertical landing jet fighter as well as working on the optimum shape for the world's first supersonic passenger aircraft. By then we had also sent jet engines to the USA and Russia to help them get started in this new field of endeavour. Again, it was the early 50s when the UK licensed the US Glenn L. Martin Company to manufacture the Canberra, our first jet bomber, for the USAF. It was also in the 50s that RAE scientists came up with the idea of fitting an angled deck, steam catapult and mirror landing sight to aircraft carriers – equipment now standard on every USN carrier.

There were no car parks at the RAE because in those days everybody cycled to work. Indeed the area of ground outside the gates devoted to the workforce bike sheds would today have a housing developer making plans for a full blown estate. Apprentices worked in most departments which made them part of the scenery and meant they could wander at will without anybody asking why they were there. Only the special hangar that contained aeroplanes modified to carry the new atomic weapons seemed to have locks on the doors. Happy days and what a place for a young lad to grow up!

During my apprenticeship, I kept a well-folded sheet of ministry foolscap paper on which I had listed all the names of the aircraft I saw on the aerodrome. The list recorded 104 different types (not marks). Some 40 years later I bumped into Wg Cdr Paddy Finch at an RAF College dinner. Paddy had been Wing Commander Flying at the RAE when I was an apprentice and in charge of the test pilots I flew with as an air observer. I mentioned the sheet of paper and the 104 types. He shook his head, wagged his finger and said, "You must have missed a couple then because I had them listed on my office wall and there were 106."

As an example of how things have changed over the last half century, let me tell you what happened during my first visit to the RAE. I was a spectator at the Royal Air Force Flying Display and Exhibition held there in August 1950. The climax of the show was a 'combined operations' assault on an enemy position on the airfield. The enemy 'fort' was a large camouflaged canvas and scaffolding structure positioned on the crowd side of the copse behind which today's Farnborough display aircraft vanish after they land. The commentator explained that the RAF would first soften up the objective with an attack by four Vampire fighters each armed with rockets of the type used by the allies, five years earlier, to attack trains and other targets with their Hawker Typhoons.

Right on cue four Vampires flew fast and low up the runway from the west and, just before the 'Black Sheds' at the eastern end, they pulled up into a steep wingover and dived back towards the target in long line astern. Once settled in the dive, each aircraft fired a full load of 3" 'drains' (as such rockets were called in those days). The noise and smoke as these weapons streaked from the Vampires into the 'fort' was amazing. As the Vampires cleared stage left, a WACO Hadrian glider appeared from overhead and skidded to a halt on the grass alongside the runway. Almost before it had stopped, troops ran from it to take up defensive positions.

Under their covering fire, a section closed with the fort and quickly established that enemy resistance had ceased. At this the troops returned to the glider while some of them set up what looked like rugby goalposts some yards in front of the nose. In no time a rope was draped across the top of the 'goal' and the end attached to the glider towing hook situated on top of the nose behind the cockpit. As the last soldier disappeared into the glider, a Dakota appeared very low and slow over the Black Sheds. Under its tail was a big hook which it used to pick up the rope stretched between the 'goal posts' as it continued on its majestic passage. As the rope pulled tight the glider started to slide forward but, with the attachment point being high up, the glider adopted a nose down attitude causing its skid to dig into the soft grass. For a long moment the glider stopped while the rope stretched and stretched as the Dakota carried inexorably on its way. Then with an almighty lurch the glider shot forward and upward and the troops were gone.

Not surprisingly I was quite impressed by all this and decided that I could not wait to start my training the following month.

Looking back on my apprentice years (age 17 to 22) my main impression is of the sheer quality of the educational opportunities available to us. There were two types of apprentice, craft and student. Craft apprentices were trained to a very high level in many practical engineering skills which enabled them to take up skilled tradesmen roles in the RAE workshops at the end of their training. I was a student apprentice and as such spent three years on craft training before moving on during the final two years to working in the scientific departments. All apprentices did their theoretical studies in the RAE Technical College dedicated to the apprentice training scheme. Craft lads sat a bunch of City and Guilds exams while student apprentices were streamed into either Higher National Certificate (HNC) or Degree courses. My poor academic showing during the original selection process meant I was off to the HNC stream.

As more evidence of how the aviation world has moved on since the 1950s, there were 47 accidents to RAE Farnborough-based aircraft during the time of my training and 19 of these involved fatalities. Those numbers show how much designers, engineers and pilots had still to learn about aeroplanes in those days. Indeed I remember one of the scientists that I was working with remarking that there was still a lot of work for the RAE to do because over the last year the RAF had lost more than one aeroplane a day.

A check of the RAF records held in the National Archives at Kew shows the following:

Year	Aircraft lost	Fatalities
1950	380	238
1951	490	280
1952	507	318
1953	483	333
1954	452	283
1955	305	182

I expect such numbers will seem incredible to many people today.

On a happier note and as an example of the sort of inspirational background to which I was exposed, another scientist who knew of my interest in becoming a test pilot said he had something to show me. He took me to a room in another building, opened the door and asked,

21

"What do you think of that?" I found myself looking at an ordinary wooden chair surrounded by a small U-shaped console made of bits of plywood on which was mounted a variety of instruments and switches. When I asked him what it was he said it was the cockpit of the future. I queried why it had not got a control column whereupon he pointed to a small hand controller on the right hand part of the console and said that was it. The year was 1954 so 20 years before such a 'fly-by-wire' cockpit first flew in the General Dynamics YF-16.

Returning to the educational opportunities on offer, I don't suppose the classroom lectures were any better or worse than those at many colleges at that time. However, I am certain that the practical experiences available to us were second to none in the aviation world. While my passion for aeroplanes meant I was motivated to make the most of this (I was the only member of my year to qualify for air observer duties for example), it was the overall quality of advice and instruction provided by my apprentice masters and the test pilots I flew with that proved invaluable during my subsequent test flying career.

The first scientific department I worked in was Structural and Mechanical Engineering or SME as it was known. For reasons I never understood they had a section that dealt with parachutes. My apprentice master, John Picken, was trying to solve the problem of why some of the parachutes used to drop heavy army equipment were misbehaving.

SME Flight had a US Fairchild C-119 Flying Boxcar for these heavy drop trials which used a fairly simple and common sense procedure. First the rear cargo bay doors were removed then the load, such as a Jeep or a small artillery gun, was lashed to a platform which was secured inside the cargo bay. The drop was initiated by firing a small drogue parachute out into the airflow behind the aircraft. This drogue was spring loaded to open and, once inflated, its lanyard pulled a larger 10 ft diameter 'extractor parachute' out of its pack on top of the load. Simultaneously the lashings tying the platform to the aircraft floor were released, the extractor chute inflated and the platform slid out, helped by rollers fitted in the cargo bay floor. Once the load was clear of the aircraft, a static line attached to the aircraft pulled the rip cord of the three large main load-carrying parachutes.

At least that was the idea. The problem was that a significant number of the extractor chutes were failing to inflate and taking up what was known as a squid condition. Here the parachute is fully deployed from its pack without any tangle of the lines but for some reason the canopy fails to inflate. The name 'squid' was appropriate because the canopy looked like the body of a squid with the lines being its tentacles. In the world of parachute jumping, the term 'roman candle' is sometimes used to cover a similar condition.

It does not take much imagination to realise that a C-119 with no doors and a load free on its rollers trailing a squidding extractor chute that could inflate at any moment, is in a dodgy condition to leave the Larkhill range on Salisbury Plain and return to Farnborough.

John Picken felt that the problem was aerodynamic and suspected that the peripheral hem was taking up a negative alpha that prevented the canopy spreading. Therefore he wanted to study the deployment sequence in detail including recording the drag throughout. He also wanted to pre-test a batch of these extractor chutes for correct operation before using them to drop loads.

SME Flight also had a Lincoln, RF538, that was fitted with a glider towing hook under the rear fuselage just behind the tailwheel. They removed the rear gun turret and fitted a suitable Perspex enclosure from which to observe a parachute towed behind the aircraft on a long webbing strop. This enclosure had a chute in the floor through which the parachute could be dispatched into the airflow. A 64 frames/sec high speed movie camera was fitted to a suitable bracket while drag was measured using an electrical strain gauge bonded to a short metal link fitted into the strop close to the tow hook fitting. The signal from the strain gauge was measured on a manually adjusted oscilloscope. Those were the days.

Since John Picken suffered from airsickness, I was pushing at an open door when I pleaded to be allowed to replace him for the airborne tasks. Anyhow what was the point of owning an apprentice if you were going to do such chores yourself?

The parachute to be tested was loaded before flight into the rear fuselage and attached to the strop with a loop of nylon cord. The strop went down the chute and round underneath the fuselage to the tow hook. With the aircraft flying at the desired test speed it was then just a matter of starting up the oscilloscope, switching on the camera, throwing the parachute down the chute and taking a note of the oscilloscope reading. After the test was complete, the aircraft flew down the runway at low level while I leant down the chute and used a knife attached to a pole to saw away at the nylon cord loop and jettison the parachute over the airfield. By today's standards this was all very low tech but what a simple and cheap way to do the tests and get the information needed.

Later, after we showed the technique worked and to save landing after every streaming, we used to get airborne with a whole batch of test parachutes in the fuselage. Then, having jettisoned the first, I would reach down with a hook fitted to the other end of the knife pole, pull the strop back up the chute and attach the next parachute to it with a fresh nylon cord loop.

One day, while cutting off a new length of cord from a big drum of the stuff, I managed to let the drum fall down the chute although I did keep hold of my end of the cord. I watched in dismay as the drum unwound itself in the slipstream. Needless to say I was hauling in my end as fast as I could but in seconds we had 50 yards or more of line steaming behind us and the drum was long gone. Another day we were measuring the drag of a new drogue type device (rather like a huge windsock) when I got the knot wrong and could see it was slipping as we towed the drogue back for jettisoning. Sure enough the thing came off a few miles short of the airfield. The response of the department to the loss of this test article was, "You know where it went so you go and get it". Accordingly I was dispatched on my push-bike to try and find it in the wood we were flying over at the time. Of course I never did.

Since I am by nature a hoarder, I still have the sole documentation associated with my becoming an RAE Air Observer at that time. As the copy of my RAE Form A/36 shows, we were categorised according to our experience once the training exercises were completed. My initial category in the Lincoln was 'TRG'. After an appropriate number of such flights the pilot, Flt Lt John Greenland, who I still see at ETPS association functions, signed me off and I was upgraded to a C category limited to 10,000 ft. With many trials going on which were more exciting than towing parachutes, I naturally made a nuisance of myself until by the following April I had my A category as well as an ejector seat clearance.

It really was a different world in those days. Even very junior people like me (if they showed willing) could be given real responsibility and allowed to get on with things. I trust you are starting to get a feel for how this sort of upbringing could make a big impression on a young lad!

RECORD OF TRAINING FLIGHTS

DATE	AIRCRAFT	TIME IN AIR	PILOT
11·5·53	LINCOLN RF528	·30	
11·5·53	" "	·40	
13·5·53	" "	·30	
13·5·53	" "	·25	
14·5·53	" "	·15	
2·7·53	" "	1·25	
7·7·53	" "	1·00	

TRAINING COMPLETED SATISFACTORILY

O/C. _S.M.E._ FLIGHT

DATE _8ᵗʰ July 1953_

R.A.E. FORM A/36

RECORD CARD FOR AIR OBSERVERS AT THE ROYAL AIRCRAFT ESTABLISHMENT

NAME M̃ʳ J.F. FARLEY

OBSERVER No. 328

CATEGORY TRG. | C | B | A |

DEPARTMENT ~~MECH.ENG.~~ TO DEPTᵗ

I CERTIFY THAT I HAVE READ AND UNDERSTOOD R.A.E. STANDING INSTRUCTION No.14

John F. Farley

SIGNATURE OF HOLDER

THE HOLDER IS AUTHORISED TO FLY AS AN R.A.E. OBSERVER IN THE CATEGORY STATED ABOVE

_____ G/CAPT.

COMMANDING OFFICER, EXPERIMENTAL FLYING DEPARTMENT, R.A.E.

DATE 11/6/53

MEDICAL CLASSIFICATION

27/5/53. Category C.

REVIEWED

DECOMPRESSION TEST

14/4/54

REVIEWED

ENDORSEMENTS

DATE	SUBJECT & SIGNATURE
28/5/53	CAT "C" Qualifying Lecture
/5/53	Oxygen Lecture
21·4·54	Ejection Seat Lecture

LIMITATIONS OF CATEGORIES

TRAINING:— LIMITED TO 10,000 FT., FLIGHTS OF 2 HOURS AND NO AEROBATICS.

CAT. C:—— LIMITED TO 10,000 FT.

CAT. B:—— LIMITED TO 25,000 FT.

CAT. A:—— NO HEIGHT LIMITATION.

NOTE:—— FLYING IN AIRCRAFT FITTED WITH EJECTION SEATS NEEDS SPECIAL ENDORSEMENT ABOVE ON PARTICULAR TYPE OF AIRCRAFT. USE OF PRESSURE-BREATHING EQUIPMENT NOT PERMITTED WITHOUT ENDORSEMENT ABOVE IN THIS SUBJECT.

Without going into too much detail, three other flight test programmes on which I flew are worth a mention. Two were when I was working in Armament Department and one during my time with the National Gas Turbine Establishment (NGTE) also located at Farnborough. My apprentice master at NGTE was Ray Holl, a scientist working to develop a practical re-heat or afterburner as it became known once the idea crossed the Atlantic. The engine was carried under another Lincoln SX971 flown by Flt Lt Norman Kearney.

NGTE Lincoln

The aircraft had up-rated Merlins and could get well above 30,000 ft. It was unpressurised and gave me my first experience of the bends. They were brought on by charging about looking after instrumentation scattered the length of the aircraft. Decompression sickness (of which the bends is just one symptom) was only then starting to be understood by the doctors at the RAF Institute of Aviation Medicine (IAM). This was triggered by a boffin getting out of a long high altitude trip in a Valetta, saying he felt groggy and being sent home. He collapsed and died in his lounge later that evening. The penny then dropped that the pilots flying at 40,000 ft in unpressurised Meteor 7s were only getting away with it because they did not have enough fuel to stay up there long. Time as well as height was clearly important. This has parallels with scuba diving where you can go very deep if you don't stay there but can be in real trouble if you hang about at only medium depths.

One day Norman Kearney mentioned that the BP111 then being flown by Aero Flight fleet was a handful. Naturally I asked why and he explained that, because of the short coupled delta wing design, a mere ¼ inch movement of the stick top at high speed resulted in 6g being recorded. He explained that the aircraft had fully powered controls to prevent flutter and other transonic problems so feel was provided by a simple stick centring spring. This spring offered negligible resistance to pilot input at tiny deflections so pilots who had flown this aircraft were extremely unhappy. He left me in no doubt that something would have to be done about these new fangled fully powered controls in order to give them the same feel as pilots had with manual controls. If not people would be breaking aircraft right, left and centre.

BP111

Not lacking in youthful arrogance it was clear to me that if the boffins could not come up with an idea to give the pilot the feel he needed then I would have to do it myself. After a couple of question and answer sessions with Norman, I felt I understood what was needed to obtain reasonable 'stick force per g' values and to mimic the feel of manual controls as speed increased.

It seemed to me that an electrical system was the easiest thing to vary as speed changed but my electrical engineering skills were not up to specifying some of the details. Fortunately there was another apprentice in my year who was a fully paid up electrical ace (certainly compared to me) so Alan Cole and I worked together on a design and put it into the RAE Suggestion Scheme system. I include the Introduction to our suggestion here because it is a useful reminder of control issues from those days.

"Originally the hinge moments on aircraft control surfaces were of such a magnitude that they could be applied by the pilot's limbs acting through a suitable lever and cable linkage.

As the speed of aircraft increased, the control surface hinge moments grew larger and the pilot was assisted in overcoming them by numerous devices varying from aerodynamic balancing and spring tabs to modern power boosted controls.

In all of these methods, a percentage of the forces applied to the control surfaces (and hence the airframe as a whole) was 'fed back' to the pilot enabling him to 'feel' the loads he was imposing on the airframe.

With the advent of modern high performance aircraft it has been found a big advantage to use irreversible controls. Here by definition a force exerted on the control surface cannot 'feed back' into the actuating system and move the pilot's controls.

The problem that now arises is that the pilot can no longer 'feel' the loads he is imposing on the airframe. This results in the possibility of his inadvertently overloading the airframe.

In an effort to counteract this, 'spring feel' was incorporated in the control column, so that the pilot has to do work against springs to move the controls.

This is a step in the right direction but is by no means a complete answer for the following reasons:

(i) When the aircraft is flying at a low airspeed – e.g. landing – very large movements of the control surfaces may be required to control the aircraft. To obtain these large movements the pilot may have to give full stick deflection leading to very high stick forces (due to the 'spring feel') whilst at this low speed the stresses in the airframe are still very low.

(ii) At high speed, however, only a small stick deflection is necessary to overload the airframe, and the pilot is able to obtain these small deflections easily without encountering much 'spring feel' resistance.

Hence there is a very necessary requirement for stick forces to increase with air speed."

We went on to describe a system that used the like poles of an electromagnet to resist movement of the stick and where the strength of the magnets varied with aircraft speed.

Naturally Alan and I were well pleased when we received a letter thanking us for our efforts plus a nice cheque from the director of the RAE, Professor Arnold Hall. This eminent man went on to become Chairman of the Hawker Siddeley Group and, as I mention in Chapter 8, some years later he even entrusted me with one of his daughters for a flight in Harrier G-VTOL.

Our magnetic system never flew but feel systems based on hydraulic pressure were developed shortly afterwards. These 'Q feel' systems as they became known (Q being the notation for the ½ ρV^2 term at the heart of so much aerodynamics) allowed pilots using irreversible controls to still experience feel. For those interested in such details our complete suggestion is included as Annexe A to this chapter.

Two of the trials I flew on with Armament Flight were destined to provide déjà vu feelings years later. The first was in an early Canberra to drop a large magnesium parachute flare that weighed 4,000 lb. The idea being that such a device would be dropped over the front line at night to allow close support aircraft to help our troops with their pilots using the only tactics they knew in those days, namely daylight ones!

Because our prototype Canberra had no bombsight fitted, the brief was that the flare should be released on a countdown from the radar range controller at Larkhill. The store was also to be released from as high an altitude as the aircraft could reach. We had spent some minutes between 41,000 and 42,000 ft trying to get the last bit of height when there was a loud double thump and both engines stopped.

The cause was a compressor stall due to high rpm being used at very low outside air temperatures on these early standard Avon engines. For any engine men it was a classic $N/\sqrt{\theta}$ surge. This was not really a problem as all we had to do was relight them. In those days I didn't realise that you had to descend to get inside the relight envelope and neither did the pilot. To cut a long story short, he tried at once so the engine went straight back into surge, over-temped and had to be shut down again. This happened several times with both engines until, as we went through 10,000 ft, the pilot announced he was going to do a forced landing at Boscombe. This was too much for the navigator who made it very clear that, if he wanted to do that with 4,000 lb of magnesium flare in our bomb bay, he could do it on his own. To emphasise his point, the navigator proceeded to take the safety pins out of my seat because in those days we flew with them in as the professional aircrew did not trust these new fangled bang-seats. Then he took out his own, strapped himself in to his seat alongside mine and with much élan threw both sets of pins complete with their big red disc labels forward onto the floor alongside the pilot. After this the intercom went very quiet. At 8,000 ft the pilot got one engine going and so we set off for Farnborough where we landed normally. Later I heard the navigator telling some others about the trip and he made the remark that he wished he had had several other people he could name with him rather than me as he did not think they would have sat quietly through the event.

It is amazing how invulnerable one feels when young!

The déjà vu bit came nine years later when I was back at RAE to do the ETPS course in 1963. Jerry Skyrud (a USN Commander and the senior student on the course) and I were allocated the Canberra for some fuel consumption tests. There were several flights involved so we took it in turns to either fly it or sit in the back and write the numbers down. On this occasion I was in the front, we were about 42,000 ft and Jerry was exhorting me to get a few hundred feet higher to fit his desired test point when, you guessed it, there was a boom, boom.

I explained to a slightly concerned Jerry that I had been there before and that we had at least 25 minutes of gently gliding down before the ground would become any sort of a factor and that the engines would relight very nicely below 10,000 ft. You go a long way in a straight line getting fuel consumption data so we reckoned our position was somewhere off Lands End. Accordingly we made a quick call to ATC to get a steer. That was when we found we had R/T failure. We were above complete cloud cover so made our best guess as to the easterly heading needed and got on with the long glide. As we neared 10,000 ft a tiny hole appeared in the cloud and there, right in the middle, was the only unique navigation feature in the whole of southern England, namely the new white concrete taxiway leading to the western extension of runway 25 at Farnborough. Therefore down we went, re-lit the Avons and landed. It turned out that ATC had been trying to contact us for some time so our late and unannounced arrival resulted in an irate Chief Test Flying Instructor, Wing Commander Stanley J Hubbard, standing by the door as we got out. As is often the case when senior people have built up a head of steam, they tend to speak their preconceived mind first rather than enquire what happened. When we eventually got a word in edgeways, our version of events produced a long silent hard stare of the 'I wonder if they are having me on' variety. Aircraft recorders have their uses post such events. Incidentally, Jerry was responsible for the best 'one-liner' on our course, as I mention in Chapter 16.

Stan Hubbard had quite a reputation and was not to be trifled with. Any student who did not realise this only made that mistake once. A very experienced RAE Aero Flight test pilot from the 1950s, he was known around the aviation world as either Stanley J or 'Ball of Fire', the latter because he invariably rounded off any description of a past aviation drama with those three words. For those who have never met him, I believe it reasonable to suggest that, if he had been born in the USA then Chuck Yeager would never have got past flying the Mustang. I say this because, big though Edwards is, it could not have contained both men and the smart money would have been on Stanley J. The only time I ever had the nerve to pull his leg arose from an overwhelming sense of well being at finding I was alive after the school parachute jump. This was carried out using the boom exit of a Beverley flying over the Solent and was aimed at improving our observation under stress.

After our group had been fished out of the sea and taken ashore, fellow student Terry Gill and I were sitting on a jetty leaning up against a large wooden bollard while letting the water run out of our kit. We were both conscious that Stan had his back to the same post on the other side. Terry started to ask me what I had noticed during various phases of the jump so I gave him a wink and said "Nothing". When he asked, "Why not?" I said, "Because I had my eyes shut." "Good grief, when did you open them?" "When I felt my feet get wet," I said. At this Stan, who was a parachuting nut and had completed a course in combat jumping with the USMC, came round the corner with a look of fury on his face just in time to realise that he had been had.

Another student on our course was USAF Major Bill Pogue, later to be Astronaut Bill Pogue of Skylab IV fame. In 1963 Bill was a pilot and excellent mathematician but he badly wanted to be an astronaut. Bill reckoned that his age and blood pressure could both have been better for his chances but that his maths would help redress the balance. In those days astronaut applicants also had to be graduates of a test pilot school hence Bill was very keen not to fail the course. One day I saw a look of despair come across his face which has stayed with me until today. We were both doing the school high mach number handling exercise at the time on the Vampire T11. This aircraft had some absolutely gross characteristics between .82M and .87M and was a very violent ride by any standards if pushed any faster. We were allowed five sorties for the exercise and, as each dive was of very short duration, we were very pushed for time to carry out the investigation.

As I went out for my final sortie Bill mentioned he too only had one trip left and asked if I had found any features worth reporting. I thought he was joking at first but realised he was serious when he said, "I'm within .01M of the airframe limit and I've only picked up very slight airframe buffet so far". I pointed out that the T11 did not have an airframe limit. He looked puzzled, pulled out his T11 Pilot's Notes and pointed to an airframe limit of .72M. I explained that he had wasted four of his five flights creeping up to a limit on the aircraft that only applied when fitted with ferry tanks and his aircraft was clean. That is when he had that look of total despair. However his eventual VTO in the Shuttle got him a thousand times higher than my Harrier ever did.

Returning to my apprenticeship, the RAE had an outstation and weapons range at West Freugh on the coast of Luce Bay some eight miles south of Stranraer. I was privileged to walk about the beach there looking for bits of an experimental type of (inert) bomb after it had been dropped. As some compensation for this chore, I was allowed to fly up in the Farnborough Lincoln for the drop. Fifteen years later I walked out to a development Harrier at Dunsfold to examine its flying qualities when carrying six of a 'new' bomb called the BL755. It was déjà vu time again when I realised that these were no less than the production version of what the RAE had been experimenting with all those years earlier at West Freugh.

I only ever saw two UFOs. Not funny craft full of aliens, just things in the sky that I could not recognise. The first was while in the Lincoln as we started a drop run at West Freugh. I was looking out of the starboard side when I saw something coming towards us. I shouted a warning to the crew and then, because it seemed to be going to pass below us, I crossed over to the other side to look for it there and saw it again going away. Nobody else saw it. It was a matter of some concern because we were on the range which was supposed to be clear and we were under radar control for the drop. The radar man saw nothing either. As you would imagine, I took a fair bit of stick that night in the mess bar although not from my crew who knew me and kept very quiet.

The trouble with seeing something you don't recognise is that it is difficult to know how far away it is when you don't know its size. In this case what I saw went beneath us and, since we were at about 10,000 ft, it could not have been that far away. As to estimating its speed, the unknown size and distance issues apply again but as I saw it for several seconds both sides it was not going particularly fast. When asked what it looked like, my best description was to say, "The front view of a Vulcan but with no fin". In other words, a sphere with two slender cones sticking out. It seemed uniformly dark grey, it had no distinguishing detail such as windows, left no trail and made no noise that I could hear over the racket in the Lincoln. It flew with the point of one cone first. The only sensible conclusion was that I imagined it or had some floater in my eye. What bothered both me and the crew was that I first saw it out of one side and then was able to spot it again on the other side after it went under us. It was never explained.

The other UFO event was during the course at ETPS when I was doing that high mach handling exercise in the Vampire T11. The aircraft had no effective cockpit demist or heating system so in many circumstances the inside of the transparencies got covered in ice. In those days there was nothing unusual in this and the cockpit contained a small sponge in a leather pouch which was soaked in glycol before flight. At the top of the climb, I used this sponge to clear myself some view for the dive and in the process saw a small silver dot above me. I was at 40,000 ft yet this looked way higher. In fact it reminded me of how, in the late 1950s, we were scrambled in our Hunters in Germany to intercept unknown blips coming from the east, only to find they were returning U2 aircraft and naturally way above us. Those were black though. This was silver. As I watched trying to work out what it could be, it exploded in a cloud of white smoke. Shortly after that I saw what seemed bits of wreckage about the size of a Hunter fuselage falling down some way out beyond my port wingtip. I was over Boscombe at the time so imagined it was some sort of high altitude trial that had gone wrong. I therefore told ATC what I had just seen and got on with my exercise.

A couple of hours after landing back at Farnborough I was asked to go to ATC where I was told that what I had seen was a particularly large silver met balloon that had burst at high altitude about that time. The 'wreckage' I had seen was the instrumentation package falling down. The most interesting thing to me was that the biggest bit of the package was about 3 ft long. Thus my 'Hunter fuselage' some way away was clearly something much smaller and closer to me. Yet another example

33

of the problem of estimating distance, size or speed of something in the sky when you have no idea what you are looking at.

Whether I was an apprentice, a student on the ETPS course, an RAE Bedford test pilot or a company test pilot at Dunsfold, I naturally attended most of the Farnborough Air Shows. Since I have devoted Chapter 8 to Display and Demonstration Flying, I will leave my airshow stories until then, apart from this next one which I feel is more related to research and design than airshow.

I have a special memory of watching the Russian jet VSTOL Yak-38 and Yak-141 being towed round the taxiway at Farnborough two days before the 1992 airshow. They had both just emerged from an An-124, the 38 in one piece and the 141 minus just its fin caps, showing that folding wings have their uses even away from ships.

My initial reactions to seeing a type for the first time can still surprise me. Watching the Yak-38 seemed just the natural conclusion of a story previously limited to pictures. I recalled being in a room under the MOD main building, back in the 1970s, trying to make sense of grainy images and later some infra red cine that allowed a degree of flow visualisation of Yak-38 exhaust gases. Now at Farnborough, the sight of the small swivelling yaw reaction control nozzle, almost hidden from view under the rear fuselage, brought back to me the voice of a puzzled USMC Harrier pilot just as if I had heard him the day before, not some 15 years earlier. That Marine, back from a brief spell in formation with a Yak-38 operating over the Mediterranean, had expressed surprise that he could find no evidence of side blowing reaction control jets and wanted to know how I thought they might control yaw in the hover.

My first impressions of the Yak-141 were something else again. To one used to the Harrier, standing at the side of this large aircraft was an extremely exciting business. It is no exaggeration to say that practical VSTOL operations are all about successfully managing the engine exhaust. The Harrier has a remarkably cool and low velocity exhaust but even so it can still damage itself, or its operating site, unless correct nozzle angle and throttle procedures are religiously observed. With this in mind a close look at the large diameter after-burning main engine between the booms of the 141 was truly awesome.

Once out from underneath, I stood for a long time saying out loud to myself, over and over again, "Holy shit". A passer-by, seeing me standing there and looking stupefied asked, "What do you think of it?" I replied, "It looks as if it could do a lot more damage than the SC1," but I don't think he got my point.

Yak-141 with main engine nozzle deflected

Such subjective initial reactions aside, Farnborough International 1992 did improve our ability to assess Yakovlev's VSTOL efforts and compare them with the Harrier. However I will leave my detailed thoughts on these matters to Annexe B at the end of this chapter as I suspect they will be of limited interest to many readers.

By the end of the 1980s the old RAE buildings were looking increasingly unsuitable for a modern research establishment. As a result a completely new range of buildings started to appear on the Cody site just outside the southwest corner of the airfield. By 1999 the move was complete and the MOD handed over the original RAE site to the developers. Many of the new buildings were given names so you can imagine how honoured I felt in 1997 when the occupants of one lab chose to name it the Farley Building which I was invited to formally 'open'. The building was purpose-built to do research into the problems of people communicating in noisy and vibratory environments such as tanks, helicopters and military cockpits. I can only assume they thought that spending many a happy hour sitting a few feet in front of the engine of a hovering Harrier qualified me to appreciate the importance of their work. I certainly saw it as a wonderful end to my time at the RAE.

(This document looks distinctly quaint by today's standards but it was written and the figures drawn well over half a century ago!)

Annexe A

A METHOD OF INCORPORATING OPTIMUM FEEL IN A FULLY POWER-CONTROLLED AIRCRAFT

by

A.J. COLE & J.F. FARLEY

SUMMARY

The following is a method of stiffening up the control column of an aircraft as its airspeed increases.

The stiffness incorporated in terms of stick force to produce a given g and stick force per g against airspeed is fully variable in its characteristics and may be adapted to any aircraft type.

The effect is to put the stick force required to bring about a structural failure of the aircraft beyond the physical capabilities of the pilot at any airspeed.

INTRODUCTION

Originally the hinge moments on aircraft control surfaces were of such a magnitude that they could be applied by the pilot's limbs acting through a suitable lever and cable linkage.

As the speed of aircraft increased, the control surface hinge moments grew larger and the pilot was assisted in overcoming them by numerous devices varying from aerodynamic balancing and spring tabs to modern power boosted controls.

In all of these methods, a percentage of the forces applied to the control surfaces (and hence the airframe as a whole) was 'fed back' to the pilot enabling him to 'feel' the loads he was imposing on the airframe.

With the advent of modern high performance aircraft it has been found a big advantage to use irreversible controls. Here by definition a force exerted on the control surface cannot 'feed back' into the actuating system and move the pilot's controls.

The problem that now arises is that the pilot can no longer 'feel' the loads he is imposing on the airframe. This results in the possibility of his inadvertently overloading the airframe.

In an effort to counteract this, 'spring feel' was incorporated in the control column so that the pilot has to do work against springs to move the controls.

This is a step in the right direction but is by no means a complete answer for the following reasons:-

(i)   When the aircraft is flying at low airspeed, e.g. landing, very large movements of the control surfaces may be required to control the aircraft. To obtain these large movements the pilot may have to give full stick deflection leading to very high stick forces (due to the 'spring feel') whilst at this low speed the stresses in the airframe are still very low.

(ii)   At high speed, however, only a small stick deflection is necessary to overload the airframe and the pilot is able to obtain these small deflections easily without encountering much 'spring feel' resistance.

Hence there is a very necessary requirement for stick forces to increase with airspeed.

OPTIMUM 'FEEL' CHARACTERISTICS

These are dependent to a large extent on the personal opinion of individual pilots but two points may be fixed to the satisfaction of all.

(i)   Airspeed zero. Stick force zero lb at all deflections.

(ii)   Airspeed maximum. Stick force x lb at maximum permissible deflection.

N.B. x lb = maximum force that pilot is able to apply.

These points are the lower and upper limits of the characteristic curve. Of the possible relationships in between, fig (i) and fig (ii) seem (on a limited number of enquiries) to be equally popular.

These curves do not allow for change of airspeed, considering this we arrive at fig (iii) and fig (iv).

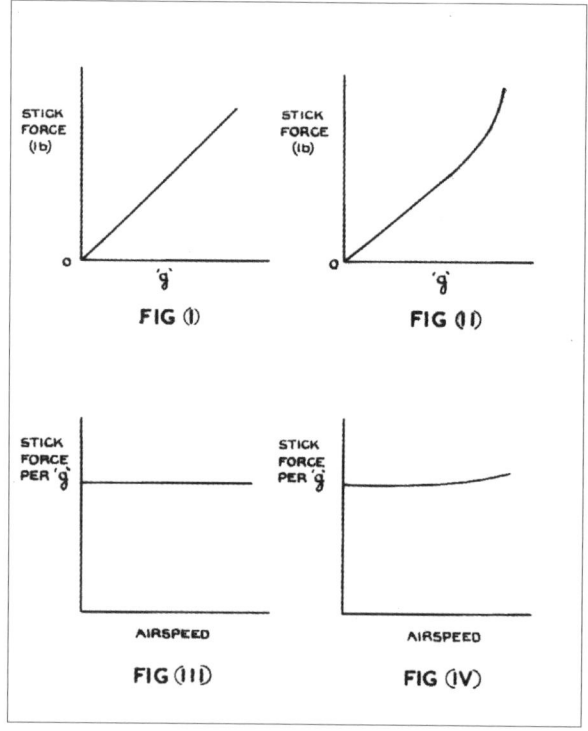

Of these (ii) seems more popular.

At this stage it is only necessary to point out that whatever characteristic might be chosen (as a result of exhaustive analysis of pilot opinion) it can be obtained solely by changing the windings on two potentiometers.

GENERAL

In effect the requirement is for a "variable rate spring". The type of 'spring' envisaged is composed of two electromagnets with windings arranged so that ends of the same polarity are presented to each other. The 'spring' is thus a compression type. The rate is controlled by varying the current through the coils, such variation being governed by the airspeed.

A schematic of the system is shown in fig (v).

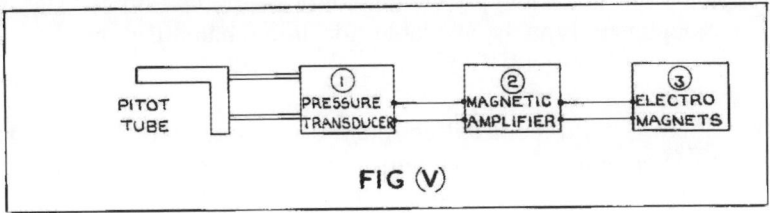

FIG (V)

The three stages shown in this fig and training and safety devices to be incorporated are dealt with in more detail as follows:-

1. PRESSURE TRANSDUCER

(To make it possible to obtain a variety of feel characteristics the output current of the transducer does not necessarily vary linearly with the differential pressure of the pitot head.)

Possible types of pressure transducer systems considered are set out below:

(a) The differential pressure acts on a bellows or aneroid capsule and via a mechanical linkage moves a potentiometer wiper, producing a variable voltage.

The way in which this potentiometer is wound would provide the necessary airspeed to stiffness characteristics. As an alternative to a wound potentiometer a carbon potentiometer track with a varying cross-sectional area might be used.

(b) A carbon pile. The pressure variations acting through a diaphragm change the compressive force on a stack of carbon plates and thus their resistance. This has two disadvantages: the pressure/resistance characteristic is necessarily a straight line and carbon piles have a very high hysteresis effect. The first might be overcome by the introduction of distortion, i.e non-linearity in the magnetic amplifier stage and the application of

39

the (preferably amplified) signal to a moving coil system which would drive the wiper of a non-linear potentiometer, however the second is insuperable and prohibits the use of a carbon pile transducer.

(c) A well tried and proven type of pressure pick-up, the variable inductance type is available for immediate use, in the size required (approx 0-10p.s.i.)

This could be used in the normal oscillator circuit. The disadvantage of this system is that the translation from this variation of frequency to a variation of d.c. level would require the use of relatively delicate thermionic equipment. It is not felt that this could be tolerated in such a vital function in the aircraft.

From the above it appears that (a), the bellows system, is the most practical choice.

DESIGN CONSIDERATIONS OF A BELLOWS TYPE TRANSDUCER

Two major points to be allowed for are:-

(i)   The bellows must be large enough to give a reasonable deflection and operating force with the rather small pressure change of 0-10 psi. available.

(ii)   The bellows must not be so large that its mass is such that the accelerations of the aircraft materially effect the potentiometer wiper position. (As much as 8g might be expected from a fighter aircraft.)

By careful design and by positioning the bellows correctly relative to the axis of least acceleration (the fore and aft axis) the conflict between these factors may be reduced.

A suitable design is shown in fig (vi).

The slightly oversize cylindrical support will in the event of acceleration forces in any direction other than fore and aft prevent distortion of the bellows.

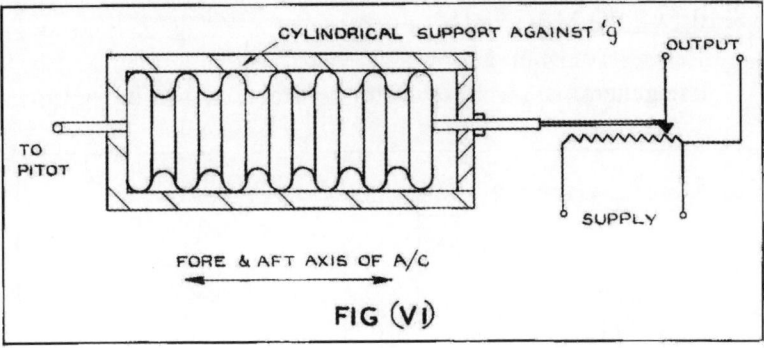

If the bellows is mounted as shown with the fixed end facing forward, at take-off or retraction of dive-brakes the acceleration which may distort the bellows will increase the output current and hence slightly stiffen up the feel, (the opposite effect occurring on touch down and applying wheel brakes). These forces will normally be less than 1g and are not considered a disadvantage.

2. MAGNETIC AMPLIFIER

The design technique of magnetic amplifiers for the control of a large number of appliances is well advanced. With current gains in the region of 20 for a single stage no difficulty is anticipated in amplifying the current from the transducer to that of the magnitude required for the magnets.

The output can be rectified and smoothed to prevent eddy current losses in the electromagnets.

This part of the circuit necessitates the use of a 115V 400c/s supply. (This will probably have to come from a separate three phase alternator to that already in existence for the feeding auto-pilots and flight instruments since these may be affected by the load of the 'feel' mechanism).

By the provision of more than one control winding to any stage, a corrective voltage may be applied to alter the shape of the overall characteristics of the amplifier, if this is necessary.

3. ELECTRO MAGNETS

The general layout for elevator control is shown in fig (vii).

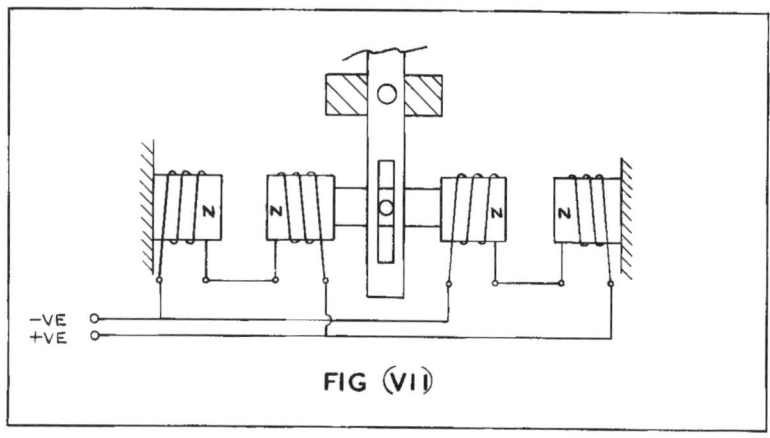

FIG (VII)

Two horse-shoe electromagnets are fixed to a bulkhead fore and aft of either an extension of the control column or a lever actuated by some part of the control rod. (If necessary some distance away from the cockpit.) Two similar magnets are fixed to the lever so that they move with it.

The windings of the coils are arranged to give the polarity shown. With current flowing through the coils two equal and opposite repulsion forces will centralise the stick.

When the stick is deflected the repulsion force increases with deflection. The magnitude of this force is inversely proportional to $(deflection)^2$. This type of characteristic is undesirable. To alter the characteristic to that required a further winding is incorporated on each magnet. The sense of these windings is opposite to that of the main windings and the current fed through them is controlled by a potentiometer.

The position of the wiper is dependent on stick position. As the deflection is increased the current flowing through the demagnetising coils is increased and the rate of increase of the repulsion force is thereby reduced.

Also directly linked to the stick movement is the switching arrangement shown in the complete diagram, fig (viii). The purpose of this is to cut out the unwanted repulsion force of the two magnets that are being separated.

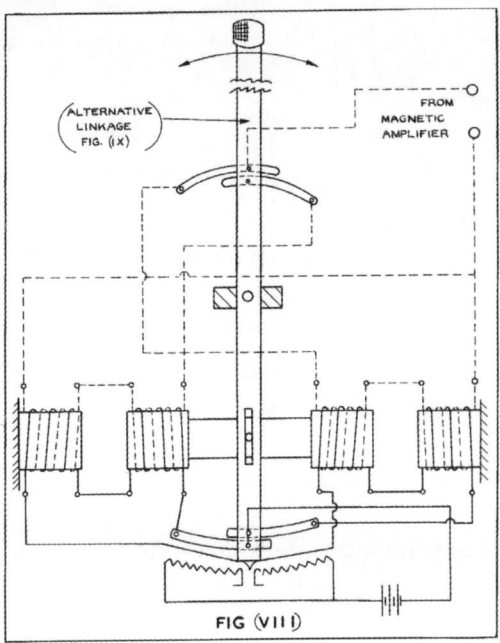

ALTERNATIVE LINKAGE FIG. (iX)

FROM MAGNETIC AMPLIFIER

FIG (VIII)

METHOD OF TRIMMING THE AIRCRAFT

Tail units used on modern aircraft are mainly of two types:-

(i)   (Large Bomber Aircraft) A variable incidence tailplane and stick controlled elevator.

(ii)   (Smaller Fighter Aircraft) One piece 'flying tail'.

Trimming on an aircraft using a type (i) tail is accomplished by varying the incidence of the tailplane. On an aircraft fitted with a type (ii) tail the 'no-force position' of the stick must be changed.

In the event of this feel system being used on an aircraft with a type (i) tail the feel system is unaffected by using existing trimming methods.

When a one piece flying tail is used the <u>feel system</u> must incorporate a device for changing the 'no-force position' of the stick.

43

A method is outlined below with a sketch, fig (ix).

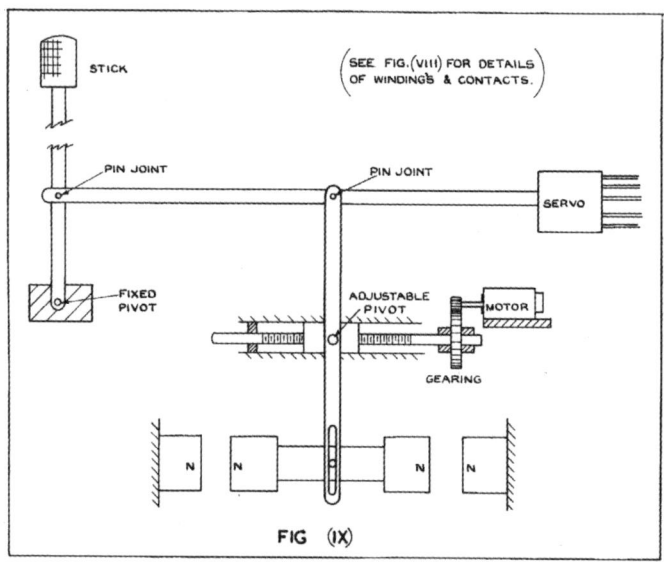

FIG (IX)

The pilot's trimming control takes the form of a three position switch situated on the top of the control column. A straightforward method of moving the 'no-force position' of the stick is to move the pivot of the lever to which is attached the moving pair of electro-magnets.

The pivot pin is carried in a sliding block attached to a nut. The nut and hence the pivot position is moved by a lead screw driven by a reversible motor. The direction and duration of the rotation is controlled by the three position switch. (Nose up. Off. Nose down.)

The amount of movement involved is not large and can be easily accommodated by this method.

SAFETY

Two safety systems may be incorporated.

(i)   Automatic substitution of constant feel
(ii)   Manual substitution of constant feel

The electrical circuit is shown in fig (x)

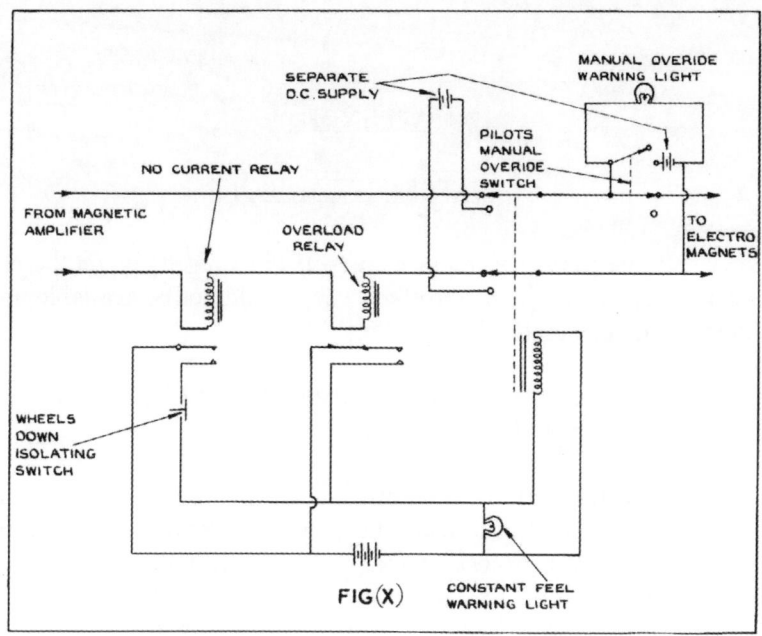

FIG(X)

(i)   Automatic

Between the magnetic amplifier and electromagnets there is placed a change over switch, operated by a solenoid. The current to the solenoid is switched by either of two relays. One is a relay which holds open the contacts whist current is flowing through it, the contacts closing when the current drops below a predetermined value. The other relay only closes should some fault occur causing an overload current to flow. The relay which operates on no current is rendered inoperative by an isolating switch which is open circuited in the 'wheels-down' undercarriage position.

(ii)   Manual

Should a fault develop in the supply to the electro-magnets, the automatic substitution of constant feel would operate. Should this too develop a fault, the pilot will again be without 'feel'. A switch should therefore be incorporated for emergencies whereby the pilot may select a second constant supply to the electromagnets, again producing constant feel.

Warning lights may be provided to show the condition of the system.

45

APPENDIX 1

CATAPULT TAKE-OFF

In the case of a catapult take-off the aircraft sits on the catapult at zero airspeed and with zero feel. Feel would not be available until the aircraft had accelerated.

This is the state of affairs existing both on cable control aircraft and with this feel system.

With the bellows type transducer situated as described, due to inertia effects a high g assisted take off will provide a feel during the acceleration run in excess of that normally available at that airspeed. This is considered an advantage.

Should it be decided that more stick-force was necessary at standstill and during acceleration, the manual switch described under 'Safety' could be used for take-off and after safety height had been obtained, the switch could be opened giving automatic airspeed controlled stick forces.

APPENDIX 2

PITOT-STATIC DISTURBANCE AT MACH 1

The system should be unaffected by any high frequency fluctuations or impulses in the pitot-static pressure difference, due to the inherent inertia of the bellows and its low natural frequency.

Annexe B

**Thoughts on seeing the Yak-38 and Yak-141 aircraft at
Farnborough 1992**

The most obvious difference between the Yak and the Hawker way of achieving VSTOL is the number of engines. Yak use three on both the 38 and the 141. Two vertically mounted lift engines are just behind the cockpit with one horizontally mounted thrust vectoring engine further aft. On the other hand Hawker chose a single engine with four interconnected swivelling exhausts to vector the total installed thrust for both horizontal and vertical flight.

The Yaks need all three engines to work in the hover and the failure of any one will cause a violent and immediate change in pitch attitude since all the engines exhaust at some distance from the aircraft centre of gravity. The Harrier engine is virtually at the CG so, should it fail in the hover, the aircraft falls but with no great attitude change. With over 800 Harriers delivered, this has happened only once since 1960. (That USMC aircraft hit flat bending the wings and gear. The pilot did not eject but was unhurt).

Yak deal with VSTOL failures by automatically ejecting the pilot should the aircraft attitude exceed certain limits. Vladimir Yakimov, Chief Test Pilot for Yakovlev, quoted these for the Yak-38 as: 15° nose up, 10° nose down and 20° in roll. These values are increased to 25° nose up, 20° nose down and 30° in roll in the Yak-141. Yakovlev say the seat has a 100% success record with 21 auto and 13 pilot initiated ejections.

If we assume all engines have the same reliability, the Yak concept is more than three times as likely to suffer an engine problem than the Harrier. This is because a three engine installation is inherently more complex than a single one and such installation aspects can contribute to thrust loss causes. There is also the matter of lift engine starting system reliability at the end of every sortie, assuming that there is no runway within range that is long enough for a conventional landing.

Combat damage of powered lift and control systems also needs to be considered. A Harrier pilot only needs high rpm, a variable nozzle angle and reaction controls to carry out a safe VL. These items can be checked quickly at any speed below 500 kt by opening the throttle fully (to check rpm response) then momentarily pulling the nozzle lever back (to check nozzle rotation) and, while the lever is still back, moving the stick and rudder (to check the reaction control air supply or 'duct pressure' behaviour is normal).

A Yak pilot suspecting damage will have to suck it and see when in the circuit. To be fair, this is no worse than the way that a conventional aircraft pilot has to wait to see if such things as his gear, flaps, weight on wheels sensors, thrust reverser, braking chute, hook, wheel brakes, tyres and nosewheel steering will do the necessary to stop his aircraft on the narrow, cross-wind, 500 metres strip that the brochure says is OK.

The Harrier concept has major problems not present with the Yaks. They stem from needing one very large engine close to the CG and include aerodynamic distortions due to exhaust flows passing close to the airframe; a short air intake that is poor for efficiency, surge margin and head on signature, one compromise engine and intake design to deal with the conflicting requirements of low and high speeds and a general lack of flexibility in overall layout.

The Yak engine configuration has problems beyond the engine failure case. For example, the total installed thrust is not available throughout the flight envelope, the lift engines take up valuable volume that could be used for more internal fuel and their weight effect is similar to carrying around a couple of large but 'dud' weapons. The blast, vibration and temperature environment under the fuselage centreline during VSTOL limits high tech stores carriage to the wings (unlike the Harrier where it is possible to splay the nozzle efflux 15° either side of the vertical viewed from behind). Once a Yak has its lift engines running for takeoff, any holding point delays will warm and soften asphalt surfaces (or concrete block seals) so that they erode when the aircraft later moves forward. This actually happened at Farnborough when the Yak-38 had an unexpected 20 minute hold before lining up for its first pre-show qualifying sortie.

Despite such configuration induced problems, Yak were quoting a 141 internal fuel load of 4,400 kg for an 11,650 kg empty weight (37.7%) which compares with early Harrier Is at 5,000 lb for 12,500 lb (40%) rising to some 43% for later Harrier IIs. However, given the better optimisation of the Yak cruise engine, wingborne range and endurance are likely to be in the same ballpark for both concepts. This was certainly not the case with the earlier Yak-38 which was observed to fly sorties of only about one third the endurance of the Harrier.

Intake ingestion of foreign objects is a problem for both concepts. However, careful pilot control of thrust vector angle versus groundspeed has shown that Harriers can operate from loose surfaces. The Yak engines require a non-erodable surface for routine operation. A ship's steel deck would be ideal, especially if it was fitted with a gridded area at the deck edge.

Most of the foregoing is by way of background. What was new to me came from talking to Vladimir Yakimov and Alexander Dondukov, Yak's Chairman and General Designer, from watching videos of their operations back home and seeing both aeroplanes fly.

A cockpit brief in both aircraft showed that, so far as pilot operation is concerned, the Yak's VSTOL controls are perhaps even less demanding on the pilot than the Harrier's simple nozzle lever. Understanding how this is achieved, given the inherently complex Yak three-engined concept, is to appreciate the remarkable hydro-mechanical control engineering achievement on the 38, which has none of the 141's fly-by-wire facilities. However, such comparison presumes familiarity with Harrier piloting techniques.

The Harrier pilot has two engine controls mounted side by side on the left console: a normal fighter type throttle outboard and alongside it the special 'nozzle lever'. Pushing this nozzle lever fully forward points the jets aft while pulling it back progressively increases the downwards deflection of the exhausts, up to a maximum angle of 18° forward of the hover position.

This nozzle lever is sometimes used as a configuration change selector and sometimes as a flying control. Examples of the selector type of use being pulling the lever back to select the nozzles down, for example prior to doing a VTO, a hover, or a VL. The actual height control of these three manoeuvres is then done by throttle adjustment. An example of the lever being used in the control sense is when it is moved progressively forwards, from its hovering position, to control speed and flight path angle during an accelerating transition, the throttle remaining fixed throughout. Another example is the use of the nozzle lever to control the airspeed during a fixed throttle slow approach when weight precludes a VL. Such control/selector uses (and habits) must not be confused (like accidentally selecting the nozzles aft in the hover!)

On the other hand, despite his three engines, the Yak-38 pilot has only a single throttle handle operating in a fore and aft slide on the left cockpit wall. On the left hand console, in a similar position to the Harrier's nozzle lever, is a lever which is used only as a selector for choosing the VSTOL or conventional mode of the flight control system. This lever never has a control function.

In VSTOL mode, use of the single throttle gives height control through thrust modulation of all engines, while stick forwards and back gives pitch attitude control by differential thrust modulation of the lift and main engines. A trimmer-like switch on the top of the stick controls the vectoring nozzle angle and the limited rearwards component of the lift engines thrust. As on the SC1, this switch is a case of push forward to go faster, pull back to go slower. It has no other function or mode so confusion is unlikely. Additionally, the display of the vectoring nozzle angle is clear and shown to the pilot as it would appear to an external observer of the side elevation of the aircraft, with the needle indicating the direction of thrust. This gauge has a line to mark 60° on the Yak-141 from which angle the rest of the transition can be automatic if desired.

Playing such mode change tricks with the control systems in order to simplify the piloting task is nothing special in the world of fly-by-wire, but to make it all happen in the Yak-38 is an astonishing achievement. Vladimir Yakimov suggested I would "find the control system very interesting". He went on to repeat the point. However I believed him the first time.

Watching videos of the Yak-38 doing short takeoffs and rolling landings and operating vertically from a mobile hide completed my education on Yakovlev's achievements with a configuration which is intrinsically problematical. The mobile hide was a lorry like container, the sides and ends of which folded down to become the pad showing the benefits of folding wings again.

After this briefing the flying rehearsals and demonstrations were just as I expected: routine wingborne operation of both types, including takeoff and landing but with hovers thrown in mid-sortie. All slow flight was carried out with remarkable attitude steadiness but then you don't bow to the President at the end of your show with a Yak unless you want to eject and plant the aeroplane in his tent.

So what conclusions should we draw? It is very dangerous to

oversimplify what are complex issues but, at that stage of VSTOL history, it was difficult to avoid the conclusion that the Harrier concept represented the best way to do a military sub-sonic VSTOL job. Supersonic flight, with its requirement for high exhaust gas velocities, is a very different matter and it simply would not work to immerse the existing Harrier configuration in such velocities and temperatures. On the other hand, the Yak solution to powered lift, proven in the 38 and developed further in the 141, is suitable to drop in to the plan view of a Mig-29 or a Su-27/35.

Looked at like that, putting the Yak-38 in service becomes a very sensible stepping stone towards an ultimate supersonic goal and a far cry from being a poor attempt at doing 'a Harrier' as suggested in the 1970s by many who should have known better.

Chapter 4

RAE Bedford

On the 4th November 1964 my boss, Sqn Ldr Jack Henderson, stuck his head round my office door, said "Lunch" and disappeared. As it was 12.30, I dropped what I was doing and followed him out of the Aero Flight pilots' block at Bedford.

Parked in a slot right by the entrance was a plain dark green 10 cwt Bedford van which served as our runabout. In the way of Ministry transport in those days it was an extremely basic set of wheels. By the time I arrived Jack was already in the driving seat and his deputy, Lt Cdr Paul Millett, was joining him in the front so I made for the double doors at the back. The back of the van was completely empty and I squatted down on the wheel arch for the short drive to the mess just outside the airfield boundary. As a flight lieutenant posted in at the beginning of the year, I was the most junior of the four service test pilots whose collective job was to fly a variety of aircraft for the civilian scientists at Bedford. The fourth, Flt Lt Clive Rustin, was away that day.

There were no windows in the back so I watched the road ahead through the wire mesh divider between me and the cab, the better to keep my perch on the wheel arch as Jack was not hanging about. Half way to the mess I realised that he and Paul were talking about me. Essentially Jack was asking Paul's advice on whether I was ready to be launched in the 'Fred', as WG777 the Fairey Delta FD2 was affectionately known. Paul clearly had his reservations. Thanks to its reheated Avon, the FD2 accelerated faster than most aircraft of that era and Paul was afraid I would get left behind and so exceed the limiting speed for getting the wheels locked up and raising the droop nose. He made a big point to Jack that the last time this happened the thing had been up on jacks for weeks while the hangar crew tried to readjust the various gear and nose linkages, micro-switches and sequence valves involved. On the return journey after lunch, Jack and Paul continued their debate about whether I was fit to be let loose in the Fred. With hindsight their whole conversation was a big stage managed exercise but it did not seem like that to me at the time.

I had not been back in my office many minutes before Jack came in asking if I would like to fly the Fred that afternoon. I thought, "Oh shit" but heard myself say, "Of course, Jack".

FD2 or 'Fred'

As you can imagine, when I opened the throttle to start the takeoff roll there was no way I was going to let this thing run away with me and nothing was going to stop me getting the nose high enough to nail the speed below the dreaded 250 kt. After unstick, at about 170 kt, I quickly selected the gear and nose up and got on with a pretty determined pull which settled the IAS at 220 kt. From this position of advantage I watched all the bits do their thing and was rewarded with a full blown sequence of lights and 'dolls' eyes' showing that retraction was happening and finally that the aircraft was clean. (Dolls' eyes – properly known as magnetic indicators – were round and a bit less than an inch in diameter. They showed either black when all was tucked away or white if bits were still travelling. They were much in fashion in those days.)

Once clean, the best climb speed for the Fred was 450 kt IAS changing to 0.85M at about 13,000 ft, depending on the temperature of the day. Therefore I lowered the nose and started to let the speed build up.

With the experimental aircraft on Aero Flight it was normal to use 'continuous voice', this being a system that allowed you to transmit on one frequency to ATC and receive on another. Thus you could talk as if on the phone without having to wait to speak or even press a transmit button. There was also a room in the pilots' block where a safety pilot could join in on the conversation, plus watch real time telemetry data from the aircraft. On top of this you had your own dedicated air traffic controller who just looked after you. All this sounds great (and indeed it was) but it also meant that the ground pilot as well as ATC could hear every breath you took so those on the ground were never in much doubt about how well you were getting on – or not as the case may be. That afternoon I had none other than Jock Connell, the senior air traffic controller at Bedford, looking after me. Clearly with Jack Henderson as my safety pilot (and it sounded as if Paul was by his side), the first team was handling this flight.

Then it happened. As the speed reached 450 kt the aircraft went into a violent pitching oscillation.

I had never experienced a pilot induced oscillation (PIO) before, nor had Jack mentioned the possibility of one in his brief. Luckily, from the depths of my apprenticeship, I remembered a conversation with an RAE test pilot where he had told me that when guys got into a PIO (thanks to these new fangled powered flying controls), the only way to recover was to let go of the stick. I did just that and the oscillation stopped dead. Just then Jock Connell came up with "97 (my call-sign), amber one 5 miles ahead turn right 180 on to east." I quickly put in a bunch of right aileron aiming for a 60° bank before pulling round to avoid the amber one airway which was the main UK north-south route for airliners. Immediately the Fred started another oscillation. This time it was the mother of all lateral oscillations. A roll PIO. I let go of the stick as if it was on fire and at once the aircraft became steady as a rock. Of course my heading had hardly changed so now Jock was shouting for me to start my turn immediately.

I am sure you get the picture. Every time I tried to control the flight path in pitch or roll I just set off a huge PIO. I did get it round roughly on to east and I did keep it climbing but in the process I had this wild oscillatory ride which knocked all the stuffing out of me. I was too busy to speak – just panting and grunting – while I tried to decide what to do. At one point I dimly heard Jack enquire whether I had got it trimmed yet. I also thought I could hear Paul laughing in the background. Goodness knows what the joke was – it all seemed a pretty poor show to me.

A minute or two later, roughly on east and going through 35,000 ft, I let go of the stick and closed the throttle to give myself a much needed physical breather while I decided what to do. Clearly I could not control this monster to better than 20° of heading and several thousand feet. To land it was out of the question but I needed a rest before I jumped out. At idle power my speed was slowing and now approaching 200 kt so I gingerly got hold of the stick with the aim of getting the aircraft down to a more reasonable height. Thirty seconds later I realised the Fred was now a doddle to fly so I continued to descend at this speed. At 10,000 ft all was still well. Jock even had me on a steer for base. I added some power and levelled off at 200 kt. No problem.

To cut a long story short, I drifted down into the circuit and landed perfectly normally but my brain was churning as I taxied in. Clearly I was not cut out for this sort of work and I was rehearsing my resignation speech to Jack as I continued to taxi to my parking spot on the Aero Flight apron. This was just as well because Jack and Paul were standing with the ground crew and clearly waiting for me. I shut it down, the ground crew put the ladder up to the cockpit and I climbed down noticing that Jack and Paul were still enjoying some sort of joke.

As I approached them I started with, "I'm sorry, Jack" but he put his hand up to silence me and told the ground crew to put the hydraulic ground rig on the aircraft and turn it on. With this and the Houchin electrical rig running, Jack turned to me and, shouting over the noise of the two rigs, said, "Get back in, stand on the seat and face the back". Wondering what on earth all this was about I mutely did as instructed. "Now push the stick forward with your foot." I turned round on the seat to do this and Jack shouted, "No – do it facing the back and watch the controls". Again I did as he said and felt the stick go fully forward under my boot. For a second or so I was amazed to see no movement of the controls, then suddenly all the trailing edge surfaces went down.

Back in Jack's office he put me in the picture. When the Fred was designed in the 1950s, fully powered flying controls were in their infancy and people were learning about them all the time. In the Fred's case it had none of the more modern filtration systems and so, after a fair bit of flying, silt built up in the operating fluid resulting in significant lags between the pilot's input to the servo valve and the subsequent movement of the actuator. Lags in any control system are very bad news. If you wonder why, you have only to imagine driving a car fast with a small built in delay between you moving the steering wheel and the front wheels turning. If you were to make a normal correction, nothing would happen so you would then put in a bit more input. Suddenly the thing would bite and you would realise you now had more than you needed, then, as you tried to correct the other way, it would happen all over again, leading to a nice weaving progress up the motorway.

Knowing that the Fred was due a major hydraulic system flush and clean, Jack and Paul decided to use the opportunity to give me some valuable on the job training regarding the effect of lag in a control system. Today such things are taught rather more formally at test pilot schools using variable stability aeroplanes where an instructor in the back seat can dial in a whole range of flying control problems. However, I suspect such modern experiences are perhaps a little less memorable when compared to the one Jack set up for me.

Returning to that lunchtime journey in the van, as I suggested earlier, the conversation I 'overheard' was clearly deliberately staged for my benefit. They wanted me to be concentrating so hard on checking the gear and nose retraction sequence that I would simply fail to notice how nicely the Fred handled below 250 kt. Later, at high speed, when more control precision was needed, I would trip over the lag effects and learn my invaluable lesson. Which doubtless explains why the first team was up for this trip and everyone was laughing while it was going on.

WG774, the first FD2 after it was modified to become the BAC T221

Incidentally WG777 was the second of the two FD2 aircraft built. The first, WG774, was the airframe that Peter Twiss used to raise the world's airspeed record by no less than 310 mph to 1,132 mph in 1956. It was used alongside WG777 at Bedford up until 1960 when it went to Bristol to be modified, returning to Bedford in 1966 fitted with an ogee wing as part of the Concorde research programme and reborn as the BAC T221 with a nice modern hydraulic system that took all the fun out of life.

Winding the clock back ten years to 1954 and my apprenticeship, I had been lucky enough to have a stint working with the Aerodynamics department at the new wind tunnel site then being built at Bedford. As I then lived in the YMCA apprentices' hostel at Farnborough, it involved a daily commute in an Anson or Rapide aircraft allocated to the 'Bedford Ferry' task. However, apprentices were expected to take the rough with the smooth.

My apprentice master at Bedford, Ralph Maltby, was the boffin in charge of one of the first tunnels completed on the site – the new state of the art 'low speed' 13 x 9. Tunnels are always referred to by the dimensions of their 'working section' (the part where the model is mounted) so this one had a rectangular working section 13 ft wide and 9 ft tall. The special thing about it was the very high quality of the airflow past the model which was steadier, smoother and less turbulent than the air in any other RAE tunnel to date. This was vital for accurate results when testing models at low speeds such as those involved during takeoff and landing.

In the way of life's little coincidences, the first man I met when I reported for duty at Bedford in December 1963 was Ralph Maltby. I was climbing the stairs in the Aero Flight pilots' block in my best uniform, hat on, on my way to meet my new boss and Ralph was coming down. He stopped, looked at me and said, "I know you. Take that hat off." I did as he asked and he said, "Good grief – Farley."

Walking round the hangar later that day was a sobering experience because there were so many different types of aircraft. They included the Fred and four other research prototypes as well as countless other service types employed on specialist tasks and by then I had been told that each of the four Aero Flight pilots was expected to fly them all.

Nothing in my RAF experience had prepared me for my new pilot colleagues and it took me a while to understand them. The boss, Jack Henderson, had such powers of observation that a 20 minute flight took him literally weeks of steady writing to get his thoughts down in first draft form.

Paul Millet was in the Navy, which struck me as strange as Bedford was a long way from the sea. Paul never seemed to write and was always apparently on the point of saying something to me. Then he would break off, go to the phone and try to arrange for the SB5 (or some such thing) to fly in a new configuration on a day when Jack was going to be away. To help him do this he had an uncanny knack of correctly estimating when Jack would convene one of his meetings with the boffins to obtain their first reactions to his rewritten second draft of last month's report.

The third pilot was Clive Rustin. Clive was very kind to me, took me under his wing and gave me invaluable advice on the hardware in the hangar, always assuming I had first managed to distract him from his normal preoccupation of trying to come up with something that Jack hadn't already covered in one of his reports.

Concorde research
In the mid-1960s three Aero Flight aircraft, the HP115, the BAC T221 and Vulcan XA890, played an important part in convincing the RAE scientists that their ideas for a supersonic transport using a slender delta wing were practical. The HP115 was already hard at work when I joined but the Vulcan and the BAC T221 arrived during my time.

HP115 over the Bedford wind tunnels

The HP115 was the first pure research prototype that I was allowed to fly so it will always occupy a very special place in my test flying memories. However there were other reasons why I enjoyed flying it so much. After all, with a shape like that who could doubt it was a *real* research aircraft and *real* research aircraft had to be flown by *real* test pilots, didn't they? Well not this one! This one was so easy and benign to fly it was amazing that we actually got paid to do it. In the world of research flying, the HP115 has to have been the definitive sheep in wolf's clothing.

Thanks to the lift produced by vortices over their top surfaces, slender deltas flying at low speeds can enjoy a remarkable margin from the stall. Indeed the stalling alpha can be more than double the angles we are used to with ordinary wings and even then the limit may take the form of a loss of control (known as a 'departure' in the trade) in roll and yaw rather than a breakdown of lift. The bad news is that such high alphas lead to huge amounts of drag so that as you slow down and long before you run out of lift, you reach a speed at which you need full throttle just to maintain level flight. This speed is rather naturally called the Zero Rate of Climb speed or Vzrc. At Vzrc you cannot accelerate, climb or turn so the only way to get speed back is to reduce the drag by lowering the nose, accepting the associated temporary loss of lift and height in order to accelerate. From a pilot's perspective this manoeuvre is similar to a normal stall recovery.

HP115

*74° 42'
leading
edge
sweep*

This led to the consideration that certifying the takeoff speeds of a slender delta airliner, such as Concorde, would need to be related to a margin above Vzrc rather than a margin above the traditional stalling speed. The snag with this idea was that on a multi-engined slender delta Vzrc literally leaps up if you lose an engine, requiring the very rapid selection of a much lower pitch attitude from the one you had before the engine failure.

To address such concerns the Aero Flight boffins came up with a Takeoff Director (TOD) proposal for Concorde that was aimed at giving pilots easy-to-use guidance to help them maintain optimum climb performance following an engine failure on takeoff. It used the cross pointer director bars already provided in all airliners for the ILS approach and landing phase. This meant using the vertical needle on takeoff to track the runway centre line, following the horizontal one to rotate at the correct speed and then capturing the attitude that gave the desired margin above Vzrc during initial climb out. When an engine failed, the system would at once start moving the horizontal bar down the display, directing the pilot to a new lower nose position, automatically taking into account the thrust and drag variations due to the particular AUW and ambient conditions of the day.

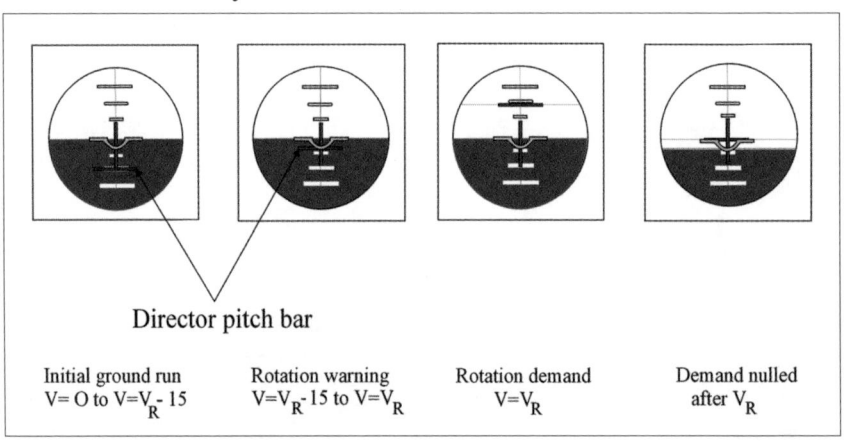

Director pitch bar

| Initial ground run V= O to V=V_R- 15 | Rotation warning V=V_R-15 to V=V_R | Rotation demand V=V_R | Demand nulled after V_R |

TOD modes as used in the Vulcan

While the HP115 and the BAC T221 were conceived to have similar aerodynamics to Concorde, they had totally different inertias. In the dynamic situation of a takeoff, the high inertia Concorde was going to respond quite differently to the low inertia single-seat aircraft because of its very different weight. Therefore Bedford was allocated Vulcan

XA890 to develop the TOD. This was an early pre-production aircraft then surplus to requirements since it had a straight leading edge unlike the shape that served with the RAF V-force.

The box that drove the TOD display contained a suitable mix of accelerometers and rate gyros and was provided with inputs from the normal Vulcan pitot-static system. The trial needed to develop the laws, or mathematical equations, that would determine just how the box moved the director bars as well as what to do about a rotate cue. It was clear that different pilots were likely to respond in different ways to the instrument display so we tried to arrange things so that the system could handle the full range of piloting techniques from smooth gentle corrections to large aggressive inputs.

The normal right hand seat Vulcan flight instruments were replaced by a panel that closely resembled that of the Trident, then in service with BEA, including the actual Trident attitude and horizontal situation instruments.

Normal Vulcan panel   *TOD panel*

After we had done some 100 hours of development flying, the Aero Flight pilots felt the laws were about right so it was time to see what airline pilots thought of them. I had strong views about this final and most important part of the programme where we had to 'sell' the system to those who would have to use it, failed dismally to keep them to myself and so got lumbered with the job of running this phase. The flying supervision chain then swung into action regarding the need to indoctrinate the visiting pilots on purely Vulcan issues. The bosses could foresee nothing but trouble with these flights and looked to me to cover all eventualities so that they might be fireproof, come what may. The standard stuff of life really.

If we were to successfully sell our work to airline pilots who were not used to development work, let alone the Vulcan, some thought was required. Because they were used to the spacious and comfortable shirtsleeve environment of a Trident, or similar, such evaluators were not going to feel instantly at home trussed up in the right hand Vulcan bang-seat, looking through a porthole to the side and a letter box type slot to the front. In fact if I was not careful, I suspected some might even change their minds before we got to taxi out. At best their minds were hardly going to be fully focused on the niceties of the TOD. Finally, there were a few Vulcan bits and pieces on the right which I could not see, let alone reach and which I would have to rely on them operating correctly when appropriate.

I pondered all this and concluded that the sortie brief should only mention the Vulcan in passing and that all emphasis would be on the TOD. This approach left me with the need to operate this two pilot cockpit without much help so I decided it was time to call in a few favours in the hangar.

The idea was that the experimental fitters would make three Perspex sheets that went over the right hand side consoles. These sheets would have holes for the switches to poke through and allow the gauges to be read. One panel was painted white and had the switches and gauges numbered 1 to 10, the second was blue 20 to 22 and the third yellow 30 to 37. This simplified the check list calls to the likes of 'Yellow panel 32 to ON' (or whatever). Having different numbers on each panel further reduced the chance of a mistake. Thus the Vulcan brief boiled down to just mentioning that there were these three panels which I would ask them to check and set from time to time.

As for the ejection seat, I explained they did not need to know anything about it. I would check it thoroughly and strap them in. I pointed out we were only flying in the circuit and this was Bedford not Heathrow so we had the luxury of the airfield and ATC all to ourselves. This meant we would land at once in response to any conceivable emergency. (To land rather than eject was also highly desirable so far as the poorly placed team in the back were concerned who, without the benefit of ejection seats, would see only the nose leg through the escape hatch should they have to attempt a bale-out.) In short our evaluators were about to fly at our very own private airstrip in a delightfully overpowered four engine airliner that could climb on one.

In the air they all loved it. As is the way of the world the older captains looked very serious and tried to come up with a significant comment (as befitted their station in life) while the young first officers said, "Want one!" and a week later sent in well-written reports. My logbook contains the names of 16 chaps who enjoyed the TOD. They include such legendary aviators as Dave Davies of the ARB (later the CAA) and Brian Trubshaw. One with whom I especially enjoyed flying was First Officer John Millett from BEA who had earlier been a flying instructor of mine at FTS. I then felt a little of what Janis Joplin described when she went back to a high school reunion as a pop star and met again the teachers who had virtually drummed her out of school. Actually, if John reads this, we thought he was one of the better ones. Good military instructors need to be hard at times because hard school works and military squadrons are not exactly flying clubs.

XA890 at Bedford

It was a real pleasure to see how this diverse bunch took to the TOD kit. A typical sortie started with them doing a normal takeoff to see the rotate demand and generally get used to the display, then I would quickly pop it back on the ground so that they could do five or six more takeoffs.

63

On the second one I would chop a throttle on initial climb out, the bar would dip and off they went at the correct new attitude.

Then came a run with the first throttle chopped at rotate and the second after unstick. Given the right weather and evaluating pilot, I later enjoyed chopping one before rotate, the second during rotate and a third as we left the ground. Sitting alongside them and watching as they climbed out over the valley at the end of RW27, with a rate of climb of around 200 ft/min, on one engine, in a strange type for which they had not been briefed said everything about the potential value of this TOD.

That was the part played by XA890. As aeroplanes go it was the only one I have flown where I always felt I had plenty of wing, whatever the manoeuvre. That wing and its low speed lift put it in a class of its own, especially when landing. There was one TOD visiting pilot who experienced the truly awesome potential of all that wing area and the occasion is worth mentioning. The chap, who shall be nameless, was a senior examiner with the Civil Aviation Flying Unit (CAFU), the organisation charged with setting the standards in civil aviation. Such worthies are not known for treating trips as a jolly but I expected him to relax his examiner attitude a bit on his day out in our Vulcan.

Sadly I was to be disappointed and, by the end of the trip, I was a tad peeved with being treated as a lower form of aeronautical life. Sure I was only a flight lieutenant with two thin blue ones against his four wide gold ones but it was my aeroplane! Therefore I decided to use some of the aforementioned wing and show him that there were other people in the world who knew about aeroplanes beside him. After he had done his final takeoff, I quietly remarked that the Vulcan had a lot of lift available and so did not need much runway for landing. I then took control and turned finals on RW24 which was half the width and much shorter than the main one we had been using.

Vulcan buffs will know that the minimum threshold speed in RAF service was 125 kt, a speed determined not by lift requirements but by the need for good lateral control in turbulence. The day was lovely, with not a turb anywhere so by half a mile out I was nicely settled on finals at 125 kt gear down and airbrakes out. At 100 ft, as the security fence slipped beneath our nose, I used my right hand to stream the braking parachute, open the bomb doors and stop-cock the two inner engines while my left kept steadily raising the nose. The lovely monster reared right up and seemed to just hang in the sky before greasing on at a very low speed. I lowered the nose, put on the brakes and stopped. Then I remarked that if he looked out of his side he would see that we were still a little short of the centreline of the main runway.

Getting no response, I looked across to find him rigid in his seat and just staring out of the front. I suspect he was in shock as we had only used the stub of 24 or about 2,000 ft. Perhaps he thought he had died and was waiting to see some pearly gates appear. Showing him what could be done with a decent wing made me feel quite a lot better though.

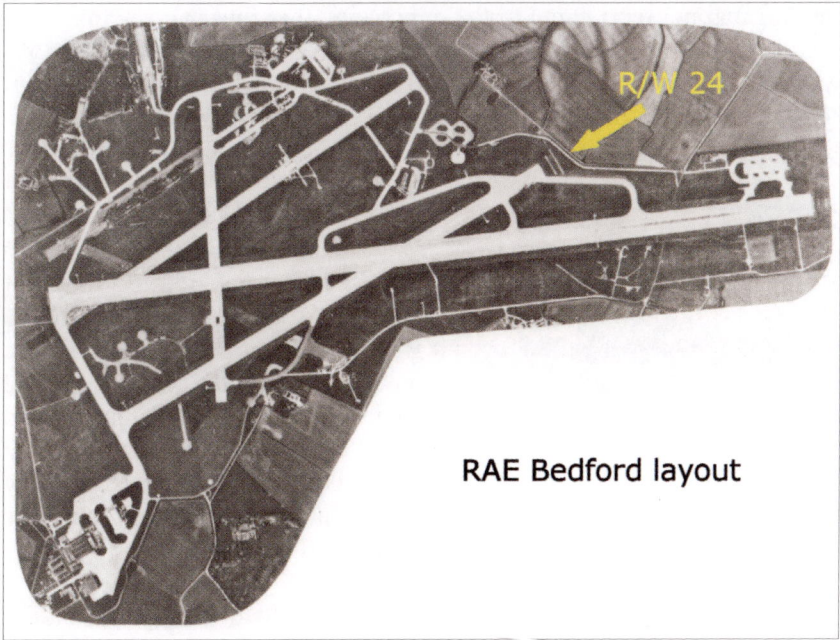

RAE Bedford layout

Bedford runway layout, showing the part of runway 24 before the main runway

The man in charge of the TOD programme was no less than my former apprentice master Ralph Maltby so, during a demonstration flight with him in the right hand seat, I insisted he try it for himself. Very reluctantly Ralph flew a circuit in the same manner as the airline pilots on their TOD familiarisation flights and clearly enjoyed himself despite his reservations. This event was typical of the very close relationship between the Aero Flight 'boffins' and their test pilots which played such an important part in the success of many of the Bedford research programmes in the 1960s.

Helicopters

Helicopters were used at Bedford for many support tasks and so in my first month I was sent back to Farnborough for a chopper conversion courtesy of the ETPS helicopter instructor, Sqn Ldr Bill Stevens. After half a dozen trips in a Dragonfly, 'Sir' sent me off on my own to practise my very limited skills. I can remember to this day how totally inadequate I felt on those early solo trips. Sitting in the hover and flying by numbers over a local farmer's field just north of the Hogs Back, I wondered how I might cope if I had any serious sort of emergency – or even a minor one for that matter. I came to the conclusion that I was a very long way short of being in possession of the sort of correct instinctive reactions that I felt I had acquired with fixed wing. However, as with so many flying concerns, the only solution is time practising things in the air and, just as importantly, thinking about them on the ground.

Aero Flight had a piston-engined Whirlwind 7 helicopter modified to drop large free-flight models of aircraft like the FD2, the HP115, the BAC T221 and Concorde. These model trials were to bridge the data gap between wind tunnels and full scale, especially when it came to stalling or spinning which nobody was keen to do for real on the types mentioned.

I used to love a day of model dropping. Typically it started at Met Briefing on a misty morning when the met man said that a high was established and because of the lack of wind the visibility might not pick up all day so normal Bedford flying was unlikely. At this point, the model-dropping boffins would rush to get a model from the store, the hangar would prepare the Whirlwind and I would go to the mess for a stack of sandwiches. By mid-morning all would be ready for the off. We ferried the model, attached to a special cradle under the Whirlwind, to the drop site inside the Larkhill range complex north of Boscombe. The trip down usually took a good hour or so and, once cleared onto the range, we would land to prepare the model and ourselves. There were three of us – a boffin, a model technician and me. The model needed off-loading to fit batteries and check out the timer controls, recovery parachute and so on while we needed our sandwiches.

Apart from ATC communications, the team were on their own. No bosses, no phones (those were the days!), no in-tray, fine weather, plenty of grass, a super model aeroplane to play with plus our very own chopper. What a terrible job.

The drop height was anything up to 10,000 ft so the climb took a little while. Once at height the model was lowered on the end of a cable that came out under the belly. The trick then was to try and get it flying steadily on the end of the long line at the appropriate scale speed for the launch. I did my best to follow the instructions of the boffin who was leaning out of the main cabin door and observing how it flew. When all was right he hit the release and the model did its thing.

We now needed to fly down in big circles round the model and keep it in sight. This usually needed an autorotation and a fair bit of speed in order to lose height as quickly as the model. After the model recovery parachute popped, it was a case of trying to land as close as possible to where it finished up because the things were jolly heavy to lug any distance. The ground condition varied a lot on the range and one needed a bit of caution in picking a touchdown spot which was often sloping. I never had the chopper fall over or get stuck but I do remember one day having to climb back in pretty smartly as the little wheels started to slowly but surely disappear from view on a surface that turned out to be softer than it had looked from the air. Once the model was crutched back up under the chopper all that remained was a nice evening trip back to base. All things considered, a day out to die for.

Other jobs for which we used the choppers were more obvious. The Short SC1 and later the Hawker P1127 jet lift aircraft were eventually coaxed into some pretty small restricted sites with the aim of demonstrating the operating site flexibility that comes with being able to land from a hover. We had two such sites cut in woods near the airfield and we used the Whirlwind to accustom ourselves with the visual cues inside these holes. The engine in the P1127 in those days had a one hour

67

life when used in the hover or partially jetborne. Only with the nozzles aft did it offer a 25 hour life. With this sort of time pressure, the Whirlwind was invaluable to sort ourselves out before the expensive jet aircraft trials.

One day I was lucky not to break the Whirlwind. It had been drummed into me during my chopper conversion that if the engine stopped you had to push the collective down really fast or you risked the rotor slowing down catastrophically quickly. On the other hand, I knew that Boscombe were unhappy to release fixed wing aircraft to service without showing that a two second pilot reaction time was feasible following critical failures such as an engine failure or autostab hard over so, when doing an air test on the Whirlwind following a routine rotor head change, I thought it would be a good idea to snap the throttle shut and wait for a count of two before lowering the lever. I think I felt it would just sink a bit and so what as I was at 5,000 ft. As the proper chopper pilots reading this will know, I was wrong. The thing instantly pitched violently nose down and started rolling as well. In moments the speed was very high and, as I instinctively tried to get the nose up, my pull accelerated the rotor above the rpm limit to a number I could not believe. I crept home where the consensus was I was lucky not to have lost the rotor.

Whirlwind 7 and JF in the 'Hole in the wood' restricted site

In order to try and put some consistency into pilots' comments about aircraft handling matters, the research community uses something called the Cooper-Harper Rating Scale. In the 1960s it was just called the Cooper Rating as Mr Harper did not offer his refinements until later. The scale consists of Levels 1 to 10 plus a written description of the circumstances associated with each number. The evaluating pilot selects the words that best express his feelings and so the appropriate number is established. A rating of 1 is as good as it comes while the paragraph associated with Level 10 has words like 'uncontrollable' and suggests escape is uncertain (bang seats not being universal in test aircraft, at least for the first 60 years or so).

I once experienced what I felt was Level 9 handling in a Whirlwind Mk1. It belonged to the Blind Landing Experimental Unit (BLEU), also based at Bedford. Unlike our model-dropping Mk7 which had a dual hydraulic powered cyclic control system, the Mk1 had only single channel power with manual reversion should that fail. One night, while assessing a new BLEU aerodrome lighting proposal for VSTOL aircraft, I had a hydraulic failure and found the now manual stick wanted to thrash about all over the cockpit. Indeed it needed rather more strength than I seemed to have to hold it in anything like the right place. More by luck than judgement, I managed a vertical landing in the middle of a runway and went off to complain loudly that, following a hydraulic failure the thing was at least a 9 and should never have been cleared to hover with that sort of handling. I became very embarrassed when I was promptly informed that without hydraulics this mark of Whirlwind was not cleared to fly slower than 60 kt and so needed a rolling landing to prevent the stick being snatched from one's grasp. Ignorance seldom results in bliss when it comes to aeroplanes.

I never considered myself a proper helicopter pilot as I just used them for a few specialist tasks. However I honestly believe that for the good of his or her soul, every aviator should have a go in one – at least once. As an ego busting experience for a fixed wing 'ace' there is nothing like it.

Gust Research

In the mid-1960s the new breed of swept wing jet airliners were offering to fly their passengers above the nasty stuff called weather but in so doing suffered a spate of what were termed 'jet upsets'. These involved suddenly going from a nice sedate cruise in clear air into a pretty violent descent, sometimes losing several tens of thousands of feet in height and more than once shedding an engine pod during the ensuing manoeuvre and recovery.

These events attracted the attention of Aero Flight because, while such incidents might have been expected if the aircraft had been in a thunderstorm, it was far from clear why they should happen out of a clear blue sky. Soon it was established that these upsets were due to a combination of a seemingly new phenomenon called 'clear air turbulence' (CAT) and the limited stability and control characteristics of those early large swept wing designs, once they exceeded their certificated speed limits.

The boffins felt that they knew very little about the precise nature of the air movements underlying CAT. Accordingly their gust research team took advantage of the emerging capabilities of instrument recording systems and modified a two-seat Meteor NF11. Internally the radar was replaced with instrumentation recorders (big things in those days) while externally the nose was fitted with an impressive probe and suitable vanes to sense airflow direction ahead of the aircraft. Thus equipped off it went in search of CAT.

This was easier said than done as we were reliant on Met telling us where the upper air conditions might be favourable for CAT. It was pretty dull old stuff. To forecast CAT, the Met men looked for areas having a considerable wind speed variation over a small height band as can be expected in the vicinity of jet streams. At a guess the ratio of flat calm flights to those with some chop was about one in ten, while I personally never found severe CAT. Since we had it, the instrumented Meteor was also used to get a more modern feel for the insides of thunderstorms as they are pretty bad news when it comes to normal aviation. At best they can give you a very nasty ride and at worst they will have your wings off, while in between they can cause you to lose control while flying on instruments.

The Meteor NF11 was a good strong aeroplane, very suitable for the job, although it had no bang seats. It was made of metal and also very simple so far as systems were concerned, which meant no wild results from a lightning strike. Some years ago I asked an F-16 guy exactly what he thought about his fly-by-wire flight control system should he encounter a thunderstorm. Because very bad language has no place in this sort of book, I will leave his reply to your imagination.

Gust research Meteor WD 686

That said the F-16 has a mostly metal structure which is good when it comes to containing the results of a lightning strike. Many years later, while flying the 'plastic' winged Harrier II out in the States on engine out trials at Edwards, I arrived first thing in the morning to find the carbon fibre wing being wallpapered with rolls of aluminium kitchen foil from K-Mart. I asked why (which I did a lot in those days) and was told that in the event of a lightning strike the high voltage stuff would have something to make it feel welcome besides the fuel and hydraulic pipes inside the wings. Mmm. Still the AV-8B had an ejector seat which has to improve most odds.

There is a long history of lightning strikes being relatively non-events on aircraft which have a well bonded metal structure. This is good news since the traditional side effects of strikes on things like compasses and one's nerves are rather less important than a chunk of structure failing. However, being in a modern plastic general aviation aeroplane could be food for thought and in my book is another very good reason to stay clear of thunderstorms. Although in saying that, I am well aware that I am no expert on the triggering of strikes and it may well be that the experts feel that such aircraft are very unlikely to be hit, given the great reduction in metal components.

I have twice been in an aircraft that has been struck by lightning. Once was in the gust Meteor and then, a few days later, in a Trident going on holiday with the family. The big flash and bang in the Meteor set me up for a nicely nonchalant response to the Trident experience because as we know currency really does help in the aviation business. I was squeezing past a steward and his trolley at the time and his face was a picture. I really did think the poor chap's eyes were going to pop out of his head. Fortunately my proximity to him allowed for a slightly conspiratorial mutter in his ear that it was only a lighting strike and nothing to worry about. He gave me the sort of look that I suspect religious leaders enjoy from members of their flock fairly routinely but for me it remains a novel experience to this day.

It may seem a statement of the obvious but the effect of gusts is to momentarily distort the airflow around an aeroplane. How bad this distortion is depends on the speed of the gust compared to the airspeed of the aeroplane's lifting system. *Fig 1* should make the effect clear. The gust shown is acting purely upwards which will momentarily increase the alpha. To make the angle effect obvious I have used a gust speed that is very large, about a third of the IAS, as experienced by microlight pilots. Just what effect this angle change has on the g one feels depends on two aircraft related factors, the lift curve slope and the wing loading.

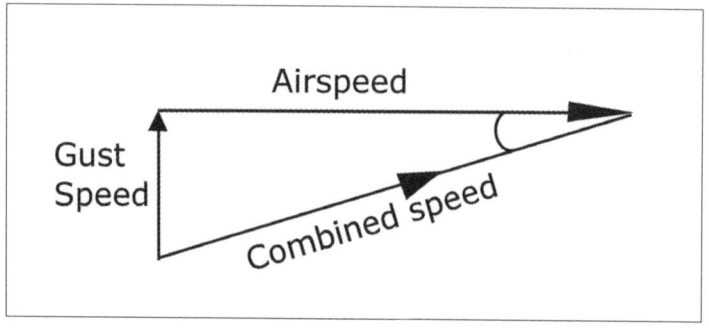

Fig 1

The lift curve slope (for details see Chapter 10 Lift and Drag) is nothing more than the angle of the C_L versus alpha line. The steeper this line, the more the lift will leap up for a given angular increase in alpha while the shallower the slope, the less will be the change in lift. In general, the higher the aspect ratio of a wing, the steeper will be the slope of the curve while for low aspect ratios the flatter it will be.

The effect of wing loading is pretty intuitive. You slip through a gust better with a high wing loading aeroplane than in one with a low wing loading where the ride will inevitably be relatively wilder. The boffins at Bedford had a favourite standard for evaluating the likely effects of turbulence and this was the '15 ft/sec sharp edge gust'. This phrase means just what it says. The gust had a speed of 15 ft/sec and arrived instantaneously. Since knots need to be multiplied by 1.69 to turn them into ft/sec, a general aviation light aircraft flying at 100 kt is doing 169 ft/sec so in the triangle of *Fig 1* the Airspeed value is 169 and the Gust Speed value 15 which, according to my tangent tables, makes the increase in the alpha 5° as near as matters.

At an airspeed of 200 kt the angle becomes 2.5°. For a slower aircraft doing 50 kt, the angle change is doubled to 10° which is why microlight pilots have such a rough time on gusty days!

Given how easy it is to distort the lifting system round a microlight, consider a hovering Harrier. Here the lifting system speed is the speed of the jet efflux which is very high indeed compared to any gusts. This is why the Harrier sits nice and steadily in the hover alongside a ship despite a high wind over the deck and local turbulence from the superstructure. In the same circumstances the pilot of a similar weight Sea King helicopter is only too well aware of how the slower speed lifting system he is using is being distorted by the gusts and hence requires continuous control inputs to hold station.

Before going any further with gusts, it is important to remember that in real life most gusts will have a component in more than one aircraft axis and will not just blow upwards as in *Fig 1*. A pure lateral gust will not affect the normal g but will affect the aircraft motion in yaw (weathercock effect) and roll (via dihedral effect – and please remember that the dihedral *effect* depends on more than just the dihedral *angle* of the wing). With a vertical gust the longitudinal stability will determine what pitch attitude change results from the gust. Hit a gust that has both lateral and vertical motion and you will get some combination of all we have described. Plus don't forget the effect of a gust component along the direction you are flying, which will result in a sudden increase or decrease of your airspeed.

Now we can easily see why the extreme gustiness inside a thunderstorm can be pretty much an unknown so far as the effect it is going to have on your aeroplane. A big enough vertical gust could have the wings off, a big enough lateral gust could make you fear for your fin while the general mayhem could reduce your accuracy of flight path control to the point that you go up or down thousands of feet without having much say in the matter.

Of course it may only be a weak thunderstorm but without weather radar how do you know this? What about icing? What about freezing rain effects which are at their worst should you fly your nice cold airframe into a mass of super-cooled water inside a thunderstorm. Then there is hail. Do you really want to dimple your leading edge (or worse) with hail the size of golf balls?

All in all it was not surprising that Aero Flight conducted a lot of gust and thunderstorm penetration trials around the world to help quantify some of these effects. By the time I left Bedford, as well as the trusty Meteor, they had the prototype Canberra PR9 (WH793) and a Scimitar (XD231) fully instrumented for gust research. While I flew these from time to time, I counted myself lucky to be able to plead that the powered lift aircraft needed a lot of my time.

Powered lift research

SC1

Aero Flight already had the Short SC1 jet vertical takeoff and landing research aircraft when I joined them. This used four lift engines for vertical and low speed flight and a fifth for normal wing borne flight. Two of these aircraft were built to RAE specifications and their origins can be traced back to 1951 as discussed in Chapter 6 which deals with the VAAC programme.

A moment's thought about doing a vertical takeoff using any sort of jets makes one realise that the engine exhaust is going to bounce off the ground and create very rough conditions underneath the aircraft before it lifts off. This is going to do nothing for the steadiness of the aircraft just as it leaves the ground and is less than desirable when initially testing a new type.

Such conditions leave you torn between trying to do a prudent slow and progressive lift, while hoping the considerable time spent in 'ground effects' do not cause you to lose control there and then, or alternatively a mad dart up and away from the ground into clear smooth air where you just hope you will find the controls work when you get there.

The solution is to dig a hole in the ground and cover it with a grating strong enough to support the aircraft. The jets can then pass through the 'ground plane' leaving you with an aircraft that seems to be in 'free air' or 'out of ground effect'. Of course you need to make provision for the air that has passed through the grid to exhaust well away from the aircraft but that is hardly difficult.

SC1 on the 'grid' at Bedford

Apart from helping pilot handling, extensive use of the 'grid' at Bedford, or the 'pit' as the same device was known at Dunsfold, certainly reduced the scatter of VTO performance measurements during the 1960s.

Another benefit was that you could spend a minute or two with either the lift engines running or, in the case of the P1127, with the nozzles in the hover position without cooking the rubber tyres. That sort of practical consideration was a big help with carrying out last minute checks, instrumentation calibrations and so on.

Hawker P1127

In 1964 as the junior test pilot on Aero Flight I never expected to be given what I thought was the best job going at that time. This was to go to Dunsfold and collect XP831, the first prototype P1127, bring it back to Bedford and become its project pilot. When you get that sort of opportunity you don't go around asking why, you just get on with it and thank your lucky stars. Some considerable time later I did ask Ralph Maltby and he said it was a matter of money. What else?

As mentioned earlier, the engine in XP831 had a one hour life when flown with the nozzles down and 25 hours when flown nozzles aft like an ordinary aircraft. Understandably the boffins had more questions about flying on the engine than flying on the wings. The very short life when used at low speed was because the engine had to be thrashed to generate sufficient thrust to equal the aircraft weight even with only one or two minutes of fuel on board. After an hour of such jet lift time had been accumulated (usually in flights of only a minute or two), the engine had to come out and go back to Bristol for a strip overhaul. Since that usually involved considerable replacement of the blades in the hot end, the one hour life was certainly not a conservative estimate. The cost of this overhaul was £60,000 – quite a lot of money in the mid-1960s. This gave an overhead of engine direct operating cost of £1,000 per minute, to which had to be added all the other costs associated with flying a prototype and rather naturally concentrated senior people's minds.

As Ralph explained to me many months after I took XP831 to Bedford, "We did not want to talk to you until you had done at least one of all the VSTOL manoeuvres (vertical takeoff, hover, vertical landing, rolling vertical takeoff, rolling vertical landing, accelerating transition, decelerating transition, short takeoff and slow landing) and we reckon you couldn't do that lot in less than 15 minutes total time. Because we had to invest a quarter of an engine life in such a conversion we chose you because you had most of your tour remaining."

Much of the flying done with XP831 at Bedford involved the nitty gritty of data gathering, the bedrock of so much research. However, given the unusual nature of the aircraft and its capabilities, it was always going to be interesting work for all concerned. This especially applied to the need to develop new test techniques to establish as far as possible steady state data with an aeroplane that was in those days a pig to handle as well as introducing the new major variable of nozzle angle which rather increased the number of flight conditions that had to be checked!

Once we had flown the P1127 into the 'Hole in the Wood' restricted site and later had a successful press event showing off this 'new jet fighter capability', the boffins wanted to know if we could do it again at night.

Since the aim was to make things as operationally realistic as possible, I finished up doing this with only a couple of tiny battery driven red lights in a field a mile short of the 'hole' for range clues, plus three white ones in the hole. The aluminium pad was illuminated at the last moment using the dipped headlamps of a Land Rover parked in the entrance to the site. Both the deceleration to the hole and the subsequent VTO and acceleration away were by far the hardest instrument flying I ever did and I discuss some of the particular issues and solutions I used on this occasion in the specialist Chapter 13.

There were so many differences between flying the Short SC1 and the Hawker P1127 that the phrase 'chalk and cheese' comes to mind. By the time I finish this comparison you may be inclined to feel that it all boils down to 'Hawkers got it right and Shorts got it wrong'. However that is far too simplistic a view and involves hindsight – and believe me in 1964 hindsight about jet VSTOL was in short supply.

At the simplest level both aeroplanes were similar because both were single-seat fixed wing jet aircraft that could take off and land vertically. Both could fly on their wings, both could hover, both could transition to and from the hover and both used pure jet thrust to achieve all this.

However, the design teams at Shorts and Hawkers used very different solutions because they started from very different positions. The Short SC1 was specified, designed and purchased to enable the RAE to do research into jet VSTOL. On the other hand, the Hawker P1127 was conceived by a fighter design house with a long history of supplying fighters to the Royal Air Force as a possible way of achieving a jet fighter that could land and take off vertically. It was not originally designed to a government specification but to meet a need, as perceived inside Hawkers, that the RAF (and others) needed a VSTOL capability to counter the possibility that their conventional aircraft could be grounded by attacking their runways.

This difference in objective was fundamental in determining why Hawkers finished up with a single-engined vectored thrust aircraft that they hoped they could make work but which had the potential to become a fighter, while Shorts filled a small airframe with four lift engines and one cruise engine to meet Specification ER143T.

One level up from my 'chalk and cheese' comment, may I say that it took me very many flights in the P1127 before I could climb down the ladder without offering up thanks that I had not bent the thing. Yet after shutting down the SC1, I always felt relief that it had not suffered one of several possible nasty failures.

Why this big difference in how I felt after a flight? The SC1 had five Rolls RB108 engines – four for lift and one for propulsion. The aircraft was very heavily autostabilised and used full authority autostabilisers in pitch and roll which had priority over the pilot when it came to the reaction controls. Plus there was a manual mechanical back-up control mode intended as a last ditch option for emergency use. The pilot controlled the thrust from the lift engines using a helicopter-like 'collective' throttle with the left hand. For reasons we shall come to shortly, the SC1 had very easy handling and later it was established that this good handling even extended to the manual mechanical back-up control mode but the aircraft was a real problem to operate due to very complex systems and the five engines which had to be looked after.

On the other hand, the Hawker P1127 had a single Bristol Pegasus engine for lift and propulsion plus the aircraft was always mechanically controlled by the pilot and had optional low authority autostabilisers in pitch and roll. Piloting wise, the P1127 had demanding handling due to two controls for the left hand and intake effects. However it was a delight to operate as it had no potentially dangerous systems and only one engine to be looked after.

To sum up, the Short SC1 was demanding to operate and easy to handle while the P1127 was easy to operate but had demanding handling.

I think the differences in operation hardly need explanation. In the case of the SC1 you were operating a five-engined 'bomber' all by yourself. It had none of the benefits of automation that would be available today and so you had five of most things to deal with when it came to starting it up. In the air after takeoff and getting on your wings, it was necessary to shut down the four lift engines because they were very thirsty even at idle. Before landing the process of restarting them, one at a time using bleed air from the cruise engine, was also easy to get wrong. In some circumstances this had to be done on short finals at below 500 ft. Then there was the issue of the full authority autostabs. These had 100% access to the roll and pitch reaction controls and, unless you kept an eye on a gauge that was quite low down on the right side of the instrument panel, the first indication that they had used up all roll control was when you moved the stick and got no response. Not good.

Compare that to the operation of the P1127 which was in effect a single-seat fighter of the day, say a Hunter, with one extra lever in the cockpit to set the nozzle angle and two extra instruments – neither of which needed much attention. One instrument showed the nozzle angle set (but so did the nozzle lever) while the duct pressure gauge showed that the reaction controls were available (but so did moving the stick). P1127 handling, however, was quite another matter.

The reasons why the P1127 handling was so demanding are rather less obvious. However, I will try to explain them to you so that you will understand why handling the SC1 was so easy. As shown in *Fig 2*, the throttle box incorporated the throttle and the nozzle lever and was positioned on the left hand side of the cockpit where your left hand would naturally fall when sitting in the seat. The throttle worked as with any jet fighter – forward for more thrust and back for less. An inboard slim nozzle lever set the angle of the nozzles – pull it back and the nozzles were rotated downwards and so the aircraft went slower, push it fully forwards and the nozzles pointed aft making the aircraft a conventional jet.

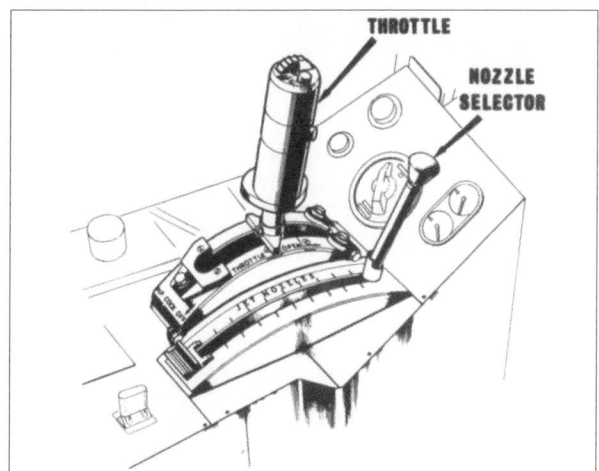

P1127 Throttle box

Fig 2

While this was a brilliantly simple way to achieve the full range of VSTOL manoeuvres, it necessarily posed a piloting trap. Should you move the wrong lever, it might not be possible to recover from the mistake depending on what you were doing at the time. For example, raising the nozzles in the hover would have you dart forward and downwards very rapidly, as has happened more than once in public.

The other problem stemmed from the intakes and meant that, if left to its own devices, a P1127 flying slower than about 100 kt wanted to go tail first. The pilot literally had to use his feet to keep the aircraft pointing into the airflow. This was directly analogous with the need for the pilot of a tail-dragger aeroplane to use his feet to stop it swinging and ground looping when landing, especially in a crosswind.

The reason for this was that the aerodynamic stabilising effects of the P1127 fin were no different from any other aircraft so faded away as one got slower. Unfortunately there was a *destabilising* force that *increased* as flying speed reduced and so defeated the residual efforts of the fin. This force was called intake momentum drag. It exists on all jet engine intakes and gets greater as rpm are increased. Thus whenever you were flying slowly and necessarily using jet lift not wing lift, up went your rpm and up went the intake momentum drag.

To understand why this destabilised the aircraft directionally we need to look at the airflow round the aircraft when viewed from above. In *Fig 3* I have tried to indicate that everything is fine when the aircraft is pointing directly into the airflow.

Fig 3

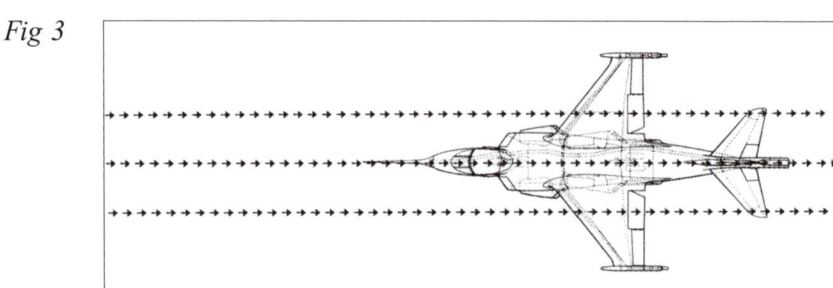

However, what happens if the aircraft starts travelling slightly sideways through the air because of a crosswind or a deliberate move by the pilot is shown in *Fig 4*.

Fig 4

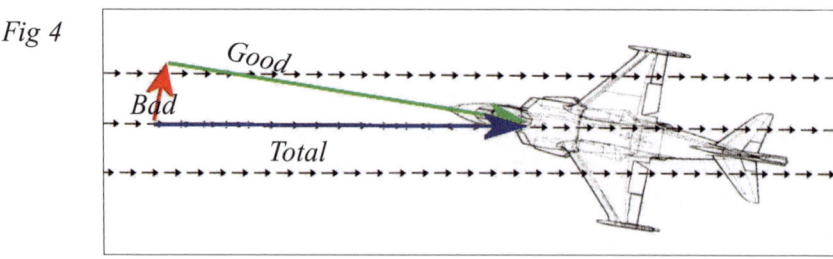

With the total airflow – represented by the 'total' 'blue' arrow – now coming at an angle to the nose, we must think about its two components as shown, the 'green' being that part which is straight on the nose and the 'red' that part which is blowing directly across the nose.

The 'red' arrow is of course the troublemaker because its effect is felt at the intake which, is well ahead of the centre of gravity and so opposes the fin. Should the pilot allow the aircraft to swap ends and fly tail first you might think it would just be embarrassing for him because in his debrief he will be told to try harder on the rudder. Sadly he is unlikely to make the debrief because, at speeds greater than about 70 kt as the aircraft goes seriously sideways, the leading wing will generate much more lift than the other and the aircraft will roll out of control, thanks to what is termed 'rolling moment due to sideslip'. Such asymmetric lift can easily swamp the aerodynamic and reaction controls.

Clearly some exotic technology was called for to help the pilot keep the aircraft pointing into the airflow. In fact all that was needed was a simple wind vane as seen on any church steeple. It is mounted in front of the pilot and always shows him where the airflow is coming from as shown in *Fig 5*.

Fig 5 The wind vane

I hope that by now you will have appreciated why the P1127 had demanding handling.

With that in mind, let us consider the SC1. As the picture of the SC1 in *Fig 6* shows, the lift engine intake momentum drag arrow acts vertically down through the centre of gravity, regardless of which way the aircraft is pointing with respect to the wind, allowing the fin to do its job even

81

as speed reduces. This lack of directional instability made the SC1 easier to handle in the hover and at low speeds.

Fig 6

The arrow shows the benign direction of the lift engine intake momentum drag in the SC1

Add to this that when jetborne the pilot had only one control to operate with the left hand and it becomes clear why the chances of the pilot making a handling mistake in the SC1 were much less than in the P1127.

As experience was gained at Bedford with the un-autostabilised P1127, it became clear that the best way to fly the SC1 was in the mechanical back up mode which did not use the autostabilisers thus eliminating the serious problems that could arise with autostabiliser failures and so was very good for one's peace of mind. That way the attitude control system became just like the P1127 with the stick position showing how much reaction control authority you had used.

Although handling wise the SC1 and the P1127 were very different, both aircraft did great jobs in teaching the UK how best to proceed with the development of jet VSTOL.

Hunting H126

Another interesting aircraft that was on the fleet when I joined Bedford was the Hunting H126 Jet Flap XN714. Like the Flying Bedstead and SC1, whose origins I cover in Chapter 6, this was another aircraft specified by government scientists to check out their new ideas in flight.

The only difference was that the scientists this time were working at the National Gas Turbine Establishment (NGTE) situated on the south west corner of the RAE Farnborough site. Both RAE and NGTE boffins were working at reducing the dependence of future aircraft on ever longer runways. They saw the 'jet flap' as a way to increase the maximum lift coefficient of a wing enabling an aircraft to fly slowly on takeoff and landing and so use a short runway.

Essentially the idea was to squirt a very high speed jet of air out of a long thin slot along the trailing edge of a wing and to be able to direct this jet sheet down at typical aerodynamic flap angles for takeoff and landing. As can be seen in *Fig 7* this was achieved in the H126 by having the Orpheus turbo jet engine exhaust into a vertical chamber (the 'dustbin') from where two thirds of it were piped out to the wings. From there it exhausted via fish tail nozzles arranged so that it could emerge as a sheet of high speed air along the whole of the trailing edge of the wing.

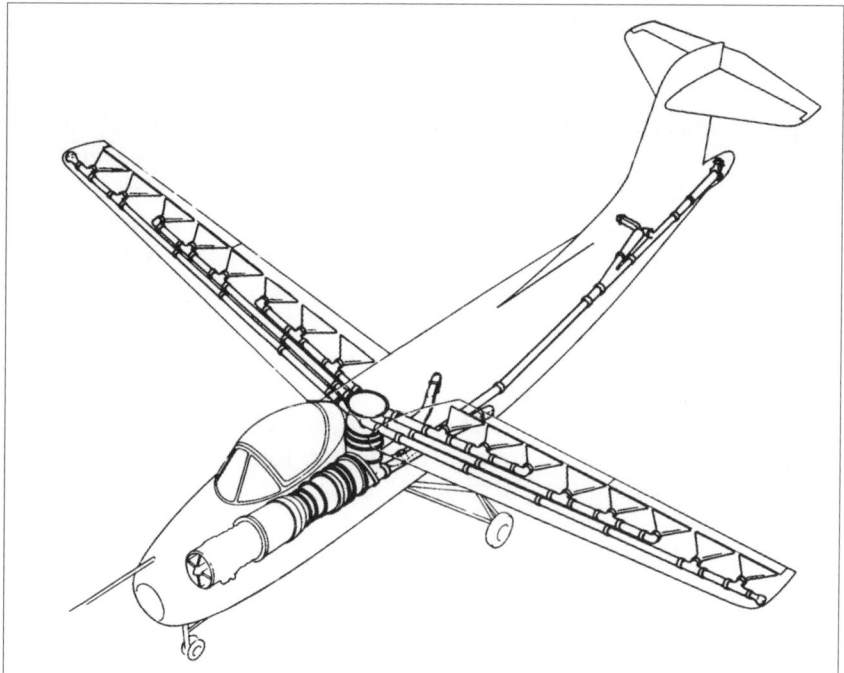

Fig 7 H126 Jet Flap ducting

The angle of this sheet could be adjusted between zero and 60° using a narrow metal flap to induce the flow downwards. Not surprisingly the ordinary air approaching and passing over and under the wing reacted to this high speed sheet of air as if it were a mechanical flap, hence the name 'jet flap'.

The other third of the air that entered the 'dustbin' was ducted to small jets on the side of the fuselage to provide ordinary thrust with a little going to the tail to allow reaction controls to augment the normal aerodynamic tail surfaces when flying at low speed.

It was a fascinating aircraft to fly for two reasons. Essentially the wing was one great jet pipe and as a result the extent of the panel of fire warning lights on the right hand console had to be seen to be believed. More importantly, it completely demonstrated the effectiveness of the NGTE ideas by enabling us to fly at speeds which, when inserted into the normal equation for the lift of a wing, gave a lift coefficient of 7! This number was somewhat artificial as it did not take into account the direct lift effects of the deflected jet sheet (the same simplistic sum for a Harrier drifting around at the hover would give a lift coefficient approaching infinity). However, slow flight was certainly demonstrated!

Not surprisingly the H126 had a vicious wing drop at the stall as one wing always let go before the other. If you were on top form, you might contain the subsequent roll to 90° but how many days are we ever that sharp? There was also zero warning. Although IAS readings in the 40s were very possible at a safe height, we used a minimum of 90 kt when lower so the aircraft always appeared to fly in a very nose down attitude to observers on the ground.

The big snag to the Jet Flap principle was the complexity of the ducting and, even with today's turbofans which are able to produce huge quantities of relatively cool air (removing the fire hazard), the concept was never employed.

To conclude this chapter, the overriding recollection I have of my time with Aero Flight at RAE Bedford is what a joy it was to be able to do research flying in the days when the aim was to acquire knowledge rather than to make money.

Chapter 5

Kingston, Dunsfold and the Harrier

One day I was an RAF flight lieutenant and the next I started 23 years as a civilian working at Kingston and Dunsfold. Because of this I left writing this chapter until I had finished the rest of the book because I could not make up my mind about what to put in and what to leave out.

The people at these two Hawker Siddeley Aviation sites, together with their opposite numbers at Bristol, where the Pegasus engine was born, gave the world the Harrier flying machine. In doing this, they showed everyone how to make the first effective military aircraft that was not dependent on long runways or large aircraft carriers with their catapults and arrester gear.

Of course the flying machine was only the start. To turn it into a useful military aircraft required it to be fitted with many complex systems. While this work was overseen by Kingston and Dunsfold, the credit for developing much of the eventual military capability of the Harrier goes to another Hawker Siddeley site at Brough, as well as to companies such as Smiths and Ferranti, as they were then. Given that so many people just think of the Harrier as a 'Jump-Jet', it is important to record that, when it went into service with the RAF in April 1969, it was their first aircraft equipped with a Head Up Display and an Inertial Navigation system. In those days these represented the very latest capabilities. Indeed, when one of these new Harrier GR1 aircraft won the Great Air Race from London to New York in 1969, it was refuelled over the Atlantic by Victor tankers whose navigators were much less certain of their position than the Harrier pilot, Sqn Ldr Tom Lecky-Thompson, in what some considered was his 'toy' jump-jet.

In several quarters the misconceptions about the worth of the Harrier family and the prejudice against it have persisted since the earliest days of the programme but I do not intend to waste space on them here. It was sufficient thanks for everyone working at Kingston and Dunsfold that, after the Falklands War was over, Admiral Sir Henry Leach, RN First Sea Lord and Chief of the Naval Staff said, "Without the Sea Harrier there could have been no Task Force". In the same vein history also records that the US military are not given to buying their aircraft from overseas unless those aircraft are pretty special.

In 1966 the Dunsfold team working on what was to become the Harrier included three pilots: CTP Bill Bedford, his deputy Hugh Merewether and Duncan Simpson. As Bill was due to retire, he recruited my then flight commander on Aero Flight, Sqn Ldr Clive Rustin, to join the team. Fortunately for me he did not mention this detail to Hugh or Duncan until after the event. On hearing about it they had other ideas and the upshot was that I got the job. Clive went on to fill several senior test flying posts at Farnborough and Boscombe and I am glad to say we remain very good friends!

A couple of events that happened shortly after I joined Dunsfold will show how much I had to learn about life in industry in those days. I was allocated a small office that was equipped with an oak desk that had seen better days. At the weekend I returned to the airfield, drew the keys to the pilot's block from the guards at the main gate, lugged my desk outside and, using a sanding disk and my drill from home, stripped the old varnish. With the desk back in my office, I gave it two coats of Rustin's Plastic Coating and went home well satisfied with the result. This plastic coating was a superior type of two-part epoxy varnish with which I happened to be familiar as it was produced and marketed by Clive's chemist brother, Ronnie.

First thing on Monday morning a fairly gruff chap who announced that he was 'The Convenor' came into my office and enquired what I had been doing over the weekend. "Improving my desk. Looks good, eh?" was my reply. I was then treated to a dissertation quite remarkable for the number of words per breath, as well as its varied vocabulary of which any RAF drill sergeant would have been proud. It seemed Dunsfold employed carpenters specifically to do this sort of work. When I enquired as to why a job that clearly needed doing had been neglected, the answer I got was very long but not entirely clear. Later on, as the years went by, Joe Daly and I both realised we came to work with Dunsfold's interests at heart and so developed a considerable mutual respect for each other.

Later I was asked to do some night circuits in one of the development batch Harriers to check out the cockpit lighting. The airfield had no runway or taxiway lights so, if the Dove communications aircraft had to come back after dark, the firemen laid out some 'goosenecks' down the sides of the runway. These were watering-can-like metal containers full of paraffin with a wick sticking out of the spout. When the wicks were lit, the resultant yellow smoky flame could be seen for a mile or so, allowing visual circuits. I was briefed to start with a short takeoff and then to come round for a slow landing. Off I went, banged down the nozzles at the appropriate speed and climbed up into the black night. On the downwind leg I could not pick out the expected two parallel lines of goosenecks marking the runway and thought I was looking in the wrong place. Then I saw what I thought were lights in the hangars and office buildings to the north of a large black area. At that point ATC remarked that my takeoff had blown out the goosenecks and would I hold while the firemen went out and relit them. Hoping that nothing would require an early return, I duly waited for 15 minutes or so before a vehicle appeared and completed the relighting.

Not best pleased with my night's work, I wrote my limited report and went home. The next morning I went into a local hardware shop and enquired about rechargeable battery powered lanterns. They produced a brochure that showed one with a nice heavy lead acid accumulator in its base and a neon tube about a foot long on its top. I arranged for 50 to be delivered to the aerodrome and went back to work. When they arrived, I got the carpenters (I learned you see) to arrange some racks in the fire station and for the electricians to sort out the charging arrangements so that the firemen could look after the batteries. A month or so later, I had a very uptight clerk from Kingston on the phone wanting to know what I had been doing buying all these lights and charging them to the company. To cut a long story short, my education continued while someone called 'The Buyer' explained to me the error of my ways and how the company had administrative systems to ensure those sort of purchases were properly handled. Mind you, we had done our night circuits by then so I felt I had done my bit to keep the programme on track. In the services one got it in the neck if you failed to show initiative. Civilian life was clearly different. Needless to say the lamps did sterling service for many years.

In my early years with the company I was very much the junior pilot to Hugh and Duncan and quite right too as they had so much more time in the Dunsfold test pilot role than me. As such I did not always get the pick of the daily jobs going so was very pleasantly surprised when I was given the 'rough ground heavy weight STO spec point' to fly. Since that description will not mean much to other than Dunsfold insiders, let me explain. The contract to develop the initial Harrier for the RAF allowed us to obtain stage payments when we achieved a number of what were termed 'specification points' or effectively technical milestones in the flight test programme.

One such 'spec point' was to show that the aircraft could take off at heavy weight from a rough grass strip using the short takeoff technique. The rough grass strip was defined by the RAF as one where a Land Rover driver could reach 40 mph without losing control. During the build up to this spec point, Duncan had done a number of increasingly heavy STOs from a specially surveyed strip on the airfield and the next flight was to be at the spec point weight. Well chuffed to be asked to do this important point, I got briefed and found that at this high weight and, with the modest engine fitted in those days, a speed of 108 kt was needed before lowering the nozzles. As I taxied out towards the start of the surveyed strip, I was quite impressed with the bumpiness of the ride.

Then it dawned on me that at 108 kt I might have considerable difficulty in reading the airspeed indicator accurately. Since it was a spec point, accuracy was vital and the test instrumentation records would clearly show if I got it wrong. I was just thinking that perhaps I had been set up and the trip was not such a super present after all when with a big bang the nose fell on the ground. Obviously that was wrong, so I shut it all down and got out and started wriggling under the front fuselage to try and see if the nose leg had broken or whether it had decided to retract.

As I did this I could see and hear the 'dramatic society' setting off towards me from their post near the control tower. The fire engines were followed as usual by the ambulance driven by the last fireman and contained the nurse scrambled by the crash alarm from the sick bay. Almost before the ambulance had stopped, the nurse got out and started running towards where my feet stuck out from under the nose shouting "Mr Simpson, Mr Simpson are you OK?" I slid out from underneath and was greeted by, "Oh! It's you." Following this she turned on her heel and returned to the ambulance. Some days you find out who your friends are and I always looked at Duncan in a different light after that. I had been fortunate that the fatigue-weakened leg had gone when it did and not at 100 kt thirty seconds later but as we know the devil always looks after his own.

A few weeks later the same fatigue failure at the top of the leg struck another of the development fleet. This time the pilot was Sqn Ldr Mike Adams, the Operational Requirements Liaison Officer at Dunsfold. Mike had his nose drop to the ground while on the taxiway so the sudden violent jolt injured his back quite badly.

As an aside, Mike came top of my course at ETPS while I was only second. I was later told by a staff member that they had found it hard to choose between us and decided that a fair distribution of the spoils was that Mike should get the coveted McKenna trophy, while I would be given the job that we both wanted on Aero Flight at Bedford, which certainly suited me.

The RAF wanted the Harrier to use SNEB 68 mm diameter rockets. These were carried in one of two types of pods under the wings. The training pod, known as the Matra 155, was a collection of tubes open at the front and back and so could be refilled after use. However, the crude aerodynamics of the nose of this pod meant that it had a lot of drag. On the other hand, the operational Matra 116 pod had a streamlined nose cone of a composite material through which the rockets punched their way out and then, as the last of the 18 rockets left the pod, it automatically jettisoned itself for minimum weight and drag during the remainder of the sortie. Rather naturally there was concern that, as the 116 pod was fired, fragments of the nose cone could finish up entering the engine intakes.

Matra SNEB 68mm rockets

Training
(Matra155)

Operational
(Matra116)

Accordingly a flight development programme was drawn up where the aircraft was fitted with a 116 pod on each of the four pylons and it was planned to fire single pods at varying speeds and positions on the wing while filming what happened to the nose cone debris from a chase aircraft. I was briefed for the first of these sorties by our most senior flight test man, Ron Cooper, who explained that he wanted me to fire the pods in turn starting with the left outboard at 250 kt and increasing speed by 50 kt for each subsequent pod. For these trials the cockpit had been specially fitted with an aluminium panel that had four big switches in a row with which to arm the chosen pylon. I enquired as to what I used to fire the selected pylon and Ron said the trigger on the control column.

Careful to keep everything switched off, I got airborne and flew towards the live firing range in Lyme Bay, joining up on the way with the camera aircraft from Boscombe Down. This was a two-seat Hunter flown by no less than Tom Lecky-Thompson of Air Race fame with Rob Addie as the photographer. When cleared by the range controller, I dived at the first speed, selected the port outer pylon and started the countdown on the radio for the benefit of the Hunter. When I got to zero and pulled the trigger nothing happened. I discussed things with the Hunter, reselected the same pod and we set off downhill again. Nothing. To cut a long story short, we went through this palaver five times, all with considerable tension but all with no result. By which time, as you can imagine, the Hunter crew were talking amongst themselves about how Dunsfold pilots never could sort out switches and so on.

The Hunter was just about to leave and return to Boscombe when I asked for one more try. They were reluctant but agreed. I reasoned to myself that we could hardly have four duff pods and perhaps the armourers had set the aircraft up to use the bomb release button for the firing. Down we went again and, as I got to zero and pressed the button, all four pods fired at once. I can still see and hear those 64 rockets as they shot off trailing smoke and flame. Later I heard that in the Hunter, Tom and Rob were certain that nothing would happen when suddenly the whole front of the Harrier disappeared in smoke and flame whereupon Tom cried "*****! He's blown up" while out of the middle of all this mayhem they heard a disembodied voice say, "How about that then?"

Since I flew this last dive at the fourth speed briefed for the starboard outboard pylon, we actually achieved a salvo firing at high speed in one hit and so eliminated our cautious build-up programme of many flights.

Sometimes the good guys get lucky, especially as the engine did not mind what went on.

Sea Harrier

The people at Kingston and Dunsfold had the distinction of producing the Sea Harrier, which was the last of all British fighter aircraft. Since I worked on the programme for many years, please excuse me if I write about it here in some detail and from a very personal perspective.

My earliest memory that is relevant to the Sea Harrier story is from 1966 when things did not look good because the government had just cancelled two VSTOL programmes, the P1154 and the AW681. At the time Clive Rustin and I were both on Aero Flight at Bedford flying the P1127 and Short SC1. Appalled that the government might abandon the world lead that we knew the UK had established, we sat down to consider how best to demonstrate the potential of our aircraft should the worst happen. We felt that people might get the message if we hovered over the Thames, alongside the Houses of Parliament, before landing vertically in the grounds of the Palace of Westminster. On a point of detail, it also seemed desirable to demonstrate the precision of control in the hover that had been achieved with these two designs. We would do this by simply pushing in a couple of stained glass windows on the southern face of the building, using the long instrumentation probes that stuck out from the nose on both aircraft.

What has all that to do with Sea Harrier? Simply that it sums up exactly what the Sea Harrier programme was for me, namely a continual struggle to convince people of its merit. The struggle before it was ordered was to explain and demonstrate just how good it could be and, later during development, to put across how good it actually was.

How I came to do my first landing on a ship was an example of what I mean. It was May 1969, a mere month after the Harrier went into RAF service and just after Sqn Ldr Tom Lecky-Thompson had won the London to New York Air Race as mentioned previously. The participation had been brilliantly commanded by Group Captain Peter Williamson, the RAF's first Harrier station commander. He believed in the aircraft enough to risk his career by authorising the race himself, while his lords and masters were still trying to decide whether to allow it. After his team won, Williamson got a signal telling him to go ahead.

91

With the race over, Williamson found himself in New York with Tom, two Harriers and no ground crew. There were two Harriers because Andy Jones had ferried one out earlier to act as a spare for the one that Sqn Ldr Graham Williams used for the New York to London leg of the race. As part of the drive to support the yet to be agreed USMC Harrier buy, Kingston asked the Ministry to be allowed to do a short US demonstration tour with these two Harriers. Permission was given and an HSA main board director, Barry Laight, plus Bill Bedford who was now a sales executive, were dispatched to the US with me as their pilot.

I had met Tom before at Boscombe Down where he was a test pilot but I had never met Peter Williamson. However, the three of us instantly hit it off as a team of believers. Peter talked the RAF into letting us have a five man ground support team from the VC10 transport crew at New York and we were all set. After a few days demonstrating in the Washington area, flying from Andrews AFB, Tom and I flew the aircraft to the Navy airfield at Norfolk.

Looking over the site with USN Commander Bob Thomas, I pressed him to let us get away from the airfield and fly from a road alongside the dock in the Norfolk base. There was even the flight deck of a carrier moored alongside the dock-side road that would provide a grandstand for the VIP guests. As Bob and I were looking at this venue, I spotted the brand new USS La Salle moored out in the bay and suggested to him and Peter that we could include a landing on its aft helicopter deck, shut down, get our ground crew to add some underwing stores, then restart, take off and complete the demo before finally landing back on the road. This would show the Harrier's unique ability to operate from a small deck without any of the starter trucks (or 'yellow gear' as the USN call it) and the special training that the USN needed to operate its carrier based aircraft.

Our plan was agreed thanks entirely to Peter Williamson's impressive display of confidence at a meeting we had with the USN, where he indicated that his team was only doing what came naturally to us all back in the UK. He didn't bother to say that we had only met up for the first time earlier in the week or that I had never landed on a ship. He just accepted my judgement that it could be done. When Laight and Bedford heard of the plan that evening, they said I was to do no such thing in case the engine failed to start on La Salle. They also tossed in many other 'what ifs' for good measure. I told them I was sorry but it was Peter's plan and I was just doing as I was told. He owned the aeroplanes and so I was flying for him. I added that great strides had been made from the early P1127 days and that it was now time to show the aircraft had matured. If we were not prepared to demonstrate our trust in our product ourselves, how could we expect others to buy it?

In the event it was all a great success and as we know the USN bought the Harrier for the USMC. Indeed some years later when the company decided to launch a house journal I was moved to write the following:

I didn't realise it at the time but an event, ordinary enough in itself, on the afternoon of Monday 19th May 1969 was to become a memory to which I would often return. One of those experiences we can all recall years later as if it happened only yesterday.

I was walking slowly along a road in the US Navy base at Norfolk, Virginia. It was a pleasant early evening – mild, calm and quiet with a pale sun low on the horizon. On either side of me were the sort of buildings, cranes, oil tanks and railway sidings which mark the middle of any large industrial or military complex. A few yards behind me, two VSTOL Harriers were standing in the middle of the road on the spot where they had landed an hour or so before. Apart from the three men in overalls with their tractor and tow bar, everybody else who had been there earlier – the top brass, military and civilian, people from the base, photographers and television crews – had all gone. As I walked alone I said out loud to myself, "Well mate. We did it".

"We" were two Harriers, an RAF Harrier pilot, a small team of RAF officers and ground crew and me. "It" was a full week of demonstrations of the aircraft with flying at New York, Washington and Norfolk. The aircraft had flown every day except the Sunday. The entire programme had been met, despite it being doubled due to demand as the week progressed. The ground crew had never worked on the Harrier before, the pilots had not planned the flying manoeuvres together beforehand, let alone practised them, yet everything had been immensely successful.

To get a satisfactory result like that when everyone is unrehearsed, under pressure and working out of their normal environment required a bit of luck but above all it needed an outstanding aeroplane. Not a theoretically brilliant and capable aeroplane (there are lots of those) but a genuine real life practical aircraft which is reliable, easy to maintain, easy to fly and so far ahead of the competition that there wasn't any. When I turned my back on those two Harriers and walked down that road, I was convinced that the original prototype P1127 that I had started on in 1964 was now such an aeroplane.

On the programme for the last demo of the week was me taking off from the road and landing on the USS La Salle anchored in the nearby bay. Once on the ship I shut down the engine, the ground crew loaded a pair of hundred gallon drop tanks and two rocket pods, then I restarted and flew back for more manoeuvres before landing on the road. There are only two points of interest about this story – the USS La Salle was not an aircraft carrier and I'd never landed anything on a ship before, let alone a jet fighter.

Back to 1966 and the cancellations I mentioned earlier. The Royal Navy did not enjoy that year either, because that was when their proposal for a new large aircraft carrier CVA01 was cancelled. Fortunately, the RN was subsequently able to make a case for a new 'through deck cruiser' class of ship from which to fly their anti-submarine helicopters. By 1971 the first of these, HMS Invincible, was ordered and the RN then seriously set about trying to get some Harriers to fly from it.

Since by 1971 the RAF Harriers had been cleared to fly from ships, the attitude of the procurement system was why not just make a few more and give them to the Royal Navy? That, as they say, was a good question. The short answer was the Kingston design team, plus the RN planners, believed that changes were advisable for various engineering, piloting and operational reasons if the Harrier was to be optimised for use at sea.

A few examples should demonstrate what we had in mind. An aeroplane that is going to spend much of a 20 year or more life at sea in a salt-laden atmosphere should be made of materials less vulnerable to salt water corrosion than the magnesium alloys used extensively in the Harrier airframe and engine. Maintenance on a ship that is rolling, pitching and heaving is harder than anywhere on dry land so it would pay to spend money on improving access to equipment and the basic reliability of some components, rather than just accepting a lower availability due to longer maintenance times.

Flying controls that are fine when sliding into a hover alongside a fixed landing mat can leave you less than happy when the landing spot just won't keep still. When you routinely have to taxi around the very edge of a wet and slippery lurching deck and within a couple of feet of several other very expensive parked aircraft, the handling and failure cases of wheel brakes and nosewheel steering systems take on a whole new degree of importance.

The Harrier had a weapon system that was designed to attack ground targets by day with the help of a ground-based forward air controller who could see the target and guide the pilot in the final stages. That package of kit is spectacularly useless when your job is to locate enemy sea or air targets over miles of featureless sea. Add a cockpit with no rear view and the idea of relying on the Harrier for the air defence of a fleet was silly.

Despite good reasons such as these, the mantra at the Ministry in those days was 'minimum change', which meant that every single change from the RAF Harrier standard of the day had to be fought over tooth and nail. No wonder Harrier Chief Designer, John Fozard, was fond of referring to the Ministry at that time as a condom on the penis of progress.

By far the biggest issue was raising the cockpit eleven inches in order to give the pilot a decent view all round in air combat. In the RAF Harrier of those days, looking to the rear just gave you a view into the top of your own intake, arguably the one place in which an enemy aircraft would not be hiding. Why it was like that in the first place and why the RAF did not object at the time is not a Sea Harrier matter, so I will not go there.

One day the MOD Chief Scientist, Sir Herman Bondi, was scheduled to come to Kingston to hear our pitch on the 'raised cockpit' as it was known. Kingston was well used to hosting top ranking military officers and civil servants and we knew when to put on a clean suit and get our hair cut in order to make such folk feel wanted. This day was no exception and John Fozard (who was a formidable aeronautical intellect with a marked physical presence and dominated his design team in the manner of a semi-benevolent dictator) was to lead an engineering drawing and slide presentation on the merits and cost effectiveness of the proposed change.

Fozard briefed us just before zero hour. He said that we had to convince Bondi and his team of the need for the raised cockpit because it was his office that had the final decision on whether it would go ahead. He went on to say Sir Herman was not an aeroplane man but a scientist with a background in astronomy and relativity. Therefore, we should be patient in explaining aircraft matters.

Fortunately I knew somebody who had worked with Sir Herman in the past and he had already briefed me. As a result, I was probably the only member of our team not surprised when this eminent scientist entered the room casually dressed and without any advisors. I did feel sorry for John as he was clearly put off his stride by this. Things only got worse when our visitor started interrupting his prepared presentation and asking very astute and detailed aircraft questions which were not easy to answer.

At the end of his pitch, which had clearly not gone as well as he would have wished, our leader visibly pulled himself together and announced that such a complex issue was understandably difficult to grasp using the two dimensional medium of drawings and slides. He said that arrangements had therefore been made for our visitor to examine a full scale raised cockpit mock-up in the nearby experimental workshops, offering the benefits of three dimensions to help his appreciation of the various issues.

"If you would care to step this way, Sir, our deputy chief test pilot will be glad to show you just what the raised cockpit will be like." The reply was cool but instant. "That is not necessary, thank you. I am used to solving four dimensional problems on paper." For us ordinary mortals in the team who it must be said sometimes found difficulty in keeping our end up in John Fozard's office, it was a moment to treasure, especially when later Sir Herman agreed to the raised cockpit.

As we lobbied for the Sea Harrier programme, I was asked to fly quite a few senior individuals in the back of our company Harrier two-seat demonstrator, G-VTOL. One, the 4th Earl of Kimberley, was due to speak in the House of Lords in a debate two days later and our PR people were most anxious to impress him with the need for Sea Harrier before his speech. He was extremely aristocratic but far from young. Such mature people cannot be briefed, fitted out in full kit and trussed up in an ejector seat without an appropriate level of TLC.

In addition, if such passengers are to stand any chance of settling down in what is for them an extremely alien environment, you need to talk to them casually and steadily throughout the whole start up process and when taxying out. The chatting needs to continue throughout the STO and initial departure which must be as gentle as possible. Once away from the airfield, the ride should emulate the way an airliner flies because to do otherwise is to invite, at best, a complete lack of appreciation of what is going on and, at worst, a very sick passenger. Accordingly that was how I treated this gentleman.

Just after we passed the end of the runway, after fierce but unavoidable acceleration during the STO, I had time to take a good look at him in the rear-view mirror. His head was on a swivel, he seemed to be very pleased with the view outside and completely at home. More than a little surprised, I suggested that we could increase speed and try to find a warship in the Channel. He readily agreed to this and, soon after crossing the coast, I spotted a frigate and very gently reduced speed to a hover alongside the helicopter platform on the back of the ship. Then, with the crew staring up at us, I remarked how easy this whole hovering capability made flying to a ship. "Indeed Sir, I hope you can see how easy it would be for us to move across and land on board. However without the prior approval of the Captain, I think we had better not."

He was so enthusiastic and apparently immune from motion effects that I suggested that we accelerate away and return using the procedure for coming alongside in poor visibility. I explained this involved slamming on the brakes when the ship appeared out of the murk. Accordingly the Earl was subjected to us flashing towards the ship at low level and high speed before a sudden full power reverse thrust deceleration at the last moment had the aircraft roaring, shuddering and shaking to a very abrupt stop alongside. As it all calmed down in the hover, he remarked "Does that put a strain on the machine?" which I consider to be the top remark that a G-VTOL passenger has ever uttered. Later his obituary in the Daily Telegraph showed that it was not at all surprising that he performed the way that he did in G-VTOL. For those who are not easily offended, Annexe A includes his obituary in support of that view. Hansard for 24 April 1975 gave the Earl's contribution to the Harrier debate in the House of Lords and made it clear that he was also no slouch at picking the bones out of his brief and flight in G-VTOL.

The Navy planners had certain specification missions that they required the aeroplane to perform. One of these involved carrying a Sea Eagle anti-ship cruise missile under each wing. This was a much bigger and heavier weapon than anything in the RAF close air support and ground attack inventory and was itself only in the early stages of development. In order to get the Sea Harrier development contract, we had to show that this and the other specification missions could be flown using existing development Harriers. In typical Kingston style, we chose to demonstrate the Sea Eagle case by carrying and firing an existing missile, the Martel. This was larger and heavier than the more modern Sea Eagle would be and was in service with the Buccaneer.

I well remember the day I did the Martel firing flight. I had to take the aircraft from Dunsfold to Boscombe Down where the missile was to be fitted by a specialist live Martel handling team. After taxying to a special safe area, I shut down and they fitted the beast. When all was ready, they strapped me in and sent me off with a variety of throw away lines like "I hope you know what you are doing" and "Whatever happens, we don't want that thing brought back here." I tiptoed airborne and set off for the firing range.

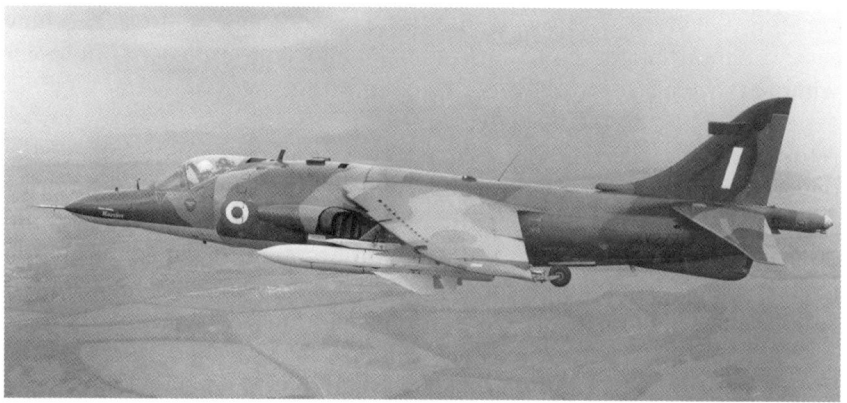

Martel firing flight

The Martel had a big motor that put out a large exhaust plume which was not the sort of gas that the Pegasus engine thrived on, hence the need for the trial. In the way of things, the required firing conditions of 5,000 ft resulted in us being between layers of cloud over the sea facing due south off Lyme Bay which was not the ideal situation if the engine coughed with the smoke.

After pressing the button, I remember being instantly extremely impressed with the sight and sound of this very large 1,800 lb firework streaking away into the cloud ahead, followed quickly by pleasure at the way the Pegasus ignored it and finally being slightly concerned that the boffins had done their burn out sums correctly. It was well known that I was not a Francophile and it suddenly occurred to me that I could have been set up. I never heard where it went. I didn't ask either because what mattered was we had ticked off another requirement towards getting the

Sea Harrier development contract. Two years later in 1975 we were given the actual go-ahead.

XZ450 was no run of the mill Sea Harrier. It was the first one to fly, the first one displayed in public, the first one up the ski-jump, the first one fully equipped to fire Sea Eagle and the first one shot down during the Falklands War.

It was ready for its first flight on Sunday 20th August 1978 and we were all keen to see what effect the changes had made. So keen in fact that we had not waited for the paint shop to do their bit. Accelerating south away from Dunsfold and enjoying the much better view from the raised cockpit, I gave the stick a quick left/right, left/right. The aircraft seemed to accelerate noticeably quicker in roll than the Harrier, to the point where my helmet was hitting the side of the canopy. That was not expected. The rest of the trip produced no further surprises and I returned to the airfield for a chance to look at the roll control in the hover. I had a vested interest in this being better because, as I describe in Chapter 14, one of the changes that I had proposed was a reduction in how far you had to move your hand sideways in order to reach full reaction control deflection or an increase in lateral control sensitivity, if you prefer it.

I was delighted to find that with this change it was much easier to keep the wings level in the hover. So much so that I found I could trim it and then let go of the stick long enough to take a small camera out of a pocket and snap a security man who was watching nearby. That sort of thing would not have been possible with the previous standard of reaction controls.

It was decided at the debrief that I had been wrong about the roll acceleration. The aeroplane was not behaving differently, it just felt like it. Sitting higher above the roll axis meant the head would put more force on the neck for the same aircraft manoeuvre. Ten days, 11 flights and several coats of paint later, I took off in XV450 from the ski-jump at Farnborough. The Sea Harrier was ready for that year's SBAC show with three days in hand on a 13 day programme, five of them devoted to painting it. Things had gone better than many had thought possible, once again the story of the Harrier as far as I am concerned.

SBAC Farnborough 1978

Three-and-a-half years later on Friday 2nd April 1982, I happened to be airborne in XZ450 doing stalling tests while carrying two Sea Eagles, two Sidewinders and two 30 mm guns. When I landed, the balloon had gone up over the Falklands invasion. We stripped out our test kit and the aircraft flew to HMS Hermes at Portsmouth that weekend. The fleet sailed on the Monday which was also the day I arrived in the US to get on with AV-8B development flying.

Every evening I tried to find out what was going on from the US TV news. As a result I was probably more up to date than if I had been in the UK as the US public were being fed much Argentinean video. Then on the 4th May I hit the TV switch as soon as I reached my room after work and, as the pictured appeared, I was looking at the wreckage of XZ450. It lay among rocks and I could see the serial number on part of the wing. The camera zoomed into a detail shot of the reaction control linkage hanging out of the tip. Realising there was nothing fake about the film, I was also sad that XZ450 was the first to be lost. Later I was to hear that the pilot, Lt Nick Taylor, had been killed when hit by ground fire as he attacked Goose Green.

It is possible the loss of Nick and XZ 450 actually helped to save many other men. When the Argentines found the Sea Eagle control panel in the wreckage I suspect they thought XZ450 was just another Sea Harrier and were shocked to find it had Sea Eagle air launch capability. They were not to know it was the only one so fitted and must have wondered if the Sea Eagle was in service with the force. I have always felt this must have been a factor in why, apart from the Belgrano episode, the Argentine Navy did not approach the task force. If they had used their aircraft carrier, the 25 de Mayo, there is little doubt that many more lives would have been lost on both sides. Nine years earlier I had flown a Harrier GR1 demonstration from the 25 de Mayo when it was passing through the Channel on its delivery voyage from Holland and, while they seemed interested, they eventually purchased cheaper, second hand A-4 Skyhawks from the USN. If they had bought Harriers, one can only guess how things might have worked out.

The Sea Harrier was a remarkable British aircraft. I shall always count myself very lucky to have been associated with it.

Ski-jump

Falklands footage left the public in no doubt that our Harriers took off from their ships using a curved ramp, commonly referred to as a ski-jump. The idea was conceived in 1973 by Lt Cdr Doug Taylor RN during a year spent at Southampton University where the RN had sent him to carry out research into new ship launch techniques for aircraft.

I first learned about the idea when our senior performance man at Kingston, Trevor Jordan, rang me up at Dunsfold late on a Friday afternoon and asked what I thought about running up a curved ramp at the front of the ship in order to improve takeoff performance.

I am afraid I was extremely dismissive of the idea. I explained that I had only that day returned from a week on board a USMC Harrier ship where the main concern of the pilots was that the stick was hitting the front stop just after leaving the deck during a heavy weight short takeoff. In other words, they were very short of nose down authority and "Now you want to add a nose up pitch rate from going round a ramp!"

By way of background, the Harrier had always been a bit short of nose-down control when flying with the nozzles partially down because the deflected engine exhaust induces airflow down on top of the tailplane.

101

This situation, while containable after a runway takeoff, was made worse operating from a ship because of the area of rising air just ahead of any carrier flight deck. As a result, it was not uncommon for pilots to find they were pushing against the front stop for a second or two after launch. This was something that nobody enjoyed and exiting a curved ramp with its built in nose up rate of rotation seemed likely to turn a bad situation into outright loss of control.

Adjustable trial ramp at Bedford

After the weekend I rang Trevor to apologise for my outburst and to talk sensibly about what the performance advantages of the ramp might be. The upshot was that Kingston did some computer simulations of Doug Taylor's idea and wanted to build a trial ramp at Dunsfold. I favoured Bedford as a location as I felt that way we would have the support of Aero Flight's VSTOL boffins.

I had little doubt that, if we went ahead with plans to do it in house at Dunsfold, the MOD would want Bedford's view before agreeing to anything so giving them a stake in the project from the start seemed sensible. In the event a fully adjustable trial ramp was built at Bedford so that we could start tentative flight trials at exit angles around 6° and build up progressively to 20°.

The ski-jump takeoff was a development of the flat deck launch which was itself a development of the runway short takeoff (STO). Like most things, it is easier to understand the issues if one starts at the beginning.

A Harrier at maximum weight will be too heavy to do a VTO by some two or three tons, depending on the version and the load it is carrying. Therefore it needs to add that much wing lift to the engine thrust in order to get airborne. This means accelerating along the surface, with nozzles aft, to a speed at which the wing can lift two or three tons then lowering the nozzles and flying away on a mixture of wing lift and engine thrust.

During a runway STO the bicycle main gear, which is mounted well aft of the CG, resists rotation so you cannot raise the nose in the normal way during takeoff but have to make do with what the wing can provide in the normal ground attitude. This means an alpha of only 8° instead of the 12° available if you could rotate. However, once off the end of a ship's deck you are free of this undercarriage constraint and can quickly rotate the aircraft to 12° which provides considerably more wing lift. This is why a flat deck ship allows a heavier load to be flown than is possible from the same length of runway.

However, all of this ship advantage vanishes in rough water. If the ship is pitching, you could get to the end of the deck when the bow is down and so finish up diving towards the sea. Pulling out from this dive requires the ability to increase g which means a considerable margin of lift is needed so you must schedule a lighter starting weight. Thus a rough sea can seriously degrade your load carrying ability.

However, with a ramp that has an exit angle greater than any conceivable bow down angle of the ship, then every launch starts with a climb! Make the ramp angle considerably greater than that needed to counter ship motion and you really start to gain performance and find you need less initial run than from a flat deck which leaves more of the deck space behind you for other activities.

The secret in appreciating how this increased performance comes about is to realise that a ramp gives you *time* in the air even if you have *zero* lift. If you drove your car up a 15° ramp at 70 mph, it would fly for quite a few moments before it fell back towards the sea. Replace your car with a Harrier where the engine can already support 70% of the weight then, even without any wing lift, it will only sink below the ramp induced climb angle at 30% of the normal effect of gravity. However the wing clearly provides some lift so gravity drags you down even less than that which means you continue upwards for many seconds before your climb rate reduces to level flight, let alone a sink. If you use a nozzle angle off the end that gives about 10 kt per second acceleration, then the flight time that the ramp provides allows the airspeed to build and you fly happily away. In effect you are accelerating to flying speed along a runway in the sky. This is exactly the same as an ordinary aircraft accelerating for a number of seconds along a normal runway in order to get flying speed.

Finally, safety is improved compared to the flat deck case because, even if the engine or nozzles fail as you leave the ramp, we know the aircraft will 'fly' for some time so allowing you ample time for ejection.

Why is the handling better? Because the ramp rotates the aircraft and delivers it into the sky in the right attitude and climbing, things the pilot has to make happen during a standard aircraft takeoff. Indeed, to convince the boffins during those early ski-jump trials that it was all as easy as said, I did a launch without touching the stick for 35 seconds after leaving the end. At the debrief they stared in considerable disbelief at the straight lines on the instrumentation traces that showed no pilot input before agreeing with me that doing nothing was as low a workload as you can get.

However, what about the nose up pitch rate that I had been worried about? By an amazing stoke of luck this nose up rate was exactly equalled by a nose down pitch rate that the ramp imparted to the aircraft during the brief period its nosewheel was in fresh air but the main wheels were still hard on the ramp.

There was another potential problem that involved undercarriage fatigue life. When you hit the ramp the aircraft was pushed up at about 3g courtesy of the undercarriage. This would obviously impact on fatigue life and not surprisingly no allowance for this had been built into the original undercarriage design ten years earlier. When the sums were examined, though, there was a big fatigue factor that had been incorporated for the heavy weight rough strip case I mentioned earlier. In the event the services were not using this and it proved enough to handle the ski-jump case.

The ski-jump really was the best example of a total win-win aviation idea that I have ever come across.

The Skyhook

Chapter 8 mentions several demonstration sorties that I flew from ships and on one of these I landed vertically while the ship had considerable deck motion. Initially pleased with my easy and safe arrival despite the extreme ship motion, I suddenly became very concerned as the ship continued to roll and lurch making my aircraft slide about the slippery deck in such a way that it could have gone over the edge. Back at Dunsfold, I debriefed the other pilots and said I was off to see the chief designer to try and get him to come up with some way of grabbing and physically restraining the aircraft after touchdown. I knew such equipment was used with helicopters and clearly the Harrier needed help as well because the concept of a floating aerodrome, where all aircraft control on the deck depends on friction, had obvious limits for safe operation. It seemed ridiculous that we had to lose the possibility of a real rough water operational capability when the aircraft was not limited for piloting reasons.

Two days later one of the Dunsfold pilots, Heinz Frick, came into my office and said he felt the way to solve the whole issue was to use a smart crane to grab the aircraft as it hovered alongside the ship, even relieving the pilot of the need to do a landing. The Skyhook was born.

G-VTOL hovering under the Skyhook mock-up

Clearly after being hooked on to the crane, the engine could be shut down and the aircraft moved aboard and deposited wheels up in a suitable maintenance and rearming cradle. Heinz's idea went down very well at Kingston and they started the preliminary design of such a system. The crane would have its hook end space stabilised while its ship end moved about with ship motion. Indeed, as we were soon to find out, the offshore drilling industry used similar space stabilised cranes to drill into the sea bed from a barge tossed about by the waves. The concept is also like an upside down flight simulator motion base where the cockpit is deliberately waved about on top of a base that is fixed in space.

With computers and robotic systems already developed and in use, providing the smart crane was not going to be difficult. However, the design of the capture head required an understanding of how accurately a Harrier pilot could hold station under the capture hook while the engagement process took place. We guessed that the pilot could hold position inside a two metre cube but guessing is no good so we got the local fire brigade to bring one of their telescopic turntables and we established, using a camera on the top, that when we hovered alongside it we did so within a one metre cube. Later the turntable changed to a Coles crane fitted with a serious mock-up of the capture head as shown in the picture above.

The Skyhook concept offered considerable potential for operating Harriers from modest sized ships and various designs for these were considered by Kingston.

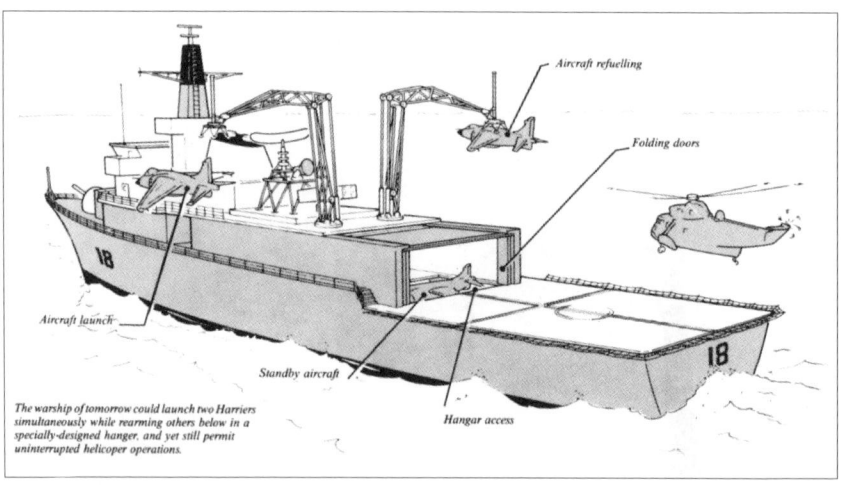

The warship of tomorrow could launch two Harriers simultaneously while rearming others below in a specially-designed hanger, and yet still permit uninterrupted helicopter operations.

Harrier forward picket ship concept

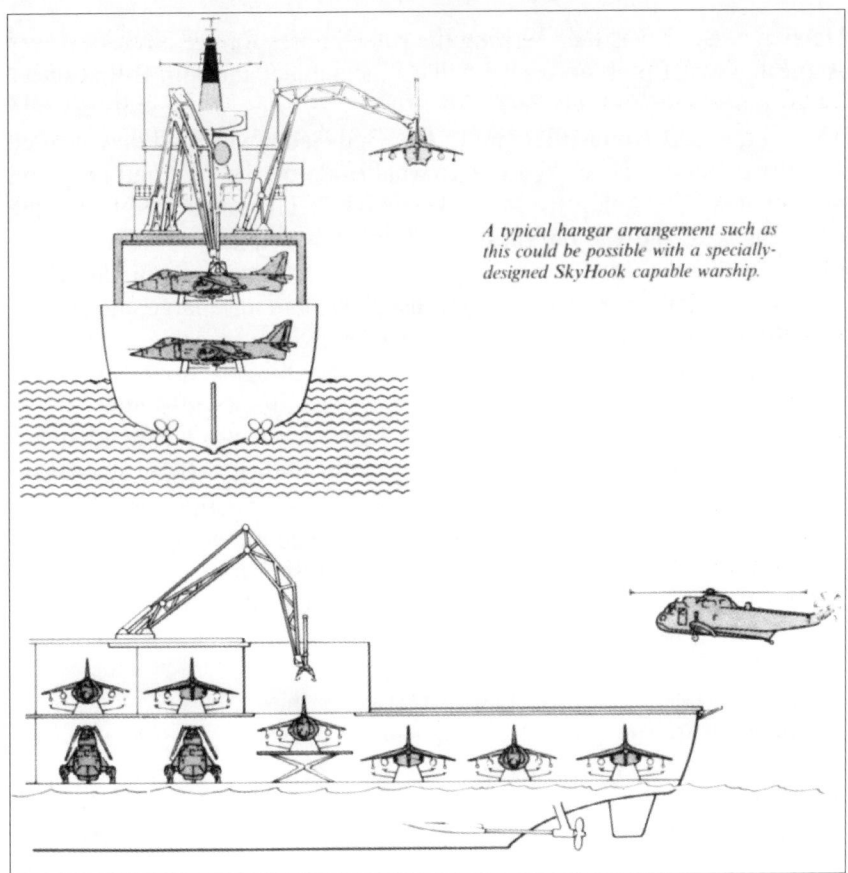

A typical hangar arrangement such as this could be possible with a specially-designed SkyHook capable warship.

Skyhook ship internal layout

In the event, big ship navies were not persuaded of the Skyhook notion and, in the absence of such support, the company was not prepared to finance the manufacture of a working head and associated aircraft modifications to enable actual capture trials. There is, of course, no doubt that big ships are nicer places for Admirals to have their cabins and large flight decks are better for hosting cocktail parties and parading marching bands so perhaps they had their reasons.

The USMC and the AV-8B

My first experience of the USMC was at Farnborough (where else?). I was in my office at Dunsfold when the phone rang on the Thursday of the 1968 show week and PR told me that Bill Bedford had been approached at the show by a couple of Marines who wanted to fly the

107

Harrier. Since I was then writing the pilot's notes for the aircraft, it was suggested that I pick up what I had on the subject and join Bill at once.

There I met Col Tom Miller and Lt Col Bud Baker who said they wanted to do two flights each. "You tell us what to do on the first and we'll tell you what we are going to do on the second". They also said they were going back to the US on Tuesday. To put this request into context, we must remember that at that time we had no two-seater, no simulator, the limited autostabs were not used because they were unreliable, the aircraft was still seven months of development away from being cleared for RAF service and all the aircraft were owned by the Ministry not HSA.

All this brought a fair rush of blood to the corporate head. My only input was to suggest that, if I had anything to do with it, Miller and Baker would need a week for a VSTOL conversion and another week to do a worthwhile evaluation. Hugh Merewether backed me on this and the two weeks were agreed. For those interested in putting themselves into Tom and Bud's shoes I have done a detailed write up of a typical single-seat conversion at Annexe B to this chapter.

It is a matter of history how effective Miller and Baker were in completing this task and selling the Harrier in Washington. At that time they were USMC visionaries working in the Pentagon and not at all part of the USN evaluation system. Nevertheless, thanks entirely to their missionary skills, the USN was quickly tasked to send a formal Navy Preliminary Evaluation (NPE) team of test pilots and engineers to Dunsfold the following January and Hugh asked me to look after them.

Clearly these NPE flights were going to go into a lot more detail than had been possible with Tom and Bud's quick look. Accordingly I spent the first two days with the NPE team going through all the aircraft systems and briefing them on every handling or other issue we had come across in flight. I did this because it seemed to me that, if they stumbled across an unexpected problem, they would immediately tear up their test plan and concentrate on the problem. I felt they could easily spend so much time doing this that they might fail to experience all the good aspects of the aircraft.

During the briefings I saw a lot of looks passing between the team members but was too naïve to realise that this was because at home they lived with the 'lying, cheating contractor' mindset and so could not believe I was telling them about the bad as well as the good. Again it is a matter of history that the eventual NPE report was extraordinarily glowing and suggested only minor things that needed to be addressed if the aircraft was to be used in the USMC expeditionary role.

As the programme progressed I spent a lot of time with the USMC but three very minor events happened quite early on which, when taken together, were destined to earn me a very useful but totally unjustified reputation for boldness with the Marines.

The first happened when I was at the USN flight test centre Patuxent River, or Pax as it is usually known, helping them put the first marine aircraft through their Board of Inspection and Survey (BIS) trials. The aircraft had an ejection seat that required five servicing pins to be stowed in a housing on the right hand cockpit glare shield. The pins were all different lengths, diameters and types and only one sequence of stowing them in the unlabelled holes would work. It was a truly dreadful bit of kit that I had totally failed to get the Kingston drawing office to change before delivery. Out on the pan, I noticed a large Marine top sergeant in the cockpit getting more and more irate as he tried to deal with this thing. Being a good company man, I went over to apologise for our deficiencies but, as I climbed up the ladder, he let rip with a tirade of abuse about Hawkers, the Brits and the bloody Harrier.

As I had only come over to help, I felt a bit put out by this. I waited for him to draw breath then, acting as if nothing had happened, commented what lovely weather they had at Pax and asked if he was pleased to be on the Harrier. This wound him up again. Eventually I got in, "Surely you are not having trouble with that pin stowage are you? That's a specially designed intelligence test. If you can't deal with that, you shouldn't be in the cockpit."

I clearly remember his fist starting to come up from the area of the right hand console and arc towards my face. Then strangely, its range held steady at about a foot and I realised that I was being yanked bodily backwards off the ladder by Bill Scheuren who had been the lead pilot on the NPE team. I had been talking to Bill on the pan and he had fortunately followed me over to see how I would deal with this guy who I later found out had a reputation for direct action. Subsequently I overheard Bill talking to his colleagues in awed tones about this Brit who was prepared to take the rise out of Sergeant X. Bill was a remarkable guy, a USMC major, the first Pax test pilot to fly the Harrier and at that time the only indigenous American to be commissioned in the Corps. He used to swagger a lot.

Later that week he took me to a semi-formal dinner of 50 or so chaps from the Pax test squadrons. They were celebrating something or other that had not sunk in. I was just happy yarning away at the bottom of the table with the small Harrier team. Then I realised everybody was looking my way and the base commander was on his feet saying that he understood that there was a Brit pilot over with a strange hovering jet and he thought it appropriate that I say a few words about flying this unusual aircraft.

In those days everybody wanted to know how hovering the Harrier compared to hovering a helicopter. Therefore, after describing how and why it was so much easier and altogether more sensible than a helicopter, I told a hoary old joke suitably modified to emphasise this point. I explained that, just before coming out to the US, I had to do a prolonged performance hover just after lunch and dozed off in the middle of this zero work load procedure. Having nodded off, I had a dream of the future where I was walking down a street of small shops, one of which had a window full of glass jars containing brains from people who had died that one could buy to transplant if not satisfied with one's own. Their prices ranged from a few dollars for those that had been well used up to one on the top shelf that was priced at $10,000. I asked the shopkeeper why this one was so expensive. "That, Sir, is the best brain in the house. A truly wonderful brain from a man who went on to design helicopters. It is as good as new and has never been used."

The reaction of the audience to this punch line surprised me. It was not just the silence but the way people turned to look at each other. Then somebody clapped at the back of the room and gradually the cheering and table banging started. "Funny lot," I thought. As we mingled after the meal, Bill took me to meet an old man in his eighties who was the clearly revered private guest of the base commander. "Sir," said Bill, "I'd like to introduce John Farley". We shook hands. "Loved your story, perhaps we should talk some time," said the old man. His name was not mentioned. "Nice to meet you, Sir," said I and we moved away. The next day as I approached the crew room, I overheard somebody retelling my punch line. The reaction this time was:

"Jeezus, he told *that* in front of Frank Piasecki!"

The final event in this trilogy happened at the next Farnborough Show. I was just making my way from the bar in our chalet carrying a pair of large gin and tonics needed by some guests when one of the receptionists appeared with a USMC pilot. I placed the glasses on the bar, shook hands and explained that I couldn't stay to chat right then because, as soon as I had got rid of these drinks, I had to go and do my demo. He seemed a little surprised but I had no option but to say, "See you later" and with that I picked up the drinks, delivered them to my guests near the door and left. Later back in the chalet, I was pleased to see the Marine was still there so went up for the promised chat. "Great show" he said, "I can see why you needed the gins." I thought he was joking of course, so grinned and said, "Yeah, well without those we wouldn't be able to touch the nozzle lever would we?" and got on with our chat.

On my next visit to the latest USMC Harrier squadron forming at Cherry Point, there was a message at the gate that I should go to the Marine Air Group Headquarters, not the Squadron, as the MAG commander wanted to see me. I thought this strange but naturally did as requested. Imagine my surprise when the colonel immediately jumped all over me and said he understood that it was my habit to drink before carrying out displays and as such I was not a fit person to visit the pilots in his crew rooms. I thought it was a wind up of course and initially played it that way which proved to be a bad error on my part. Over three decades later my mind still boggles at the notion that I could be a bad influence on anybody in the USMC.

When the USMC started flying Harriers, they had only four changes from the RAF Harriers of the day. These were US insignia instead of RAF roundels, a different radio compatible with the USMC ground units, a US standard attitude indicator and, most importantly, the ability to fire Sidewinder air to air missiles. This last change was because the USMC realised from day one that the aircraft had the potential to be used as a fighter and not just for ground attack. The RAF aircraft did not get the Sidewinder modifications until they were on the ships on their way down to the Falklands in 1982 which I felt was leaving it a little late.

The original USMC Harriers were given the designation AV-8A. A decade later they were replaced by the AV-8B. The first thing to say about this new aircraft is that I loved flying it and yes, I realise I did not say the same thing about the Sea Harrier earlier on in this chapter.

Perhaps it is inevitable that people will try to compare the UK Sea Harrier and the US/UK AV-8B. I loved flying one but not the other. Does this mean I think one is better than the other? Certainly not, because they were designed to do very different jobs. My comment reflects how I felt about my participation in the two programmes not the aircraft themselves. As I hope I explained earlier, it so often seemed a daily struggle to get the Sea Harrier to happen and to continue. In such circumstances you just don't have the time to enjoy, let alone love, what you are doing because you are too busy worrying about doing it.

In the US I enjoyed my AV-8B work very much indeed because I never for one moment doubted that it would lead to something and produce a better version for the USMC. Of course the programme required plenty of technical problems to be solved but to go to bed thinking about such matters was the height of luxury so far as I was concerned. Indeed, before I became one, I thought this was all that test pilots did.

The seeds of what it would be like to fly the AV-8B were irrevocably planted by the USMC planners in the mid-1970s. After a brief foray into the possibility of a supersonic version, called the AV-16S, the USMC settled for what became the AV-8B. The USMC wanted the B model to carry twice as much load for the same distance as an AV-8A could go or take the maximum load of the A model twice as far. All this was to be achieved without needing more space in which to take off and land. That was what they wanted and so that was what they said, a point I shall return to later.

Such a 'doubling of the payload / radius of action' would have been easy with a bigger and better Pegasus engine but there was no money for that, so it was to be a case of using airframe brains rather than engine brawn. McDonnell Douglas, Kingston's chosen partner to support the AV-8A in USMC service, was given a contract to study this far from easy job. They came up with a new wing, beautifully optimised for the cruise using DC9 airliner expertise. This bigger wing would carry extra stores and fuel, as well as provide the greater lift needed to maintain STO capability with more stores. Vertical performance was to be increased by a package of changes that included better intakes and cold nozzles. Further VTO help came from saving weight by making the wing structure largely out of carbon fibre rather than metal and making the under-fuselage strakes larger. These big strakes would give the aircraft an extra push up by trapping more of the jet energy that rebounds from the ground surface during the start of any VTO.

In order to flight test these proposals, two existing USMC AV-8As were fitted with the new wing and intakes at St Louis. They were designated YAV-8Bs. I got my first trip in one in November 1979. Because of the possibility that this aircraft could form the basis of replacing early RAF Harriers, a UK evaluation team was dispatched to see how it was shaping up. The team included three pilots, Sqn Ldr Bob Iveson, an RAF Harrier flight commander who would concentrate on the tactical potential of the new aircraft, Wg Cdr David Scouller, CO of the Boscombe Down fighter test squadron to assess service release implications and me from Dunsfold to examine the VSTOL and conventional envelope limits. This excellent composition meant that we could each fulfil the responsibility that we had at home, thus providing our masters with an evaluation that covered all aspects.

Before leaving for the US, I went to discuss the trials with Ralph Hooper, father of the P1127, then Chief Engineer, Kingston. I left his office literally amazed with what happened between us. For the first time in 15 years of working for him (in the way a priest works *for* the Pope and not *with* him), I had found myself disagreeing with Ralph over a basic technical issue. It concerned the large fly-by-wire flaps fitted to the YAV-8B. Ralph wanted to stick to the existing safe and simple method of controlling the flaps that had been used on all Harriers to date namely a single hydraulic jack rotating a shaft that linked both flaps together. Although it was possible to do this on the B, weight could be saved using the method chosen by St Louis. Their solution was two independent flaps, each with its own actuator and a computer to ensure they moved as one. Also, these new flaps were so big they had to be moved in step with the nozzles, only going fully down after the pilot selected nozzles down on takeoff and coming in just ahead of the nozzles as they were raised during acceleration to wingborne flight. This co-ordination would also be looked after by the computer.

Ralph was concerned that these flaps introduced a whole range of failure cases, some of which could lead to an instant crash if they happened during takeoff or landing. He pointed out that much of the credit for the Harrier's success to date was down to Kingston avoiding such design risks like the plague and I should at all times be prepared for the worst and not trust such devices as they were a big mistake. I replied that, while understanding his views, I felt the only way to get the improved lift and reduced weight was to move to such systems. I was happy to see the flaps operated this way in 1979, because by then the F-16 had shown several years of reliable service and that whole aircraft was controlled by fly-by-wire, not just its flaps. As I left his office, I remembered ten years earlier my judgement that it was reasonable to land on La Salle and shut down. Now I felt the time had come to lean on computers in order to move forward with VSTOL.

The UK team duly arrived at Whiteman AFB, a more suitable airfield for an intensive evaluation than St Louis International Airport but we were thwarted when the trials aircraft, the second prototype, crashed during its ferry flight from St Louis. The engine had surged and the McDonnell Douglas pilot, Jack Jackson, could not get a relight and was forced to eject. Fortunately for Jack the seat worked as advertised and he was unhurt. However, it was not just as simple as switching to the other prototype because the initial testing of the pair had shown the need to reduce wing related drag and the necessary modifications for this were only fitted to the one that crashed. As a result the formal UK evaluation was called off.

However, when the dust settled, it was decided that I should do three circuit only flights on the remaining aircraft. This would allow a quick look at the VSTOL improvements and meant my journey was not in vain. At once I was most impressed by the great increase in lift that was available from the new wing and the large flaps. Weight for weight it knocked about 40 kt off the sort of speeds previously needed for a short takeoff or slow landing. I had expected the lift would be there but it is always nice to prove it in flight.

What I was not prepared for was the dramatic increase in safety that I found during transitions. To appreciate the significance of this, one needs a bit of background. Previously the most dangerous handling characteristic of the Harrier had been its tendency to roll out of control if sideslip built up during transition to or from the hover. This meant the pilot had to use precise foot movements on his rudder bar during transitions in order to keep the nose pointing the way the aircraft was travelling through the air. If he failed to do this adequately then one wing would be slightly ahead of the other and this leading wing would develop more lift than the trailing one and the aircraft would try to roll upside down. The control available to the pilot from his stick to counter this was quite limited hence the danger if he did not use his feet accurately enough.

I was used to evaluating this problem by flying at mid transition speeds and deliberately pushing on a little incorrect rudder, using the stick to keep the wings level, until the rudder caused two thirds of the available stick travel to be used up. The amount of rudder needed to reach this point was really very small. When I tried this test on the YAV-8B, I got to an unbelievable full rudder pedal travel. In addition, the amount of stick I needed to keep the wings level was so small I could not detect it amongst the normal activity needed to fly. I had to let go of the stick, still at full rudder, to be sure it needed any correction at all. What a splendid improvement!

Before pilots of the AV-8B, GR7 and GR9 tell me their aircraft are not quite as good as that, I must add that a little of this benefit had to be sacrificed later in the programme to allow drooped ailerons to be used on STO to further increase lift capability. However, even with the increase in rolling moment due to sideslip caused by the drooped ailerons, the new wing reduced the magnitude of this handling problem to a perfectly acceptable level.

The following March saw me back at St Louis on the YAV-8B programme and then in April we reconvened the whole UK team at Whiteman for the full evaluation of the remaining aircraft, now modified to the latest standard. This time everything went as planned and it was a great success.

The remaining YAV-8B did much good work in the period before the first four development batch AV-8Bs were available, including a couple of periods at Edwards looking at engine handling at the edge of the new wing's envelope and even beyond it on occasion. However the situation at Edwards with its cloudless skies, miles and miles of flat lakebed to glide onto if need be and no worry about Gatwick traffic, was very different from my normal Dunsfold stamping ground and enabled me to concentrate on the technicalities. No wonder I loved that flying.

August 1980 found me back at Whiteman, this time because McDonnell Douglas were planning to present the YAV-8B at the Farnborough Air Show a month later. I was asked to work up a routine that would convincingly demonstrate the performance improvements that were now available. This caused me some concern because I knew it would be difficult to achieve. The world was used to seeing Harrier VSTOL and it would look no different when done by the YAV-8B. The better controls or the extra weight, even the greater safety, would not be evident to those on the ground. However, I felt the extra lift from the new wing might just be put across. My plan was to do a very short takeoff allowing the speed to build quickly as I pulled up into a loop. Once on my back at about 1,200 ft over the middle of the airfield, I would roll to 80° of bank, then use the big wing plus the flaps and the nozzles to fly a very tight 360° turn high up where it would be easy for all to see. That would be new Harrier behaviour. When I flew to practise this manoeuvre it became clear that the serviceability of this development machine was very dubious. After several aborted trips, I began to think that we were in danger of going to the show and then not getting airborne, which would not be good PR. McDonnell Douglas was also having problems with the Atlantic transit arrangements and it all looked pretty dodgy. Despite this nobody wanted to say stop.

Then the aeroplane made its own mind up and showed that it knew best when one day the nose sank noticeably as I taxied out. The bemused ground crew had seen it too so were not surprised when I shut down on the spot. It transpired that the nose leg had an internal fault and there was no spare and no time to repair it. I patted the Y's nose, thanked it for doing that there and not at Farnborough, went home and borrowed a Sea Harrier from the RN for the show.

By early 1982, McDonnell Douglas had the development fleet of four AV-8Bs for the test programme nearly ready to fly. Ship 1, as they called it, had done extensive hover tests in 1981 but, when it was flown conventionally, the engine unexpectedly gave a single self clearing pop surge during the climb to high altitude. Not only was that unexpected but the St Louis area was certainly not the place to investigate that sort of behaviour. Neither was that aircraft the right one for the job as it lacked the back-up hydraulic power supply and pilot oxygen systems needed if one was to go around routinely stopping and starting the engine at altitude. This job had always been planned for Ship 2 so, as soon as that aircraft was ready, it was time for me to go to St Louis again. I got my first flight in it at St Louis in April. How wonderful it was to enjoy the new bigger cockpit, properly laid out with a bubble canopy and a modern TV screen type instrument display. Kingston did good aeroplanes but their first decent cockpit had to wait for the Hawk. Why they were weak at cockpits is a long story and not worth wasting time on here.

By mid-May, Charlie Plummer (the McDonnell Douglas test pilot who had the misfortune to get the original pop surge fright at St Louis) and I were at Edwards ready to demonstrate in a programme planned to take six weeks that Ship 2 would do everything the Marines required. Unfortunately, Ship 2 did not agree with the planners. Our initial trials showed that surges happened all too easily. Given it was a British engine behind a US intake, there was scope for argument as to the cause! In the event I was left to await a replacement engine while Charlie went back to St Louis to do something useful.

JF and Ship 2 out of St Louis

Of course I wanted to go home and get on with the thousand and one things that a Chief Test Pilot is expected to do. At this time they included a little matter of the Sea Harrier and all the modifications that were being done in support of the Falklands War, where the shooting had started a couple of weeks earlier. However it was not to be. Getting approval for me to do engine testing at Edwards had not been easy as the authorities there saw deliberate 'engine out' work as high risk and invoked a variety of procedural hoops for the driver to jump through to make them look better at any subsequent board of enquiry. A Brit civilian flying a USMC aircraft on a USN programme and doing a high risk trial at the USAF test centre particularly got their attention. If I went away there was no guarantee that I would get back in again. Anyway that was how the St Louis suits saw it as they rushed around in circles sorting out another engine.

In the end all was well. Jack Jackson came out to join me and we took it in turns flying chase on each other using an AV-8A. It took five different build standards of engine, three of the intake and a year, not six weeks, before the engine airframe combination did everything that was asked of it. In the process I enjoyed two hours gliding over my favourite lakebed.

We also measured how fast it would go. That answer was a lot slower than the Sea Harrier. At the same rate of engine and fuel usage it was over 80 kt slower but the USMC had not specified it had to be as quick just how much they wanted it to carry and how far they wanted it to go. Interesting point don't you think? So now you see why it is wrong to say one was better than the other. They are different machines, each with strengths and each with weaknesses. I loved them both.

Supersonics

Many people have asked me why we never did a supersonic Harrier. My answer to them all was that the Harrier layout did not allow it. To fly supersonically requires not just an engine with enough thrust to overcome the drag of flying at such speeds but an engine specifically designed to produce a very high speed exhaust. In other words the nature of the thrust is important, not just the amount of it.

For the benefit of non-aviation specialists, the physics behind this are remarkably simple. The thrust of a jet engine is calculated by multiplying together just two numbers, M and V. M is the mass or amount of air passing through the engine in a given time (pounds per second using the units I was taught at school) while V is the speed *increase* that the engine imparts to the air as it passes through the engine (feet per second in my day).

With both the Harrier (a typical subsonic fighter) and the F-16 (a typical supersonic fighter) the product of M x V is about 20,000. However, the difference between the two aircraft is that the Harrier engine gets its 20,000 by using a big value of M and a modest value of V while the F-16 engine uses a modest value of M but gives it a bigger V.

It is pretty obvious that when flying at high speed you need the engine to exhaust the air out of the back rather faster than you want to fly hence it is the nature (or speed) of the exhaust that determines the top speed of your aircraft not just the total thrust. While 20,000 lb of thrust is plenty to get a small fighter supersonic, it will only do so if the V component of that 20,000 is big enough.

The Harrier engine deliberately uses a small V because a big V would have the ability to damage the surface below it during a VTO and, if not the surface then the under-surfaces of the aircraft itself. Additionally and very importantly, an engine that produces a big V can only do this by making the exhaust very hot. Immersing the bottom of a Harrier and its rubber tyres in such a hot environment would clearly not work.

Thus, if you want to use VSTOL to provide operating site flexibility, you must keep the V (and the temperature) of the engine exhaust as low as possible. Helicopters are subject to the same physics regarding thrust so, in the case of a large 20,000 lb helicopter, it uses a *huge* M (captured by the rotor) and gives it a very small V (the downwash we can feel or see blowing stuff about under a helicopter) but the product is still 20,000.

Finally think of the hard time that hot fast exhausts on the Harrier would give the rear fuselage and tail in normal flight.

All this means that you need a different configuration of aircraft from that of the Harrier if you want to produce a practical supersonic vertical landing aircraft.

Hawk

When I was CTP and concentrating on the Harrier, I was fortunate to have three outstanding test pilots to whom I could delegate all aspects of the Hawk programme. They were Andy Jones, Jim Hawkins and Chris Roberts. These were men who I could rely on to do the job as I would have done it myself or better. Who can ask for more? While Andy and Jim did the majority of the early development work, I had to ask Chris, who had only just joined the company, to take on the less glamorous but vitally important job of training overseas customers 'in country'. While this did not challenge his test flying skills, the job did call for a high degree of diplomatic, managerial and commercial talents, which he exhibited to the full.

Final comment

In my view not enough people involved with military fighter procurement are aware of the many piloting advantages of being able to hover before landing. Indeed the same applies to many pilots who have not flown the Harrier. In the 1980s I wrote a paper on this subject where I tried to list and explain them. Apart from the USMC, where I was preaching to the choir and some of the Harrier fraternity in the UK, I don't think it was well received. Reading it again a quarter of a century later I would not change a word so I have included it as Annexe C for those who like a bit of history.

Annexe A

From the Daily Telegraph 28 May 2002

The 4th Earl of Kimberley, who has died aged 78, achieved a measure of fame as the most-married man in the peerage; once known as "the brightest blade in Burke's", he worked his way through five wives in 25 years before settling down contentedly with a former masseuse he had met on a beach in Jamaica. Johnny Kimberley was a jovial extrovert whose interests included shark fishing, UFOs and winter sports – for much of the 1950s he was a member of Britain's international bobsleigh team.

There was a serious side to him too: he played championship tiddlywinks, bred prize pigs, and as a Liberal spokesman in the Lords advised the electorate to vote Conservative, whereupon David (now Lord) Steel sacked him. Once on the Tory benches, he took a keen interest in defence and foreign policy, although not in social reform. "Queers," he declared, "have been the downfall of all the great empires." However, it was his frequent trips to the altar, and those shortly thereafter to the divorce courts, that most naturally caught the eye of the public. His first marriage, in 1945, was to Diana, daughter of Sir Piers Legh, Master of the King's Household and a former equerry to Edward VIII; Kimberley had met her on a blind date at the Ritz.

The wedding took place at St George's Chapel, Windsor, and was attended by the Queen, Princesses Elizabeth and Margaret, and King George VI, who proposed the toast to the bride and her groom, then a Guards officer. But Kimberley already knew that he had made a mistake. "I couldn't stop it," he said later, "because the King and Queen were there, and I was in my best uniform." Several years ago, in racy memoirs which were then unpublished, he wrote that on honeymoon he had more fun chasing mice around the bedroom than his new wife, and within a year the marriage was all but over.

"I gave the butler a note to give to her saying that it wasn't going to work out, and that since her mother was sailing for America that night why didn't she go too? That night I found a lovely girl and realised what I'd been missing not having a proper romp. After that, I never stopped."

By now Kimberley was a free-spending, hard-driving member of London's beau monde, taking weekends at Deauville, losing heavily at all-night chemmy sessions with John Aspinall, and bedding as many women as he could. "Sex. I just couldn't think of anything else," he recalled later. He claimed among his conquests Eartha Kitt and Glynis Johns, and even tipped his hat at Princess Margaret, though she declined the honour. One night, he was caught naked by an irate husband in a hotel cupboard.

His second marriage, in 1949, was to Carmel Dunnett, one of the five daughters of Mickey Maguire, sometime welterweight champion of Australia. Kimberley was introduced to her by her elder sister (a daughter-in-law of Lord Beaverbrook), whose affections he had already enjoyed. They were married at St Moritz, and in 1951 she presented him with an heir, Lord Wodehouse.

"It went quite well for three years," the earl remembered. "Then I found out that she had been knocking off one of my chums. I wasn't all that upset, but it was the fact that one had been made a fool of." They were divorced in 1952. She was later murdered in Spain in 1992 by her third husband, Jeremy Lowndes, who then confessed the crime to Kimberley's son.

Number three was Cynthia Westendarp, a Suffolk farmer's wife whom the earl met at Newmarket. After she contracted polio, he invited her to recuperate at Kimberley, his seat near Wymondham, Norfolk, "and she never moved out". They were married in 1953, and divorced in 1961. Three years before that, he had sold Kimberley, a Queen Anne brick mansion built on land held by his forebears for five centuries – "it was the easiest way to get rid of Cynthia. All I could think about was buying a new Aston Martin".

Next up was Maggie Simons, a 23-year old fashion model and the daughter of a cafe owner. She refused to sleep with him until he proposed marriage, which he did within a week. They were married in 1961 but "we both drank a fair amount and had fearful fights". Kimberley's fourth divorce came through in 1965. He was 39.

His fifth marriage, in 1970, was to Gillian Raw (nee Ireland-Smith), "and that was a disaster from the word go. She was a very successful girlfriend, but it didn't work as a wife". He had met Janey Consett, a soldier's daughter, in the Caribbean some years before, and now decided to "sugar off" with her instead. Once more divorced, he married her in 1982, and happily it proved to be sixth time lucky.

Annexe B

THE SINGLE SEAT CONVERSION PROCESS

When I converted the first two USMC pilots to the aircraft in 1968, we had no two-seater, no simulator, the limited autostabs were unreliable so were left switched off and the aircraft was still seven months of development away from being cleared for RAF service.

I propose you sit back and let me treat you as I did Col Tom Miller and Lt Col Bud Baker. Which one you choose to be is up to you. Tom was a quiet mature gentleman while Bud was the classic young Marine from haircut to attitude. Both were very experienced A-4 and F-4 pilots.

As with flying any new type there needs to be a bit of ground-school first but, in the case of experienced people, I liked to give them that info when they are sitting in the cockpit and I am standing on the ladder. A comprehensive left to right check of the cockpit covering every switch, control and instrument allows one to introduce the nature of the electrics, hydraulics, fuel and other systems as you come to them. The development batch Harrier that Tom and Bud were sitting in had little new to offer aviators at their level apart from the nozzle lever that was next to the throttle as in *Fig 1* and two gauges which I pointed out but said we would talk about later.

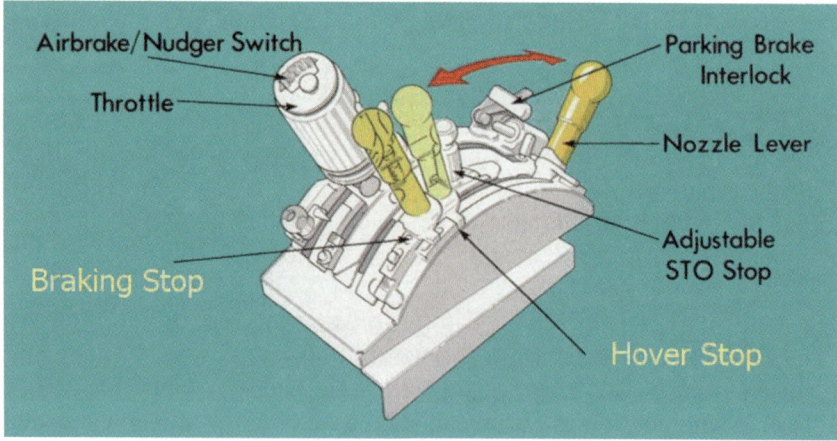

Fig 1

Having got the 'trivia' out of the way, it was time to adjourn for a coffee and a serious crew room chat about the differences that flowed from the VSTOL capability.

I am sure you will have no problem with the idea that being able to swivel the thrust of a jet fighter from the normal aft direction to straight down in order to hover was brilliantly simple. The way the lever worked was push it forward and the aircraft went faster, pull it back and the aeroplane went slower. The throttle was standard in that it was push forward for more thrust.

Having provided the necessary vertical thrust to counter the weight, you can 'fly' without having any airspeed. The next issue is how to control the aircraft attitude when the normal aerodynamic controls are completely ineffective. The answer is reaction controls or puffer jets as they are known as shown in *Fig 2*. These take the form of a pipe supplying high pressure air to the wingtips, nose and tail. There are shutters over the various ends of the pipe which are mechanically linked to the normal aerodynamic controls.

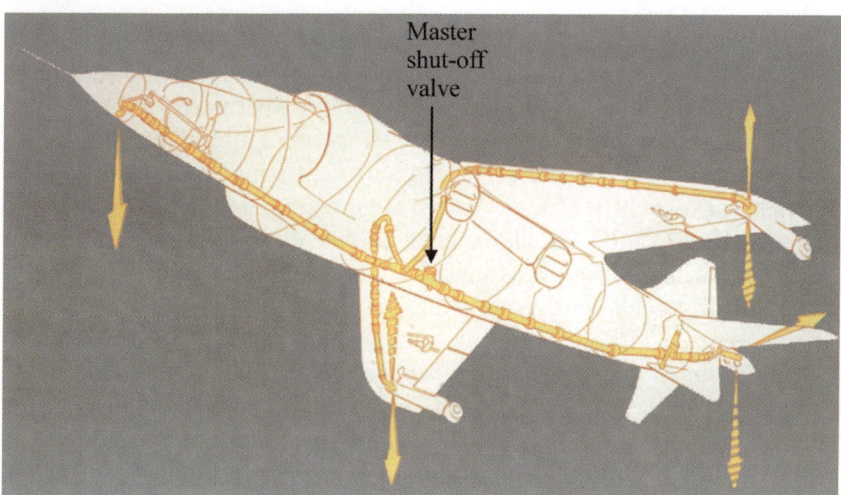

Master
shut-off
valve

Fig 2

When any flying control surface is centralised its associated puffer shutter is closed but, when that control is displaced, the shutter opens allowing the puffer jet to blow that corner of the aeroplane in the direction the aerodynamic surface would move it at normal airspeeds. The two new gauges are an air pressure gauge in the duct feeding the puffers and a nozzle angle gauge. The VSTOL bits and pieces really are that simple.

I shall start you off with a very low fuel, light weight, taxi-only sortie using nosewheel steering via the rudder bar and toe brakes. The aircraft thrust/weight ratio will be 1.3 to 1. This taxi session will finish with a nozzles-aft full power acceleration down the runway as if for a conventional takeoff. At 60 kt you should chop the throttle, slow down and return to dispersal. In fact most people doing this were so surprised by the 1.3 g acceleration that they reached 80-90 kt before chopping the throttle (1.3 g from a standing start being enough to get you to the legal limit on the motorway in 2.4 seconds). By the way, Bud objected that he did not need a Brit civilian to tell him how to taxi an aeroplane so his eyes glazed over during my brief and he was later clocked at 120 kt before he got the power off. Job done actually because, when he returned, he was clearly shocked that this little toy with kiddie wheels on the wingtips and no reheat could leave him so far behind. The end result was that he soaked up every other brief like blotting paper and did brilliantly thereafter.

I hope you appreciate now that the reason for that taxi session was to teach the lesson that you should never move the nozzle or throttle lever over the full range without first thinking about what would happen next. That is all it takes to stay ahead of any aeroplane. Think it through before you act and so cut out the surprise element. I could have said that the Harrier was a small aeroplane with a huge engine until I was blue in the face and Bud would never have been convinced until he experienced it for himself. Therefore it was necessary to set him up to be left behind while still in an inherently safe situation on the ground.

Having rammed that point home, the way was clear for their first flight which was to be a vertical takeoff followed by an immediate vertical landing. The brief was easy and went like this: "Start up and taxi out as before, park the aircraft into-wind on a suitable bit of concrete near the end of the runway and do the normal takeoff checks. When ready you now have to do four things that you did not do during the taxi session. No, put that chinagraph away and listen. If you cannot remember these four things then you should not be getting in the cockpit. Number one is to ask ATC for takeoff clearance. Everybody knows you have to do that so that just leaves three new things. Number two, select the nozzle lever back to the hover stop which is as far as it will go without lifting it into the reverse thrust position or 'braking stop'. Number three, place the throttle fully open. Yes, I do mean place it fully open, I do not mean creep it up gradually to see what will happen. As soon as you place it fully forward the engine will accelerate quickly and the aircraft will rise up off the ground."

"But you said there were four things to do, what is number four?" Ready for this question I rudely pointed at the speaker and shouted, "LOOK OUT OF THE WINDOW!" Then more moderately, "I do not want you looking in the cockpit as you open the throttle because there is nothing there that will help you". It is essential that the pilot looks out and, as the aircraft leaves the ground, keeps the attitude picture constant. The stick should be used instinctively to hold the wings level and the pitch attitude steady while the feet should be used to keep the nose pointing into wind as it was before lift off. I told pilots to feel free to throttle back a little as soon as they left the ground and so descend back for their first vertical landing.

Staying with you as the student, this would be the easiest first takeoff in a new type you had ever done. It is not necessary to accelerate to an unstick speed that you have not seen before nor to rotate using a force and displacement on the controls that you are not sure about, nor try to capture a nose up attitude that you have never seen before, nor try and relate that to the climbing speed and so on. The VTO into the hover and back down for a VL is just an exercise in straight and level flight and maintaining the attitude picture you see outside while standing on the wheels until you are back down on the ground again.

It really is that easy, except you won't believe me when I say you will not throttle back enough after lift off and so you will go up to 50 ft plus with me saying, "Less power, less power" on the R/T. Eventually you will move the throttle back the 2-3 cm needed to kill the climb and you will start to creep down. Despite being told to keep it flat, you will raise the nose and try to do a landing flare as you see the ground coming up and will have to be shouted at again: "DON'T RAISE THE NOSE". When it eventually touches, but not before, you must chop the throttle to idle or the engine thrust plus the energy stored in the compressed undercarriage will push you back up into the air and you will have to do it all over again.

Regardless of how it went, I would make sure you did not do another lift but taxied in and shut down for a coffee and debrief. When people walk out to do their first VTO, they always think they will be the first person not able to do this 'press-up' as briefed then, after they have done it, the realisation that it is so easy hits hard and suddenly they want to do a display. This tendency to go from under-confident to over-confident in the Harrier is normal but very dangerous and must be stamped on. That is why I allowed only one new manoeuvre per sortie which enabled a heavy critical debrief to be applied before the next attempt.

After four or five of these single press-up sorties, you will do one properly, no wobbling, straight up to 20 ft or so and straight back down to the same spot. You are now ready for the next exercise which is height control in the hover. This time climb well up towards 100 ft and try and stabilise your height. Then deliberately come down a bit and stop it again. Then down for a landing and coffee. You will probably do the repeat of this perfectly and so will be ready for sideways translations in the hover on your next sortie. For those you deliberately put on 10 to 15° of bank and hold it until you get to the edge of the runway or pan you are hovering over where you will have to reverse the bank to stop the motion and wait while it moves you back to the centreline.

It may sound very boring and repetitive when written down like this but I assure you it is not. However, don't think that having gone solo in the hover the main problems are all behind you. Any aeroplane is likely to bite a pilot with such an attitude and the Harrier has a few more teeth than most.

I did not want to concern you with this before you hovered but, as an example of how previously well established military jet pilot reactions must be changed when you are in a Harrier, imagine the fire warning light comes on. Previously you have been brought up to chop the throttle to idle and wait for a while in the hope that a high power hot gas leak is the cause of the light. If the light then goes out, there is a chance that you can land using reduced power. If you are in the hover or partially jet-borne in the Harrier, such an instinctive reaction of the throttle hand will cause a crash there and then. Thus you must master a new reaction to a vibration, bang or light, namely expedite a landing or eject. After all, if you are in the hover, you are only a few seconds away from being able to do a vertical landing.

The justified confidence that comes from doing good hovers must be tempered by realising that it is always going to be easy to move the throttle when you meant to move the nozzle lever and the other way round. Such a simple and natural mistake is nothing to do with an error of skill such as misjudging a landing flare. The very concept of the single lever which allows such remarkable operating site flexibility from a fast jet also sets pilots up to make such pure mistakes. That is an important part of why the Harrier is so easy to crash.

The next thing on your conversion is to investigate some forward speed. This time, from a steady hover into wind over the runway, lower the nose a little – say 5 or 10° – and allow the aircraft to move forward. Snatch a glance at the airspeed indicator and see how easily it comes off the bottom stop of 24 kt. Once the ASI does move, gently raise the nose back up through the hover attitude to a similar amount nose up. This will kill the speed and get you back to the hover. You will notice the reduction in forward view when the nose is up and the need to keep your head on a swivel looking out both sides to re-establish the hover. Then carry out another vertical landing. After a coffee, do that again and this time keep the nose low until you have 50 to 60 kt on the ASI before slowing back to the hover. Raising the nose like that is what you will have to do at the end of your first full deceleration from wingborne speed. This decelerating transition (as the manoeuvre is called) and the accelerating transition from the hover are next on the VSTOL agenda.

Before doing these transitions on days when the weather was good, I often sent people off on a purely conventional sortie (with the nozzle lever kept fully forward throughout), not because it was part of the VSTOL conversion process but just because they were itching to get a conventional feel for the jet.

Today as befits your usual luck, there is a front coming in from the west and we have only got another hour or so before it clamps, so your first conventional wingborne trip is not on. Therefore I suggest you go and do a circuit that includes both transitions. Big stuff, two new manoeuvres in one sortie!

These two transitions are totally different in nature and both will seem extremely natural to you when you do them but neither will give you any sense of flying in a grey area between wings and engine. However, I do not expect you to believe this until you have experienced it for yourself. To help your confidence, take a look at the diagram in *Fig 3* showing what happens to the vertical and horizontal thrust components when you rotate the nozzles 15° aft from a steady hover.

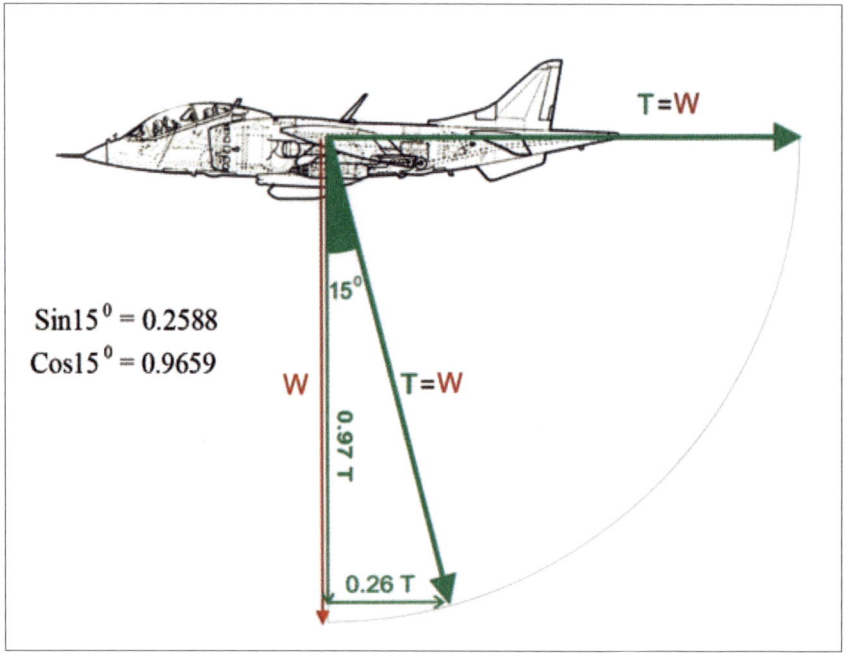

$$\sin 15^{\circ} = 0.2588$$
$$\cos 15^{\circ} = 0.9659$$

Fig 3

While such a change loses you only about 3% of your engine 'lift' (or gives a 0.03g sink if you prefer), it provides a very smart forward acceleration of some 0.25g. Pure piloting magic! This is why Harriers are able to leap forward from the hover without any obvious sink. That 3% vertical loss represents about 1% on the rpm gauge so, if you add a little throttle before you move the nozzle, you will get no height loss. However, even without that touch of throttle, the rush of lift from the wing as the IAS increases will soon have you well up and away. I bet you never realised the Sine/Cosine relationship could be so useful!

Therefore let us have a brief for this double transition of yours. Pull the nozzle lever back to the hover stop, open the throttle fully and do a normal VTO. Maintain the unstick attitude with your right hand and the heading with your feet then, once clear of the ground, transfer your left hand from the throttle to the nozzle lever. As you rise through your normal hover height, start the transition by moving the lever forward. Make the first forward hand movement 2-3 cm or so which will move the nozzles about 10°, pause there with your left hand while concentrating on maintaining the hover attitude and keeping straight with your feet as the speed starts to build. Once you are happy that you are keeping straight, progressively move the nozzle lever forward until it will go no further. You will then be flying on your wings.

The question, of course, is how fast should you move the lever? Consider the two extremes. If you just slammed it fully forward, the aircraft would fall to the ground. On the other hand, if you did not move it at all (the ultimate in too slow), the aircraft would just continue its vertical climb. Therefore the rate at which you move the lever becomes your height control. If you are happy with your flight path as you accelerate, then the way you are moving the lever is just fine. If you are climbing more than you need, then feel free to move it a bit faster. If you are barely holding height, then slow the movement down a bit. Should you really overdo it and cause a sink, then pull it back a little until you are once again ready to continue the acceleration. This is a lot easier to do than it is to write about because the seat of your pants tells you so much.

This operation of the lever is the new thing and so is likely to be your main concern. However, the task that will stretch you and give you the highest workload is the need to keep straight using your feet. This you must do as the aircraft is directionally unstable below about 120 kt. If you relax and let it swap ends, the outlook is bad. If it gets away in yaw between 60 and 90 kt, the leading wing will provide so much more lift than the other one that it will swamp your lateral control and the aircraft will roll onto its back. Since nothing comes down much faster than a Harrier with its nozzles pointing upwards, you will die. Although you must be concerned, there is no need to be scared. Keeping the nose pointing straight ahead is vital but not difficult. Indeed it equates with the job of keeping a tail-dragger straight during takeoff and landing. As you will not always have the luxury of operating directly into wind, there is a simple wind vane or 'yaw vane' mounted on the nose in front of the windscreen to help you keep zero sideslip. It works just like the string on gliders and points to where your IAS is coming from. Should it point to your left, then left foot is needed to get the nose back into wind and stop any rolling moment developing.

Back to when you feel the nozzle lever has reached fully forward. You are now flying on your wings and still accelerating like mad so throttle back and hold the speed anywhere between 200 and 250 kt. Leave the wheels and flaps down. Turn towards a 1,000 ft downwind leg using 45° of bank and fly a normal jet circuit aiming to be on finals at 200 kt and treating it as just another approach to land. Speed is not critical but, as the stall is about 150 kt, I suggest 180 as your minimum. With half a mile

129

to go and at the usual height for this range, select the nozzle lever to the hover stop, this movement being made as a configuration change, not as the operation of a flying control.

At the same time as you select the nozzles down, switch your brain to hover mode. This means you use the stick to maintain your usual hover pitch attitude, keep straight with your feet and control the height with the throttle. At first you will probably do a little balloon because of the approach level thrust that is now pointing down. However, as there is also no horizontal thrust remaining, the drag will start to slow you down very quickly. This means the wing lift will rapidly decrease and you will need to open the throttle to maintain the glidepath. Aim to level out at about 100 ft and be prepared to open the throttle quite fast once you get below 100 kt when the wing lift appears to vanish with a rush. In no time at all you will be over the airfield at about 100 ft and just needing to raise the nose a bit to kill the last 60 kt. Just as you practised previously.

I trust you now realise why I said there is no piloting grey area during these transitions. In one the lever is your height control throughout while in the other it is the throttle that controls the action. In both, your right hand is used to maintain the hover attitude while your feet are responsible for keeping the vane in the middle. After a few sorties of these transitions, you will be ready to look at them from a more operational standpoint. There is not much more to learn about the acceleration beyond getting used to moving the lever as fast as possible to give a clean flat transition which can be got down to about 13 seconds. However there is rather more to slowing down.

In poor visibility it is clearly helpful to put the 'brakes' on faster and so reduce the distance taken to stop. This requires lifting the lever up over the hover stop and pulling it all the way back to the braking stop which is the end of its slot. With this lever position the nozzles rotate forward of the vertical by some 15° giving real reverse thrust. You can increase this effect still further by pulling the nose up at the same time to the alpha limit of the wing, thus rotating the thrust vector even further forward as well as increasing airframe drag. This does little to improve the forward view and also requires you to shovel on the power because the speed fairly hurtles off. Therefore a degree of skill is creeping into this manoeuvre. Finally, just as you stop, you must momentarily take your hand off the throttle and move the nozzle lever forward to the hover position or you will charge off backwards at 0.25g. Since any deceleration has a vertical landing spot at the end of it, there are associated issues of learning when to start slowing down and how to control the rate of deceleration to finish up just where you want. It's the same with a helicopter, of course.

Once you have mastered how to fly vertically and transition to and from the hover, there only remains the 'S' letter of VSTOL to consider. Short takeoff or landing is needed when you are too heavy to hover. To fully appreciate how to fly a Harrier, you need to consider the three ways it can generate lift. The first is totally from the engine, the second is just using its wings and the third is when the engine and wings share the responsibility for supporting the weight.

As you have already experienced the first two ways, we just need to cover the third, where wing and jet lift are used in combination. This is actually much easier to sort out than you might think and also includes the easiest, safest and most high performance way to get airborne (using a ski-jump) that I have ever experienced in any type of aircraft. When I first made that comment to the boffins during the early ski-jump trials, they thought I was exaggerating. Earlier, on page 104, I described how I proved to them that I was doing no such thing.

The need to share the lift between the engine and wings, or to fly 'partially jet-borne' (PJB), arises because the maximum weight that is cleared for wing-borne flight can exceed the thrust available by some 30%. For takeoff, this requires a significant aerodynamic input leading to the short takeoff (STO) or, when landing heavy, the slow landing (SL). At the end of a normal sortie, when most of the fuel has gone, a vertical landing (VL) will often be possible. Indeed with ship operations it is essential to arrive by VL because space and obstacles preclude a landing that depends on surface friction and wheel brakes.

Back to your training. We used to teach the STO and SL techniques in a single manoeuvre called an STO hop. From a simple chart of aircraft weight and outside air temperature, you pre-computed two things, the speed at which you should select the nozzles down and the nozzle angle needed to provide the correct mix of wing lift and thrust. Typical values might be 70 kt and 60°, in which case you set a bug on the ASI to 70 and the adjustable STO stop on the throttle box to give 60° as the maximum nozzle angle.

With nozzles aft, the maximum rpm that can be held on the toe brakes is 55% or the locked wheels will simply slide. Therefore set 55% then, when ready for your STO hop, release the brakes, slam full throttle and transfer your hand to the nozzle lever. At 70 kt pull the nozzle lever back to the stop and you will jump airborne. Maintain the normal ground pitch attitude with the stick, immediately transfer your hand back to the throttle and reduce power to go straight back down for a slow landing. After touchdown chop the throttle and put the brakes on.

That is the simple procedure. However there are few things to note before your first attempt. The 70 kt will come up very quickly in 2-3 seconds so you will need to get those nozzles down pretty smartly or you will exceed the briefed speed. Remember your accel/stop during your pre hover taxi session? Next, the wing is mounted at an angle that provides 8° alpha on the ground so no rotation is necessary to make the wing lift. The best tailplane trim to set for your first few goes is 0° which is about right for being partially jet-borne in ground effect but, if you let it climb above about 10 ft main wheel clearance, you will need to push the stick forward to stop the nose rising as you leave ground effect. The amount of throttle back needed to kill the climb and start a descent will be 3 to 6 cm of hand movement. The throttle will be your height control for the landing, just as in the hover.

One final tip is not to forget the need to keep straight on the ground and in the air. You are going out to mid transition speeds and you already know that you need to be very firm with the rudder if it tries to yaw.

How much runway will you need? It rather depends on how far off the ground you let it get. If you keep it down to 10 ft then 1,500 ft should see you stopped again on your first go. Once you get the hang of how to throttle back to land, you will find you can probably do the whole thing in half that distance.

For a second sortie of these STO hops, you can try setting the tailplane trim at +4° which is half way to the +8° you will need when you want to climb out normally after an STO. With +4° set, the trick is then to pull the stick back as you pop the nozzles down to save the aircraft emulating a wheelbarrow in ground effect. Once you have got the need for this momentary back stick input sorted, you can try a few using the full +8° trim setting. You are then ready to do your first STO from which you climb away and perform what is the second half of an accelerating transition by pushing the nozzle lever forward until you are supported only by your wings.

Following your first STO into the circuit, you will obviously have to do a slow approach in order to do the landing which you have already mastered. Before we brief for that STO and SL circuit, let us consider the need for margins on this approach and how to control them. The certificated margins on the approach in a normal aircraft are based on the stalling speed of the type but, in the case of the Harrier, this normal relationship between airspeed and the stalling alpha is broken as soon as you use some jet lift. Thus it becomes essential to monitor the wing alpha. In the Harrier the equipment for this is called the airstream direction detector (ADD). Despite its name, the ADD probe effectively tells you about the wing alpha and so can be used to fly at a margin below the flaps down stall alpha which happens at about 14 ADD. The other element of the PJB approach is the engine power in use and the need to keep a margin of that below full throttle, in case of a go-around.

The easiest way to see how all this comes together is to brief for a slow approach. Fly the downwind leg on your wings with the gear and flap down, nozzles aft at 200 kt minimum. Abeam touchdown, select 30° nozzle, kill the touch of balloon with forward stick and re-trim nose down. Then select 92% rpm (from the low 70-75% that you will probably have on at the time), quickly put your hand back on the nozzle lever and increase the nozzle angle to reduce the speed back towards 160 kt. Turn finals as normal and use the stick to control the flight path.

There you are, with probably about 45° nozzle, certainly 92% rpm, still rushing along at 160 kt and nose low to control the flight path. It is now time to start seriously slowing down but to what speed? This is where it all becomes supremely simple. You do not need to know your aircraft weight or the thrust available from 92% rpm in today's ambient temperature – just slow down using the nozzle lever until the ADD needed to hold the flight path reaches 8. Note the IAS you have at that point and maintain it until you flare for landing.

It really is that easy. You have set the power to leave yourself a good margin for any overshoot then, with the throttle fixed at that value, you have slowed down using the nozzle lever and progressively raised the nose to control the flight path until the wing has reached an appropriate margin below the stall. You have now optimised the slow approach without ever needing to think of a chart or a graph and with practice you will get better at setting things up quickly. Then you will find that you can push the power up during the turn, haul back on the nozzle until you need 8 ADD, note the speed and there you are. With experience, you may well feel happy with a higher power setting of 95 or 97% and also up to 10 units of ADD for a much shorter landing roll (to say nothing of slipping the nozzle lever craftily into the braking stop as you present the jet to the ground).

There are refinements to the above that the experts will argue about, such as should you vary the throttle or the nozzle to control the speed in the final stages? I was a fixed throttle varying nozzle man myself (I liked to be sure I was not nibbling into my overshoot power margin) but later the RAF used to teach that, once on speed, it was better to fix the nozzle and vary the throttle. Such finer points do not affect the basic idea of how easily the aircraft tells you what speed to fly for optimum landing performance, regardless of your weight and the ambient conditions or your particular engine's performance. What could be easier?

Annexe C

In my experience the interests of the squadron pilot are not always given the priority they deserve when it comes to procuring the aircraft they will use to fight wars on our behalf. This paper discusses some piloting factors during takeoff and landing that I feel should be taken into account when choosing a combat aircraft. In particular it tries to explain the limited potential of STOL to provide safety and operating site flexibility. In concentrating on these piloting issues, I fully accept no account has been taken of such matters as inter-service rivalry, company self-interest, industrial partnerships or politics. While history shows there are good reasons for supposing that such non-piloting matters are likely to seriously effect the acquisition of an aircraft, surely that is no argument why all concerned should not clearly appreciate what is at stake for the pilots if such considerations are allowed to unduly influence matters

THE ADVANTAGES OF LANDING FROM THE HOVER

INTRODUCTION

A case can be made that future landing needs would be satisfied by providing a conventional or slow landing capability on land or an arrested landing at sea. There are piloting reasons why this view should be questioned. To clarify this, the advantages that result from being able to hover before landing are listed below. The reasoning behind these points is explained later. It is important to note that the term "hover" has a specific meaning in this document. It refers to a hover in free air outside ground effect. It should not be taken as necessarily implying that a vertical landing or vertical takeoff capability also exists, or indeed is needed for the hover under discussion to be worthwhile. Following such a hover, the pilot may choose to step forward into a 'rolling vertical' landing at low forward speed to avoid hot gas recirculation, foreign object damage (FOD) or damaging the surface with the exhaust efflux.

An aircraft that can hover offers the following advantages:

(a) Operating site choices are increased on land and at sea increasing operational flexibility and effectiveness.

135

(b) Peacetime landings provide valid training in the event that restricted site operations become necessary in wartime.

(c) Weather is less of a problem on the approach.

(d) The landing surface can have standing water, ice or snow that would preclude a safe short landing.

(e) A landing can be made with aircraft defects that would require ejection in the absence of a hover capability.

(f) The landing is easier for the pilot.

An examination of the reasons underlying these assertions now follows:-

PILOT WORKLOAD

A slow landing differs from a conventional landing in that ground roll is greatly reduced however important piloting problems remain so long as the aircraft cannot hover. During the approach to a slow landing, the following constraints apply:

(a) A minimum speed set by limits of lift or control.

(b) A maximum speed set by stopping ability and the strip remaining at touchdown.

(c) The approach path angle must be within narrow limits.

(d) The track over the ground must be accurately aligned with the strip in the final stages or the aircraft will leave the side of the strip shortly after touchdown.

(d) In order to avoid an undershoot or an overrun, very little height variation is allowable as the strip is reached.

Considerable pilot effort and skill can be necessary to fly within these constraints. This workload increases rapidly as the landing strip dimensions are reduced towards those needed by the aircraft when it is flown perfectly. We all know that an inability to stop, whether on foot or in any vehicle, brings with it a fundamental need to plan ahead. In the case of an aircraft, any minimum flying speed limit requires the provision of overshoot and diversion procedures, together with the fuel reserves to carry them out. These procedures bring air traffic control problems and lead to repositioning sorties and logistic complications. Because of these issues, pressure on the pilot is further increased at the very time that he is expected to perform at peak skill levels leading to the possibility of reduced accuracy and increased risk of failure. Even worse, the pilot may continue towards an inevitable accident because, under this pressure, he subconsciously rejects all options other than the approach in progress, despite the fact that the approach is beyond his capabilities or those of his aircraft.

Given a hover capability, these demanding requirements do not apply and the pilot just needs to establish a hover with the landing spot in view. This fundamental change reduces his workload for several reasons:

(a) The approach speed can be varied to suit external factors such as poor visibility or the need to fit in with other aircraft in the air or on the ground.

(b) Any descent path angle can be used so long as it is above local obstacles.

(c) The direction of the approach is not linked to the landing.

(d) Aircraft height at the end of the approach needs only to be above any obstacles and below any cloud.

(e) Because it is easy to adjust position over the surface once in the hover, acceptable position limits for the end of the approach can be measured in hundreds of metres to the left, right, forwards or backwards.

It is important to note that any trial results aimed at comparing pilot workload during different types of landing will only be valid if the landing sites chosen are equally limiting. Vertical landings on the small aft platform of a ship or in an urban car park may only be properly compared with slow or conventional landings made on a strip with a bomb crater or other genuine limit at each end. It is misleading to rely on measured short landing data obtained on a runway that is much wider and longer than aircraft performance alone would dictate. As discussed later, peacetime flying from an oversize runway is also inadequate training for any wartime restricted strip case.

SIZE OF OPERATING SITE

Since the area required for a landing from the hover is small, it is clearly easier to provide or find suitable locations for this as opposed to a short landing strip. However, it is sometimes suggested that, because a short takeoff strip has to be provided for a VSTOL aircraft to take off at max weight, then the existence of this takeoff strip means that it can be used for short landing and hence STOL is all that is necessary. This view takes no account of several reasons why an STO, even at maximum weight, can be safely carried out from a much shorter and narrower strip than is acceptable for a slow landing even at a lighter weight. First consider factors affecting strip length:

(a) An aircraft can be positioned for takeoff at the very beginning of the strip and the subsequent ground roll required to unstick can be very accurately predicted (as a function of weight and thrust), making it acceptable to plan to unstick close to the end of the strip. On the other hand, some distance will be needed for a landing at both ends of the strip to allow for scatter in touchdown position and stopping performance.

(b) The acceleration available for takeoff may well approach 1g and be unaffected by a wet or icy surface but it is difficult to design for a similar level of deceleration throughout the ground roll when landing, even in good conditions. Given slippery conditions, wheel braking effects can all but vanish.

(c) The use of full power on takeoff maximises the lift effect of thrust, reducing the speed needed to fly at a given weight. However, in order to have a go around capability when landing, some power margin must remain at touchdown. This results in a reduction of the lift element from thrust on a slow approach, compared to that available during a STO. Replacing this powered lift with V^2 aerodynamic lift can need a surprisingly large increase in V at the lower approach speeds of short landing aircraft, countering the advantage to be expected from reduced weight at the end of the sortie.

A narrower strip is acceptable for takeoff compared to landing because:

(a) An aircraft can be lined up very accurately before a takeoff, whereas there is a need to allow for lateral scatter when landing.

(b) Direction can be controlled relatively easily during the slower first part of the takeoff ground run and then the quality of aerodynamic directional control improves as speed increases. The opposite applies when landing and the use of brakes, aerodynamic devices and reverse thrust all tend to degrade directional control and stability. This stems from the use of large forces to slow down quickly on the ground and so quite minor asymmetries in those forces can cause the aircraft to veer. Experience shows that such asymmetries can also result from crosswinds interacting with the complex flow patterns around an aircraft using high power or aerodynamic devices for deceleration.

Provision must be made at the end of a strip used for landing for the aircraft to turn round and backtrack or clear the strip at the side, whereas places for landing from the hover can be provided some way away from the short takeoff strip, thus easing flow control on the ground through the land/hide, replenish/takeoff sequence. When the same strip has to be used for both takeoff and landing, a larger and more complicated site layout becomes necessary. Even in the orderly peacetime world of civil aircraft operations, the advantages and smooth traffic flows that result from using different runways for takeoff and landing are apparent for all to see.

WEATHER EFFECTS

In the absence of full autoland, pilots need time to make final visual corrections to an instrument approach before landing. The length of time taken to carry out these corrections can be shown to depend on the size of the approach error, the manoeuvrability of the aircraft, pilot skill, groundspeed, crosswind, turbulence and the accuracy of touchdown required. Provision of this time interacts through any minimum speed of the approach to determine the lower limits for cloud base and visibility. The greater the time needed then the higher the cloud base and the better the visibility must be.

Given a hover capability, speed on the approach can be reduced to suit the visibility, avoiding a minimum visibility cut off below which a landing will not be possible. Similar relaxations apply to cloud base considerations with the additional advantage that a hovering aircraft need not be constrained to a shallow approach path angle but can descend more steeply once it has passed obstructions in the chosen approach sector. Indeed the approach sector may be deliberately chosen to avoid obstacles as the aircraft is not constrained to line up the approach with any ground roll.

Crosswind is of little concern to an aircraft that can hover because it can be yawed around in the hover to point into wind for the actual touchdown. If a rolling touchdown is required, then the optimum starting position can be set up accurately while in the hover, before stepping forward for the landing. This avoids approach errors caused by crosswind being carried forward into the ground roll on a narrow strip.

Turbulence has adverse effects on the stability and control of all aircraft. Because the extent of these effects depends on the ratio of the local gust velocity and the aircraft lifting system velocity, the lower the lifting velocity the greater the distortion of flow around the aircraft for a given gust. In the case of a jet lift aircraft in the hover, the lifting system velocity is that of the jet efflux. Since this velocity is very high when compared to gust velocities, the hovering jet lift aircraft hardly reacts at all to turbulence levels that seriously degrade the control of other fixed wing aircraft and helicopters.

Water, snow, ice or sand contamination of the landing surface causes fewer problems for aircraft that can hover because of the slower nature of their touchdowns. In addition, such aircraft do not have to rely on surface friction for control of direction and speed on the ground but have reaction controls and reverse thrust to back up brakes and nosewheel steering. In many cases jet lift aircraft can use their own efflux to clean an area before takeoff or landing.

An example of poor weather capability if you can hover was provided during the Falklands War when Sea Harriers crawled up the wake of their ship in poor visibility and very low cloud base just by following flares thrown onto the water, indicating the way to the deck (like a motorist in fog lucky enough to have cats eyes leading to his garage). In this case, the only flight path limits that had to be observed were to remain above the sea, below the cloud and clear of obstacles. Since the ship was an obstacle, the top of which was in cloud, the landing pilots kept to port of the flare centreline and corrected to the landing spot once in the hover alongside the deck. Put even some of these circumstances, let alone the radio silence needed because of the submarine threat, into the recovery of conventionally arrested naval aircraft and it becomes likely that some, or even all, would have been lost when operating non-diversion.

TRAINING

Because of the scatter in conventional landing performance (whether this scatter is caused by aircraft characteristics, pilot performance or ambient conditions is immaterial), operators only clear aircraft to land routinely on runways that are much wider and longer than perfect performance requires. An acceptable peacetime accident rate is quoted as the reason for this conservatism. Common sense in the face of reality would be another way of putting it. What price the landing accident rate for the Hawk and Tornado, the F-16 or the MiG-29 if the runway width and length normally available was only that needed with man, machine and the elements all on top form?

In some quarters (although not crew rooms), it is felt that things will be routinely achievable during war without constant practice in peacetime or that accidents would be the least of people's worries. Put another way, attrition in war will only occur due to the additional element of enemy activity and that an unacceptable peacetime accident risk will not carry over to wartime.

In fact nothing could be further from the truth. If a procedure is unacceptable in peacetime due to the risk of accident and attrition, then in war it carries an even higher risk due to the extra pressures present during hostilities.

Because of the increased chance of an accident, there is no precedent in RAF or RN operations for conventional fast jet operation into limiting sized landing sites other than with the use of arrester gear or when the aircraft can hover. It is not clear what aspect of a short landing capability is going to change this in the future but, without such a change, where will be the peacetime training of the wartime case? Only a hover capability can permit this critical training.

AIRCRAFT DEFECTS and COMBAT DAMAGE

A landing from the hover is tolerant of many defects that make a forward speed landing hazardous. Indeed, where the option exists, it is the landing of choice in the event of any malfunction or suspected problem with gear, brakes, steering, tyres and flaps. There have been several cases of wheels up vertical landings in Harriers with only cosmetic damage and none with any injury to the pilot. This fall out from a vertical landing capability becomes a significant force multiplier and cost saving in the real world of operating aircraft.

All systems associated with deceleration and steering of a short landing aircraft on the ground have to be fully serviceable to achieve minimum distances. The operation of some of these (e.g. lift dumpers, reverse thrust, parachutes, tyres and auto configuration changes dependent on weight on wheels switches) cannot be fully checked in flight before landing. The need to rely on such systems is one of the reasons why commanders will not approve routine training into performance limited sites unless the aircraft can hover.

In the limit, the pilot of a Harrier only needs power, a variable nozzle angle and reaction controls to come to the hover. Therefore, as soon as combat damage is suspected and, while remaining at cruise speed, the ability to land vertically can be confirmed by simply opening the throttle to check rpm response, momentarily pulling the nozzle lever back to check nozzle rotation and by moving the stick and rudder with the nozzles deflected to check reaction control response. As previously mentioned, flaps, airbrakes, gear, steering and tyres are not necessary in order to carry out a safe landing. No other type of fast jet can offer such damage tolerance and still land safely.

OPERATIONAL FLEXIBILITY

In addition to the operational flexibility that stems from being able to operate from smaller sites, the ability to hover provides further operational advantages.

Such an aircraft can, if required, operate in the VTOL mode. Whilst restricted in payload/radius of action, the VTO mode is always the ultimate in flexibility so far as dispersal, quick response time to airborne or even ease of moving aircraft between theatres are concerned, for example, Atlantic Conveyor in the Falklands.

These days Commanders rely on flight refuelling to give them operational capability in many roles from air defence to tactical strike. Few would disagree with this point of view which is why flight refuelling close to base following VTO provides a unique flexibility of operation.

Some proposals exist based on short landing aircraft being able to return to base and land between the craters. How will the length of these strips be ascertained by the pilots? How will they be defined? Will they land between the craters regardless of FOD from small debris or just on the clean areas? How will they be marked so that the pilots can identify them? Will they be able to taxi from the isolated strip to the hide/dispersal/hardened aircraft shelter (HAS) or will they be on the ground exposed and unable to taxi due to having no safe route?

A hovering capability eliminates all these problems as it allows an aircraft to land at the entrance of any serviceable HAS. When required it can also emerge from a HAS, VTO at once and deploy to the nearest available weapons or fuel if the HAS cannot be supplied for any reason. Only such an aircraft can take itself to supplies or engineering resources that have become trapped in the rear echelons. This sort of flexibility provides a force multiplier factor that is beyond value in times of disarray and tactical confusion.

SAFETY

Easier tasks tend to produce fewer mistakes so the reduced pilot workload when landing from the hover can be expected to result in fewer pilot error accidents during the landing phase, in both the lack of skill and error of judgement categories. However, if a landing accident should occur despite this, the situation is inherently safer than during a short landing because the energy remaining at touchdown is less. (The dents, scratches and lost pride associated with car accidents at city centre speeds compare favourably in most people's minds with the aftermath of high speed motorway pile ups.)

Safety also reduces attrition and the exchange rate between attrition and operational cost effectiveness is a high one.

CONCLUSION

To land from the hover offers many piloting advantages compared to doing a short, arrested or conventional landing.

Chapter 6

The Harrier VAAC programme – *a journey enabled by RAE scientists*

On the 16th of May 2005 Justin Paines, a QinetiQ civilian test pilot, pressed the 'coffee bar button' and for me a dream came true.

The 'coffee bar button' was in the rear cockpit of Harrier XW175 (the second Harrier two-seater ever to fly back in 1969) and the result of Justin pressing it was that 175 looked around, sniffed the air with its satellite navigation system, decided where Justin's coffee bar was located, took him to it and landed him safely, gently and of course vertically, on board HMS Invincible.

Harrier XW175 about to touch down automatically on HMS Invincible

This first fully automatic recovery of a Harrier to a ship was the end of a journey on which RAE scientists embarked in 1951. Yes, that is correct. The journey started nine years before Bill Bedford broke his ankle and the doctors decided the only thing he was then fit to 'fly' was the first prototype P1127 tethered to the grid at Dunsfold.

Just what were RAE (later to become DERA and now QinetiQ) scientists up to all that time ago that eventually led to the Invincible landing over half a century later? Also why was I so keen for such a capability to be developed? I will try to explain.

Inevitably the story is not short and it is fairly technical therefore I intend to start with an overview so that the reader can appreciate the remarkable achievements of the RAE and then follow that with an Annexe for those who would like more technical background.

During 1951 the senior management of RAE realised that the thrust of jet engines was increasing all the time and that one day an aircraft with a thrust greater than its weight would become possible. That raised the question of how could the attitude of such an aircraft be controlled in the hover? In an attempt to provide an answer Dennis Higton, a former RAE apprentice who had joined the Aerodynamics Research Flight at Farnborough at the end of his apprenticeship in 1942, devised a rig to investigate the feasibility of controlling the attitude of a hovering aeroplane by means of small jets mounted in the nose, tail and wingtips. The layout he first used had two jets and is shown in *Fig 1*, copied from *RAE Tech Memo 286* of April 1952 in which Higton reported his work.

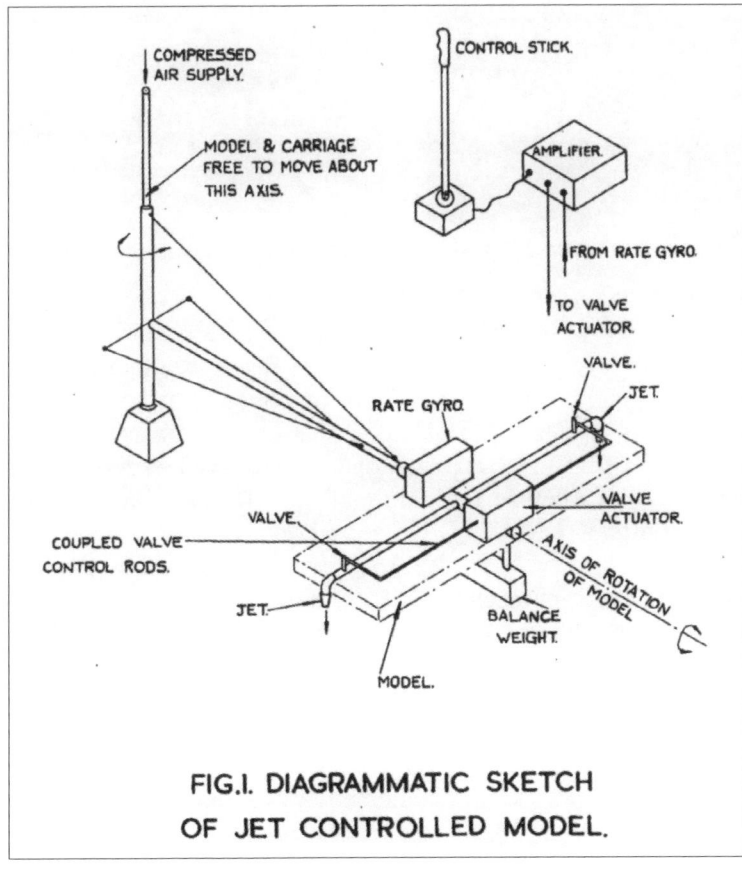

Fig 1

FIG.I. DIAGRAMMATIC SKETCH
OF JET CONTROLLED MODEL.

These early experiments showed that a reaction control system was indeed suitable and enabled Higton, working with Arthur Keeler and later Roger Duddy, to draw up the specification for a full size piloted rig to be used by the RAE. This rig, which initially hovered tethered under a safety gantry at Rolls-Royce Hucknall in 1953, flew free for the first time in 1954 and was known as the Flying Bedstead.

From those early days the scientists of the Aerodynamics Research Flight at RAE – or Aero Flight as it was usually called – worked continuously to develop and improve the handling qualities of jet lift aircraft. After the Flying Bedstead they commissioned the Short SC1 which they operated from the then new RAE research airfield at Thurleigh, near Bedford.

Flying Bedstead   *Short SC1*

The SC1 was only ever intended to be a pure research aircraft and it enabled an investigation of the 'transition' or going from hovering on engines to flying on wings at normal speeds and then back again to the hover. This world's first 'double transition' was achieved by the SC1 at Bedford on 6th April 1960 in the hands of Tom Brooke-Smith, Chief Test Pilot for Shorts.

From the start the RAE approach to the control of jet VSTOL aircraft was to use a high degree of autostabilisation to make the handling as easy as possible for the pilot. This was in marked contrast to Hawker's at Kingston who favoured simplicity as a means of reducing the number of potentially lethal control failures that, in those days, sometimes happened with such equipment. Accordingly all of the initial Hawker P1127, Kestrel and Harrier aircraft could be flown without artificial aids, relying on the pilot to compensate for inherent handling deficiencies.

With hindsight both teams were correct. The RAE approach was without doubt the ideal way ahead for the pilot but (and it was a big but) in those days autostabilisers were not reliable enough for service use. Because of this the Hawker approach of simplicity, even though it meant relying on the pilot to compensate for the lack of aircraft stability during powered lift flight, was correct during the 1960s and arguably enabled the Harrier story to happen.

Once the Harrier went into service, there was a slow but continuous programme to add devices to it that made control at low speeds easier and safer for the pilot. Not surprisingly, Aero Flight's input into the development and certification of these aids was considerable and from 1964 onwards they were helped in this work by having their own P1127.

By then six of the P1127 aircraft had been flown at Dunsfold and naturally the later aircraft incorporated lessons learned from the earlier ones. Because of this the standard of the original prototype, XP831, was by then fairly unrepresentative, so Hawkers were happy to allocate it to Aero Flight at Bedford.

First P1127 prototype XP831 in the Science Museum, London

At that time I happened to be serving on Aero Flight as an RAF Flight Lieutenant test pilot and was fortunate enough to be given the job of collecting XP831 from Dunsfold for comparison with the SC1 which was already flying at Bedford. Three years later, after the retirement of Dunsfold's Chief Test Pilot Bill Bedford, my luck continued and in 1967 I left Aero Flight, took off my uniform and joined Dunsfold as their junior test pilot.

One morning in 1970 Hugh Merewether, who was then Dunsfold Chief Test Pilot, came in to my office and asked me to represent him at a meeting being held that afternoon at RAE Farnborough. Hugh explained that it appeared the RAE boffins had ideas for making life easier for Harrier pilots and so he needed somebody to go and keep tabs on them. He pointed out that as a former RAE apprentice I was obviously the bloke for the job and anyway he had better things to do that afternoon.

At that meeting it became clear to me that the eventual aim of the scientists was to hand over the controls of the Harrier to a computer with the pilot's job changing from moving all the airframe and engine controls to instructing the computer what manoeuvre he wanted the aircraft to fly. If this happened it would mean the Harrier pilot's nozzle lever would no longer be needed because control of the nozzle angle, as well as everything else, would be left to the computer.

As I drove back to Dunsfold I was quite excited about what I had heard. After using my left hand to operate both the nozzle lever and throttle for six years, it was clear to me that it was only a matter of time before I made a mistake and moved the wrong one with potentially disastrous results. Therefore I very much welcomed the boffins' ideas although I realised it might take a few years to turn them into reality. (It actually took 29!)

We must remember that at the time of this meeting the RAF had been flying Harriers for only one year and the provision of the nozzle lever in the cockpit was seen as the simple masterpiece that had enabled VSTOL to happen. Rather naturally, at Kingston and Dunsfold any talk of removing the nozzle lever was as close to Harrier heresy as you could get, so care was needed when broaching the subject. Anyhow since the Kingston designers were all so busy coping with the USMC decision to buy Harriers, it was not reasonable to expect them to give serious consideration to futuristic ideas.

Time passed and I became increasingly frustrated at the conservative approach taken by the RAE with regard to specifying the modification of a Harrier to start flight trials in that they were not intending to split the control of the four engine nozzles. I remember talking to Kingston aerodynamicist Robin Balmer about this in the mid-70s and suggesting that if we let a computer put the nozzles down on one side only, we could get rates of roll in low speed combat that would make any opposition's eyes water. Equally by putting down the front or rear pair we could pitch in a way nobody else could even dream about.

While it seemed so obvious to me that the Pegasus offered a ready-made way to endow the aircraft with unmatchable manoeuvrability, such ideas were viewed as too way out. Not surprisingly the Kingston design office and spiritual home of 'Keep it simple, stupid' (and that is meant as a compliment not as a criticism) was not about to change horses in mid-stream and take the lead in the brave new world of computer-based control systems or fly-by-wire as they are called today.

Nevertheless by 1982 the RAE programme, now called VAAC for Vectored thrust Aircraft Advanced flight Control, had laid the three key foundation stones needed for its eventual success. The first of these was the choice of a two-seat aircraft for the programme.

Harrier XW175 in its original colours

Had the team chosen to modify a single-seat Harrier, they would only have been able to test tomorrow's ideas on today's Harrier pilots which would have hardly the best way to conduct open minded research. Incidentally NASA went this route with a modified Harrier and I suspect lived to regret their decision.

The second was installing something called the Independent Monitor (IM). The IM was essentially a special computer that was carried around in the test aircraft for many sorties during which time it was taught by the crew to recognise the safe limits of Harrier operation. It was then sealed and became the basis for the subsequent airworthiness certification of the aircraft as a research tool when it was flying using new and untried software control. When the trials proper started, the IM kept an unblinking eye on what the single channel experimental equipment was attempting to do with the various Harrier controls. If it detected anything that looked like going outside what the human pilots had previously agreed was a limit, it instantly disengaged the experimental kit and handed the aircraft back in good order to the safety pilot in the front seat.

The third foundation stone was developing Unified. This was a control strategy that was conceived by scientist Peter Nicholas and test pilot Flight Lieutenant Peter Bennett, both of RAE Bedford. This introduced the notion that if the pilot wanted the aircraft to go up then the stick had to be pulled back and to go down the stick was pushed forward. Sound familiar? Well yes but Unified was conceived for use at any speed. Helicopter pilots raise or lower a lever called 'the collective' to go up or down in the hover while Harrier pilots use the engine throttle for the same thing. The aim of Unified was to allow the pilot to fly from takeoff to landing using just the stick for height control. You may prefer to think of it as eliminating the concept of a 'stalling speed' below which you cannot fly. When the pilot asked Unified to fly the aircraft slower than the stalling speed, the computer merely put the nozzles down and used the engine as well as the wings to support the weight. This of course was what human Harrier pilots already did but only after special and expensive training. Unified enabled any fixed-wing pilot to handle a Harrier in the circuit without extra training.

Easy though Unified may appear as a concept, it was in actual fact far from straightforward to optimise and approve all the necessary software. Indeed in the beginning the Unified notion was only one of several 'control law' possibilities that the VAAC team examined in their search for the optimum way to control a jet lift aircraft, as described in some detail in the Annexe to this chapter.

150

I had to retire from my job as Chief Test Pilot Dunsfold in 1983 when I reached 50. However the VAAC team were kind enough to keep in touch with me and I was invited back in 1994 and again in 1999 to fly the aircraft and comment on how I thought they were getting on. In 1999 my safety pilot was the then Squadron Leader Justin Paines. When I got out after our couple of sorties at Boscombe, I told him that I thought the team had cracked it and that Unified was the way ahead.

Shortly after that, following a detailed and quantitative evaluation trial where the VAAC was flown by many test pilots including several from the USA (some of whom had never been in a Harrier before), the VAAC team was able to convince the US Joint Strike Fighter Programme Office that Unified should form the basis of the JSF flight control system.

There was much more to selling Unified to the US than that account might suggest. The final test pilot push was led by Justin Paines who was in no doubt that the opinion of Harrier squadron pilots on both sides of the Atlantic was bitterly divided. While some saw the attraction of Unified, others were seriously opposed to it. The opposition even included senior BAE SYSTEMS test pilots. As I saw it the opponents all had many years of successfully using the nozzle lever and arguably it was that skill that made them feel they were better pilots than those who had no such experience. It made them better in the circuit, better in the bar and probably better in bed. As for the mistakes that other Harrier pilots had made over the years, it was only lesser mortals, not people like them, who moved the wrong lever. Expecting such successful senior operators to vote for abolishing the nozzle lever was akin to expecting turkeys to vote for Christmas.

In the end I am glad to say that the VAAC team's arguments in favour of deskilling the process of flying jet VSTOL won the day, thus saving costly training as well as reducing the likelihood of accidents on the squadrons. The JSF will not enter service for some time and will likely be used for 50 years so many of its future pilots have yet to be conceived. Thankfully the aircraft is to be built with them in mind and not yesterday's nozzle lever men.

Finally, what about my wish for a 'coffee bar button'? In many of the conversations I had with Harrier pilots about the controversial idea of Unified, I was at pains to point out that although I wanted to get rid of their beloved nozzle lever, I was not a boffins' nark and against the operational pilot's point of view. In fact my position was quite the opposite. I believed that while operational pilots were over the target (and being shot at on our behalf), their views about what they need and how they should go about their job were paramount. However, once they turned their back on the target and their operational job was done, they should be able to press a 'coffee bar' button whereupon the aeroplane would then take them home safely, day or night, in any weather, regardless of whether they were exhausted, injured or (heaven forbid) it was just their day to make a mistake during their approach to land.

I know some readers will not altogether take to this notion because they have reservations about the reliability of computers and software. You should know you are not alone. At a recent software engineering management course in the US, the participants were given a question to answer. "If you had just boarded an airliner and discovered that your team of programmers had been responsible for the flight control software, how many of you would disembark immediately?" Among the ensuing forest of raised hands, only one man sat motionless. When asked what he would do, he replied that he would be quite content to stay on board. With his team's software, he said, the plane was unlikely to even taxi as far as the runway, let alone take off.

Thank goodness the computer software engineers associated with the VAAC were of an altogether better standard as demonstrated by the remarkable career and success of XW175.

XW175 aged 38, Boscombe July 2007

Annexe: Some journey details

This more detailed story starts with the thinking that was around in the 1980s and follows progress through the 1990s towards that first automatic recovery of the VAAC aircraft to Invincible in 2005.

The VAAC programme was never aimed at improving existing service Harriers. It was always about the aircraft that would follow the Harrier into service. Such aircraft were expected to be stealthy, manoeuvreable, supersonic and to land vertically when required. Unfortunately their powerplants, while endowing them with capabilities so far only seen in video games, would certainly not be capable of simple pilot operation like the Harrier's Pegasus.

Because the new powerplants were going to be complex, an Integrated Flight and Propulsion Control System (IFPCS), pronounced 'Ifpics' would be needed. This required clear thinking and unambiguous language. Thus a control used by the pilot (e.g. stick, throttle, rudder bar etc) became an 'inceptor' while a control that moved to make the airframe or powerplant do something (aileron, throttle valve, nozzle angle etc) became a 'motivator'.

The Harrier record clearly showed that pilots with appropriate training could operate an aircraft that used three hand operated inceptors (throttle and nozzle lever with the left hand, stick with the right) however the proposed powerplants required up to ten motivators to be adjusted/switched/set/varied, compared to the three on the Pegasus (throttle, nozzle angle and IGV angle – an automatic function). Clearly most if not all of ten motivators would have to be automated which made IFPCS the only game in town.

Without doubt, handing over the complete responsibility for when and how to use the wing lift and the direction and amount of engine thrust to an IFPCS computer would solve all these issues very nicely. Then the pilot would only need one inceptor to signal his request for the aircraft to go up or down and another to ask for it to go slower or faster. This and more was what the VAAC programme investigated. Many questions needed answers. What sort of aircraft response (control law) would pilots prefer when asking the computer for up or down, slower or faster? Nippy and quick? Slow but sure? Variable depending on one's airspeed? What about groundspeed? What about attitude or heading hold?

The achievement of the VAAC team was that all such matters were investigated without reducing standard levels of Harrier flight safety. The front seat safety pilot had the normal Harrier T4 throttle, nozzle lever stick and rudder bar which moved in response to the outputs from the experimental system that the test pilot was using in the rear seat. This way the safety pilot could use his ordinary Harrier skills to stay in touch with what the software was making happen – like a flying instructor watching a student.

On its own this would still be unsafe because the computer might try to do a manoeuvre that was outside the Harrier T4's performance capabilities, leaving the safety pilot in an impossible position. As mentioned earlier, the VAAC team solution for this was to come up with the Independent Monitor (IM) concept. This separate processing element within the flight control computer had a memory which contained what it was safe for an ordinary Harrier T4 to do. It continually monitored how the experimental system was flying the aircraft and disconnected it at once if it saw these Harrier limits being approached. This ensured that the safety pilot always had a flyable Harrier situation when control was dumped back to him. This combination of safety pilot and IM meant that the experimental system could be safely abused by the test pilot or it could fail with impunity. It allowed the test pilot to vary the gains of the control software even while the system was engaged in flight by using a cockpit keyboard, surely the ultimate optimisation facility. The VAAC team called this 'variable gain changing'. More accurately it was adjusting a chosen control law parameter. The parameter concerned was given a two digit number, e.g. VG45 or VG23, from a master list. The test pilot keyed the appropriate two digits to access a change.

During my 1994 flights, two very different digital control laws, out of a total of five then being flown by the VAAC team, were selectable from the rear cockpit. They were termed 'Digital Harrier' and 'CL003'. As the name implies, Digital Harrier (DH) was a digital model representing the normal Harrier T4. Flying DH should be just like flying a basic T4 with its autostabs switched off. On the other hand CL003 was aimed at producing low pilot workload through IFPCS concepts. DH was an obvious and powerful validation tool for the total VAAC system. If DH flew like a Harrier, the whole synthetic airborne system was shown to be serviceable and accurate.

At that time Wg Cdr Dennis Stangroom, OC Flying Wing at Bedford, and Flt Lt Dan Griffith, the VAAC Harrier Project Pilot, shared the

VAAC flying. Both were Harrier pilots so either could fly as safety or test pilot. I flew with Griffith but 'Wings' kindly volunteered to help me strap in and get settled. As we walked out, the Bedford pilots were concerned that with the wind gusting up to 35 kt, this was the roughest weather in which CL003 had so far been tried. The day also set a low pressure record, giving less thrust than usual and therefore less hovering time to look at things. Sod's law was mentioned. I made sympathetic noises but was actually thinking that future VSTOL pilots were unlikely to get the day off in a war just because it was blowing a bit.

After engine start we ran through a typical set of checks between front and rear cockpits to ensure that the test and safety equipments plus the auto and manual disconnect modes were serviceable. Then with our ground team in telemetry ready, Dan got us airborne.

As we turned cross wind after takeoff, he cleared me to arm the rear cockpit. I then moved my throttle lever until my 'offset' light illuminated showing synchronisation with the front cockpit inceptor position. A few seconds after this my flashing IM light went steady, indicating it agreed all was well so I pressed the engage button. I was now flying DH.

Instantly, I found myself in a Harrier at some 230 kt and 1,200 ft on a downwind leg. It felt to me that I was flying a Harrier, not DH, as there was no feeling of artificiality at all. Indeed it was as if the 10 years since my last Harrier flight had somehow never happened. After a slow approach and overshoot at 100 ft in this very familiar aircraft, using normal Harrier techniques, Dan took control and talked me through the rear cockpit selections to set up CL003.

CL003 incorporated IFPCS ideas. With DH I had been responsible for control of rpm and nozzle angle, with CL003 in use I had no such responsibility. As soon as I asked to go slower than 200 kt airspeed, CL003 would determine what mix of rpm and engine nozzle deflection would be used, not me. My left hand would only have to use one inceptor, not the two of DH. The VAAC Harrier also offered pilots testing this law a further choice of flying using only the right hand with the left hand task moving to a 'go faster go slower' switch under the right thumb.

I engaged CL003 using the two hand option. A few inputs showed I was flying a nice steady aeroplane that responded smoothly and pleasantly at

230 kt. By comparison an ordinary Harrier might be described as very light and sensitive, even touchy in some people's view.

Since the longitudinal axis is the challenge for an IFPCS, costs were saved on the initial VAAC aircraft standard by restricting computer access in the lateral and directional (L&D) axes. For L&D control in 1994 it used the existing Harrier roll and yaw autostabilisers, not the full aileron and rudder circuits so some limited L&D pilot assistance could still be needed. With the longitudinal value of VAAC proven, a full L&D system was added during the next lay up.

I moved switch S2 up and this put me in the one hand mode. A blip or two with my right thumb and up and down went the noise from the Pegasus. The thought went through my mind that this was just as promised by the VAAC team leader, Gerry Shanks, when he ran through his brief earlier that morning. I have noticed that such thoughts only arise in the air when things are going exactly to plan – and turning out easier than you had expected. As we turned finals at about two miles and 800 ft for another 100 ft low fly through, the rpm was showing 57% and the nozzles still zero. I held the speed control switch back briefly and several things happened in quick succession: the speed started to reduce, a bug appeared unwinding anti-clockwise round the HUD airspeed indication, the Pegasus noise increased and down went the nozzles. We had moved, workload free, into partially jet-borne flight.

"Set the bug to 70," said a voice from the front. It was easy to use the thumb to set this bug anywhere round the dial but Dan had in mind the need not to go too slow at our weight if the engine was not to be thrashed. So 70 in this case was an index rather than an actual speed request to the computer and it flew us through nicely at a similar speed to our first circuit using DH. Overshoot in DH had been a matter of the usual careful judgement in easing the nozzle lever forward to avoid losing too much jet lift before the wings had developed extra lift from the increased airspeed. With CL003 I only asked for 'faster please' with my right thumb and IFPCS took the strain. "That is the only way to fly," I commented.

On hearing such immediate enthusiasm for flying using one hand, my safety pilot clearly thought I was not commenting from anything approaching a full assessment of what VAAC had to offer. He therefore told me to put S2 off and use two hands for the next fly-through. This I did. The left hand inceptor had a soft but just usable detent a little aft of the mid-point of its range. "Put it in the detent when you are ready to slow down," said the voice. I did as instructed. This time the voice did not have to say "Set the bug to 70" as the detent did just that and CL003 flew us nicely through at an optimum 8 ADD and 130 kt.

I did another two hand approach but I put S2 on for the overshoot, held my right thumb forward and followed that with another one hand circuit.

Back downwind Dan said I should now have a look at a change to the control law in flight. "On the keyboard," he prompted. "Star 28 and enter." "Done," I said. "Now use the airbrake switch in the throttle handle to set the value in the window down from 100 to 15." Whatever that changed it clearly did not impress Steve Gale, the scientist responsible for developing CL003, who was on the ground monitoring the flight on telemetry. "You want VG29," he chipped in on the radio, with all the conviction of one who knows what he is talking about.

With VG28 back at its proper setting, I selected VG29 but ran it down a bit too enthusiastically, overshooting 15 and briefly seeing 2. At that point down went the nose some 10° and, as I pulled back with no apparent initial response, my "Aw shit" was followed by a voice from the front saying "Ha ha, that's got you, now look how difficult it is. That's a good demo I think!" What I had just experienced was a demonstration of the effect of changing the tailplane loop gain in the control law to an unacceptable value while actually flying the law.

Back with the optimised version of CL003 and with fuel weight reducing, it was time for me to try a snappier deceleration by setting the bug not at 70 but 40. This went very well and produced a noticeably crisper deceleration.

The fuel was now down enough for us to look at the hover. I selected the two hand mode for my first try. On finals I gradually kept bringing my left hand back until I found the detent. The speed bug showed 70. "Bring it back to 20," said the voice so I eased the left hand further back and got 20. "Now all the way to zero." As I adjusted the bug to the zero position, I saw a new and smaller actual groundspeed bug appear and unwind behind the bug I was controlling. A few moments later they were both at the top and we were at a stop.

I made a couple of tentative pulls and pushes on the stick to watch this normal flying technique for height control actually working in the hover.

Then I let go of the stick and CL003 held us rock steady as if we were becalmed in a balloon. The voice from the front said, "Try a max rate accel out". I shoved my left hand forward and off we went. The accel was so marked I instinctively backed off a little with my left hand, then I thought, "No! – keep it at max" and pushed it forward again. The resulting stutter in our acceleration came through to the watchful IM as not normal so it dumped the system. Some might see such an event as a nuisance disconnect. To me it was a demonstration of the safety system that has enabled the whole VAAC research programme to be where it is today.

For our second hover I used the one hand mode. Dan asked me to enter VG08 downwind so that I would be able to change the gain of the closed loop speed control in the hover. This time on short finals at 200 kt I set zero on the bug using my thumb in one movement. We came to a graceful stop. Just like that. In the hover I used my left thumb to adjust VG08 from 100 to 650, the max I could get. At once the aircraft could be felt shaking as the nozzle angle oscillated some 10° either side of the steady state value needed. "Press D," said Griffith. The default took us back instantly to 100 without me having set it manually. The nozzle angle went steady again.

During the development of CL003, when such a nozzle oscillation happened spontaneously, the ground monitors were able to analyse the problem and recommend a gain change which the pilot selected. Without the aircraft leaving the hover in which the problem arose, the fix was designed, incorporated and proved. That is a powerful capability to say the least. "Trim back," said the voice. Now I was using the stick switch to control the pitch attitude in the hover away from the correct one automatically provided by the system. Up went the nose but we did not go backwards because we still had zero groundspeed requested on the speed controller. "Now bow". I trimmed fully forward and down went the nose. Useful for airshows, maybe but essential if you want to land gently should the nose leg stick up.

We now had two flashing fuel low level lights or about 90 seconds fuel. "I have it," said Dan and he took control and landed. Such efficient use of all the fuel contents is normal procedure in a Harrier but not recommended if you are flying a jet that needs a runway. At the debrief the VAAC team offered a second sortie the next day, in case anything came to mind overnight that I would like to try.

In the morning there was a more normal 10 kt wind as we got airborne. The first circuit was a check of DH. "You were engaged 35 seconds after takeoff," came the voice from the front. We flew through at 100 ft and set up downwind with CL003 and S2 on. After a one hand approach and overshoot I let go of the stick when all looked set fair during the next finals turn. The IFPCS held the flight path angle well but I had to nudge the ailerons a few times to correct the bank angle. After this I decided that it was easier to fly both axes round finals as one normally would in any aircraft. With full L&D fly-by-wire added later it would doubtless be a different story.

After the third circuit I wanted the speed control law to work faster. I selected VG45 downwind and increased the gain from 100 to 130. The next time round I put it up to 150. I was happy for it to be even sharper. Then telemetry advised we might get actuator rate triggered IM disconnects if we did this so I settled for 150. For the last circuit before hover weight I gave it full thumb at the 150 gain and was rewarded with an acceleration that took 9 sec to go from 100 kt to 200 kt. Round we went again.

As we approached the hover, with 40 kt groundspeed into 15 kt of wind, I decided I wanted to move forward a little. The next thing I heard was the engine wind down and we started an obvious descent. I realised that I had reverted to Harrier (and helicopter) habits and moved the stick forward to lower the nose. With the CL003 I was flying, stick forward demands 'go down'. Making this mistake was useful though, because it showed that one could twig the problem. More importantly it showed the way CL003 will not let you sink too quickly in the hover even if you accidentally demand it. When I looked at the records later I found CL003 had limited the power reduction to 5% rpm.

I next made a couple of large stick inputs to watch this auto-limiting of descent rate in action. Then at 160 ft I pushed forward and let go altogether. The height was going down through 150 ft as I released the stick and the aeroplane stopped its descent and settled at a steady 137 ft without any oscillation. This was a performance that I thought a pilot flying a Harrier would be unlikely to equal. We then accelerated away for the last time.

The final downwind leg was flown close in at 1,000 ft. Half way round the finals turn with range less than a mile, we were pulling at 200 kt with 50° of bank and a 750 ft/min descent rate. At 830 ft on the HUD I moved the thumb switch fully back and held it. 26 seconds later we were stopped over the threshold. This descending turn, using maximum reverse thrust in a relatively lumbering two-seater, had been flown by the IFPCS with no pilot workload except for controlling the bank angle.

After those two sorties it was clear to me that I had seen a very effective demonstration of safe and easy flying at maximum performance with the opportunity to completely rethink what is the best way for future pilots to use their hands. That is what IFPCS made possible.

It was five years later in 1999 that I got my next invitation from the team and much had happened since I flew with Dan Griffith. The aircraft had been given a full lateral and directional fly-by-wire system enabling all three axes to be automated and the control laws had been cleared for use during takeoff and landing. With these improvements to the aircraft the flying between 1994 and 1999 had enabled serious comparisons of several control law modes because the controversial aspects of the Unified law were well appreciated by the VAAC team. By 1999 they had whittled down the options to three serious contenders, Unified, Mode Change and Fusion.

UNIFIED

Unified was the most radical mode. Here the pilot pulled back on the stick to go up and pushed to go down, regardless of airspeed. At any speed above 40 kt groundspeed the stick commanded flight path rate therefore relaxing it to the centre position when the aircraft was flying level maintained height. If the aircraft was in a climb or a dive, relaxing the stick maintained the existing climb or dive flight path angle. As the aircraft decelerated through 40 kt, the stick response blended to become a height rate control by 30 kt groundspeed so that in the hover, with stick centre commanding zero height rate, it appeared to the pilot as if there was a height hold.

When flying up and away on the wings lateral stick commanded roll rate. This blended between 130 and 100 kt to become a closed loop roll attitude control so that relaxing the stick to centre below 100 kt commanded wings level. Above 40 kt groundspeed the rudder pedals commanded sideslip. Decelerating below this speed they blended to a yaw rate command by 30 kt, providing a heading hold in the hover with feet central.

A throttle type left hand inceptor, incorporating two detents, commanded longitudinal acceleration as shown in *Fig 1*. Putting this inceptor in the centre detent held the current speed. Acceleration or deceleration was selected by moving the lever forward or aft of the detent, with full travel demanding maximum available performance.

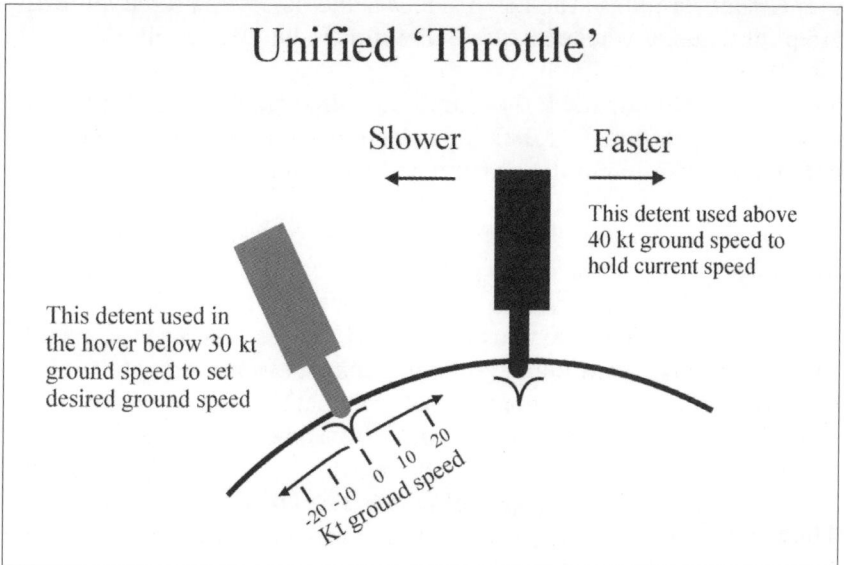

Fig 1

Decelerating through 35 kt groundspeed started a blend and below 25 kt the aft detent commanded zero groundspeed. Either side of the aft detent gave the pilot a closed loop control of groundspeed up to 30 kt forwards or backwards.

In summary, if the pilot centred both the stick and throttle when flying on the wings, the aircraft held the existing speed, bank attitude and climb or dive angle. Centralising everything in the hover maintained the existing hover height, position and heading. Such hover characteristics were the stuff of dreams for every Harrier pilot at the start of their conversion although, as discussed earlier, many experienced Harrier pilots were critical of Unified.

MODE CHANGE

Given that no Harrier or helicopter pilot pulls back on the stick to go up when in the hover, the aptly (if at first sight awkwardly) termed Mode

Change mode was conceived. At its simplest this required the pilot to select either a conventional flight or a hover mode of control. In the hover the pilot controlled height with the left hand as with the Harrier. Given the ability of today's control engineers to offer excellent handling characteristics, it was only natural that this was popular, especially with trained Harrier pilots. The down side was the risk of cognitive failure by the pilot inherent whenever a selection was required or available.

Mode Change provided the same detailed features as Unified in conventional flight but, following selection to hover mode, the throttle commanded height rate. The lateral and directional controls remained as described in Unified.

FUSION

The other main option was Fusion mode. This was designed to appeal to those military pilots who like to fly a 'back-side' approach where power is thought of as primarily controlling flight path (as opposed to a 'front-side' approach where the stick is considered to be the primary control of flight path and throttle is used to set speed).

Thus in Fusion the left hand throttle controlled flight path rate at all speeds down to 60 kt groundspeed at which point it started a blend to control height rate below 50 kt, providing a height hold when placed in the centre detent in the hover. Speed control was by a thumb wheel on the side of the throttle which commanded longitudinal acceleration or deceleration, again with a centre detent for holding the current speed, analogous to a highly augmented Harrier nozzle lever.

Like the throttle, the stick controlled flight path rate but only down to 120 kt where it blended by an airspeed of 60 kt to become a longitudinal acceleration through pitch attitude control. Thus above 120 kt, given that the pilot needed to hold the stick for lateral control, the throttle action becomes redundant. Once again the lateral and directional controls were the same as for Unified.

By 1999 Bedford airfield had closed so the VAAC team now did their flying from Boscombe Down and I flew with Justin Paines as my safety pilot. Following standard Harrier procedures we strapped in and Justin got us started. Having checked in with VAAC aircraft manager, Trevor Hartwell, and software specialist, Glenn D'Mello, in the telemetry control room, Justin talked me through the necessary rear cockpit systems safety checks. In less than a couple of minutes we were taxying and I felt I was observing a well worked up team going about their specialised business. The Boscombe circuit was busy with everything from helicopters to fast jets and it was clear we were just going to have to fit in and accept a busy R/T situation, rather than be blessed with the peaceful circuit environment that had existed at Bedford in 1994.

XW175, Justin Paines and JF at Boscombe 1999

During the taxi I followed instructions to set up the Digital Harrier (DH) control law. I had used this initially in 1994 to get settled down and to provide an up to date datum before looking at the new ideas. This time Justin warned me that the law had not been modified to take account of the totally different throws and forces of the stick now fitted which had been taken from the EAP technology demonstrator aircraft (the precursor to the Eurofighter). As a result he felt the combination provided the worst-flying Harrier ever.

Justin got us airborne into the circuit from a short takeoff (STO) and told me to put the arm switch on. Then, after synchronising the front and rear flaps and throttle inceptors, I engaged DH. Sadly, as predicted, I was flying an aeroplane that was all too easy to overcontrol and halfway round finals I let the angle of attack pass the IM limit of 12° and the system dumped. Justin put us on the ground and when we next got airborne I had the Manual Thrust Vector mode selected. This made the two main left-hand inceptors act as they do in a Harrier but with the stick providing synthetic and benign fast jet handling. This was being offered to evaluation pilots as a baseline and certainly allowed me to hover a 'nicer' Harrier than I had ever been used to at Dunsfold.

After the next STO I engaged the full trials Unified mode, fitted in a modified circuit round a Sea King going about its business on long finals, included a late jink to avoid overflying a lone ratepayer's house, continued decelerating to the hover, re-engaged following a sideslip trip, pushed the stick forward and went lower when I meant to move forward and eventually did a VL. Not entirely satisfied with my performance I asked 'Sir' if I could try Unified again.

Next time things went much more as planned. I even managed to get myself to stop moving the stick and allow the system to hold a steady attitude in the hover. The voice recording of this hover has me saying, "This is nice", which was an understatement. I also managed a few seconds using translational rate control (TRC) to fine tune the hover position by using the slew-type button on the top of the throttle.

Justin did a VTO and I had a prolonged and successful look at TRC from the throttle. Then, having set up the desired descent rate at 100 ft prior to the VL, I clicked a trigger on the front face of the stick. This locked in the descent rate and saved me having to hold the stick forward to maintain us coming down. As a result I had the novel experience of being responsible for a Harrier hover and VL and yet hands off for much of the time. Now at fuel minimums, it was time to return to the flight line. Justin asked for a hot-refuel which produced the largest fire truck I have ever seen and a bowser. The crew chief, John Elgie, came on the intercom, asked for the nozzles to be put down 30° and at idle power they plugged in the hose and gave us 3,500 lb of fuel. This ground equivalent of in-flight refuelling avoided the housekeeping procedures needed with a shut down and turnaround and is the perfect way to enhance circuit-flying productivity.

I flew the next deceleration in the Fusion mode. The thumb wheel on the left-hand inceptor was as easy to use to control the deceleration as common sense would suggest. During hover manoeuvring I blotted my copybook by leaving the wheel just outside the detent so we crept forward a bit. Since I was busy looking at flying a different law on the stick, it required the patient voice from the front to speak up before

I twigged the problem. A further circuit in Fusion allowed me to see that holding the aircraft flat in the hover and moving backwards and forwards on the thumb wheel was not such a good option as using attitude to adjust position in the way the designers intended.

Our final circuit was made using Mode Change. The important new feature here was that I was able to try using TRC with the stick as the inceptor. It was even more impressive as a natural way to adjust hover position when in flight than it had been in the simulator.

I naturally expected something better in 1999 than I had seen in 1994. Despite this, the level of improvement still surprised me. Walking into the debrief, more than a little dazed by flying some eight different aeroplanes in one sortie, I had no energy left to remove the grin from my face. Comparing that sortie with my first flight in the P1127 back in 1964, it was clear how far designers had come. In the beginning every trip in that early aeroplane required more skill than I could be sure of providing. Today this Harrier flew best when I took my hands off.

DECISION TIME

It was never going to be simple to choose the best control strategy for the JSF. There were pros and cons to all the options studied over the years by the VAAC team. As well as the technical issues, an important factor in the debate was the difference in outlook between operational and research pilots.

Operational pilots succeed in their very competitive careers by honing their personal skills to compensate for the shortcomings of their aircraft and then going out and showing they can cope better than the next guy. Indeed, without such a 'can do' attitude they are not likely to be much use in combat. An experienced Harrier squadron pilot, who by definition has successfully learned to operate two left-hand levers, is proud of this ability. It is asking a lot to expect him to vote to give it up. On the other hand, a research pilot is trying to improve aeroplanes. His job is to bring an open mind to new ideas and assess their value in reducing pilot skill requirements and the risk of pilot error. The research pilot will say that when STOVL started the options to make it easier and safer did not exist and as a result learning to use two levers with one hand was the only game in town. Now that technology offers alternatives, it becomes sensible to make a change.

For me Unified had to be the way to go. It enabled one to control an aircraft that can go from gently backwards to forwards at very high speed while using the same piloting technique throughout – surely the holy grail of aviation?

Chapter 7

Evaluating other people's aeroplanes

I left British Aerospace in April 1990 and started five years as a self employed test pilot. This gave me the chance to evaluate several interesting aeroplanes. Here I cover four of them, the Russian MiG-29, the Israeli Lavi, the US Navy T-45A Goshawk and, last but not least, the UK Slingsby T-67M.

I had only one flight in each and people often ask how one can form any meaningful opinions on the basis of so little experience. In reply I suggest that in our everyday lives we are quite used to first impressions that are valid. How many seconds does it take when you meet a person for the first time to realise that the two of you have 'clicked' or perhaps the opposite? When you drive a car for the first time how long does it take you to realise the clutch is horrible and the steering too heavy? Or that the view reversing is terrible? I suggest that, providing we have some relevant experience, we quickly form valid opinions whatever the field of endeavour. It is just the same with aeroplanes. I am not suggesting first impressions are any substitute for a full, lengthy and complete evaluation but on the other hand to suggest that they are not meaningful is incorrect.

In the case of the MiG, my aim was to concentrate only on handling aspects, with the Lavi it was about the cockpit equipment fit and ease of use and with the T-45 it was about the differences between it and the UK Hawk, although in the event the most interesting thing turned out to be the US Navy's attitude to an old man flying one of their jets. With the Slingsby trainer I needed to come up with some way of assessing it for operating from an airfield with an elevation of 6,500 ft when the only flight I had was from a sea level airfield.

Naturally any evaluation will benefit from a well thought out plan that takes into account all the circumstances that surround the trip. The plan, while initially about deciding what to include or leave out, also needs to act as a prompt for yourself during the trip and so make it easier to record your thoughts and data as the flight progresses. With each of these accounts I have included background detail on how I came to be doing the flight because of the impact this can have on the eventual plan.

Mikoyan MiG-29 UB

If you are a fighter pilot and you are ever called upon to fly against the MiG-29, you should be aware that this aircraft may have a superior aerodynamic performance to the one you are flying.

For those private pilots who can stall turn a Tiger Moth, take my word for it, you would be able to stall turn the MiG-29 as easily and reliably.

The above two paragraphs are the best I can do to give a brief introductory flavour of a very remarkable aeroplane. Neither is in any way an exaggeration although, following my report of a flight in 1990, some people clearly felt I was overstating how well it flew. Indeed after reading my views in Flight International, one person wrote to the Editor and accused me of having snow on my boots.

It was back in 1988 when the Mikoyan Design Bureau and their test pilots stole the Farnborough show with the first ever western display of their MiG-29. That occasion was truly a political and commercial watershed but the display was technically remarkable for aerospace professionals as it included manoeuvres that required a combination of engine handling, intake design and wing aerodynamics that no in-service western fighter could offer at that time.

I had many questions but two examples will suffice at this stage. How had they had developed their aircraft to pull considerably more g than ours at low speeds? How did the engines and the aerodynamics allow the pilot to start a tail-slide at 1,800 feet and take the wings and intakes to 90° alpha (as angle of attack is normally called) during the recovery? I should add that this latter manoeuvre was flown in such a repeatable way that it seemed the aircraft was on rails.

As an aviation buff whose day job allowed privileged access behind the scenes at Farnborough, I went out of my way to make personal contact with the MiG pilots.

However, this was not as easy as you might think because the Berlin Wall was not consigned to history until 13 months later. Consequently well-built minders were very much in evidence whenever one met the pilots and since any conversation required an interpreter, the whole exercise lacked the easy informality that normally exists between pilots at airshows.

It will be difficult for youngsters today to appreciate the atmosphere of suspicion and fear (even dread on some people's part) that existed between the East and West during the Cold War. This atmosphere was the normal stuff we breathed even a decade before the wall went up in 1961. Therefore, make no mistake, both the Russians and the Brits were very much feeling their way during personal contacts in 1988.

Suffice it to say that I invited three MiG pilots to the traditional dinner for the Red Arrows in the BAe chalet on the Sunday evening after the show. Things progressed further at Paris the following year such that I felt able to write to their chief designer, Michael Waldenberg, to see if there was any chance I could fly the aircraft at the next Farnborough. This resulted in a telex (those were the days) in which he agreed to talk about it when he got to the show.

Right from the beginning of the first tentative contacts with the MiG team, I had reasoned that they had no more control over their political circumstances than we had over ours, so I went out of my way not to put them on the spot in front of their minders. I felt the best approach was to concentrate on medium and low speed handling characteristics and not to push things by asking about military weapons fit and performance.

I saw no reason to change that approach as I walked to the MiG flight line caravan for my first meeting with Waldenberg. It seemed to me he had to be proud of what he had achieved and would naturally want to talk about it providing I stuck to aerodynamics. Thus after introductions, I simply took the initiative and volunteered how I had been a fan of vortex lift since my HP115 days at Bedford. I chatted slowly on through the interpreter for what must have been 10 minutes or so, asking no questions and just explaining my views on vortex lift and the frustration I felt at having to limit our research on the HP115 to angles closer to 40 alpha than the 90 they were showing with their MiG.

Sketching in my notebook as shown in *Fig 1* I went on to explain the problems we found with sideslip at high alpha. Although I was well aware that Waldenberg would know all about the HP115 programme, I wanted to give him time to size me up and decide what to say before I said to him, "You have clearly solved all these issues with the MiG-29 and I would like to know how you did it and then experience such good handing at first hand".

169

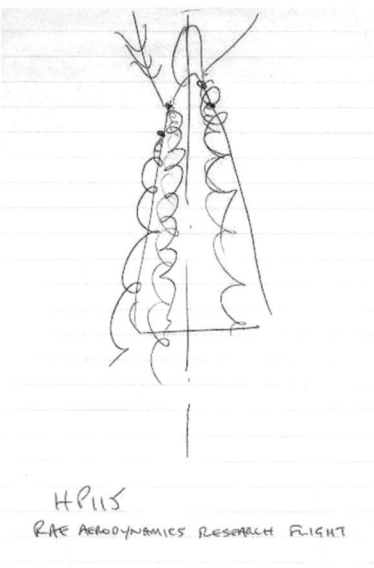

*JF sketch for Mikoyan Bureau
Chief Designer Michael Waldenberg
showing vortex flow problems on
HP115 when sideslip was present*

HP115
RAE AERODYNAMICS RESEARCH FLIGHT

Fig 1

His response was to take the book from me and make some sketches of his own (*Figs 2, 3 & 4*).

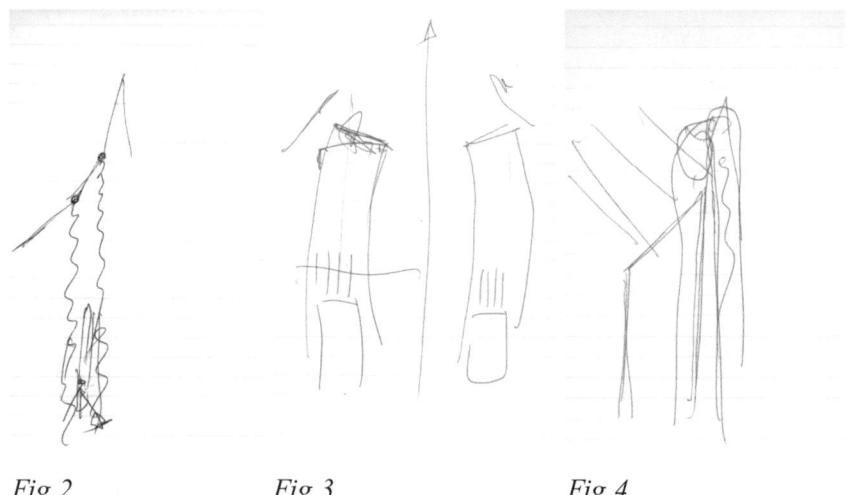

Fig 2   *Fig 3*   *Fig 4*

As he did so he was talking about how the wing and engine intake could cope with the high alphas of their display, especially the 90 alpha present during the recovery from the tail-slide manoeuvre that was a feature of the MiG-29 display. When he finished he turned to his CTP Valery Menitsky and told him to fly me "in the back seat".

170

Valery and he then had a long conversation in Russian where Valery, a real bear of a man and like most in his job no shrinking violet, was clearly deferring to his boss in a big way. Following this conversation Waldenberg left the caravan. Valery then apologised to me and said he had tried to get me cleared for the front seat "because the view is poor in the back," but the rear seat it would have to be. I was actually delighted with this because I knew that if I had been in the front I would have been distracted by the need to operate the aircraft systems and deal with any related issues, whereas in the back I had nothing to do except concentrate on the handling.

I then went away to sort out what tests I wanted to do. The next day Valery and I went through my plan, which was aimed at allowing me to be able to jot down some meaningful data as the trip progressed – not quite the same thing as going through a list of manoeuvres and reading the instrumentation after the flight!

Valery's brief was outstanding. Two examples serve to give an idea of his approach to the sortie. Firstly he said the trip would be governed by three rules. "Rule one maximum safety. Rule two maximum information for you. Rule three maximum fun for us." Secondly, when I asked Valery to take into consideration that I had stopped testing high performance aeroplanes seven years earlier, his reply was that he wanted me to do as much as possible and that the trip would proceed on the basis of "your experience and my currency". You can warm to a guy like that. Since we had no common language we agreed to limit our essential communication in the air to "Valery fly" and "John fly" with me doing all the R/T.

Clearly such an operation needed good planning and the services of a reliable interpreter. Having agreed the tests and their sequence in the flight, we went back through them all again and discussed the details. As we did so, Valery covered the flight controls, aircraft systems and limits but only in the context of this specific and necessarily limited flight.

There were two modes of nosewheel steering available from the rudder bar. Fine for normal taxying, takeoff and landing (plus or minus 8°) and coarse for slow speed in confined areas (plus or minus 30°) chosen using a change over selector. Valery briefed that he would line up the aircraft on the runway, do checks on the brakes at full cold power, release the brakes, engage full reheat and say, "John fly". He went on to say that I should start pulling the stick back at 185/190 kph (100/103 kt) aiming to

171

unstick at 220/230 kph (119/124 kt). He would select gear up. Then I should aim for 13 alpha until passing through 30° angle of climb when the alpha should be increased to 15°. After the aircraft reached the inverted I was to roll out and turn 180 towards Boscombe. He said that would be "the fun before we work". I suggest you need confidence in various aspects of your aircraft to brief a stranger to do a roll off the top after his first takeoff, especially if he is seven years out of touch.

As soon as these MiGs came to Farnborough, we realised that the intakes had internal doors to protect the engines from foreign object damage (FOD) when using rough strips. These were hinged at the top, came down and slammed shut on start up and were still shut during the takeoff ground roll.

Starboard engine running   *Both engines running*

I therefore asked about their operation and was told that the doors closed automatically as each engine started and the hydraulics came live. They opened fully on takeoff as airspeed increased through 200 kph (108 kt). I queried what would happen if one stuck shut and Valery replied with a big grin, "No practice". When I pressed him to say what would happen next he said, "We find out". I was concerned about any possible asymmetric effects but clearly their chief test pilot was not. The reason for his calmness became clear when I queried how fast they had flown with the doors shut and was told 800 kph (432 kt). He went on to say that at this speed with the doors shut one should limit alpha to 22°.

Clearly there was more to the intakes in the top of the wings than was apparent for the engines to be happy flying effectively with their main intake blanks fitted at that sort of speed!

The next day we were allocated a takeoff slot at the end of the show. A patch of bad weather was going through at the appointed time and we walked out under a 3-400 ft base with complete cover and cloud tops reported as 12,000 ft although the base was forecast to improve for our return. I pointed to the cloud, put my thumb down and indicated with my hand (how else?) that I intended to pull briefly before rolling inverted, pull again to level just under the base, roll erect again and climb towards Boscombe. Valery shrugged and clearly did not see the case for such a wimpish departure from the plan. I chickened out of doing the roll off the top because Russian attitude indicators are fundamentally different from those in the west and I had yet to see one in operation. Their horizon bar is *fixed horizontally* with respect to the instrument panel while their aeroplane symbol *banks* with respect to the panel. Pitch angle is provided by a drum that rotates behind the fixed horizon bar.

In my experience it is asking for trouble to just leap into the air when faced with something that is very different from what you are used to. I like to get my head round the issue first and form a specific plan of how I am going to tackle it. In this case, having flown plenty of line astern close formation in fighters, it seemed to me that the little aeroplane of their display would look like the rear view of your leader's aircraft against the natural horizon as he rolls and pulls round the sky ahead of you. That meant all I had to do was use my stick to 'control' my leader's bank angle remotely from behind. (How many times did I wish I could do that over the years!) That way if I wanted 'him' (actually me of course) to fly wings level or change bank angle I knew just what to do with my ailerons.

Once I got R/T clearance to start, Valery got on with it and, after the usual external checks with his crew chief on intercom, we were ready to "John taxi". The intake door indicators (a pair of vertical strip indicators showing 0 to 100% at the bottom right of the main centre panel) showed them fully shut. Taxying was no problem and the nosewheel steering was easy to use in both modes. After we lined up Valery did his checks, let the brakes off, engaged reheat and said, "John fly".

JF in the MiG-29

Because I did not want to get left behind I started rotation at 185 kph (100 kt) but overdid the pull and Valery momentarily checked my back stick, saying "No" as he did so. Once airborne, because of the brief to hold 13 alpha below 30° nose up, I didn't quite capture 15 before the need to roll under the low base. In the debrief Valery said that looking through the periscope makes it hard to assess pitch attitude once the nose is raised and that I would have been OK in the front seat. Nice guy. He also said unstick was early at 200 kph. I was looking at alpha once I started rotation so I had no idea.

We had planned to carry out the handling assessment between 4,000 and 15,000 ft near Boscombe. The cloud stopped that and after a frustrating period of no manoeuvring, we came out on top at just over 12,000 ft. The enforced instrument flying enabled me to adjust to what I felt were generally larger stick displacements and slightly heavier forces than those of a typical UK military aircraft. It reminded me more of the F-15.

Despite the scope for confusion with the attitude display, my plan to 'control my leader into doing what I wanted' worked well and I found the aircraft very stable and easy to fly on instruments. By comparison, the Sea Harrier would have to be described as a bit touchy but the SHAR did not use autostabilisers above 250 kt, whereas the MiG-29 does and they have been well optimised.

Just after we became visual on top I heard "Valery fly". A bit peeved, I studied my knee pad as I was not expecting this. I should have known better. Out of the corner of my eye I saw the stick flash to the right hand side of the cockpit. Looking up I was just in time to see three very quick rolls before the nose was yanked hard up, Valery then rolled inverted and again pulled hard. As this happened there were two loud bangs and thumps through the airframe, very reminiscent of engine surges in a Sea Harrier. Just as I thought "so much for the donks" I heard "John fly" and realised that Valery had communicated with me in a way that needed no words. He had shown it did not matter if I was a bit rough on his aeroplane and had demonstrated for good measure how the intake doors sounded as they slammed shut decelerating through 200 kph (108 kt).

Valery then had the patience to sit through my simple speed reduction at idle power from 400 kph (216 kt) until the alpha limit, at which point I had my first feel of the stall warning system restricting rearwards movement of the stick. Approaching 30° alpha slowly, the stop could be felt tapping away at the stick and trying to nudge it forward. The aircraft was by now descending rapidly in a fairly flat and easy to control attitude. I accelerated and repeated the deceleration, this time using lots of lateral stick applications as we slowed. There was excellent control response. As briefed, when I got to the limiter Valery showed we could pull through the stop to stick hard back. This needed 17 kg (37.4 lb) of pull. There was no problem and the aircraft remained under lateral control for some 15 seconds or so. Because the cockpit gauge was pegged at its max 30° reading, I later asked Valery what value we would have reached. He said flight test data showed 45/47°. For comparison, you can hold a Harrier in the stall at full back stick but the alpha would be 18° at most.

Flight test people know that incomplete data, or data noted under non-steady conditions, can be wildly misleading. For example, the speed/alpha relationship during a deceleration means nothing without knowing the power, weight and flight path angle at the time. Despite this I was keen to get some feel for the g available at low speeds. A couple of snatches of back stick, into heavy buffet and held long enough to peak the g, showed about 4 and 5g at 400 and 500 kph (only 216 and 270 kt!). These pulls were done at the low power needed to set the speeds in level flight so the wing had to be providing most of the g. In similar circumstances a Sea Harrier might have pulled half that.

We then did some tail-slides which were a total non-event. In the brief Valery had said to 'favour the right throttle' during the pitch down so I led a little with the right throttle for the first one as I slammed to full reheat, with the result that the nose did try and move a little to the right. I suspected this was due to gyroscopic precession from the engines at those high pitch rates. Then Valery did one and I watched him slam only the right throttle to full reheat, followed at once by the left one. I repeated it again using this differential slamming technique for a completely straight drop through.

I then looked at some combat reversals from steep climbs. Pulling into a 50° climb from 400 kph (220 kt) I rolled right at 240 kph (132 kt) and pulled to a wingover back downhill. I repeated the manoeuvre waiting until 200 kph (108 kt) before reversing. I did it a third time leaving the reversal until 150 kph (81 kt). There were no problems despite this silly low speed.

My first low speed loop started with a pull to 15 alpha in military power at 500 kph (270 kt) and was free of buffet all the way round. The second was planned to start from 300 kph (162 kt) in reheat but, with the burners on, it ran away from me and I did not get the pull going until 350 kph (189 kt). It went over the top at 15 alpha and 160 kph (86 kt). We were in and out of cloud between layers but I noticed that we went over the top below 8,000 ft and were recovered well above 5,000 ft. However in these circumstances I was clearly not getting anything like accurate data.

By now I realised that the intake doors seemed to spend much of their time in the 40 or 50% area and that there was no obvious kick as reheat lit, just a smooth push. Both things were unexpected so far as I was concerned. When instructing on Jet Provosts at Cranwell, I sometimes failed to demonstrate a good stall turn to students as it was easy to get stuck half way round. Not so in this MiG. I pulled the nose up as for a tail-slide but at 150 kph (81 kt) applied and held full left rudder. The nose slid round without hesitation and the wings could be kept at right angles to the horizon. I centralised the rudder as soon as we were pointing straight down and there was not so much as a wobble. Minimum speed going round at the top was 40 kph (22 kt). The whole thing inspired great confidence in the aircraft at low speed.

Valery was now pressing to return to Farnborough but I managed to hold us in a couple of orbits as we started our descent because I wanted to give time for two Hawks from Dunsfold to join us. Chief Test Pilot Chris Roberts with BAe photographer Geoff Lee in the Hawk 100, plus Warton test pilot Phil Dye in the Hawk 200 single-seater slid in just as we entered cloud.

In the circuit at Farnborough

Back at Farnborough, I did one orbit for pictures before the circuit to land. After the sort of manoeuvres I had been flying, drifting round the corner at 300 kph (162 kt) felt very easy and as if we were in the middle of the flight envelope. I only felt there was a job to be done when, on very short finals, I realised how little I could see. So I said, "Valery fly" but he ignored me. Happily at that time I used to fly a Ryan PT-22 from the rear seat which also needed you to look out both sides of the nose as you flared so I just pressed on and the MiG seemed to know how to land on the numbers.

On the numbers

After touchdown Valery took it and applied the brakes which were very impressive – but then my bike used to stop better when I used the front brake as well as the rear one. It reminded me that the only Hunter Dunsfold ever fitted with a nosewheel brake showed that such a brake was worth as much as streaming the normal braking parachute.

When we taxied in there was quite a collection of people waiting to meet us. I climbed down the ladder and one of the journalists, a middle-aged lady, was the first to speak. She said I looked glum and asked whether the flight had been a disappointment. I suggested that if, at her age, she had just experienced the best lover of her life but at the same time knew she would never enjoy him again, she might not grin either. To everyone else I remarked that when I grew up I wanted to be a MiG test pilot.

JF and Valery Menitsky

Israeli Aircraft Industries Lavi

Eleven days before the shooting started in Gulf War I, the Middle East contained hundreds of combat aircraft, including the top fighters from the Soviet Union, Europe and the USA. However the only combat aircraft conceived, designed and tested by a middle-eastern country, the Israeli Lavi, was the one I was going out to Israel to fly and that was not going to participate whatever happened.

My sortie convinced me that they had built a fighter that was easier for the pilot to use than any other type involved with the Gulf crisis in January 1991. Follow that opinion with the fact that the Lavi programme was cancelled by the Israeli cabinet in 1987 and that the Lavi's manufacturers, Israeli Aircraft Industries (IAI), fully accepted that the programme would remain dead, then clearly explanations are in order.

Before attempting those, I would like to explain what I mean by 'easier for the pilot to use', so that IAI's achievement can be properly appreciated. A modern combat pilot flying against other aircraft or defended targets on the ground has to use many systems such as radar, laser or infra red sensors, complex weapon control panels, self-defence devices to jam and decoy enemy systems and to identify himself to his friends, as well as equipment to receive and transmit tactical advice. The list is a long one. Arranging for a pilot to get the best out of all these various things, as easily as possible, while sitting in a small cockpit that also allows him a good view of the outside world is what I believed IAI had done so well. In fact, better than any other manufacturer had managed at that time.

On the other hand, if Lavi was cancelled in 1987 why was I flying it in January 1991? What made the cockpit so good anyhow? Why did IAI succeed in flying such an advanced cockpit ahead of other major and established world players? What is the Lavi like as an aeroplane? Surely something must have been wrong with the programme for it to be cancelled? To appreciate the answers to such questions it helps to start at the beginning.

Back in the 1970s, the Israeli Air Force (IAF) planners were considering what they needed to replace their A4s and Kfirs. This new aircraft had to do three jobs, the most important of which was air to ground, which would size the design. Here they wanted more payload and range options than their F-16s could offer.

The second role was air to air combat. They were very happy with the air to air capability of their F-15s but Israel could be faced with simultaneous attacks by up to seven countries in certain defensive scenarios. Because of this they needed to enhance the sheer numbers of aircraft available with a real intercept capability.

Thirdly they needed an advanced operational trainer. Quality and value for money are not just things talked about by the IAF, to them they are the basis of survival. Training is always where pilot quality starts. For an operational aircraft to have a better capability than the F-16 and still be useable as a trainer, it needed to be unusually easy to fly and economic to operate.

There was no conflict of design cases here as young reservists will always do a better job if their aircraft is easier to fly whether they are learning to fly, learning to fight, trying to stay operationally current in peacetime or engaged in combat. In addition, the better the economics the more aircraft you can afford.

Programme go ahead was given for the Lavi (Hebrew for 'lion') in 1980 using US funding. Roll out was in July 1986. A year later with most of the design envelope cleared, a senior US aerospace industry team was sent to see how the money had been spent. They had a big surprise and were shocked to find how well the Lavi had turned out. They could come to only one conclusion, namely the US would never sell another F-16 anywhere unless it was cancelled. The US had funded IAI to develop something that could kill a big chunk of their business.

On the 30th August 1987, following intense pressure from the US, the Israeli cabinet cancelled the programme by a vote of 11 to 10. IAI were still wondering if they had done the right thing at the time of my visit.

Similar in overall size and weight range to the F-16 rather than the F-15 and, using the very different aerodynamics of a close-coupled active canard/delta wing, the prototypes were both two-seaters. IAI's policy was that there were positive advantages to developing the two-seater first due to the importance of the training mission. The powerplant was a single Pratt and Whitney PW1120 giving the single-seater a thrust to weight ratio of 1.07 and a maximum speed of 800 kt/1.8M with air to air weapons and 50% internal fuel.

The Lavi

Its delta wing and canard layout was later to be seen on the French Rafael, Swedish Grippen and the European Eurofighter

Following the political blow of cancellation, IAI decided that their approach to cockpit displays and controls was too good and too important to die with the overall programme. As 'R.S.' told me, "Israel has a fundamental need for local development of unique sensors and weapons. Only that way can we meet IAF special requirements, ensure a quick response and flexibility in a changing combat arena and maintain the secrecy and surprise factor." 'R.S.' was one of four IAI engineering test pilots responsible for my preflight briefing in addition to Menachem Shmul, then Director Flight Operations and Chief Test Pilot for IAI. Menachem's pilots were all current operational reservists who understandably insisted on anonymity. "Only the boss is exposed," explained 'E.R.' with a grin as we met. To IAI the need was clear, the third Lavi prototype, which was always destined to be the avionics development vehicle, would have to be completed and flown. It would become the Lavi TD (Technology Demonstrator). The reason I came to be flying a cancelled aeroplane was because IAI wanted to develop their avionic equipments and cockpit displays and then to offer them for evaluation and sale in the most valid and professional way possible, namely fitted to a totally representative aircraft.

The briefing room in IAI's air operations building had a dozen steel tubular chairs with hard wooden seats, not that they were needed to stay awake in the particular circumstances of this visit. What was special was that one wall had a large composite photograph of the TD cockpit, clear enough to read all the captions.

Picture on briefing room wall

To anyone with experience of fighter cockpit design in those days one glance at the picture said it all – this cockpit had been designed by a pilot. The cockpit structure and the four main displays had been designed to allow the actual displays to be where any pilot would want them, namely as high up and as close together as possible with no wasted panel space, view cut off or need to look lower down than was absolutely necessary.

All too often one has heard the designers cry, "But you can't have it there, there will not be enough room for the box to fit behind the panel. Here is the best we can do". Clearly IAI was not a company where expensive suits intoned about the importance of optimising the man-machine interface as a major programme objective but then at the end of the day invited you to fly yet another poor and ordinary cockpit.

As I was to fly in the front seat which contained some indicators and controls not available in the rear cockpit, the rest of the day was necessarily devoted to aircraft systems. The pilot was provided with a wide angle field of view holographic head up display (HUD) at the base of which was the very compact Up Front Control Panel (UFCP), the keypad for all data entry. Immediately below the UFCP was a row of three multifunction displays (MFDs), the right hand one of which had colour. The hands on throttle and stick (HOTAS) switches and controls were comprehensive, seven on the stick and eight on the throttle. As is usual with HOTAS systems some of these controls and switches were themselves multifunctional.

The TD as I flew it had no radar, no laser, no infra red search and track and no radar warning system. In short the sensors were not fitted, just their display symbologies. However neither did they need to be because it was the displays that enabled one to evaluate the IAI concept that drove the cockpit design. IAI reasoned that any time one of their Monday to Friday butcher, baker, candlestick maker reservists got into this jet to train or fight he would always be doing one of four jobs:

- Going to a destination or ground target (navigating)
- Attacking a target on the ground (air to ground)
- Attacking another aircraft (air to air)
- Trying to find another aircraft (interception)

Each of these jobs needs a totally different set of sensors, displays and weapons to be selected. It can take a long time to set up the cockpit for a job change in the air and it is very easy to get a switch in the wrong place. This is a real problem and a common cause of failure during the stress of combat. The magic IAI solution was a switch on the end of the throttle, spring loaded to centre and very handy for your thumb. Hold that switch up for a moment before releasing it and *everything* needed for air to air attack was selected. Hold it down for a moment and all the displays and weapons changed to the air to ground job. Blipping it down and allowing an immediate return to centre gave navigation, while blipping it up and letting it go gave air to air interception. Four totally instinctive selections from a single three position switch. Now you see what I meant earlier about the Lavi being easy to use.

There were plenty of other examples of the thought that had gone into this easy-to-use design. Jumping in for a trip, the pilot's first action was to put a big centre off switch to either peace or war. With 'Peace' selected the APU and all the aircraft avionics got switched on and started their built-in test cycles, all that is except engine, radar and explosive countermeasures kit that could do a nasty to nearby ground crew. With 'War' selected everything would be up and running, including the engine, by the time you had finished strapping in.

Ready to taxi

In some configurations the IAF felt the F-16 was not the easiest jet to land in a strong crosswind. Therefore for their Lavi butcher and baker pilots, once they had put the wheels down, kicking the rudder just swung the nose left or right with no change of bank angle. In other words the aeroplane put in the required aileron inputs to maintain the wings level when kicking off drift. Neat or what? With the wheels up things reverted to normal so that a boot of rudder helped roll rate at low speed, just like any other swept wing aircraft. Selecting wheels down also set the optimum angles of both the leading edge and trailing edge flaps for an approach.

Perhaps you are starting to get a feel for why as a non-current oldie I was perfectly happy to taxi out, get airborne and charge about Israel (an extremely small area by the way) at very high speed pretending to attack things on the ground and in the air without a checklist or need for a cockpit related thought. Menachem had said to include an auto toss attack, letting the inertial system guide me to a target of my choice. When the HUD started to count down the seconds to pull up I pickled to preselect bomb release when the computer was ready and, as the little pull symbol started moving up the bomb fall line, I chased after it with back stick. It was easy to satisfy and up we went at the computer's choice of 4g. A voice in the back even said "Good" a couple of times at that stage. Time to impact started counting down in the HUD once the bomb was away. After impact I turned back (only a journalist would do that) and let the HUD show me the point on the ground where the system thought the bomb would have hit. It looked near enough to give the original target a very bad fright. We did all that twice and I noticed that, while moving south to set up on the second run, we got up to 550 kt TAS at 5,000 ft although, such was the smoothness and quietness of the ride, I could have believed we were only doing 300.

Since this was my first experience of a full fly-by-wire aircraft I also tried yanking in full back stick and watching the aircraft limit itself at 25 alpha. It was not quite like I expected because the aeroplane flew round the turns under obvious control. By that I mean you could detect small adjustments being made to attitude and pitch rate to hold us between 24.5 and 25 for all the world as if a very skilful pilot was demonstrating just what the aircraft could do. It was fascinating to watch.

Approaching Ben Gurion for a straight-in ILS from out over the sea, I had no trouble following the head down steering information on the ADI and in due course selected the gear down. There was nothing else

185

to do if you remember. At our weight the optimum approach was 12 alpha or about 145 kt. A small and quite instinctive flare just prior to touchdown was rewarded with a kiss and very shallow skip into a ground roll with the nose held up. At 110 kt I eased on power for a touch and go into a right hand visual. Back round to touchdown at 128 kt without a skip, into aerodynamic braking until I put the nose wheel on, under full control, at 80 kt. It just seemed the most natural thing in the world. With that flight control system the Lavi would teach well and quickly.

Trip over except for the debrief

Why did IAI achieve so much ahead of other major players? For the simple reason that Israel needs the best and IAI knows how to achieve that. They don't ask their pilots to test something, they ask them what they would like to test, which is a very different approach.

A good cockpit enhances and a poor cockpit degrades the total capability of any pilot/aircraft combination. The quality of the cockpit ranks in importance with such major aircraft characteristics as performance, agility, operating site flexibility, stealth, reliability, equipment fit and handling qualities. For me on that day in January 1991 the Lavi TD cockpit concept had just become the standard by which combat aircraft should be judged. Any future cockpit would have to be as good or better if it was to give pilots the best chance of doing their job. Meanwhile,

Harrier, Tornado and MiG-29 pilots (to name but three), you have a handicap that you could well do without. If you get a chance to talk to IAI, take it. They listen to pilots.

BAE SYSTEMS/Boeing T-45A

If you invite someone to evaluate your aircraft and write an article before it is fully developed and ready for service, one of three situations can exist: you have had a brainstorm, things have reached a point where any publicity is better than none or you are proud of what has been achieved so far. Since I had to cross the Atlantic to take up the US Navy's invitation to fly the T-45A in 1991, the flight over provided plenty of time to ponder these three possibilities.

My background on the Marines' purchase of the Harrier had taught me that NAVAIR (the aircraft procurement arm of the USN and USMC) is supremely effective at preventing one of their number going it alone for better or for worse and therefore I knew that quite a few people would have had to put a tick in the box before my invitation was issued. That ruled out a brainstorm on the part of a keen young Navy PRO. Could NAVAIR be desperate for programme publicity? No, only imminent risk of cancellation would generate that sort of pressure and continued funding was a matter of public record. That left the third explanation that NAVAIR were proud of their T-45 achievements. Were they right? Only my flight would answer that question.

The background to how the Hawk trainer became the basis of the current USN flying training programme started in 1975 only a year after the first flight of the Hawk in the UK. The US Naval Air Development Centre was looking into the feasibility of replacing the T-2C and TA-4J training aircraft with a single aircraft that could carry out both their intermediate and advanced phases of undergraduate flight training. The programme was later designated VTX-TS to indicate the Total Training System philosophy. Not surprisingly every US aircraft manufacturer submitted a paper aircraft to do the job, while the French put up the Alpha Jet and we proposed the Hawk.

It is a very expensive exercise for any company to put together a proposal for such a competition. Should you win, you will also be held to your timescales and costs but if you pad out your submission with comfort margins, you run the risk of not getting the job. Therefore there was much teeth sucking at Kingston and Dunsfold around that time because a lot of sensible people thought it would be a waste of time and money for us to enter the Hawk since the competition specified a *twin engine* solution. Generally, when any company puts in a non-compliant bid to a potential customer, it runs the risk of it going straight into the bin. In this specific case, Kingston was effectively telling the USN they did not know their own business and so had got their specification wrong. I will leave you to use your imagination about the magnitude of the uphill struggle we faced from day one before we got them to accept that a single engine solution should be considered.

The performance figures of the two real aeroplanes were not as impressive as those of several of the paper designs (surprise, surprise!) but the USN staff rated the paper jobs as higher risk (well done them) and thus the competition eventually became a simple fight between the Hawk and the Alpha Jet. You will have spotted the snag – the Alpha Jet has two engines.

Sufficient to say that in November 1981, the Navy announced the selection of McDonnell Douglas as prime contractor, teamed with British Aerospace, to develop the Rolls-Royce Adour powered Hawk aircraft for VTX-TS. After another three years of work, the Navy awarded the contract for Full Scale Development (FSD) in October 1984. This FSD plan allowed three years to build the modified Hawk and two more to show it would do the job, making FSD complete in October 1989. Not a quick programme by some standards but that was how the Navy wanted it and the chosen rate of working reduced the costs.

Naval airmen who are determined to do it the hard way (without a hover capability) face many difficulties when flying onto and off a ship at sea. This in turn means there is a lot involved in navalising any non-VSTOL land based aircraft. Firstly, it needs a stronger undercarriage and airframe to take the arrested no-flare touchdowns together with a means of attaching it to the catapult and holding it back, under tension, before launch. It will also have to fly slowly enough not to overstress itself or the wires on touchdown and must be able to get airborne again (called bolting) if the hook fails to pick up a wire. The small size of the touchdown area, plus the obstruction of the ship's structure, calls for an accuracy of flying that has no parallel in normal airfield operations. This demanding approach path also passes through the 'burble' of turbulent air just behind any carrier. Therefore exceptionally good handling qualities and performance are required in the approach configuration.

When the Navy flew their initial T-45A trials in November 1988, their complaints centred on changes made to navalise the baseline Hawk. They listed five major problems: engine and aircraft performance, speedbrake effectiveness and pitch transients, lateral and directional stability, longitudinal stability and stall characteristics.

The fixes for these 'big five', as they became known, involved a lot of work. The engine was changed from the Rolls-Royce Adour 861 to an existing higher thrust version, the 871. This engine had a specially modified fuel control system to reduce acceleration times, including a fast idle throttle stop that was automatically engaged on the approach. A redesigned higher lift version of the wing was fitted incorporating a retractable leading edge slat. An aileron ratio changer was added giving 3° more aileron travel with gear down. The longitudinal controls were balanced and the tailplane increased in size. The new wing was fitted with fences and vortex generators to preserve stall handling at the maximum lift coefficient. The speedbrake travel was increased and a tailplane interconnect added to automatically take care of the trim change. The fin was increased in size, the rudder was fitted with an anti-float device, the nosewheel doors were arranged to close with the gear down, a yaw autostabiliser was introduced and an aileron/rudder interconnect brought in below 217 kt. A low authority nosewheel steering system was provided for takeoff and landing.

That was the background to how, eight long years after I retired as a Dunsfold test pilot, I found myself in the States and about to fly one of the FSD T-45 aircraft. My sortie was to be flown at the Naval Air Test Centre (NATC), Patuxent River, which is situated on the picturesque Maryland coast about an hour's drive south of Washington DC. The USN wanted me at the main gate at 07.00 Monday morning so, holed up in a hotel the day before, I considered what my evaluation priorities should be for this one flight. It did not take me long to realise that I should concentrate on the effectiveness of the fixes for the 'big five'. These changes set my priorities for what manoeuvres to do on this limited one flight evaluation.

I was met at the main gate and hosted warmly throughout by the NATC public affairs office. The obligatory and very thorough medical tests at the base hospital (including anthropomorphic measurements, several blood and urine tests, two X-rays, ECG, audiogram, eyesight tests and a dental check before even getting to see the doctor) were followed by an aviation physiology lecture using computerised visual aids, a decompression chamber run, parachute suspension training and a shot up the ejection seat training rig. Initially I saw this as the manifestation of a reasonable 'make him wish he had never become a PR nark' attitude by the military but you can take it as read that I was not a happy bunny because at home my wife had already raised the issue of my 60th birthday party. I was very close to walking off the job a couple of times, indeed so close that I rang the UK to explain that I might not be doing the trip.

I heard later that a visiting Admiral had gone for a 'quick trip' one day, finished up dead for some reason and that quick clearances to fly in a Patuxent River fast-jet had been hard to get ever since.

I was to fly a pre-production aircraft that was inferior to the proposed service standard. The wing was not fitted with the latest moveable slat but had its shape set at the 'retracted slat' condition. There was a high gain nosewheel steering system cleared for low speed taxi use only and the engine fuel system lacked an extra shot of fuel now agreed upon to improve engine response to any throttle up. Further significant restrictions were a max speed of 450 kt/0.8M, a max g of 5.5, no stalling with gear or flaps down and no spinning.

JF in the USN T-45A

Lt O P Honors, a USN test pilot at NATC, was to fly me. 'O.P.' as he liked to be called, said he would occupy the rear seat and asked how

I would like to handle the admin aspects of the trip. I requested that he dealt with the checklist, radio and navigation, leaving me free to concentrate on handling matters. He finished his safety brief by saying he would select the seat interconnect system so that I could eject us both if I thought it appropriate. In my book acts of faith don't come much greater than that. As we put our kit on, I recalled just how much I preferred the standard US torso harness fitted to this aircraft compared to the UK Simplified Combined Harness (SCH) used on Hawks and Harriers at home.

The US harness can be adjusted to give an immaculate fit, giving much greater comfort when suspended by the parachute risers which as I mentioned earlier they made me do but, thankfully, with the top ends attached to the hangar roof. When I connected this harness to the seat, I got a more positive feeling of restraint than I was used to with the UK system. However that was really just a personal problem because, according to the RAF Institute of Aviation Medicine survey of UK military aircrew in the 1970s, I was blessed with a 3 percentile thigh diameter. Before you get too excited, that just means that 97% of RAF aircrew at that time had more meat on them there than I did and so they did not run out of strap adjustment on the SCH as I did. When we were ready to start, 'O.P.' commented that at under five minutes it was quick and easy to fire up a T-45A and get under way. Maybe it was compared to then current USN trainers but such things are relative and I had been spoilt by the Pegasus in the Harrier. The Adour needs 5 pilot actions, 4 indication checks and over a minute before it is at idle. Compare that with the Pegasus which needs 2 pilot actions, 1 indication check and 40 seconds. Indeed in 1969 a Pegasus achieved a VTO within 1 minute of pressing the starter button.

Taxying out to the runway at all but very low speeds, the linear high gain nosewheel steering was a bit over sensitive for me and it was clear why the Navy would be getting a low gain setting for use at higher speeds. Since the RAF Hawk did not have nosewheel steering, I chose to control direction by differential braking. This was easier than doing the same thing with an RAF aircraft because the rudder bar and brake pedals had been improved on the T-45A, allowing the heels to be kept on the floor and the brake pedals were at a better angle with greater travel and hence provided a better feel for how much brake you were using. As ever with an Adour, we had to wait the necessary 20 plus seconds at full throttle after line up and before releasing the brakes to allow the engine temps to settle and engine clearances to stabilise. This process, which is not by any means restricted to the Adour, enables the compressor tip clearances to reduce and so allow max thrust to develop before releasing the brakes. No problem perhaps while waiting for a catapult launch… but still a case of 'Hail Pegasus!'

Accelerating down the runway, I found it easier to track the centreline than in an RAF Hawk. Clearly being able to keep your heels on the floor with the modified brake pedals allowed better control. At 120 kt I raised the nose to unstick and, with the trim that was set, this was an easy pull of moderate force. There was no oscillation in pitch and the T-45A felt as steady as a rock after only one wobble of about 5° in bank as I got used to its different aileron gearing. I was keen to fly a heavy fuel load circuit, just as a student would have to do from his or her first catapult launch, in order to check for any sluggish characteristics that might not show up with a light fuel load at the end of the sortie.

I had briefed 'O.P.' that to generate the worst possible student scenario, I would leave the gear and flap down and initially bank the wrong way into the circuit, then correct violently the other way while putting out the speedbrakes. I wanted to do this because the press to transmit button on the throttle was just above the speedbrake selector so a student might by accident operate the speedbrake switch while responding to a sudden call from ATC to go the other way! Because the T-45A has more aileron travel than the Hawk, such a ham-handed use of full stick at low speed and high weight would expose any tendency to adverse aileron yaw indicated by the aircraft being hesitant to reverse the turn. Despite my best efforts at finding fault, the aeroplane behaved perfectly. No yaw built up, roll response was crisp and the heavy aeroplane continued to accelerate up the climbing turn with the speedbrakes out. Admittedly the outside air temperature was ISA, but there seemed a lot of performance in hand to cope with less thrust on a hot day.

 On the downwind leg, I had my first look at an indexer in action. Navy pilots live by this instrument when flying the circuit in any of their aircraft. It is mounted to the left of the head up display and looks like the diagram here. The lower arrow lights up red when fast (and so wasting available lift) while the upper one comes on green if the aircraft is too slow (and so in danger of stalling). At the optimum alpha, the centre circle lights up white and the arrows are out. I queried the colour logic of the arrows with 'O.P.' who chuckled and muttered that he thought he'd learned it in his pram.

It occurred to me that the best way to think about the arrows was as pointers showing you which way to move the nose (up when fast and down when slow). Couldn't be easier really, especially if you happen to be a GA pilot and wedded to controlling speed on finals with the stick and not the throttle. Those who know me will realise I abhor this concept as you can't use it to get speed back at low level in the final stages of the approach. It works in the USN because they have a Landing Safety Officer (LSO) on the ship who demands that you go around if you are not 'on speed' well before you get close to the deck. The LSO stands by the 'meatball' (as the ship's glidepath aid is known) looking up the approach and can tell how well you are flying the indexer because there are green, white and red lights on all USN noselegs that tell the LSO what the cockpit display is showing. As for the colour logic, how about 'green says you won't pull the arrester hook off' and 'red that you will'?

On our first heavy circuit the indexer gave an on-speed condition between 120 and 115 kt. Before leaving the circuit, I did two more heavy touch and goes using the meatball. This precision glidepath aid is fitted to all carriers and is stabilised against the effects of ship motion. Its purpose is to show the pilot whether the approach is too high, too low or just 'on' the optimum flight path into the arrester wires. One is installed alongside every runway at NATC to help with Navy testing. Despite our high weight during these circuits, I did not detect any sluggish characteristics with the engine or airframe. We left the circuit and climbed to 20,000 ft. There were no directional trim changes with power or speed, an improvement over the Hawk where the rudder trimmer gets considerable use.

Stalling the new wing in manoeuvre was interesting. Starting at 250 kt with a slowly increasing pull, the buffet built up steadily between 17 and 21 alpha and at the stall there was moderate lateral and pitch unsteadiness. Doing the same manoeuvre at 300 kt gave a burst of light to moderate wing rock at the 4g stall. The changing characteristics with speed seemed to me a useful instructional point, enabling students to experience a variety of behaviours at the stall such as they might find on different types in the future. The control forces in pitch seemed heavier than I remembered with the Hawk. On the other hand, snatching the stick back certainly gave less stick force per g and, although I did not think this difference was serious, 'O.P'. said a dashpot was going to be added to the longitudinal control run to meet the Navy rules for a snatch. A pull at 21,000 ft and full throttle reached 5.2g at 330 kt/0.7M.

Speedbrakes and tailplane   *Speedbrakes open*

Recognising that the new speedbrakes could affect the tailplane, I selected them out in a turn near the stall but there was no trim change, just a mild buffet. Putting them out hands off at 340 kt also gave no trim change. The new interconnection clearly worked perfectly. At our maximum allowable speed of 450 kt/0.8M, a good rough stir of the stick did not induce any oscillations. To me that was a big plus, since many vehicles do not behave nicely when handled roughly at their maximum speed (on the road or in the air!)

Turning at the 5.5g limit was a non-event and the fairly rapid anti-g valve response rate gave quick suit inflation, hence good protection. As with the Hawk at high speeds and so lower alpha, the dihedral effect gets very small and can even be made to change sign, producing slight right roll from left rudder. This is a totally academic point as the rudder forces are very high and nobody is short of roll rate from aileron at those speeds. Back at 10,000 ft with 1,700 lb of fuel we had a look at clean 1g stalls. From a steady state 140 kt and 76% rpm, a small nose up attitude change was used to commence a very slow speed reduction. The stall warning pedal shakers, set to come on at 20 alpha, started at 125 kt. Ignoring them and slowing further gave a 40° wing drop to the right at 112 kt. Recovery was immediate on checking the stick forward just an inch or two.

This was followed by a gear down, full flap and speedbrakes out deceleration. This had to stop at the stall warner as we had no slat out capability. The indexer showed the on-speed condition in level flight at 17 alpha, 110 kt and 81.8% rpm. Further slow deceleration set the stall warning going at 20 alpha and 100 kt, a suitable margin from the on speed conditions. The aircraft was still buffet-free and rock steady at this point. It was then that 'O.P.' insisted that I should take a few moments out to enjoy the view and have some fun. "I know you are busy but…"

NATC Patuxent River and
Chesapeake Bay

It was a wonderful scene, not a cloud in the sky, excellent visibility and the whole of the picturesque Chesapeake Bay area, with its many inlets and hamlets, was spread out below. Ideal for the lazy looping and rolling aerobatics that followed. For me, the increased control forces compared to the Hawk made the T-45A feel bigger and heavier than it really was. Very nice though for all that. Then it was back to work.

Nose leg with catapult bar   *Non-bounce main gear*

There were still two more things I wanted to look at concerning approach handling. At 4,000 ft we lowered gear and flap and, with the indexer showing on speed, I cycled the speedbrakes to get a feel for the rpm change required. It was negligible, say in the 1% region. With speedbrakes out again and level flight with the indexer on speed I chopped the throttle and waited. It took 6 seconds to reach the stall warning. No problem there. We entered the busy mixed traffic NATC circuit with 1,200 lb of fuel. I now knew enough about the aircraft to realise that its excellent handling qualities in the approach configuration would allow me to turn my back on it and just try and sort out my purely personal struggle with the demands of the meatball. Five touchdowns later, we turned off the runway having been airborne 65 minutes. The fuel state was 350 lb.

Three points struck me during those circuits. Firstly, on a couple of arrivals alongside the meatball I slammed to full throttle and selected speedbrake in as we hit. The engine accelerated very rapidly in a most un-turbofan like manner and the aircraft appeared to leap back airborne in its own length. I knew when I had closed the throttle in previous touchdowns that the undercarriage gave no tendency to bounce, hence it was clear to me that the Navy had got the safe student bolter capability they needed by the Rolls-Royce mods to improve engine acceleration times. Remember also this aircraft lacked the eventual extra shot of acceleration fuel.

A bad student error but still one that must be safely accommodated within the short carrier deck, is chopping the throttle to idle for a couple of seconds on touchdown before slamming it open again. I did this and it still gave a creditable bolter. The short but definite ground roll that resulted would need measuring, not guessing. For the cognoscenti the approach idle stop remained in despite the weight going onto the wheels, courtesy of some timer logic, thus helping the engine recover from the student's error.

Secondly, when there was a lull in the R/T and I complained for the umpteenth time to 'O.P.' about the lack of any lights in my cockpit, he suggested I check the cockpit night lighting switches. Sure enough the panel master was on, automatically dimming all cockpit light indications to the levels needed at night. With that off, the status panel and gear indications came on and I thought how much they all helped!

Finally, a couple of circuits from the end, 'O.P.' suggested I swap hands and control the meatball with the throttle and the indexer with the stick, whereas up to that point I had used throttle for speed and stick for mirror. Certainly this change fitted in nicely with the indexer thoughts mentioned earlier. However, in my view, this very special ship approach case does not mean it is sensible to teach stuffing the stick forward on an ordinary GA approach to increase speed because as I keep saying you cannot use the method when close to the ground.

Our final landing was the only full stop one of the trip. It was also the only event where 'O.P.' made any unprompted prior comment. "It will be very squirrelly after touchdown, so stay on the rudders. It basically wants to leave the side of the runway." I treated it like a tail-wheel single piston during the roll-out and we stayed on the white line. Once again most things are relative. That problem would be history with the final nosewheel steering standard.

To end we must go back to the beginning and ask ourselves was NAVAIR right to be proud of the T-45 as its future Navy trainer? My view is very much so. It has a modern, light, small, long life and fuel efficient turbofan that accelerates with the best of the previous turbojets although these were heavy, large, had short times between overhaul and positively drank fuel. A rapid response to throttle is absolutely vital for student safety because all of us can be slow to see the need for something when we are learning. If, just before touchdown, a carrier student is slow to realise the need for power *and* the engine is slow to respond, the aircraft quite simply sinks below the level of the deck and disintegrates against the stern of the very hard ship. Such an error by a Hawk pilot at an airfield might leave embarrassing wheel tracks in the grass before the runway but that is hardly the same problem. As for the airframe, although it is necessarily stronger and heavier than the Hawk, the T-45A has been given more lift and so enabled to fly slower. At the same time it has been endowed with very precise approach handling. That way it becomes safe for a student exposed to the demands of flying a deck.

T-45 in its element

Looking back to those days now, I am certain that these improvements were difficult to achieve and that at times those involved must have had their doubts about getting there. However the development team were successful so the students reap the benefits. Another indication that the potential of that early version of the T-45 was achieved is that today the USN is investing in a glass cockpit update to make the type representative of the operational aircraft now coming into service. The T-45A (analogue cockpit) and T-45C (later digital cockpit version) look set to be the US Navy trainer of choice for a long time yet.

Slingsby T-67M

At the beginning of 1992 the United States Air Force (USAF) was in the process of selecting an aircraft for its Enhanced Flight Screener (EFS) programme. They planned to buy 120 and to operate them at two sites, one of which was the USAF Academy Colorado Springs which is situated 6,500 ft up in the Rocky Mountains. The aircraft would be used to assess the suitability of candidates for military flying training and to stream them for fighter/attack or transport/tanker courses.

T-67M

To meet the EFS requirements, Slingsby Aviation fitted their successful T-67 Firefly with a six cylinder 260 hp injected Lycoming engine in place of the more usual four cylinder 160 or 200 hp from the same manufacturer. In 1991 the aircraft underwent a USAF evaluation at both US sites. A few weeks before the contract decision was to be made, Slingsby's looked for some independent publicity and invited me to fly their demonstrator and comment on whether I thought it was up to the high altitude USAF job.

Slingsby Aviation Chief Test Pilot 'Norrie' Grove briefed me: "Except for the engine, this aircraft is unchanged from when you flew it at Farnborough last year. We started by attaching ballast to the 200 engine version and progressively tested the effects of the forward CG change until we had reached the weight needed to fit the 260. With the spinner now seven inches further forward we made a new lower drag flush cowling. I will leave you to judge the result."

Norrie Grove and JF

Getting in was a pleasant experience and immediately reminded me of why I like the T-67 family of cockpits. The large, clear, one piece canopy is easy to swing back and up, giving good access to the seats and the load space behind. The unusual but remarkably comfortable seats, moulded into the structure of the cockpit, give a stylish uncluttered appearance. Most importantly, their design eliminates any possibility of loose items becoming lost down the sides or underneath the seats.

With the single exception of the flap lever operating slot, which is well protected by stiff nylon brushes, the cockpit interior is completely sealed, making it impossible for even a small foreign object to migrate from the cockpit into the works. Once seated there is ample elbow room and the five point safety harness provides excellent restraint for negative g manoeuvres, as well as preventing any possibility of the lap straps riding up and allowing the occupant to slide forward underneath them in the crash case. Given the fixed seats, the position and travel of the control columns is important. The short stubby sticks are far enough back for the shortest arms and also do not obstruct the view of the panel. The relatively small stick travel at full deflection accommodates even a large occupant without body fouls, while the rudder pedals are easy to adjust for leg length. Finally, the view is good, helped by the one-piece windscreen and a well chosen coaming line. All this adds up to my idea of a good training cockpit. Given such sound basics, the detailed layout of instruments, switches and avionic equipment is never a problem. Because the cockpit was unchanged in the demonstrator, I flew from the left seat to have the instruments in front of me. However in USAF EFS service the student would sit on the right and the T-67M panel layout would be changed accordingly.

T-67M – a tidy cockpit

We were parked on softish long grass at virtually sea level Goodwood so, once ready to taxi, I let the parking brake off and gave the throttle an exploratory prod. The aircraft moved off instantly as if on the hard. Right from that moment and throughout the flight, I was continually impressed by the rapid thrust response that one got to throttle up or down. The six cylinder engine was noticeably smoother than the difficult to balance four cylinder types and the overall impression was of a free revving powerplant that 'whirred' rather than 'roared and shook' when asked for high power.

Since my aim for the sortie was to assess the aircraft against the USAF EFS role when operating from Colorado Springs on a hot day, my first objective was to go to 6,500 ft and establish the full throttle level airspeed at that height. I then intended to fly this speed, minus a few knots to allow for a hot day, later on down at sea level. Naturally this same speed would need less throttle at low level and that power setting would become my 'full throttle' when flying the sea level Goodwood circuit. Not very scientific perhaps but a lot better than just guessing.

Nevertheless, a full power sea level takeoff and climb was clearly the fun way to start the flight. I asked Norrie for a suitable rotate speed: "I don't bother with one. Raise the nose when the elevators work and fly it off. Climb at 90," was his reply. Remembering the response to my initial pre-taxi throttle prod and conscious of the two other aircraft sharing the small run-up area for runway 06, I said, "Can I check full power on the brakes?" Norrie said no. I tried again – "Brakes not strong enough?" "The wheels will slide on the grass." I got the message.

We took off using mid flap into 5-10 kt of wind that was 20° from the right with 22 gal of fuel. Sea level pressure was 1,037 mb and the temp 7°C. By the time I noticed the rpm were 2,650 and the manifold pressure was 28 in, the airspeed was passing 45 kt, the half back stick was raising the nose and we left the ground at some 55 kt accelerating fast. I put the flap in and noticed we had reached the climb speed of 90 kt despite having the nose up about 25°. The ground roll was just long enough to realise that there had been a need to use right foot to keep straight. Say about 100 metres.

Despite some turns and a while without the ball in the middle, we levelled off at 6,500 ft on 1,013 mb (nearly 7,000 ft of climb) just 4 min from brakes off. The max level speed at this height was 136 kt IAS and the engine showed 2,700 rpm and 22.5 in. Throttling back to 21.5 in slowed us 1 kt.

Stalling came next. Throttle closed in level flight, the stall warning system, operated by a standard stagnation point sensing leading edge vane, buzzed and flashed at 61 kt. By 58 kt there was some light airframe buffet and by 54 kt this was more marked especially through the stick which was by then vibrating well. At this point the nose dropped a few degrees. These numbers seemed very repeatable and if the stick was held back as the nose dropped it would eventually rise again. This led to a gentle descent with the aircraft nodding in pitch. The ailerons worked throughout. At a nominal 5 kt above the stall and with the warning going steadily, I tried vigorous cyclic applications of about half control in all axes. There was no tendency for the aircraft to take charge and depart, even with bank reversals up to 30°.

With mid flap, the warning operated at 58 kt, the stick was buffeting well by 52 kt and there was either a nose drop or sometimes a slight left wing drop at 50 kt. Aileron could be used to raise a dropped wing without causing autorotation. With full flap the behaviour was unchanged, the warner started at 55 kt, the stick buffet was marked by 50 kt and the stall was at 45 kt. Trying to stall in turns at 80 kt and with medium power resulted in the warning starting quite soon. If this was ignored, full back stick was reached with the aircraft buffeting. Holding it like that for some time eventually resulted in small amplitude pitch nodding with a little lateral and directional unsteadiness. The higher the power the more likely the aircraft was to sit happily at full back stick. All very benign.

At 6,500 ft attempting a simulation of a takeoff, I applied full power from just above the stall with mid flap set. Up we went in a climbing turn at 45° bank, with 65 kt and 900 ft/min rate of climb. Repeating the simulated takeoff and climbing to 10,000 ft took 3 min 50 sec and gave an initial rate of climb of 1,200 ft/min. Clearly there was no shortage of performance there.

With 10,000 ft being '3,500 ft' above ground so far as Colorado Springs was concerned it was time to try some aerobatics. My first loop starting from level at 130 kt was a bit slow over the top but still went round. "Pull harder at the start," said someone. That I did and it went round inside 1,000 ft without losing height and came out at the original entry speed. I slowed down to 110 kt for a slow roll, failed to get the nose high enough inverted and threw it away, finishing up going downhill at 30°. Rolling erect, pulling the nose up and opening the throttle produced an astonishing burst of eager climb straight back to where we had started. Instructors would love that. My next attempt turned out much better.

Barrel rolls were happily carried out at 1.75 g. My first try at a stall turn was made starting at 110 kt and putting in the rudder at 50 kt. It went round quite well enough not to warrant a repeat.

At this point I needed to change my knee pad roll and asked the patient Norrie to take it for a minute while I fiddled in my ankle pocket. With my head down I noticed out of the corner of my eye that the accelerometer was indicating a steady 2g and the sunlight in the cockpit was coming and going. That is what happens when somebody does continuous barrel rolls. Since I knew that Norrie had just celebrated 50 years of professional flying, I don't imagine he did it for the practice.

The refuelled knee pad said a four turn spin using a standard entry and recovery was next. Idle power, 55 kt, stick hard back and full left rudder gave a smooth rolling entry with the nose fully down to the spinning attitude at the end of turn one. Holding the spin entry controls for a further three turns required only a moderate force. No oscillatory tendencies were apparent and it took about 2 to 2.5 secs per turn. Recovery was started by steadily pushing on right rudder to the stop and then easing the stick forward. The nose went lower, the rate speeded up and then it stopped rotating after about another 1½ turns. All classic textbook stuff.

Repeating the spin recovery with a less leisurely application of opposite rudder and stick forward produced a recovery in a shorter time and hence only ¾ of a turn. Exactly as expected. One done to the right was the same. The time taken to do a full four turn spin with recovery and climb back up ready to start again was 1 min 55 sec. The aircraft was certainly not struggling at this height. Because modern operational jet aircraft handling notes usually initially recommend letting go of the controls in a spin or departure manoeuvre, I wanted to take the opportunity to try that. No joy. The ailerons always floated into the spin and no recovery seemed likely without holding on opposite rudder. This applied even when the controls were abandoned after only half of the entry turn. However, the aerodynamics and the inertia values of operational aircraft are very different, to say nothing of their irreversible self-centralising power controls.

By now thoroughly sated by the whirligig ride, I returned to 7,000 ft for a quick look at Colorado Springs low level stability and control matters. At a typical speed of 110 kt the short period pitching oscillation was dead beat and the phugoid very heavily damped. Indeed it was hard to get two noticeable cycles. The period was 38 seconds. A steady heading sideslip showed up a lightening of the rudder force needed over the last bit of pedal travel. It was not overbalanced though. Trying to stimulate the dutch roll mode with a good hefty rudder kick resulted in the most obvious reaction being a nose down pitch with sideslip. The dutch roll itself was very heavily damped, with a yaw/roll ratio a bit over unity. The period was 2.7 sec.

Only a shallow dive was needed to get to the 'red line' never exceed speed of 194 kt. Once there Norrie then pointed out that the canopy frame was not bowing, in contrast to the previous versions that produced more lift (and drag) from the canopy due to their wrap-around engine cowlings. The control forces had built up pretty quickly above 170 kt, especially the ailerons which become heavy in the end. I said, "You need to drop these aileron forces, Norrie. I can hardly move the things at this speed," to which he replied, "Sorry mate. That would let you twist the wings off." A fair comment on this sort of aircraft as it reduces the chances of a young tyro overstressing a high aspect ratio wing by vigorous rolling under high g. At the 'red line' again some good jerks with two hands on the stick showed no tendency for pilot induced oscillations to start.

Descending to low level over the sea gave a maximum level speed of 166 kt IAS. I thought this excellent but Norrie said the pitot static pressure error meant we were really going 3 kt faster. Now came the need to adjust our 'full throttle' for the hot/high case. Since the aircraft had done 136 kt at 6,500 ft, I reduced speed to 130 kt (to be on the very pessimistic side) and noted the power was 2,650 rpm and 20 in manifold pressure. For the rest of the flight this was to be treated as 'full throttle' and we joined the circuit for a full stop landing to enable a simulated hot and high takeoff to follow. On short finals an aircraft ahead decided to land rather than do a promised touch and go. ATC agreed to us doing a quick orbit on finals so I opened up to the 20 in manifold of 'full throttle'. The performance that resulted enabled me to do a slightly climbing tight turn at 45° bank, still with full flap down and just tickling the stall warning. By chance this incident had shown the clearly adequate reserves of power that this engine provided for the USAF Colorado Springs case.

After we landed we did the planned reduced power takeoff. It seemed just like any other light aircraft. We trundled along for a while and unstuck after about 400 metres of the grass strip. As we left the ground and started a non-standard climbing turn direct towards the downwind leg, Norrie pointed out that I was only using 18 in manifold rather than the planned 20 in. I apologised but said that it was plenty anyway. At that point it was necessary to recognise the needs of the other circuit users and reduce our performance to fit in. I then did a flapless touch and go using 62 kt in the latter stages (book 1.3Vs = 80 kt). It climbed out at 900 ft/min in a 45° turn at 20 in. The final landing was with full flap and a last look speed of 58 kt (book 1.3Vs = 72 kt). At all times the handling was fine with no sense of roll or pitch control fading at these deliberately too slow speeds and that excellent positive response to throttle made precise speed selection very easy, even when flapless. We had used 15 gal of fuel in 90 min.

This sort of handling and performance, combined with the all-composite low maintenance structure of the T-67 family and the reliability of the Lycoming series engines, meant Slingsby could offer a military trainer that would have to be taken seriously as a very safe, practical, economic and effective machine for the job in any part of the world. Indeed, given more moderate altitude conditions, I felt the aircraft had the performance to penetrate well into the primary syllabus for any cost conscious air force. This is probably why today the UK uses a fleet of them at Barkston Heath where they are the first rung on the ladder for students aspiring to become RAF pilots.

MiG-29, Lavi, T45A and T-67M

Well there we are then, four very different aeroplanes. However in my view each had outstanding features that made them leaders in their respective fields and that is why I chose to include them here.

Chapter 8

Display and Demonstration flying

There are many issues associated with display and demonstration flying but number one for me was pre-demo nerves and being afraid of failure. Not failure as in crashing but failure as in letting the side down by not doing as good a display as the aircraft deserved. Such nerves are far from all bad as they can be what makes you focus on the job in hand with every bit of concentration you can muster. In my case this meant I did not want to talk to anybody in the half-hour or so before getting into the cockpit. I would escape the company guests and their attendant suits and shut myself in my car near the flight line while I went over in my mind what I had to do. The ground crew probably realised what was going on as they never tried to interrupt me with idle chat, indeed I am sure some of them probably had similar concerns regarding their own vital role in thoroughly preparing the aircraft.

Several times I was lucky to get away with making serious mistakes. These varied from going to put the pin in the ejector seat after flight and finding I had not taken it out earlier through to not connecting my oxygen which, while not critical at low level, was certainly indicative of poor performance on my part to say the least. Mistakes of that type are often connected with becoming momentarily distracted. Such distractions are potential killers for everyone from experienced professionals to new PPL holders.

One day I was even dumb enough to continue a high-speed aileron roll for an extra 360° because it seemed like a good idea at the time. I can still remember the excitement in the eyes of the company photographer when he came up to me afterwards and said how much he enjoyed the display and "especially that roll!" I can also remember the look on my boss's face when he came in to my office afterwards asking me what I thought I was up to. Most of all I remember raising the nose at the end of the roll and how wide the runway looked at that point.

As well as the classic displays flown at airshows, there are overseas sales tours and demonstrations which can be very demanding when operating with minimum resources. The regulation of display flying has also changed a lot over the years. For example, when I joined Hawker Siddeley there were no height limits for any displays we chose to give

Dunsfold visitors and I can remember how aggrieved I felt when the MOD Flying Orders for Contractors introduced them.

I have given many displays at all sorts of events but what follows is just to give a flavour for some of the more memorable.

Paris

When Duncan Simpson asked me to fly the Harrier at the 1971 Paris Air Show, the world was not so accustomed to what the aircraft had to offer as it is these days so I decided to try to get away from taking off and landing on the display runway. What I wanted to do instead was a VTO from the concrete apron at the bottom of the Hawker Siddeley Aviation chalet 'garden' and then return there with a VL at the end so that our company guests would be able to see the start and end of the display from close quarters in a way that was certainly not possible with normal jet fighters.

G-VTOL at Paris

Clearly I needed to speak to the French ATC at Le Bourget and so I jumped on an airliner and knocked on the door of their senior air traffic control officer. I had made no appointment as I did not want him to have time to think. However, by the end of our meeting I felt the informal approach had been a tactical error as it appeared that he was not prepared to consider such a non-standard (and perhaps show stealing) operation. As I was about to leave, he suddenly remarked that he used to fly Hurricanes in WWII and he would be happy to agree to my suggestion if I could arrange for a Hurricane to fly at the show. Knowing that at Dunsfold we had the last Hurricane ever built, PZ865 ('The Last of the Many' now with the RAF Battle of Britain Memorial Flight), I put on my best poker face and replied that I did not know if such a thing would be possible but I would enquire on my return. I then left his office quickly before my face had a chance to split into a silly grin. Of course, he probably dined out on the story of how he got the UK to bring a Hurricane to his show just by agreeing to a Harrier VTO away from the runway. Subsequently I felt that a week in Paris where I was being paid to fly a Hurricane in the morning and a Harrier in the afternoon was one of my more enjoyable air show stints.

At the next show in 1973 I was flying our company owned two-seat Harrier G-VTOL. After one display, which was timed to allow our lunch guests a good view, I got out and hopped over the fence at the bottom of the chalet garden. Once inside the chalet, a PR man showed me to the place he had kept for me at one of the tables. On my left was an attractive young lady dressed all in black complete with a French style beret. She turned out to be a very bright avionics engineer and we had a really good conversation about the reliability issues of avionic equipment in vibratory high g fighter aircraft. This was not at all what I had come to expect in such circumstances, however, I was brought down to earth when she asked if she could fly in the Harrier. Disappointed that the conversation had returned to the air show norm, I made my usual response of smiling sweetly and remarking how nice it would be if such jollies were allowed. Then suddenly I thought back to the introductions made when I had joined the table (hot and sweaty and with half of my head still in G-VTOL) and a short conversation ensued:

"Sorry, what did you say your name was again?"
"Rona Hall."
"Sir Arnold's daughter?"
"Yes"
"Well, it's his aeroplane so if he does not mind that will be fine by me."
Our chalet was laid out with perhaps a dozen round tables and I could see Sir Arnold, Chairman of the Hawker Siddeley Group, over at the far

side hosting some senior guests. There is something about a properly used female voice that allows it to penetrate hubbub without appearing to shout so, when Rona called across to her father and asked if she could fly in the Harrier, the silence that descended was absolute. Without any hesitation and with no hint of put down in his voice, Sir Arnold said, "Don't be silly dear, the pilot would never agree." At which she replied, "He says he doesn't mind if you don't."

The Hawker Siddeley Group was a very large organisation and I worked at probably the smallest site of all so there were a lot of senior individuals in that chalet who felt they should not have been excluded from this conversation. Therefore as soon as lunch was over I came under considerable pressure to rescind my offer. However, I deflected everyone by remarking that it was clearly a matter for the chairman and they should discuss their views with him not me. Some of their concerns arose because a Swiss Air Force pilot had ejected from a Harrier at Dunsfold only a few days before and blamed the engine. Indeed the officer concerned was actually at the show and talking to anyone who would listen about the dangers of flying the Harrier. Since I also knew there was actually nothing wrong with his engine, it seemed to me that there was no better way to demonstrate faith in our product than by giving the Chairman's daughter a very public flight.

Later that afternoon I managed to have a private chat with Sir Arnold and suggested the greatest risk centred round the dual control nature of the rear cockpit combined with the fact that I did not know his daughter and so had no feel for how she might react when airborne. I pointed out that my left hand could only hold either the throttle or the nozzle lever not both at the same time and, if she grabbed the other one in fright, the result would not be pretty. His response was to hand me some large denomination French bank notes with the instruction to take her down town that evening and use the time to decide whether I thought she was up to the trip. He finished by saying he would support me whatever decision I made.

That evening I did my best to talk Rona out of the trip, using arguments from the physical discomfort side of g, to the disorientating aspects of high longitudinal acceleration and deceleration, as well as all the ejection seat issues. I went on to discuss the problems we would have if she became scared and started to grab at things in the cockpit. She said she was confident she could cope and answered all my points with quiet, well considered comments. I said I would make the decision the next morning in case she had second thoughts in the meantime. She didn't so I decided to go ahead.

The trip went fine. She was able to communicate well on the intercom and I could see her in my rear view mirror obviously relaxed and looking about her in the way people do when they are at home in an aeroplane. I therefore expanded the envelope to include some high speed work and got her to do a roll. Then I joined the circuit and demonstrated the usual VSTOL manoeuvres.

Rona Hall and G-VTOL at Paris

One sad event at the show that year was the accident to the Russian Tu-144 supersonic airliner that occurred on the last day. I had met Valezi Moltchnov, one of the pilots who was flying it that day, at the Hanover show a year earlier when I was displaying the first development Harrier and Valezi had one of the Tu-144 prototypes minus the very important canards that appeared later at Paris. He had come up to me as I was nosing around under his aircraft and finished up giving me the complete tour. We had got on like a house on fire and his English was probably better than mine. As a result, we later talked aeroplanes for several days as we wandered around the show. He was as sharp as a tack, as evidenced when I asked whether he had any hobbies and he replied, "Reading Flight and Aviation Week". However, one probably had to have lived through the height of the Cold War to appreciate just how meaningful that was coming from a Russian in 1972. One night Valezi and I went to a shooting club in Hanover with his boss, Tupolev CTP Edward Elyan and German WWII fighter ace Adolf Galland. Not surprisingly, Galland thrashed me at shooting. I would have liked a return match in a hovering vehicle but life is not always that fair.

Back to Paris 1973. On the Sunday and last day of the show, fellow Dunsfold pilot Andy Jones and I were watching the Tu-144 display with considerable interest. We had been amazed earlier in the week at how much slower the aircraft could land now it was fitted with the canards. These retractable mini wings, when extended during takeoff and landing, generated so much nose up force that on the approach the wing trailing edge control surfaces were now deflected downwards giving in effect a delta with flaps down. At Hanover, without the canards, the aircraft had been like Concorde, the HP115 and the T221 and needed the trailing edge controls to be up for the approach and landing flare. This meant these three aircraft were in effect fitted with flaps working the wrong way round and so reducing lift. The lower approach speed possible with this new 'flapped delta' allowed the Tu-144 to land on the display runway 03 and exit at the second turn-off, which was a distance of some 1,200 metres.

However, to do this their touchdown was so close to the start of the runway that Andy and I felt they were either leaning on their luck or had some form of sensor to tell them the height of the wheels. If it was just down to pilot skill and judgement, then there had to be a chance that the next arrival would be a little too soon and in the mud or a little too late in which case they would not make the turn-off. Either way it had to be worth watching!

Their display sequence included a touch and go on 03, followed by an initial steep climb then an immediate turn onto the downwind for the final landing, a manoeuvre almost amounting to a wingover given the cloud base during the week was below 2,000 ft. On the Sunday however, there was not a cloud in the sky and their initial steep climb after the touch and go was continued straight ahead to perhaps 4,000 ft. Then suddenly the aircraft violently bunted to level flight. Both Andy and I gasped at seeing such a push in that class of aircraft. As we looked at the retreating aeroplane flying away level, we had time to say to each other that it looked as if they were going home and we were going to be denied watching another full stop landing. Then down went the nose and the aircraft made as if to descend and turn back to the downwind leg. When it was about half way to the ground and having rolled left through 90°, so giving us a side view of the dive, something made me say to Andy "He's going in".

Even though it was still a long way up, that something which suggested to me that the crew had lost it was a mixture of height, unchanging steep nose down attitude and rate of descent. Suddenly the picture looked wrong. I have seen many aeroplanes come to grief at air displays and, if you are a display pilot yourself, you develop a feel for when the picture is wrong. Just as I said that to Andy, the aircraft started to pull out of the dive and for a moment we both felt it might just miss the ground but it broke up at about 1,000 ft.

My belief is that whatever caused the bunt caused the accident because I don't believe the engines could have swallowed the appalling flow into the intakes produced by that much negative alpha without surging. Some people noticed an orbiting Mirage above them as they climbed but I did not. However, if the crew had unexpectedly seen another aircraft not far above them, then the sudden push we saw would have been instinctive. If the engines did all surge, then this would have necessitated a shutdown and relight which would have required a pretty determined dive to obtain the necessary windmilling rpm. My guess is that, as they were busy trying to get some engines restarted, they suddenly saw the ground coming up and overcooked the pull, possibly due to the very nasty view of some 230 ft electricity pylons that were right across their flight path.

To finish on a very much lighter note, I had a Sea Harrier to display at Paris in 1981 and was pressed by our marketing people to carry some stereo sound recording equipment in the cockpit. It seemed there was a Japanese record company that specialised in producing records of authentic aircraft noises and they wanted to add a Harrier display to their repertoire. This went according to plan but they asked afterwards if they could take a set of cockpit photos. I pointed out to my marketing man that there was a classified control panel in the cockpit associated with carrying nuclear stores which I would need to cover before that could happen. This was done and the pictures were taken. Then some time later I was sent a copy of the final record which included an excellent booklet of very high quality cockpit photos that had no cover over the relevant panel. The eventual explanation was that the pictures they took in Paris were not of sufficient quality so, when back in Japan, they rang PR at Kingston where a helpful assistant was happy to forward them some nice professional file shots of the cockpit.

Farnborough

At the 1978 Farnborough show I was displaying the first Sea Harrier from the ski-jump and doing customer demonstration rides in the evenings with G-VTOL. During the week I was approached by one of our marketing people to fly a Mr Ma, an experienced MiG pilot in the Chinese Air Force and reputed to be deputy commander of their fighter command.

However Mr Ma did not just want a ride, he was looking to fly basic VSTOL manoeuvres himself. Mr Ma did not speak English and I did not speak Chinese. John Parker, who brought the message, was no idiot and he freely admitted that he felt it was not on but he had been told to ask me anyhow. I said I would ponder the idea in the bath that night before deciding.

The next day I said I would fly Mr Ma and let him handle the aircraft during VTOL but with two conditions. These were that the flight would not take place in the madhouse of Farnborough but at Dunsfold and that I required the marketers to rent three top class interpreters for the day. They briefly quibbled that three was too expensive and unnecessary but agreed in the end and a date was set.

I had previously flown a couple of pilots with whom I had no common language but they did not expect to handle the aircraft in the hover. Pilots are pilots the world over and waving your hands about when briefing is a pretty international language plus I could always write down the numbers associated with such a trip on a piece of paper and see that they understood those even if the interpreter had made a mistake. However, this Mr Ma trip was way beyond that sort of thing and was without even common numerals.

My plan to deal with this was that I would write down every word of a basic brief keeping it as clear and short as possible and that each of the interpreters in the room would have a copy to make their task easier. I would then go through the brief, expanding parts as necessary, with one interpreter working and the other two monitoring. If either of the monitors did not agree with the worker, they were told to put their hand up and we would do that bit again until there was agreement. After all, with one interpreter how do you ever know that *he* has properly understood *you* let alone been successful in passing on the message to the other person?

We also had to communicate in the aircraft and with no room for doubt. This still needs care even with two English speakers as it can be quite noisy during VSTOL and there is a fair amount of buffet and vibration at times, plus the view outside is far from normal for a fixed wing pilot experiencing it for the first time. Therefore I told Mr Ma that the only words to which he should respond were when I said his name. He should disregard anything else he heard, whether it was me talking on the radio or air traffic control or another aircraft. However, if he heard 'Mr Ma', he should look at me in my mirror and, when we had eye contact, I would slowly and clearly speak a message in Morse using a combination of up to four dots and dashes. For example 'Dit dit dah dit'. If he felt he had got that correctly he should nod his head but he should shake it if he was in doubt and I would repeat it.

TAKE OFF AND LANDING

. .	Vertical Take Off	*(handwritten Chinese)*
. . .	Hover	*(handwritten Chinese)*
. . . .	Vertical Landing	*(handwritten Chinese)*
. -	Short Take Off	*(handwritten Chinese)*
. - -	Slow Landing	*(handwritten Chinese)*

CONVENTIONAL FLYING

-	Turning	*(handwritten Chinese)*
- -	Rolling	*(handwritten Chinese)*
- - -	Stalling	*(handwritten Chinese)*
- .	Engine Handling	*(handwritten Chinese)*

COMBAT VECTORING

. . - -		*(handwritten Chinese)*

He had the briefed list of manoeuvres on his knee board and the instructions for carrying them out written in Chinese and I had the same list in English. I had allocated a unique set of dots and dashes to each manoeuvre. To make life easier, all wingborne manoeuvres were just a number of dashes, all engine borne cases were just dots, while partially jet borne manoeuvres used a mixture of dots and dashes as in the example above.

For each manoeuvre I would fly a demo and then shake the stick as the instruction for Mr Ma to repeat it. I would then hold my hands up to show him that he was flying the aircraft. However, when he was flying and felt the stick shake, he was to let go and give me control.

Before we got to this airborne stuff there were naturally issues about ejection, as indeed there were during the Rona Hall flight. Ask yourself how do *you* as the captain ensure that the rear seat occupant goes as soon as possible in a real emergency, but *never* ejects because of a misunderstanding? The answer is quite simple. I told them not to eject unless they saw me go, when they should follow me at once. If this seems a bit like the captain deserting the sinking ship, then I am sorry but I cannot think of a clearer and more doubt free way of communicating and getting the rear seat occupant out as quickly as possible.

In the event, the 45-minute trip went like a dream and I never flew anybody in G-VTOL where I felt more certain about what was going on in the other cockpit than I did with Mr Ma which only goes to show the value of a good pre-flight brief.

A bad idea! G-VTOL smoke system at Farnborough 1976

For 1976 John Fozard, our chief designer, decided that G-VTOL should have a smoke system fitted to the nozzles to show the crowd the nozzle angle in use at any point of the show.

Sadly it did not quite work out like that. If the aircraft had any forward speed even when the nozzles were fully down, the smoke immediately turned the corner and streamed behind the aircraft. During my first rehearsal in front of the Flying Control Committee, I had the smoke on and was doing about 200 kt when I lowered the nozzles to the vertical to decelerate to the landing pad. At this Bee Beamont remarked to the committee, "What is John doing now? It looks like an inverted run by the Flying Scotsman".

One of the most impressive people I ever had with me in G-VTOL was the broadcaster, Raymond Baxter. At Farnborough in 1974, Bill Bedford, then the Hawker Siddeley Aviation sales manager, suggested to Raymond that he should take a ride in G-VTOL. Raymond being Raymond, was very keen to do this and in due course the word filtered down through the HSA PR system and I was asked to take him along during my display.

At that time my knowledge of Raymond was limited to his Farnborough commentaries and of course seeing him on Tomorrow's World and I am afraid my initial attitude to having anybody, not just Raymond, as a passenger during my display was pretty negative. Like any fast jet display, it took the aircraft to its g limits and involved violent rolling manoeuvres which were not really passenger stuff. Then there was the little matter that the rear cockpit was designed for an instructor so it had full dual controls together with flap and undercarriage selectors that overrode those in the front cockpit. It seemed to me any one of these items, not to mention the throttle and nozzle levers, were all too handy for a passenger to grab in the heat (or perhaps cold) of the moment. Compared to a Rona Hall-type passenger ride, flying in the back during a display was a very different exercise. As if realising what was going through my mind, the PR man said, "He used to fly Spitfires during the war you know". That changed everything for me. Now I was being asked to fly a man without whose efforts, and those of so many of his generation, I would simply not have been free to live the life I did. At once the trip changed from being hazardous to something that just needed careful planning and briefing.

That evening Raymond and I met up and went to where G-VTOL was parked. I took to him instantly because for some unknown reason he treated me like a gentleman. Forty-five minutes later he had hoisted aboard the principles of how the Harrier did its VSTOL thing and we both had a clear idea of the kit he would use to record his commentary.

We then got airborne on a shake-down flight to Dunsfold so that Raymond could see for himself the manoeuvres involved and the recording equipment could be checked out. Imagine my delight when

I gave him control en-route and he did a couple of splendid twinkle rolls. The phrase 'duck to water' very much comes to mind. After a while, we reluctantly dragged our minds back to the task in hand and I flew while Raymond talked.

To hear a polished talker do his act is one thing but, to be with him at the time and know the extremely difficult circumstances in which he is finding just the right words, is to be left in awe of a consummate professional. By the time we had done a second trip to sort out a few snags in the recording system and returned to Farnborough for a run through of the actual display, we were both very happy and confident with our plan. On the day therefore, I had no concerns and just got on with my normal routine as if I was on my own.

As I did so the man in the back talked in his totally polished way throughout the display. We finished with a couple of high speed rolls followed by a 5g break in full reverse thrust where he was faced with losing 450 kt in a 180° deg turn, arriving stationary at 1,000 ft above the field, before the nose went down very steeply to set up a vertical landing on a pad.

Raymond Baxter in G-VTOL at Farnborough 1974

Raymond handled all that without turning a hair as indeed he handled so many other commentary flights. A couple which spring to mind include with Duncan Simpson in the first Hawk, again at Farnborough and when he flew with the Red Arrows.

However, what else would you expect from a 14-year-old who pretended to be 16 in order to fly as a passenger with Cobham's Flying Circus? What else would you expect from a man who flew countless low level Spitfire 16 sorties against V1 and V2 sites during the war? Quite apart from the fact that he was being shot at, aeroplanes in those days were not as well designed as they are today. Therefore they were much harder to handle. Raymond did not survive that period just on luck. He had an aviator's talent and an aviator's hands.

Four years after our initial Harrier trips together, he produced another brilliant commentary when he explained live to the audience what it was like to go up the ski-jump at the 1978 Farnborough show. Impressed though as I was with his various performances in the Harrier, for me the best airborne commentary he ever gave was during the RAF's 75th Birthday flypast over Fairford and I include it here because I can think of no better way to show how brilliant he was with words and as a mark of respect for somebody it was my privilege to know as a direct result of my flying at Farnborough.

During this birthday flypast, Raymond broadcast live from behind the pilot in the Battle of Britain Memorial Flight Lancaster as it led a formation of current RAF aircraft across the field. You will have to imagine the background sound of four Merlins as well as the strains of the Royal Air Force March which the producer mixed in behind Raymond's words. He had just less than one minute to do justice to 75 years of the Royal Air Force and he used 116 words.

"If ever there was a flying shrine to courage, you join me there now. In these confined spaces brave men fought and died.

The history of the Royal Air Force is punctuated by great names both within and without the Service. Some defied the politicians, some defied the accepted rules of technology, some defied the enemy in the face of fearful odds.

But the people who made the Royal Air Force what it was and is today are anonymous. They are the men and women who were, and still are, prepared to serve and simply go on doing the job in hand, to the best of their ability whatever the circumstances and however great the cost."

Given less than a minute, how could anybody improve on that?

São Paulo

The São Paulo Air Show held at São José dos Campos airfield in 1973 set several records so far as I was concerned. Brazil was certainly the furthest we had travelled for a one week event although, having gone that far we used the opportunity to display G-VTOL to several other countries in South America including Paraguay, Bolivia, Peru and Equador, where we spent several days at Quito which, at just under 10,000 ft above sea level, was a high altitude record for Harrier operations. At the hotel where we stayed outside São Paulo the night porter was shot in the early hours over some sort of protection dispute with the locals. My room was over the foyer so I was not in any doubt about what was going on and the blood and mess were still in evidence when we went to work the next morning. A few days earlier in Rio de Janeiro, a pedestrian had tried to cross the road outside our hotel during the morning rush and did quite well to get half way, since it was six lanes wide. The VW on top of him was abandoned until the rush was over so the later drivers had to demonstrate the sort of skill we see during an F1 start when somebody stalls near the front of the grid.

The show itself was noteworthy for two reasons: the Colonel running it and the suicide of one of the participants at the end of his slot. The good Colonel had actually attended the previous Paris show as an observer so he knew it was customary to hold a formal brief for the pilots before the flying. When this was over, one of us asked what the minimum display height was and he replied, "Above ground level". When questioned as to exactly what he meant by this he looked somewhat pained and said, "Don't hit the ground". After the brief, a few of us Europeans decided we would use 50 ft and so what if everybody else flew lower than us. The suicide happened on the Saturday when a participant flying a Decathlon for a ten minute slot failed to land on time and proceeded to fly up and down the runway doing rolls that became lower and lower. Since it was obvious what would happen if nobody shot him down first, I told our team I intended to retire inside our chalet until it was all over. Ten minutes later I saw a wing fly past one of the skylights so went back out to join my team.

G-VTOL and the Christo in Rio

One day we were scheduled to fly a demonstration from the Brazilian aircraft carrier, Minas Gerais, so were given a time and position for the rendezvous plus a radio frequency. Since I was no longer a beginner when it came to finding ships, I told the ground crew to add a pair of 100 gal tanks and fill everything up, even though the position was only 80 miles or so off the coast. Off we went and, when we got to the appointed place, sure enough there was no ship in sight, let alone an aircraft carrier.

After 30 minutes of square search, I returned overhead our airfield to check my navigation then went back to the rendezvous. There was still no ship and no answer on the radio. Then I had a sudden brainwave and went to the ship's home port. Lo and behold, there she was, tied up against the wall. Actually I was quite pleased because John Glasscock, our Director and General Manager, was on board for the demonstration and it was nice for him to see first hand how these sort of overseas tours were not actually all sun and sand at the company's expense. Later it turned out they had decided to slip the voyage for three days but had forgotten to tell us. Overall the trip took 1hr 25 min which is why I wanted the tanks fitted.

In one of the other countries I complained to a British embassy official that the locals seemed to have a sort of mañana mentality. He looked thoughtful for a while and replied that he did not think they had a word which indicated quite that sense of urgency. South America is not the same as the UK.

Indian Navy

I was particularly frightened and my colleague, Robbie Roberts, had realised it. It was 1972 we were trying to get on board the Indian Navy aircraft carrier, Vikrant. The weather was not too bad as there was no cloud but the visibility at low level was decidedly murky, only about a mile in a humid sub-tropical haze over the sea.

As I was always pointing out in those days, you can slow down when coming in to land in a Harrier and poor visibility is nothing like the problem that it is for the pilot of a conventional fast jet. Alas, Robbie and I were not in a Harrier but in an Indian taxi, being driven at high speed through the narrow streets of Bombay's dockland in a way that defied belief. Robbie, who was then one of the Kingston sales team, had been an observer in the RN Fleet Air Arm and a former Gannet squadron commander so his help was always invaluable when I was checking out a new ship.

Once aboard we were quickly engrossed in the details of planning the first Harrier operations, which were to take place eight weeks later. A meeting was held with the ship's officers and the engineering, administrative and flying control aspects were quickly dealt with. All that remained was a period on the flight deck to decide what markings I wanted them to paint.

We settled for a centre-line 2 ft wide down the length of the axial deck, a white line across the bows of the ship for the 'nozzles down' indication and a dotted line down the starboard side of the deck, parallel with the centre-line. This last one being a 'wingtip safety line' behind which all other parked aircraft, men and equipment would be positioned while a short takeoff was in progress.

The Harrier to be used was Hawker's two-seat demonstrator G-VTOL, now fitted with a Rolls-Royce Pegasus 11, the definitive 21,500 lb. thrust engine, specified for incorporation in the RAF and US Marine

221

Corps Harriers then on order. It was the first time that the longer and 1,500 lb heavier two-seater had been taken to a ship. As a result, Robbie and I had been at some pains to point out that we had only estimates of our performance from Vikrant. This meant that it would require cautious test flying, rather than a simple sales demonstration, if we were to establish what weights we could lift from what deck runs in the hot monsoon conditions expected off the Indian coast in July.

Later the ferry flight to India was uneventful, the route being Dunsfold, Naples, Akrotiri, Tehran, Kuwait, Masirah, Bombay. The ground crew followed along each leg in a Hawker Siddeley 748. In Bombay the team met up with the monsoons, an intensity of rainfall that someone used to shopping in Woking cannot be expected to comprehend. Sufficient to say that, although the Harrier arrived at Bombay only 20 minutes late on plans laid two months earlier, we were a day late arriving at Cochin, the Indian Navy base on the south-west tip of India.

This meant Capt R H Tahiliani, the Director, Air Staff Division, Indian Navy, who was one of those to fly in the rear seat, only had one day for work-up flying from the airfield prior to going on board Vikrant. Since the Captain had not previously flown the Harrier, it meant that he had to train very intensively to reach the standard necessary for him to control the aircraft himself in the confined environment of the deck. The morning of the first day allocated to the ship dawned hot and humid but fine and the short flight out to the ship with a vertical landing on the stern was completely straightforward.

As he climbed down to the deck, Capt Tahiliani remarked that he had been the first Indian Navy officer to land a Sea Hawk, the ship's current equipment, on Vikrant so he was particularly pleased to take part in the first landing of the Sea Hawk's potential replacement. Due to the test flying aspects of the initial takeoffs, it had been agreed that I would fly the aircraft solo for the first day and Capt Tahiliani and two other officers would join in on the second day.

Examination of the deck markings showed that they had been painted just where I had asked but unfortunately the 2 ft wide centre-line, down which the Harrier would run, was painted in high-gloss paint which was very slippery indeed in the wet. Since the Harrier is controlled directionally by nosewheel steering during the takeoff run, it was clear I would have to run slightly to one side of this line.

This caused some concern because close to the bow was a large mass of steel in the form of a catapult shuttle (or hook) which was jammed in its track and could not be moved. This obstacle was only 8 ft from the left outrigger wheel when the nosewheel tyre was just clear of the left hand side of the Harrier line. Running to the right of the line would have taken the wingtip uncomfortably close to the parked aircraft. However, there happened to be an additional line already painted on the deck 7 ft to the left of the Harrier line and parallel with it so it appeared that all would be well if I kept myself between those two lines.

G-VTOL landing on Vikrant

This was how the matter was left and, after a short period of taxying round the deck to familiarise the deck handlers with the Harrier, I was all set for the first takeoff. This was done at a light weight down the full length of the 660 ft deck. The technique used for the first takeoff worked well and was retained in principle throughout the two days.

It consisted of free taxying the Harrier into position at the start of the run, running up to 55% rpm with the brakes on and the nozzles pointing aft. On being given clearance to takeoff, the brakes were released, full throttle applied and the left hand moved from the throttle to the nozzle lever as the run began. The aircraft was steered via the nosewheel using the rudder bar and then finally, when the white line across the end of the deck reached the bottom of the windscreen, the nozzles were lowered to the desired angle of 50° using a preset stop. There followed a short period off the end of the deck when I reflected how lucky naval aviators are that they do not have to climb over anything after takeoff and then it was time to jettison fuel and return for a landing on board.

A second sortie was made at the same light weight to allow me to feel certain I had got used to the technique and then the ground crew started increasing the weight by putting more fuel into the Harrier.

The third takeoff was done with full internal fuel and the fourth through to the eighth were also at full internal fuel but the distance of the starting point from the front end of the deck was reduced to as little as 370 ft.

Whether you use a free run or a catapult to get airborne from a ship, maximum performance in terms of weight or deck run depends on how much sink off the bow you are happy to accept before climbing away. I was used to the RN standard of a 15 ft sink and needed to establish the weight, run and wind conditions that gave this, hence the progressive reduction in run at constant weight. The remaining takeoffs on the first day were made with the Harrier as heavy as we could make it by filling the external 100 gal drop tanks and gradually reducing the run again. Eventually we got the distance down from 660 ft to 585 ft, still at the maximum weight.

All the flights took the same form with a takeoff performance test, then a fuel dump to a vertical landing on the stern, followed by a vertical takeoff into an acceleration round the circuit and another vertical landing. On the eleventh flight, the aircraft was landed back at Cochin for the night with the whole Hawker Siddeley and Rolls-Royce team, as well as our Indian hosts, well pleased with the day's activities.

On a personal note, I chose to stay strapped in all day with drinks and sandwiches being handed up as required during the turn-rounds. This surprised some but, as any pilot will realise, I was thus able to stay focused on the job in hand without the distraction that would have been inevitable had I got out and started talking with the visiting brass between launches. The blazing sun ensured I sweated out any need for a comfort break. Indeed the seat harness at the end of the day was soaked through with sweat. What we can do when young and enthusiastic!

On the second day, with confidence in the available performance, I was more relaxed and sociable and Capt Tahiliani flew in the rear cockpit for the first six flights. Despite his inexperience in the aeroplane and the fact that he was currently employed in a senior staff post, he had no difficulty in taking control of the Harrier outside the hangar at Cochin and twenty minutes later flying entirely unaided into a hover astern of the ship.

This, of course, was one of the main reasons why the company chose a two-seater for the demonstrator. We used to say that the Harrier could be flown by any pilot trained on modern military jets but back then people still tended to doubt us until they tried it for themselves. By the end of his six flights on the second day, Tahiliani had flown a takeoff on the full length of the axial deck and had accompanied me on the first angled deck takeoff using the short (317 ft) angled deck run. In addition, I demonstrated a cross deck vertical landing just aft of the island to show the technique used if the ship is not steaming into wind.

Then the Commander (Air) of Vikrant, Cdr Grewal, a Sea Hawk and helicopter pilot, found himself delighted with the Harrier and carried out a decelerating transition to a hover alongside the ship, followed by an accelerating transition back to wingborne flight with no assistance from me other than the odd word of encouragement.

The three remaining flights that day were with Sea Hawk squadron commander, Cdr Raju, in the second seat. On these flights we covered a vertical takeoff from the bow of the ship and a medium weight 310 ft deck run STO. This particular takeoff allowed those on the bridge and in flying control the novel experience of looking down into the cockpit of a modern aeroplane about to do a free takeoff from a starting point over half way down the deck. This resulted in many "I just don't believe it" type comments.

Having filmed our sorties, the conclusion of our Indian hosts was that the aircraft needed a total operating strip no wider than 32.5 ft. Later I talked them into allowing an extra 6 ft making 38.5 ft overall. Watchers of HMS Invincible class ships will have noticed the 'tramlines' painted

225

on the deck which resulted from this Indian experience. I realised on Vikrant that it was very nice to have your left and right limits shown so clearly when accelerating in a confined space. The problem with a single centre line is that, as soon as you wander away from it, you have no option but to steer back. This tends to make you weave and overcorrect while tramlines on the other hand allow you to relax because you can see that you are doing well enough.

During the two day exercise G-VTOL flew 21 sorties in an ambient temperature of 30° C and demonstrated the validity of our tropical brochure performance figures. The exercise also showed what could be done with minimum support away from base and that the Harrier could be handled by existing military jet pilots with very little special training.

I lost half a stone and was tired for a week afterwards but that's show business. Talking of which, the first Indian Navy Sea Harrier was the last Harrier I ever flew at the Farnborough Air Show. That was in 1982, ten years after the Vikrant trials.

Spanish Navy

One day the phone rang in my office at Dunsfold and on the other end was the leading UK spy pilot of the Cold War period who wanted to know if I would help him with a plan he was hatching. It was 1972 and I had no hesitation in saying yes.

To understand my keenness to help, you need to know that the voice belonged to Sqn Ldr John Crampton DFC AFC and Bar RAF (Rtd) then Kingston's Technical Sales Manager for the Harrier. On no fewer than three occasions in the early 1950s John had been the CO of an RAF Special Duties flight charged with deep penetration flights over the Soviet Union, flights desperately needed to obtain radar pictures of key targets for subsequent use by western bomb aimers in the event of WWIII.

The flight was equipped for this job with three USAF RB-45C four jet reconnaissance aircraft plus a spare that was never needed. At that time US politicians were unhappy at the thought of the mayhem that could follow the shooting down of any normal USAF aircraft flying uninvited over the USSR. Enter John and his team, plus a lot of mystified RAF airmen using gallons of paint stripper to remove all markings from some

US aircraft in an empty West Raynham hangar. Naturally the detailed account of those trips would be much more interesting to you than any Harrier story of mine, but that is a tale that should be told only by the man himself.

It is interesting to look back on how John's colleagues regarded him in the early 1970s. I don't think many had any appreciation of his secret past. Some knew that he had been the CO of the RAF's first Canberra squadron, in itself no minor thing to have on one's CV, but small beer compared to the responsibility of executing the overflight missions. So how do you stop colleagues picking up clues about your past exploits as a spy pilot? Well, all you need to be is a two metre tall ex-Harrovian with a natural conversational manner suited to playing the lead in a social farce in a London theatre. In short the sort of bloke who makes Hugh Grant seem like a builder's labourer. One of our best operational pilots? Him? Great cover.

However, make no mistake, John Crampton sold the Harrier to the Spanish Navy. In doing this he was helped by a Spanish friend with great contacts at the top of that service but he most certainly did not have any help from John Glasscock, the Director and General Manager of Kingston and Dunsfold and his boss. Indeed, that worthy gentleman, when presented with John's original plan, refused to even pay for his air fare to Madrid, causing John to hitch a lift in an HS 125 biz jet that was going out from Hatfield. This lack of help from his boss was actually perfectly reasonable because at the time our Government had broken off diplomatic relations with the Spanish Government over Gibraltar.

There was also the major problem that a Spanish Act of Parliament explicitly prohibited their Navy from operating fixed wing aircraft as this was deemed to be the job of the Air Force. Overall, the idea of a Harrier deal with the Spanish Navy was just not sensible. But then, neither was flying all over the USSR at .65M and 35,000 ft twenty years earlier and as we know John had cracked that, hence my desire to help him.

What follows concerns the flying that I did from the Spanish Navy aircraft carrier, Dédalo. It is worth recounting because it did not go entirely as hoped and is also a good example of how we went about things over 30 years ago. In those days at Kingston and Dunsfold, significant enterprises were planned and executed by very small numbers of people. 'Meetings' were a rarity, diplomatic clearance for overseas flights was left to the salesman involved and if anything looked a bit of a grey area then the salesman, plus me and the crew chief, would come to a decision. We did not go bothering anybody else. After all, between us we knew about the distant country plus what was involved in servicing and flying aeroplanes away from base (which by and large we reckoned our bosses did not) so we made our own minds up about whether something was sensible.

The Dédalo, which started life in 1943 as the USS escort carrier Cabot, had an unobstructed flight deck of wooden planks plus a small 'island' on the starboard side. In 1972, thanks to that Act of Parliament previously mentioned, she only flew helicopters. With the help of John Crampton's Spanish contact, we made a visit to the ship while she was in harbour for a refit. I had with me another member of the sales team, Robbie Roberts from the Vikrant story. It sounds an awful thing to say but before that visit I felt that a Spanish ship was unlikely to provide the professional standards of the RN and USN to which I was accustomed, so I was keen to have Robbie's view. I was especially thinking of ATC, fire fighting, flight deck handling and refuelling issues.

I could not have been more wrong. As we left the ship, Robbie grinned at me and said, "Better than some of our steamers, eh?" I remember shaking my head in slightly stunned agreement. Accordingly a few months later I took off from Dunsfold in a Harrier GR1A, XV770, rented from the MOD and fitted with a few extra bits to make it compatible with shipboard ops.

These extras were such mundane things as tie down lugs on all four undercarriage legs and a minor electrical modification that gave permanent nosewheel steering whenever you turned off the anti-skid switch. The only way to directionally control the ordinary Harrier on the ground was to engage a nosewheel steering button on the stick and then steer the nosewheel with the rudder bar. Since there was no differential braking as a backup for steering, it was only sensible to have a second electrical circuit to engage steering when operating within the confines of a flight deck.

With the Dédalo cruising somewhere off the east coast of Spain, the flight was a fair old jaunt from Dunsfold so I had asked the hangar to fit a couple of 330 gal ferry tanks to give me plenty of reserves should a game of hunt the ship become necessary. As I mentioned earlier, this had happened to me before, so I had learned the hard way to include such an eventuality in my fuel sums. After a dull high level flog across France,

I coasted out again and in due course started my let down. Once I got below cloud, there she was, exactly where she said she would be and pressing on in a calm sea. She even answered my radio call at once on the briefed frequency, completing a truly class act. After burning off some of the remaining fuel with a few passes at a little above normal helicopter speeds, I was welcomed aboard following a simple vertical landing on the stern.

Arriving on Dédalo

Robbie marshalled me to a suitable tie down spot and I began to feel we had done the right thing in coming after all. Mark you, only a few days earlier I had doubts anew when my favourite spy pilot mentioned that, as the Spanish Navy was intending to buy a warplane for their ship, they had said that they expected us to bring guns and ammo and demonstrate blowing their splash target out of the water.

The next day the weather was forecast to close in so we lost no time in flying three sorties, culminating in a gun attack on the splash target. Gun, not guns, as one of the two 30 mm Adens did not fire. Sadly the armourer Dunsfold had sent to the ship had been chosen by the unions on a 'buggin's turn' basis, rather than because he was the sharpest firing pin in the armoury. As a result, he cocked one gun with an air bottle that had insufficient pressure which left that gun half cocked. Nevertheless the rounds the other gun sent into the splash seemed to satisfy the onlookers.

Time then for the end of demo debrief while the crew put the tanks on for the trip back home. Judging by the drizzle that was just starting, plus the lowering cloud base, the sooner I set off north the better the end of my day would be.

On Dédalo. John Crampton is fourth from the right

First there were a large number of Admirals and assorted staff who wanted to ask questions. Crampton had made it very clear beforehand that, should we get any questions on the conversion of Spanish helicopter pilots to the Harrier, I should explain how simple that would be. Accordingly, when the very first question was on that topic, John naturally remarked that his colleague, Mr Farley, was the right man to answer. I looked at the Admiral and said that, while a 600 hour Sea King pilot (the typical Spanish Navy pilot at that time) would have no difficulty in coping with Harrier systems, I did not consider it would be safe for him to fly it without some prior fixed wing training. Our spy pilot went white. Naturally the Admiral followed with, "What sort of training would that be, Mr Farley?" Since at that time the Spanish were allowing the US to fly nuclear armed alert bombers from a Spanish base, I figured they had the odd connection with the States, so I suggested they should send their pilots to the USN to do the courses necessary to join an A4 Squadron, less the carrier landing qualification, after which I would be happy to check them out in the Harrier.

Departing back to Dunsfold

After a few additional minor questions, I was allowed to launch for Dunsfold. I entered the cloud at 300 ft with a light going home heart and started to climb. That feeling changed at 5,000 ft in solid cloud when a major electrical failure killed my HUD and some head down instruments plus the inertial navigation system and both radios. Left with only a standby artificial horizon and E2 compass, there was clearly no way I could navigate, overfly France or return to the boat. My only chance was to get below the weather while I was still over the sea and then try and fly visually to a coast. I did not enjoy the last bit of that let down nor the next 25 minutes low flying over the water in very poor visibility. Flying at 300 kt seemed too quick so I eased to 260 but any slower and I knew I would not be able to manoeuvre if anything suddenly appeared out of the murk. Left of north were the hills of the eastern Spanish coast while right of north was the Marseilles air traffic control zone.

As was usual when I took off from a ship in the middle of nowhere, my head had no real idea of where I had started from or exactly where the climb and descent had taken me so I stuck with north on the E2 and put my eyeballs on the windscreen. Suddenly there was a coast. I pulled out a topo of the south of France (was I glad I had brought that, although nobody could see the point when I had ordered it a couple of weeks before) and tried to guess whether Istres needed me to go left or right along the coast before going north. I guessed correctly and a few minutes later saw a runway threshold appear out of the murk.

I threw the gear and flaps down then two things then happened at once. To my right I saw the leader of a pair of Mirages who were just about to enter the runway slam on his brakes as I passed his nose, while my own nose started going up and up against full forward stick. In my state of twitch I had completely forgotten I was carrying those ferry tanks and had started a max rate deceleration with the nozzles forward of the vertical in the braking stop. This was banned with ferry tanks because you could not contain the resulting nose up trim change. It pitched up a long way, probably 30° or more and I remember thinking, "Hover it," so I opened the throttle and was rewarded with the plastic bumper on the bottom of the underfin stroking very gently on to the runway, followed by the nose coming down and eventually the main wheels making contact, then the nosewheel. What that Mirage pilot thought of my tail-first touchdown and mega stop I have no idea, I never met him.

The next day my Dédalo crew were diverted to fix me and I went home. I never mentioned the full pod of ammo and the one up the spout to the people at Istres. Careless talk can complicate things. Back at Dunsfold a week or two later, we learned that the US wanted us to supply an extra batch of aircraft to the USMC so they could let the Spanish navy have them. We also learned, that when the Admiral asked me that training question, he did so knowing they had provisionally booked slots for their pilots in the USN fixed wing system. As a test pilot it pays to tell the truth and to always carry a topo.

French Navy

During 1973 our marketing men were asked if we would let two French Navy pilots fly G-VTOL from their carrier Foch at night. I never expected any sales were likely to result from this exercise but the company decided to go ahead anyhow. The experience was notable for me in that it included a night recovery to the ship in extremely bad weather, possibly the worst I have known, together with a daytime operation where there was such extreme ship motion that there was a moment after landing when it looked as if G-VTOL was destined to slide over the side.

A night of visual circuit bashing with the French pilots had gone well and, after landing on the final sortie, I looked at the fuel and said that we had enough for one more VTO and quick circuit providing we turned in at 3 nm instead of the radar vectored 5 nm visual approaches that we had been doing. We launched and turned downwind but the ship had vanished. I looked up at the canopy and saw moisture streaming on the outside. Realising we had probably gone into cloud, I took control and nipped down to 400 ft but could still not see anything. At that point Don Riches, another Dunsfold pilot who was on the ship to give me a hand, came up on the radio and said they seemed to have steamed into a bank of low stratus. I asked how low and he said he could not see the masthead lights. G-VTOL was not the aircraft for this situation as it had no HUD, no radio altimeter and no autostabs. I took control, told my (now) passenger to let me know at once if I went below 200 ft and set about doing a slow stepped down approach.

I was creeping down at 60 kt at about 250 ft steering 278° when the radar man said, "1 mile go right 2 degrees steer 276". I distinctly remember saying to myself, "Oh no! Don't do that to me – not now". Which did he mean? Go right 2° to 280° or go left 2° to 276°. I decided to go for the number rather than the direction, inched left and levelled at about 100 ft. Suddenly, just ahead, the ship loomed out of the black so I hit the braking stop and we came to a halt just astern.

After landing with a really silly fuel state, I shut down, put the pins in, opened the canopy, stood up on my seat and turned to give the rear occupant the biggest bollocking of his service career for not saying we had gone below 200 ft. Then I saw the look on his face and let him off.

Because we had been training with the French pilots, I had wanted to set everything up in my favour so I had asked the ship to behave as if they were at conventional flying stations. This meant that they steamed steadily into wind and as a result they had seen nothing of the Harrier's potential for more flexible operations when flown by a fully trained pilot. When I was saying goodbye to the Captain the next morning, I apologised for this and asked if he would like me to demonstrate what a trained pilot could do. For example, would he like me to get airborne and have him try and stop me land on his ship.

I can still see the Gallic grin that spread across his face.

We were in the Bay of Biscay and there was a good blow with quite a swell. I got airborne, turned downwind and watched the ship with some interest as it turned across the swell, threw out the anchor and wallowed crosswind plus started to pour thick smoke over the flight deck. In other words, he did everything that conventional arrested aircraft cannot handle. In particular, conventional pilots do not like any smoke obscuring their view of the deck when they are on final approach. Harrier pilots on the other hand, love smoke because it shows them where the hot air from the funnel is going so they can avoid it entering their intakes and losing them thrust.

By the end of my second orbit the situation had stabilised, the ship was rolling nicely, the smoke was over the middle and aft part of the deck but the bow was completely clear. I elected to land into wind across the deck up by the bow. This I did, timing my final descent to hit when the deck was roughly level. As I chopped the throttle and put the brakes on, I was feeling quite pleased with myself. Suddenly the whole situation changed as the ship rolled to port and I started to slide backwards so it required a quick burst of power with the nozzles aft to stop it. Then equally suddenly, as the roll went the other way, I was sliding forward and grabbing for reverse thrust while French navy deck-handlers rushed at me with chocks and chains to lash me down. However, thanks to their brave services, I was spared the embarrassment of telling Mr Glasscock that his aeroplane was at the bottom of the sea.

Dunsfold

Many private demonstrations of VSTOL manoeuvres were flown for visitors at Dunsfold and they were very much part of the day to day operations throughout the Harrier programme. In the early days 'pop' surges as they were called were not that uncommon. These were by nature very transient events and the picture below is the only one I have ever seen. It is a print from a 16 mm film of the demo and only one frame had the surge. It happened about a foot up after a VTO from the taxiway. The symptoms in the cockpit are a loud bang and the feeling of a big thump through the airframe.

Pop surge during taxiway VTO at Dunsfold

Spitfire

During the 1991 Air Show season, I was privileged to fly the Old Flying Machine Company Spitfire IX MH434 for 18 trips. Mark Hanna briefed me and without exaggeration I can say it was the best pilot-to-pilot brief I have ever had. Therefore I knew what I had to do but at the same time I was extremely concerned in case I bent it. It was eight years since I had stopped flying professionally and during that time my limited flying had been mainly in a few light aircraft. This was hardly a level of currency to make you feel confident when tackling a National Treasure.

My concern not to bend the thing dominated my thoughts until I passed over the Duxford hangars after my first takeoff. Until then all I was thinking about was executing the brief leaving no mental horsepower to appreciate or enjoy the trip. The takeoff was all about what you would expect – no forward view, keeping straight, power on gently, making sure you kept the power back within the conservative limits set, keeping straight, raising the tail very carefully and not beyond a slightly tail low attitude in order to keep the prop from hitting the ground on bumpy grass. Did I mention keeping straight? After unstick there was an instant need to change hands to get the gear up using a combined gear and flap hydraulic selector gate on the right, the operation of which was anything but instinctive.

Then, over the hangars, I looked out sideways and saw the wing. That may seem a strange comment to make but these days you are so often sitting out in front of whatever you are flying and so cannot see the airframe. Anyhow, there was the wing, at which point it actually sunk in that I was flying a Spitfire. I shouted out loud "Yes," and then felt a right idiot a moment later for such un-cool behaviour.

A few minutes earlier, when walking out to the aircraft, I had passed Ray Hanna and he had mentioned that he didn't want to see me doing any straight in approaches at airshows. He wanted a nice turning final until the flare, otherwise I could expect my cards. I said something on the lines of "We will have to see about that" and got on with thinking about the trip.

Little did I realise the significance of what Ray had said until I came in to land. In handling terms, this frightening monster had become a pussycat on finals. By that I mean it was light on the controls, with excellent response about all axes and it flew really slowly as well. In plain English, it was a light and floating aeroplane, not a lead sled. The end result was a feeling that the Spitfire was aerodynamically totally happy and not going to bite you. Of course you could see absolutely zero out of the front but that was easily fixed by doing a turning final.

Suddenly it all became clear – all those wartime movie shots of tight turning finals, with wings levelled only in the flare, was not a bunch of aces showing off at all (as I had previously thought) but the natural and easy way for anyone to land a Spit. It helps that the aircraft is quite clean, even gear and flap down, so it needs only a trickle of power as you approach the flare. This of course means there is not much change in the lift or control circumstances in the flare when you eventually ease off the last bit of throttle.

Some modern pilots who are used to fully powered controls might be a little surprised at the muscle needed to get manoeuvrability at higher speeds but that is manual controls for you. Flying display manoeuvres with a restricted boost setting required you to be gentle and flowing or you could easily finish up slow and in the buffet, going nowhere and needing quite a while to build up energy again. I am however quite sure that with a boost of +12 or more, it would have been an altogether different aeroplane.

However, regardless of the power available, one thing would not have changed, namely given the slightest touch of less than zero g, the engine would cut. I understand the injected Me109 was naturally a much better bet in that regard. Having the freedom to push to evade must have been important. Needing to roll and pull in order to get the nose down quickly would take a lot longer, perhaps too long.

I have not mentioned what it is like to sit a few feet behind a Merlin that is firing up, idling, at high power or whatever because I am just not good enough with words to do that experience justice.

John Farley and the OFMC Spitfire IX returning from Belgium

The worst aspect of operating the Spitfire was dealing with engine temperatures on the ground. It naturally had to be warmed up before doing the power checks but then you only had a minute or two before you either had to get airborne and avail yourself of some ram flow through the radiators or shut down again.

The best aspect was its exquisite lateral control at touchdown. The finest I have ever experienced.

Annexe

Over a quarter of a century ago a Royal Navy Sea Harrier display pilot asked me how I flew steep climbs after a VTO. The following is what I sent him. It is important to remember this was written in the days when Harriers all had 201 sq ft metal wing and simple flap systems as well as hydro mechanical engine fuel systems. These notes would need modifying for use with a 230 sq ft carbon fibre wing aircraft.

Steep climbs from a VTO

Crowd safety

For maximum crowd safety the climb should be carried out on the B axis going away from the display line. This is also good from the display point of view because the manoeuvre looks best when viewed from behind, as it is not obvious then whether the aircraft is pointing say 70 or 80° nose up. Plan views are also generally more spectacular, interesting and unusual compared to side views. The bad news is that fixing the climb track means living with any cross or tail wind – see later.

Performance

In theory, providing the aircraft has the performance to hover clear of ground effect for 30-40 seconds (out of wind as needed for the climb track) without running out of water or reaching the dry limiter, it is clearly *possible* to rotate the fuselage 60° nose up from the hover attitude and sit there in the hover at 20° nozzle. Whether you would want to do that without a reasonable prospect of gaining some 300 ft or more during the nose up period is another matter. I wouldn't. If you agree with me on that, the practical approach is to have some 3% rpm in hand (before the dry limiter if there is a chance of running out of water) that can be applied at the start of the manoeuvre. Having said that, if the manoeuvre can get well underway for 10-15 sec of good full power wet, it is clearly not the end of the world to get a dry limiter cut back once climbing at say 50-60 kt, providing the nose is lowered as soon as that happens and before the airspeed has a chance to decay.

The performance and engine count situation will always be considerably better if a rotation about the nozzles is started from a VTO because the engine will not start hot soaked and, if the quality of go is very good, you can tell at once that the subsequent climb will be easy.

It is worth remembering that, in the event of any rpm cut back (for whatever reason), while nose high and at low IAS, it is important not to stuff in full forward stick as that would cause any upward velocity to be turned into an airflow at minus 90° alpha which does nothing to maximise upwards forces.

The aim in an emergency level off must be to try and capture 10-12° alpha (thus optimising wing lift as well as avoiding any stall effects) and make all subsequent decisions on the basis of the flight path angle and IAS that results from holding that alpha. A nozzle angle of 20° has to be the optimum until the crisis is over. It goes without saying that, if the rpm is falling to a value below that likely to be caused by normal dry limiter operation (I have seen as little as 92% on a 40°C day in Kuwait while pulling a lot of bleed with a hot soaked engine), then the sooner the limiters are overridden the better.

Handling

I was always very careful to use the same seat height setting and tried to train myself to recognise the left hand reach required for 20° nozzle at every available opportunity such as when taxying. I certainly checked the nozzle angle gauge once the climb attitude was nearly right but still felt it important to practice the ability to accurately feel a 20° nozzle selection in case one day I forgot to check the gauge. On one occasion with a two-seater at Paris in 1973, I got it wrong for some reason and attitude control started to feel a bit sloppy during the climb. Sure enough there was the gauge showing 10° nozzle. I eased it back to 20° and all became sweetness and light.

Of course we all know that the vane can point any place it likes, even at 50-80 kt, providing we have no wing lift due to no alpha because what you haven't got can't be asymmetric. However, it is lethal to have the vane far out with significant alpha and at mid-transition knots. Therefore, when faced with a crosswind, I always got the vane back into the middle *before* rotating by deliberately going sideways downwind. With that done, I accepted the subsequent cross track drift and got on with doing the manoeuvre.

Going up steeply, while clearly drifting sideways to the onlookers used to worry some people as they saw this as evidence of sideslip. In general though they were the same people who thought the manoeuvre also carried 80° alpha in total disregard of the release to service. In these

240

crosswind circumstances getting the vane in the middle before rotating is best done from a hover, rather than during a post VTO ascent. On the occasions that I mentioned earlier when there was a gale up runway 25 at Farnborough and I had to VTO from a pad into wind, then yaw 90° right, I *did* throttle back, keeping the height at 20 -30 ft while sorting out the necessary downwind groundspeed before reinstating the power and then rotating. Clearly some people might have the ability to do one smooth co-ordinated VTO, yaw round, set off sideways, roll wings level again and rotate but I did not feel confident to do that and preferred to do one step at a time.

A tailwind is really a non event always assuming you can handle it during the initial hover before rotation as its effect reduces as you build up speed. For any observer looking side on, it does nothing for the apparent steepness of the climb but it is probably the nose attitude they notice most anyway.

The *handling* emergency during the climb that needs thinking through beforehand (in the same way as the *performance* problem of an engine cut back that I mentioned earlier) is the development of sideslip during the climb. Whether due to wind shift with height or something else, if the vane does wander out, the first thing is not to change anything suddenly because after all it is just the vane that is out a little and a roll has not yet developed. Lowering the nose to a small alpha has to be *the* good thing to do and remember, if the stick is still centre, the rolling moment cannot be much. If the stick does wander out then things are getting dodgy and all the more reason to reduce alpha as soon as possible.

I say lower the nose and keep alpha low because the roll we don't want is related to the product of alpha, IAS^2 and sideslip angle and this has to exceed the roll puffer power we have available before control is lost.

Make any one of the three terms zero and the product vanishes and with it the roll danger. We normally teach to keep sideslip zero but, if alpha is kept negligible, the end result is the same even if a lot of slip is present. Nevertheless beware a high angle of *negative* alpha, as that will just roll you the other way.

Of course it must be remembered that, when pointing straight up, going in with rudder in order to yaw the nose round to put the vane in the middle will result in the first part of a stall turn entry! In fact, if one was truly vertical with the vane say out to the left, if you applied right aileron

241

you would roll the aircraft round the vertical and convert the slip to harmless alpha.

Nozzle and stick co-ordination during rotation
(plus the benefits of cheating a bit)

Given a nozzle angle in the hover of 81° and a need to go no less than 20°, we can only raise the nose to 61° in the steady state. However that probably looks like 65° or a bit more due to the slight nose up sit of the aircraft in the normal hover (such sit being needed to keep the nosewheel off until the mains have hit on a VL). However, if the initial rotation is done by leading a little with the nozzle so that the aircraft picks up a few knots forward and the attitude is only about 50° by the time 20° nozzle is set, then it is easy to continue to raise the nose until the nozzles are actually pointing say 10° forward of the vertical as this just slowly kills the forward drift rather than actually making the jet go backwards. As to how I used to judge the way the co-ordination was going, I used the seat of my pants. Too much nozzle too soon and you can feel yourself lurching forward.

In my day I turned the HUD off for displays because the early kit was extremely unreliable and would often show a normally responding but quite incorrect pitch or roll attitude when flying around in VMC. For us, at that time, the HUD was a thing to be checked and reported on, indeed a potential gotcha, not an aid to be used to control the aircraft. Also, importantly, I used to fly the P1127 (XP831) and later the Kestrel all long before HUDs were fitted and so I in no way felt any loss when I turned it off. I realise none of that applies anymore and I am sure that today the HUD is a very useful bit of kit for displays.

Other odds and ends

Engine reliability and performance during the manoeuvre when compared with a flat VTO and horizontal acceleration have to be better.

During a flat VTO, there is considerable distortion of the air flow at the front face of the fan as the air is entering the intake from above and turbulence can develop inside the top of the intake. During a steep slow climb, the intake is broadly pointing the way the aircraft is travelling and the air gets a much better run in to the fan. This increases the surge margin for any given set of conditions. Also, if the rotation follows a VTO, you are getting the intakes as far away from any rebounding and recirculating hot air as soon as possible. Which of course means less risk of thrust loss.

Given a hydro-mech fuel system, if the engine runs down and, if there is time, I think it is always worth selecting manual as a last resort before ejecting. I know we are supposed to go to idle for a changeover but I hit manual one day in G-VTOL at full throttle as the rpm went down through 82% circa 100 ft after an STO and it screamed back up in a most satisfactory way. With the throttle fully open, the uncontrolled rate of accel was something else but no surge because of all the bleed being pulled. On the same topic, I once did a session of momentary engine chops back to 80% rpm after good VTOs while going up flat and fast through 300 ft. The idea was to see what attitude change might ensue from engine failure. The nose always went down a bit, as did the right wing, but nothing to cause concern from an ejection attitude standpoint. All good news.

Chapter 9

Test Flying

It might be useful if I attempt a definition of test flying as opposed to research flying of the sort that was carried out at RAE Bedford. For me test flying is a highly structured and organised activity where the aim is to establish whether a given aircraft meets the requirements of a designated military or civilian licensing authority.

When the Wrights developed their first aircraft, although they certainly went about their task in a structured and organised way, they were not trying to meet regulations, they just wanted to fly. The same could be said for all the early aviators. They were most certainly brave men and women but I consider their activity to have been pioneering rather than test flying as it is practised today.

Given the lack of regulation, there were a great many accidents, especially during the barnstorming decade of the 1920s. As a result many aviation leaders in the USA believed that Federal regulation was necessary to give the public confidence in the safety of air transportation.

Therefore President Calvin Coolidge appointed a board to investigate the issue. The board's report favoured Federal safety regulation. To that end, the Air Commerce Act became law in the USA on 20th May 1926. The Act created an Aeronautics Branch and vested that entity with the fundamental regulatory powers needed to ensure civil air safety including:

Testing and licensing pilots
Issuing certificates to guarantee the airworthiness of aircraft
Making and enforcing safety rules
Certificating aircraft
Establishing airways
Operating and maintaining aids to air navigation
Investigating aviation accidents and incidents

Given this list, regulation had clearly arrived and for me represents the start of formal flight testing of civilian aircraft as practised today. There then followed several iterations of regulatory bodies before today's Federal Aviation Agency (FAA) was formed in 1958.

In the UK the Government created the Air Registration Board (ARB) in 1936 to examine civil aircraft and issue certificates of airworthiness. Previously such activities as there were had been dealt with by a civil aviation department inside the military establishment. In 1980 the duties of the ARB were taken over by the Civil Aviation Authority (CAA) that we have today.

Given the UK military had a civil aviation cell back in the 1920s, it is not surprising that the military led the way with a document titled 'Design and Airworthiness Requirements for Service Aircraft'. Known to a generation of designers as Air Publication 970, the same document was to become Aviation Publication 970 and then today Defence Standard 970. The contents of '970' continually evolved to meet changing times and knowledge. For example, I well remember that in the 1960s it required military aircraft to be stable about all three axes when flying in the circuit. Since the Kestrel (and Harrier to be) did not have such characteristics, it was necessary for the Dunsfold pilots to educate the system in order to obtain an exemption.

When controlling any aircraft, the presence of stability greatly reduces workload and is to be desired. However it is also true that human pilots can readily control a mildly unstable aircraft provided they are given appropriately sensitive and powerful controls with low forces and no lost motion around centre. It does mean that they cannot take their hands off the controls but, whereas hour after hour in the cruise like that would be unacceptably fatiguing, a few minutes in the visual circuit was shown to be immaterial. In the end the exemption to '970' was accepted in order to obtain the benefit of VSTOL.

Without wishing to get too sidetracked into detailed Harrier issues, it would have been perfectly possible to add autostabilisers to make the aircraft meet the stability requirements but only by introducing some very nasty failure cases which the designers were determined not to inflict on service pilots. Half a century later, the dramatically increased reliability of such systems has allowed them to be safely used in the modern versions of the Harrier.

In 1943 the business of test flying took a huge step forward with the setting up of the first school for teaching test pilots their trade. The Empire Test Pilots' School (ETPS) came into being in no small part thanks to the lobbying of Wg Cdr Sammy Wroath who was its first Commandant. Up until that time, test pilots were chosen from the ranks of experienced pilots who had survived accident rates that no youngster would believe today. Natural selection if you like.

How much better that pilots involved in flight testing were formally introduced to the theory and practice of aircraft design and specialist test techniques, based on the collective test flying knowledge of the day. Initially based at Boscombe Down, ETPS briefly moved to Cranfield, before 20 years at Farnborough after which it returned to Boscombe in 1968.

Given the obvious benefits of this school, three other test pilot schools were formed using the ETPS model. The USAF started one at Edwards (1944), the USN at Patuxent River (1945), while the French opened their École du Personnel Navigant d'Essais et de Réception (EPNER) in 1946. It was initially at Brigny-sur-Orge before it moved to Istres in 1962. In more recent years, we learned that there was one at Gromov in the USSR. Since the graduates of No 5 Course at ETPS in 1947 included two Chinese pilots (referred to by the staff as Right Wing Hi and Left Wing Lo), I am sure there is also a school in China. Of course it took a while before graduates of the various schools filled the majority of test pilot posts around the world but in the end it became the norm.

Wg Cdr Derek Collier Webb, a flight safety specialist at the centre of the UK test flying scene, has published comprehensive data of all the UK flight test related accidents, military and civil, between 1940 and 1971.

The following table summarises his work and shows a big reduction in accidents over the period. Clearly the main factors that produced this decline were the end of the urgent wartime needs, improvements in aircraft design and test pilot training and an overall reduction in the number of aircraft on test.

Period	Number of accidents
1940 - 1944	497
1945 -1949	331
1950 - 1954	188
1955 - 1959	110
1960 - 1964	66
1965 - 1969	36
1970 - 1971	11

Over the years I was a full time test pilot (1964-1983), the average UK flight test accident rate dropped from one a month to one every couple of years or so. However the public perception continued to be that a test pilot had a dangerous job. Clearly the numbers today no longer support that view.

By chance in 1951 I was cycling round the perimeter track at Farnborough and watched Dunsfold's CTP, Wimpy Wade, take off in the P1081. We learned later that the aircraft had crashed and Wimpy had been killed.

P1081   *Hawk 200*

It was not until 35 years later that Dunsfold lost another test pilot when Jim Hawkins was killed flying the prototype single-seat Hawk. I suggest that, if the company had gone to an insurance broker the day after Wimpy's accident and asked for a quotation to insure his replacement and other pilots to develop the first swept wing fighter and then the first swept wing fighter that could takeoff and land vertically without actually being sure how they were going to do this, they would have been given a silly quote or even laughed out of the office.

However, had the Company then gone on to say that there would be 17 test pilots working at Dunsfold over the next 35 years and ask for a quotation to insure their children to reach the age of 30, I believe the quote for such cover would not have been expensive. However over those 35 years that team of 17 pilots was to lose six children. I appreciate that one should not draw conclusions from the statistics of small samples but what those numbers suggest to me is that, because being a test pilot is perceived as dangerous, special care is taken by the people associated with all aspects of test flying and not just the pilots themselves. On the other hand, being a child is not viewed the same way at all. The reality may well be opposite to the perception.

In 1992 as a self-employed test pilot I was asked if I would go to Indonesia and carry out flight trials on a CN-235 twin turboprop aircraft in order to collect all the data necessary to build a simulator. The request took the form of a phone call from designer Desmond Norman of Islander fame, with whom I was already working on various trials involving certification of modifications made to existing civil aircraft.

I thanked Desmond for the job offer but remarked that one did not normally fly an aircraft to collect data for a simulator but purchased the manufacturer's simulator package. He said that he appreciated that but Aeronautical Systems Designers Limited (ASDL), the company contracted to build the simulator for the Indonesian internal airline, Merpati, had fallen out with the aircraft manufacturer who flatly refused to help them in any way. Therefore they had no alternative but to rent an aircraft from Merpati and employ an organisation to design and execute the flight trials and provide the data they needed.

Merpati CN-235

What followed provides a suitable illustration of my views on test flying and how to go about it safely. The company chosen was Kollsman Systems Research and, at a meeting with all the interested parties in Burgess Hill, ASDL tabled a large list of tests and those present considered them one by one. When it came my turn to comment, I merely said yes to each one including several that were outside the certificated envelope of the aircraft. This raised eyebrows among the Kollsman team as they considered such items to be 'high risk' especially as I had never flown a CN-235. At this stage I suspect Kollsman felt that they were faced with a cowboy test pilot who was well out of his depth. Accordingly they required everybody to agree that for the high risk tests their flight test engineer, who would normally fly with us and control their recording systems, would turn everything on just before takeoff and then exit the aircraft. After the flight he would then get back in and do the necessary to wind everything down.

Once we were out in Indonesia and had been flying for a few days, the flight test engineer said that now he had seen the technique I used to fly the 'high risk' points, he was quite happy to stay onboard the aeroplane in future which I took as a nice compliment. Indeed at the post trials wash-up, Kollsman went so far as to say that, if they ever got another request for a similar flight test programme and needed a pilot they would know who to call.

I used what I call the 'iterative' approach, not just for the high risk tests but for all of them. Here each step forward is sufficiently small that if you run into any unexpected problem, you can quickly retreat back to where you were before and know everything will be fine. Whatever the parameter you are changing, be it speed, angle of attack, sideslip and so on, you set the size of the step or the rate at which you are changing things according to the inherent risk of the particular flight condition.

An example from the CN-235 tests should help to illustrate what I mean. To enhance the training value of their simulator, ASDL wanted it to be representative of the aircraft when that was taken beyond its normal envelope. This was a very laudable aim. In particular they wanted data on how the aircraft would respond to an engine failure that happened at maximum weight on a hot day and with the pilot not flying correctly. To this end they wanted the fuel turned off to the critical engine at a speed five knots below V_1 and the takeoff continued. Normally of course, if an engine fails below V_1, you abandon the takeoff and stop. Naturally turning the fuel off rather than throttling back the 'failed' engine is an irreversible step for that particular takeoff and so this test point was well up on the Kollsman high risk list.

Instrumented yoke

Cockpit cameras

We were flying from Surabya, an airfield on the coast of Java so I explained at the briefing that I wanted to put in an extra 300 kg of fuel above the test weight, do a very gentle takeoff in case we had a real engine failure, then climb to 1,500 ft over the sea. Once there, I would put the aircraft in the takeoff configuration and ask the Merpati captain in the right hand seat to turn the fuel off to the critical engine. With full power on the remaining engine, I would then slow down to a speed 5 kt less than the required test speed. If I could not reach this speed without running out of rudder or aileron, I would simply lower the nose a little to pick up some speed, restart the engine and return to say the test could not be done. In the event I did not run out of control, I then wanted to see a rate of climb at the test speed less 5 kt of at least 400 ft/min because on the test takeoff we had the town of Surabya off the end of the runway. If the climb rate was below my chosen minimum, we would again return and declare that the test could not be carried out. If both requirements were met, we would then restart the engine, land, burn down to the precise weight and fly the test takeoff.

I trust you can see that with that sort of build-up doing the actual test takeoff was not in any way risky because we had been flying slower and heavier than the test conditions only a few minutes earlier. The technique was thus a mixture of the iterative approach and common sense.

When a practising test pilot I was prepared to use this approach, without further help or special briefing, to carry out any test, on any aircraft with only two exceptions. These were spinning and flutter, for which I needed help because the normal pilot-controlled iterative approach was either not possible or did not guarantee safety. The iterative approach cannot be used in fully developed spinning tests because you are either in such a spin or you are not. You cannot be in a bit of a spin then choose to back off a little. As I discuss in more detail in Chapter 12, there is no law of aerodynamics which says that if the controls of an aircraft can make it enter a spin, they can also make it recover. This is because at spin entry the aircraft is flying slowly close to the stall and has no great rates of yaw, roll or pitch. Once in a developed spin, the airspeed may not be very different from that at entry but the rates of pitch and yaw can be high. By applying a whole lot of new inertia-based forces to the aircraft and without actually doing such a spin, you cannot be sure that the controls can deal with these additional forces.

Therefore I required help. Since it is hardly professional to abandon an aircraft under such foreseeable circumstances with no regard for those on the ground, I insisted the aircraft be fitted with some sort of emergency spin recovery system. This traditionally takes the form of an anti-spin chute and jettison system which clearly involves company expense. Then, in the event that the anti-spin system failed to do the job, I required a parachute for me and a suitable exit for baling out. While with most aircraft it is easy enough to make arrangements to wear a parachute, ensuring there is a suitable exit for a manual bale-out can again require expensive temporary modifications.

Flutter tests are very different. They most certainly need to be done in an iterative way but it is a complex iterative way not a simple one. The reason for this is that the time from the first symptoms of flutter being apparent to the pilot can be as little as a second or two before a major structural failure of the airframe.

For those who may not know what the term 'flutter' involves, it is an oscillation of some part of the airframe, such as the wing or tail, caused by the interaction of aerodynamic forces with the structure. At its simplest, the aerodynamics make the structure bend slightly and this change of shape results in a slight change to the aerodynamics round the aeroplane which in turn causes its shape to change yet again and so on.

An everyday example of flutter can be seen on a hot day when a window fitted with venetian blinds is open and the blinds partly closed. The wind blowing on the slats of the blind can cause them to lift slightly, which in turn can make them change shape so as to reduce the lift and the slats drop down a little, thus getting their lift back and so the cycle starts to build up until the whole blind is rattling away. The easiest cure is to reduce the draught blowing through the window, making the aerodynamic effects less and giving the structure of the vanes a chance to stop changing their shape.

An aircraft can suffer from many types of flutter ranging from simple control surface flutter, where a hinged surface is flapping about through an ever increasing deflection, to examples where the whole wing or tail surface is oscillating in a very violent way. To prove that an aircraft is not going to suffer from flutter in any part of its flight envelope requires that the airframe is specially instrumented with very sensitive sensors that can detect small oscillations. Then when the pilot uses one of several ways to induce such oscillations in flight, the instrumentation can show whether such oscillations are safely damped. Ideally, this instrumentation will transmit its information to the ground based test team so that they can clear the pilot to move on to the next point or warn him to slow down and quit because the damping is reducing in a dangerous way.

There is much more to the business of flutter testing than I have touched on, including extensive pre-flight ground based resonance testing of the airframe. My aim here is solely to leave you in no doubt that a test pilot needs help with flutter and cannot rely on a simple cockpit-based iterative approach. I have lost personal CTP friends as recently as 1976 and 1990 to catastrophic flutter testing events, so I can think of no better way to end than to quote the words of the famous aerodynamicist Theodore von Karman:

> *"Some fear flutter because they do not understand it,*
> *others because they do."*

So much for the simple nuts and bolts of how to fly safe flight tests and get the data needed. In many ways the easy bit! Now I want to turn to a different and much more controversial side of test flying.

I first became aware of what I will call company cultural issues in connection with flight test thanks to Bill Waterton and a book he wrote in 1955, shortly after he resigned from his post as Chief Test Pilot for the Gloucester Aircraft Company. I was given the book at the end of my apprenticeship and I soaked up every word. It had a dedication and a preface and I can do no better than quote from both:

The dedication included these words:

"To those few who design, build, operate and fly aircraft and put ideals, practice and common-sense above profit and self advancement.

To the many unheard of and un-honoured pilots who have devoted – and given – their lives to the air and the aeroplanes they loved.

To those frustrated designers, aerodynamicists, engineers and test pilots who have laboured honourably for their beliefs"

Perhaps the language of the preface that followed is a touch old-fashioned and some may see it as a bitter rant but the message is clear for all that. The book had the title The Quick and the Dead:

"I wanted to call this book "Suck it and see", for in those four words is the essence of experimental test flying. Despite the calculations and tests which go on before a plane takes the air for the first time, in the end it boils down to just that. But, as you see, I didn't get my way with the title; I failed in that small matter, and failure is the real tale of this whole book. For I feel that I have broken faith, with myself and with my fellows.

I experienced in the RAF many aeroplanes which were far from what they should have been. I didn't like it, for a plane which is not as practical and foolproof as human endeavour can make it is a dangerous, or potentially dangerous, vehicle. It is not appreciated just how a switch in the wrong place, resulting in an awkward movement by the pilot, can mean, in case of emergency, the difference between "going in" and "getting away with it". I left the RAF and went into the aircraft industry, wide-eyed, as a Sir Galahad eager to slay and put down the avoidable evils which beset my beloved mechanical birds.

For seven long years I did my best to put good, safe, world-beating aeroplanes into the hands of young, inexperienced squadron pilots of my old service. Despite a few minor triumphs I don't think I accomplished a lot. I didn't accomplish or bring into being a fraction of what I consider I ought to have achieved. Looking round the aeronautical field, I don't think others have done a great deal either. But I am out of it all now and so in a better position to say what I feel I must.

This book is not likely to make a mark as a treatise on how to win friends and influence people. If that were its object it would have been done on more stereotyped lines. As it is, it is just possible that a number of people will have quite a lot of things to say about what is written here. That is expected; I've been called a lot of things, very occasionally to my face – very frequently à derrière. It will be surprising if this book provokes anything new in invective.

Those who know aviation will recognise the evils to which I refer. The shirking of responsibility by jumped-up people in a jumped-up game. The old school tie habit of covering up and passing the buck. Greed, inefficiency, and "couldn't care less". All these are rife in larger quantities than aviation will stand. And the end product is that mess I have so often identified on the mortuary slab. But the blame is rarely laid at the right door. For aeroplanes do not fail as a result of "just one of those things". They fail or crash because of incompetence anywhere along the line, or through overconfidence, carelessness, laziness, untruthfulness, or the pursuit of wrong ideals. They fail or crash because somewhere, sometime, someone has boobed, and for no other reason. All these are human faults, and to my knowledge no other of man's creations will show up human failings, wherever they be, more quickly or more ruthlessly. The sea is a hard master; the air even harder, for its foibles are so often invisible.

All this being so, I often wonder if it does not account for the lengths human beings go to try and deceive one another over air matters, for aviation has bred a prize collection of artful dodgers. The measure of their deceptions is invariably directly proportional to their lack of first-hand knowledge of flying. And, "you cannot shoot a line about an aeroplane with impunity", for those who fly will not be fooled; "suck it and see" will reveal the truth."

The next clue I got that not everybody in the aircraft business was interested in making better aeroplanes came from Eddie Rigg, one of the test flying tutors on my course at ETPS in 1963. Eddie opened our eyes to what went on at meetings. I quote from his lecture notes:

"A conference can be defined as an assembly of people representing different bodies or interests who meet to debate the various courses of action and eventually decide on the best course to adopt. In fact no conference is ever thus. In real life these same people meet to engineer the course of action which will best suit their own interests and preconceived opinions. Various tactics are employed including procrastination, haste, falsifying the minutes of the meeting, making hollow verbal promises, failing to invite the opposition to the meeting, etc."

Eddie went on to say:

"These tactics are best opposed by adopting a highly methodical and watertight position. Make thorough preparation for the conference. Ensure that you have all the necessary background to support your arguments and demolish those of the opposition. Do not let glib assertions go unchallenged but ask for the facts, and the foundations for the facts if necessary. Make sure that all important decisions and promises are recorded in the minutes. Make your own separate record of the proceedings and compare it with the official minutes when they are published. If the minutes are wrong, write to the secretary of the conference immediately to establish your disagreement."

During my early years in industry those words were my daily text. I saw them, as I am sure Eddie Rigg intended, as another test flying technique that needed to be studied and put into practice.

The test pilot's contribution to the design, development and production of an aircraft varies greatly. Part of this variation is naturally due to the quality of the individual involved. However, I believe the effectiveness of any test pilot's contribution will depend more on the culture of the organisation that he serves than on his inherent worth as a pilot. I believe that inside the right culture the use of a merely competent pilot will still result in fine aircraft being produced.

Given the right culture and an exceptional pilot, the aircraft will be even better for their purpose and the real bonus will be that the manufacturer will sell many more of them and make more profit.

The opposite is also true. Get the culture wrong and the result will be a relatively poor aircraft that has a limited future and a profit to match, even if the design team includes the best pilots that the world has yet seen. Clearly I believe a lot hinges on this thing I call culture. I also believe the test pilot's contribution should include marketing and making money, rather than just sorting out the stick force per g or stopping wing rock at high alpha, as many might expect.

In the military world, the simple technical merit of the product was often overcome by political expediency plus there was less of the beneficial element of market competition that exists in the civil world to justify spending money to improve the product.

My definition of a good culture is when the company is making the aeroplane in order to give the user (who is of course a pilot) the best buy aeroplane for his job and by so doing make a fair profit from the project.

If on the other hand the organisation is trying to beat the opposition by convincing the customer (not the user) that it is in their interest to buy Brand X regardless of how good it actually is then that is my definition of the wrong culture. Such a culture has no interest in how the user (a pilot) fares as he goes about his daily job in Brand X, this culture sees the customer as the only player.

In these circumstances, especially if the customer is not too bright, or if the manufacturer goes behind the military customer's back and lobbies the customer's political masters naturally telling them only what they want to hear, then the company (now probably a member of a consortium of like-minded cultures) gets away with an aircraft specification that has more to do with what suits company vested interests than what the operational pilot needs.

No doubt some would see my good culture as naïve and the bad culture as what successful project management and today's business is all about. I disagree with them. I prefer to regard the good culture as one that values professional integrity and does not expect to make money at the short term expense of the customer. Rather it understands that, given integrity and trust, they can work together to their mutual advantage over many years.

In this context the views of HRH The Duke of Edinburgh are interesting. In an essay simply titled "Test Pilot" and published by Hamish Hamilton in a book called *Men, Machines and Sacred Cows*, the Duke says

"I have to confess that I have frequently speculated – like Walter Mitty perhaps – whether I would have liked to be a test pilot. I thought it idle to speculate on whether I could have been a test pilot – I do not like hypothetical questions. After a little reflection on the subject, I came to the conclusion that a test pilot had an impossible job."

"... I suspect that the test pilot's greatest difficulty is that he is, in effect, a critic. It is true that his criticism is intended to be constructive, but still he is a critic and critics are seldom popular."

So where does all this get us?

I believe that the job of the test pilot is simply to do what he can to improve the quality of the aeroplanes that his fellow pilots use on a daily basis out in their operational world. However, in working towards this simple objective, it is possible that greater demands will be made on his honesty and his integrity than on his flying skills and physical courage.

So far I have only mentioned the *problems* that the pilot has when making his contribution and people problems at that rather than technical ones. Despite this I am happy to report that by virtue of his position, a test pilot does have some undeniable *advantages* which make it easier for him to put some things right, should he choose to do so.

256

Therefore perhaps Prince Philip was not right when he said the job is impossible. It may be difficult at times but certainly not impossible given what I call Plan B. When, as a test pilot, you find a problem with an aircraft, Plan A is to properly investigate it, correctly and convincingly communicate the results of that investigation to the development team and then do what you can to help the development and implementation of the fix. That is your contribution. You should not expect a medal or pay rise for doing this well as it is just your job.

If you are fortunate to be serving a good culture, then you will be helped at every stage of this process by good people. These people will greatly increase the value of your contribution. They will coach and encourage you in such a way that your value, as the man who operates and reports on the machine, will be magnified many times over compared to what you might have achieved on your own. I can say this from personal experience because I have been fortunate to have the privilege of working with some of the best people in the flight test business. Does this sound like an impossible job? Far from it. For me it was quite simply the best job there was.

If, on the other hand, you are working for the wrong culture, shake hands with HRH because you are really up against it. In the worst case you will be actively opposed at every point. Your professional judgement will be called into question and the views of other pilots quoted to counter your own. Of course there is nothing wrong with using a second and different opinion providing it comes from someone who shares your idea of a test pilot's duties. On many of these occasions, however, one observes that the second opinion is selected from the ranks of those who can be relied upon to toe the company line, an action perceived as rather more likely to assist their personal advancement.

So now is it impossible, just like the Duke said? No. Now is the time to move forward with Plan B. Plan B is about telling the truth to the customer's pilots. Sooner or later they will come to evaluate the aeroplane, then, thanks to your briefing of the problems they will be able, in a wonderfully short period of flying, to put their fingers on all the issues as well as demonstrating a remarkable ability to conceive just the right concept for the necessary fix.

I never found that telling potential customers the truth cost us any orders. You just have to make your mind up whether the product you are pushing has more going for it than against it. If it has, then come clean about it, warts and all. If you find out, or know before, that it would not suit the user for technical reasons then say so, or don't get involved in marketing it in the first place. A pilot who understands his product and the users' needs can be very effective in obtaining a sale, especially if he passes the users' checks for honesty. Equally, pushing out an unjustified company line will quickly lose you all credibility.

One problem when using Plan B is that the investment in programme time and money prior to the customer's pilots flying may be such that it is too late to act on their recommendations. Now the customer (not the user this time) has got to be made to realise that changes are necessary. That may not be an easy thing to make happen.

In doing this, I have even had the customer's top man, a one star civil servant in MOD (PE) called Director Harrier, complaining to my company (behind my back of course) that I was rocking the boat during a meeting in the US. I wanted a different navigation system fitted to the one he was pushing to use as government furnished equipment. There is no need to go into his motives, let me just say that he was not my idea of a straight guy. He made the mistake of suggesting that my job was to fly aeroplanes and not get involved with project policy. Yes my job as a test pilot was to fly the aeroplanes but it was also to see that the data I got in flight was properly employed in improving the breed. I am happy to say that when the aircraft went into RAF service it was actually fitted with the kit I had recommended.

I suggest those whose duty it is to criticise but who give way under management pressure are letting down their fellow airmen no more and no less. In my view such men are not test pilots, they are just pilots who fly flight tests.

Chapter 10

Lift and Drag

Lift

If you are somebody who understands Lift you may choose to skip what follows. On the other hand, if you are not totally sure about how aeroplanes stay up, you may find it of interest as it describes how I have taught the topic at a summer school for the last ten years. The students are sharp, specially selected 16 to 18-year-olds and the course aims to encourage them to join the aerospace business. The lesson is the first they get on day one and is called 'An introduction to aerodynamics' with a subtitle of 'plus why helicopters cannot fly fast'. Although it may not be obvious from this, the lesson is almost entirely about Lift.

In my view when it comes to something as basic as aerodynamic lift there is no such thing as a weak student only an incompetent teacher. Since I also hate oversimplified or misleading explanations that do not bear close examination, I gave myself some simple rules when putting together this lesson. Nothing was to be factually incorrect and where possible the way I put it across would include life lessons that would help the students understand other topics where maths are involved. It also had to send them away understanding the term angle of attack (or alpha as I refer to it in this book) – the key to all matters Lift.

I chose to start by explaining and discussing the things that affect the lift on an aeroplane. Not how lift arises but what a pilot does to control the amount in use and what the designer can do to maximise the amount available. Ten years ago I used chalk and blackboard but today one has the benefit of PowerPoint and being able to show on a screen really good words, diagrams and interesting pictures.

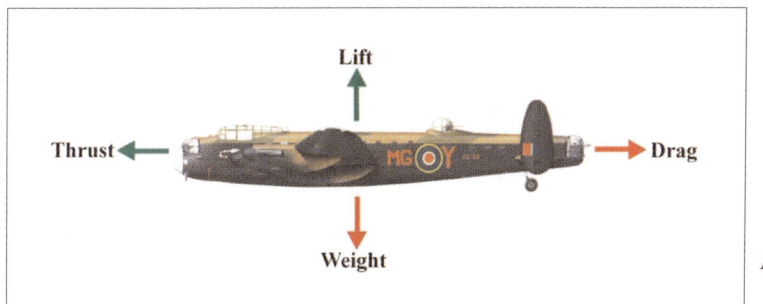

Fig 1

Once a nice picture of a Lancaster has grown arrows showing Thrust, Drag, Lift and Weight, as in *Fig 1*, I explain I am going to concentrate on Lift because that that is the clever bit that enables us to fly. Then I hit them (remember it is first thing in the morning!) with the equation:

$$L = C_L \tfrac{1}{2}\rho S V^2$$

It is in very large, bold font and I announce this is the formula that enables us to calculate the lift a wing can produce. One can almost hear the groans and can certainly see the looks of dismay on some of their faces – after all they have come to the course expecting to have fun with aeroplanes not to be reminded of how much they hate maths. This is intended as life lesson number one by making the point that formulae enable non-mathematicians to get their heads round quite tricky concepts, providing people realise they are just shorthand for a lot of words. I then explain what the shorthand means in simple English. As I read out what the formula says my words go up on the screen:

"The lift (L) on a wing is equal to something called the lift coefficient (C_L) – which I will explain in a moment – multiplied by one half, multiplied by the density of the air (ρ), multiplied by the area of the wing (S), multiplied by the speed of the wing through the air (V) and multiplied by this speed again."

We then have a side conversation where they agree that dividing by two is not too difficult and that they are probably aware that the density of the air we live in varies with height. It is relatively 'thick' down where we are but it is so 'thin' as to be virtually non-existent up where the Shuttle goes round in orbit. Since any wing uses the air to fly we must clearly take the air density into account.

Because both sides of any equation have to be equal, life lesson number two is that we do not have to bother with units when using an equation if all we want to do is understand how the 'subject' of the equation (in this case Lift) varies as we change the size of the other terms. For example, if we halve the value of the air density we will halve the lift if nothing else is changed. Similarly doubling the wing area doubles the lift – not altogether surprising.

On the other hand speed (V) needs watching because it is a squared term so if we double our speed we have the potential for four times the lift.

This means we must be careful when slowing down, as halving our speed will result in only a quarter of the lift we had before – unless the pilot changes something in addition to the speed. Looking again at the equation, it is clear that the pilot cannot change the wing area (S), nor the density (ρ), nor the half term so the only thing left is the Lift Coefficient (C_L). Thus we realise that whenever pilots pull or push on the control column they are varying just one thing in the Lift equation, namely C_L.

It is now time to get to grips with Lift Coefficient, what it represents and how pulling and pushing on the wheel or stick makes it change. The Lift Coefficient of a wing is just a number and it has no units. The maximum possible value of the number for any given wing is called $C_{L\,max}$ and this number varies from wing to wing. Thus $C_{L\,max}$ can be thought of as a measure of how good a particular wing is at producing lift and naturally depends on the shape of that wing both in cross section and planform.

I go on to reiterate the key point that the amount of C_L in use at any time in flight is directly controlled by the pilot (or autopilot) in order to control the height of the aeroplane when it is in straight and level flight. Pilots vary the amount of C_L in use by varying an angle called alpha (α). Just what is this angle and how does it affect C_L? *Figs 2a* and *2b* provide the answers to those questions.

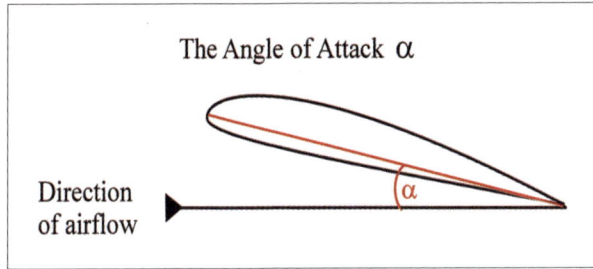

N.B. The angle is taken from the chord line joining the leading and trailing edges not the undersurface

Fig 2a

I emphasise that alpha is about the angle between where the aircraft is pointing and the direction it is travelling. The penny usually drops on this when I explain that at an air show a jet fighter doing a slow flyby has its nose high (even though it is not climbing) while when it goes by on a fast pass it does so in a flat attitude. In the first case the V^2 term in the lift equation is small and so a lot of C_L (and thus alpha) is needed to keep the lift equal to the weight but when flying fast the V^2 term is huge so only a tiny amount of C_L (and thus alpha) is needed for the same amount of lift.

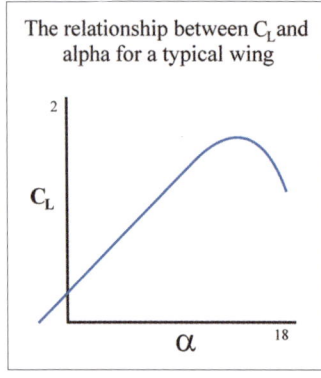

The relationship between C_L and alpha for a typical wing

C_L

α 18

Fig 2b

Doubtless you can see how easy everything is after that. Showing them *Fig 2b*, I ask why C_L starts reducing at very high values of alpha and so we get on to the stall and the turbulent airflow that happens when air finds it too difficult to follow the contours of the top surface of the wing.

Later in the morning they see all this happening in a wind tunnel with smoke injected to visualise the flow. Having sorted out just what factors affect the lift on a wing, I ask the question, "So why don't helicopters fly fast?" and explain they now have enough information to work out the answer for themselves. I then prompt them with four diagrams. The first, *Fig 3a,* shows the V experienced by the blades of a two bladed helicopter rotor in the hover.

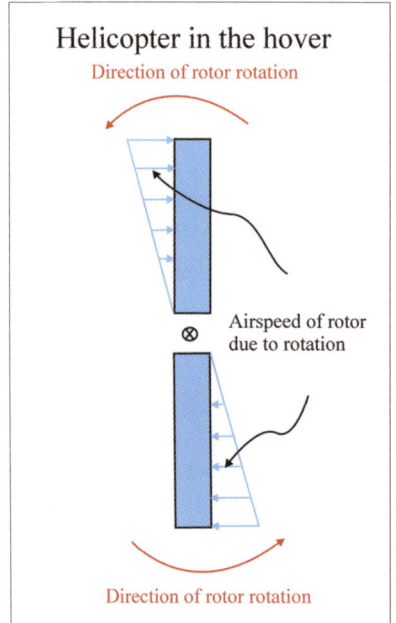

Helicopter in the hover

Direction of rotor rotation

⊗   Airspeed of rotor due to rotation

Direction of rotor rotation

Fig 3a

The point illustrated here is that the V experienced by a rotor blade in the hover is a maximum at the tip and falls to zero at the hub.

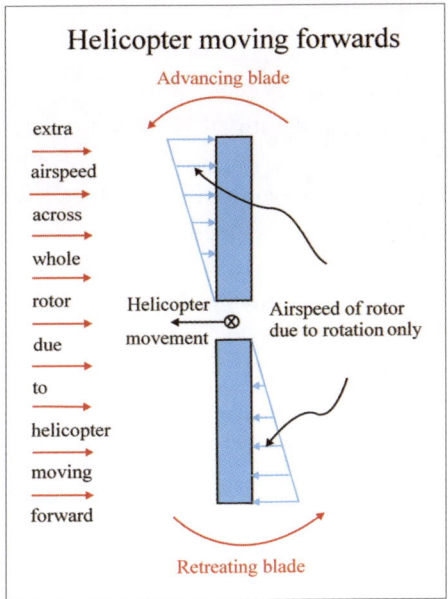

Fig 3b

Then *Fig 3b* shows how once the helicopter starts moving forward there is an extra V equal to the forward speed which is added evenly right across the rotor disc. This extra V shown has to be added to the V due to rotation to get the total airspeed as seen by the blades.

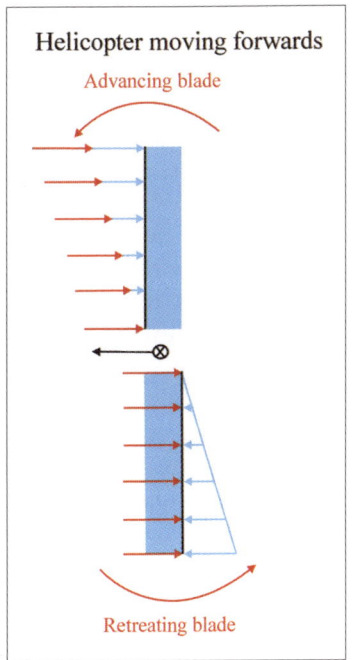

Fig 3c

The problem with high forward speeds becomes clear when these Vs are added as in *Fig 3c*, which shows that while the V of the advancing blade increases the retreating blade has its V due to rotation reduced by a 'tailwind' due to the helicopter's forward speed.

(N.B. In these diagrams with forward speed applied I have deliberately made the forward speed high compared to the rotor speed to emphasise the effect on the retreating blade.)

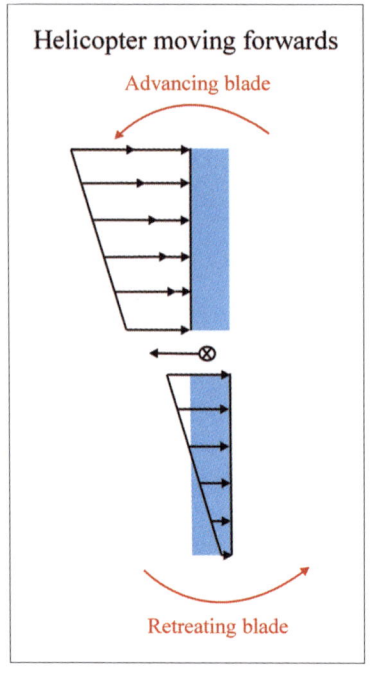

The final diagram, *Fig 3d*, shows how at high forward speeds the V of the retreating blade has very real problems with a much reduced speed at the tip and the likelihood, even at modest forward speeds, of reversed flow close to the root.

Fig 3d

I then ask the question, "Given such different values of V on the advancing and retreating blades, how are we to stop the helicopter rolling on its back as it moves forward?" This has never failed to produce at least one person who says, "Increase the C_L of the retreating blade". This is the cue for my final question: "So can we just go on increasing the C_L of the retreating blade for ever as we go faster and faster?" When somebody says, "No it will stall" we have established that the fundamental forward speed limit of any helicopter is determined by the onset of retreating blade stall.

After this one hopes that even the non-mathematically inclined students will feel they now understand something about Lift so it is time to introduce the common sense notion that we need low pressure on top of the wing for lift to exist. This allows the bright ones to show off their knowledge of Bernoulli and for Newtonians to reflect on the downwash angle. Going back to *Fig 2a* also allows one to discuss why the line does not go through the origin unless the wing section is symmetrical, plus how a symmetrical aerofoil can generate lift thanks to the way the stagnation point (where the flow splits above and below the wing) moves down and under the nose of the aerofoil as alpha is increased.

With good students I am then able to get a conversation going about vortex lift and how this can generate low pressure on the top of wings at silly angles of attack providing you have enough thrust to overcome the huge drag levels – and so we get into induced drag. This demonstrates how far you can travel on the back of the basic lift equation in just one short hour.

What I like about this very simple approach to the lift of a wing is that it requires no half-correct ideas nor oversimplifications, just acceptance of the original equation. It also firmly establishes the concept of alpha, which is what flying is all about. As to life lessons, I hope it also demonstrates the value of equations to non-mathematicians.

So far I have deliberately limited my remarks to the factors that affect lift. The lift equation I have quoted can be established experimentally from tunnel and flight measurements and does not rely on a theoretical explanation of how lift arises. Various scientists have developed theories to try and explain the observed facts regarding lift and a lot of their work has been quoted and misquoted in the piloting world in the search for a simple explanation of lift. The two names most mentioned among pilots are Bernoulli and Newton. In reality the flow round an actual three-dimensional wing in free air is very complex and not totally explained by the work of either man. However, this is a book for pilots so, from a pilot's point of view, I offer some personal comments about these contentious and oversimplified issues.

Daniel Bernoulli (1700-1782) was a Swiss mathematician who specialised in understanding the way fluids flowed in pipes. Since the air in which we fly is also a fluid, his work allows us to say:

'If you add the pressure energy and the kinetic energy of the air flowing past anything the answer will always be the same.'

In the context of this chapter 'anything' is a wing. There are four conditions that have to be met for this simplified form of Bernoulli's theorem to apply. Firstly the air has to be flowing in a streamline way and not in a chaotic or turbulent fashion. Secondly the Mach number of the flow must be low (generally accepted as 0.4 or less). Thirdly we have to agree that the potential energy (or height) of the air is unchanged by flowing past the wing. Finally there must be no external source of heat energy applied to the air as it travels past the wing. Clearly the wing of a GA aircraft flying clear of the stall meets these four conditions.

265

In practice the simplest manifestation of Bernoulli's theorem is the venturi tube of *Fig 4* where, given a steady flow of air into and out of the venturi, the air has to speed up to get through the narrowing tube. Since this means that the kinetic energy of the air increases to a maximum at the narrowest point, Bernoulli tells us that its pressure energy must fall and become a minimum at the throat which is why, in years gone by, people commonly used to power suction-driven flight instruments from a tapping taken off the neck of a venturi.

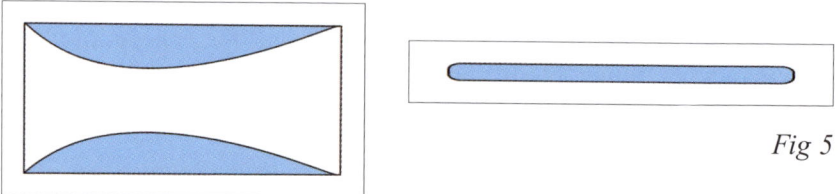

Fig 5

Fig 4

Those who like to use Bernoulli to explain lift say that if you remove the top half of a venturi, you are left with a simple aerofoil where the air above the wing would have a lower pressure than that below it because it had to speed up to travel the longer curved distance above the wing when compared to the flat bottom.

This brings us to the point where many contributors to internet forums throw a wobbly and shout "Rubbish!" The shout is often based on the notion that if that was the case aircraft fitted with such a wing section could not fly inverted. They also point out that flat plate sections, as in *Fig 5*, have been in use on tail surfaces of older light aircraft for years and the only way they could generate lift would be if Sir Isaac caused it with his laws of motion. They rant that the air travelling over the top of a flat plate has no extra distance to travel so it does not speed up thus leaving the Bernoulli fans totally bereft of a case.

However it can be demonstrated in a wind tunnel that the flow past a flat plate which has an alpha (and so is providing lift) divides to go over the top and bottom, not at the leading edge but at a point a little way behind it on the under surface. Thus the air going over the top still has to go further to get to the trailing edge so still speeds up and still experiences a drop in pressure.

For illustration purposes, consider the traditional aerofoil shape shown in *Fig 6*. The stagnation streamline is just an imaginary dividing line above which all air goes over the top of the wing and below which all air goes underneath. Where the stagnation streamline contacts the wing is termed the stagnation point (SP).

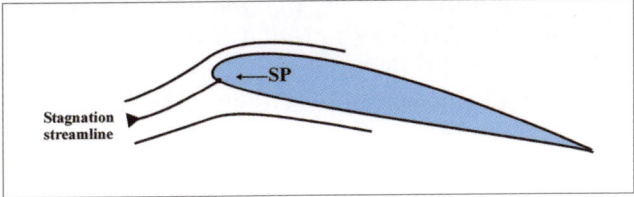

Fig 6

The key thing to realise is that the only time the SP is located right on the front of the wing leading edge is when the wing is at such an alpha that it is producing zero lift. If the wing, even a flat plate, is at an alpha that allows lift to be produced, the SP will be located on the underneath of the wing a small distance back from the leading edge. Furthermore, the SP moves steadily back under the wing as alpha is increased until the stall – and even beyond. This effect can be seen in any simple wind tunnel where smoke is introduced to enable the flow past the wing to be visualised. To understand how this can also happen with a flat plate, I offer the following explanation. Imagine it is a windy day and you are carrying a large 8 x 4 ft sheet of chipboard out of B&Q to your pickup. Being bright, you take care to hold it flat and edge on to the wind as in *Fig 5* so naturally the SP is right on the leading edge and all is well. Then out of the corner of your eye you see another chap who is carrying his sheet flat on to the wind like *Fig 7*.

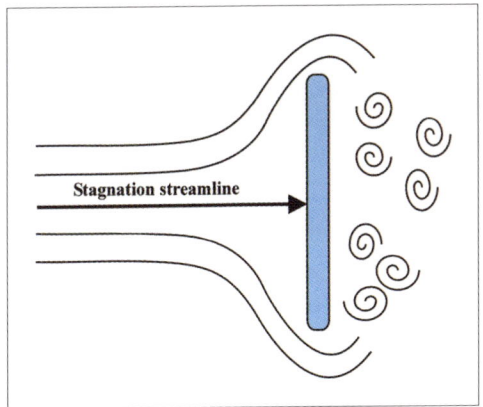

Here the SP is right in the middle of the board with the air spilling round all four sides. He realises your way is easier and starts to rotate his board towards the flat position you used.

Fig 7

Hopefully *Fig 7* suggests how, as the alpha is reduced from his 90° to your 0°, the SP has to move forward from the centre to the leading edge. If so is it not reasonable to accept that as the alpha of the sheet is reducing through say 10° (below that for the stall but not yet zero), the SP will be well on its way to the leading edge but it will not actually get there until the alpha for zero lift is reached? I apologise for that childishly simple analogy but I find such things useful so perhaps others will as well.

Before leaving Bernoulli let us reflect on the mathematical form of his simplified theorem:

$$P + \tfrac{1}{2}\, \rho V^2 = \text{constant}$$

It does no harm to remind ourselves that when flying $P + \tfrac{1}{2}\, \rho V^2$ is precisely what goes into the hole in our pitot heads. P of course is the static pressure of the air while the term $\tfrac{1}{2}\, \rho V^2$ represents the kinetic energy of the airflow. Since P is what is sensed at our aircraft static ports, the job of our airspeed indicators is to subtract the P from what goes into the pitot head leaving us with just that part of the expression that contains V.

Sir Isaac Newton (1642-1727) was a British mathematician and physicist. His third law of motion states 'To every action there is an equal and opposite reaction'. It is an observed fact that the passage of a wing that is producing lift deflects the air that it is passing through downwards – indeed the terms 'downwash' and 'downwash angle' are commonly used when discussing all sorts of aspects of flight. Because of this Newton's third law is used to explain how a wing generates lift. Clearly though this effect does not explain the observed low pressure above the wing.

Actually calculating the lift coefficient, as opposed to explaining or measuring it, is strictly beyond Bernouilli or Newton and requires consideration of the circulation round an aerofoil and the theoretical work of Lanchester, Kutta and Joukowski.

However, I repeat my view that all this theory has nothing to do with flying a safe circuit, approach and landing. That depends on understanding just what you are doing when you vary C_L. Only that understanding will enable you to stay safe in turbulence, not stall in a turn and not go off the end of the runway because you land too fast or indeed repeat any of the many ways people have come unstuck in the past. If you don't know what I mean by this, may I suggest you consider once again the lift equation:

$$L = C_L \tfrac{1}{2} \rho S V^2$$

When you are on short finals to land you have absolutely no means of varying the density of the air (ρ) nor the area of the wing (S). As to the speed (V) that needs to be whatever it should be for a host of reasons. I reiterate, the way a pilot (or autopilot) controls the lift is by varying the lift coefficient and that means varying the alpha of the wing.

Sadly – even tragically – GA aircraft are not fitted with alpha indicators. Therefore pilots are left without any direct way of realising how close they may be to the stall that takes into account their aircraft's weight, speed and bank angle. The only bit of their aeroplane that knows the alpha is the sensor that suddenly turns on the stall warning horn. Now how stupid is that? It is beyond me why no ambulance chasing lawyer has yet brought a class action for design negligence against the world's GA aircraft manufacturers for omitting such a vital piece of kit. Alpha matters to pilots in a way that Bernoulli, Newton, Lanchester, Kutta and Joukowski never will. Please remember that the next time they are mentioned at the bar and move the conversation on to something that matters and indeed could affect how long you live – alpha.

Drag

The nice thing about considering Drag after Lift is the similarity between the lift and drag equations. A sort of 'learn one get one free'.

$$L = C_L \tfrac{1}{2} \rho S V^2$$

$$D = C_D \tfrac{1}{2} \rho S V^2$$

However, the drag coefficient is more complicated than the lift coefficient because there are two sources of drag. One is due to the shape of the object, while the other arises from the presence of any lift. The part due to shape is often referred to as form drag although it should more properly be called zero lift drag, while the other is referred to as induced drag or lift dependent drag.

Let us leave the detail of these two components for a moment and return to the business of flying because people often ask for an explanation of the term 'flying on the backside of the drag curve'. The short answer is that as *Fig 8* shows, the total drag of an aeroplane in straight and level flight has a minimum value at one speed. Fly faster than this 'min drag speed' and you are said to be on the 'front side' of the drag curve. Fly slower and you are said to be on the 'back side'.

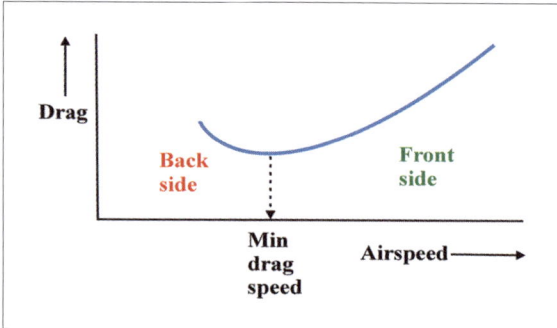

Fig 8

If you fly on the back side you will find that any reduction in airspeed for whatever reason (say a gust or just pulling the stick back a little) will result in the speed reducing still further unless you add power or lower the nose. In stability terms, an aircraft flying on the back side is said to be speed unstable while one flying on the front side is speed stable. With speed, as with any other parameter, if a stable aircraft is disturbed and then left to its own devices, it will tend to return to its original state, unlike an unstable one which will diverge further and further from its starting point unless the pilot (or autopilot) takes action to stop it.

The problem with this short answer is that it offers no explanation of why (as common sense would suggest) drag fails to reduce steadily all the way down to the minimum speed you can fly. To appreciate why drag increases as you fly slower than a particular speed we need to consider a longer explanation. What follows has served me well during a practical life in aviation so I hope it will be a help to other pilots. It also has the serious advantage that it uses common sense and everyday observations, rather than maths.

As soon as we learned to ride a bike, we became aware of the invisible hand of air resistance that increased remarkably rapidly as we tried to cycle faster or into a strong wind. Of course we didn't call it drag until the day the bike became a means of travelling to a hangar to look at aircraft. Then we realised that our bike allowed us to experience the drag force shown in *Fig 1*.

The first hint of complication in this simple world came when we read books or mixed with people who qualified the word drag – parasitic drag, form drag, skin-friction drag, surface friction drag, base drag, interference drag, wave drag, zero lift drag, lift dependent drag and induced drag. To make matters worse some of these terms turned out to be a bit like tailplane and stabilator, in that which one people used depended on where they got their aeronautical education.

Take the term 'parasitic drag'. An aero student in 1950 was expected to purchase the standard textbook of that era, a weighty mathematical volume entitled simply *Aerodynamics* by N A V Piercy, Professor of Aeronautical Engineering at the University of London and Head of the Department of Aeronautics at Queen Mary College. In it Piercy defined parasitic drag as the 'extra to aerofoil' drag of the whole aeroplane which in 1950 seemed clear enough and pretty important. Move on to the 21st century and today the Royal Air Force has this to say in their flying manual *AP3456:* 'The causes of subsonic drag have changed very little over the years but the balance of values has changed e.g. parasitic drag is such a small part of the whole that it is no longer considered separately, except when describing helicopter power requirements.' While it may be interesting to compare Piercy and *AP3456* such pondering does not help flying finals into a small strip with local obstacles, on a bumpy day, with a cross wind and on the backside of the drag curve. To do that safely needs an understanding of Zero Lift Drag and Lift Dependent Drag, especially the latter.

Zero Lift Drag is the easy one. As its name implies, it is the sum of all the types of drag that act on an aircraft other than those due to lift. Imagine if you will an aircraft holding a truly vertical flight path, it needs no lift because its weight is acting along its flight path so only Zero Lift Drag is present. The way this Zero Lift Drag behaves is also fairly intuitive. It is zero when the aeroplane is stationary and increases as the square of the speed as the aeroplane flies faster. Perhaps the squared effect is not entirely common sense but we did notice that the effort to pedal our bike into a wind of 20 mph seemed a lot more than twice the effort needed into a 10 mph wind. Too right – it was four times the effort because of the squared effect. Line A on *Fig 9* shows how this Zero Lift Drag increases with speed.

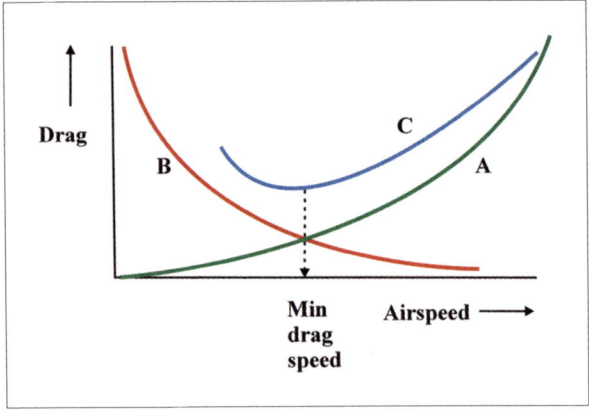

Fig 9

On the other hand Line B, which shows the Lift Dependent Drag, is certainly not intuitive. In straight and level flight its value reduces as you go faster and increases when you slow down. Lift Dependent Drag is also subject to a squared effect so at 100 kt it is four times what it is at 200 kt.

At last we have arrived at the point where I can offer my explanation of why the drag arising from Lift increases as an aircraft slows down. Glancing again at the Lancaster, we see that what we call 'Lift' is the vertical force which in straight and level flight is equal and opposite to the weight. Let us consider a wing moving through the air at a modest alpha. The air above the wing is at a lower pressure than that below it. The total force on the wing due to this pressure difference (suction) will act at right angles to the chord line or, in the case of a flat plate section, the flat plate itself. This is shown in *Fig 10.*

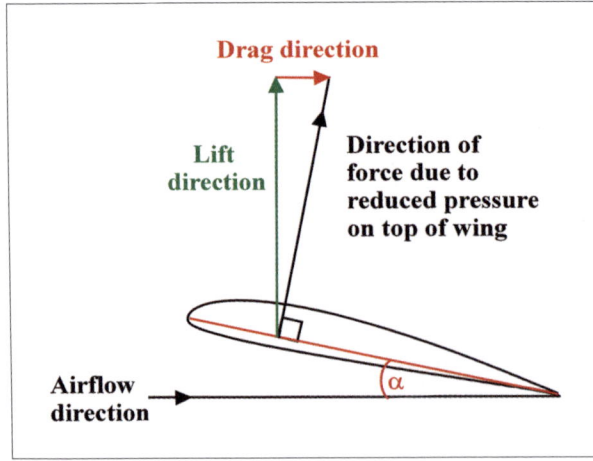

Fig 10

We now get to the 'model in my head' regarding Lift Dependent Drag. This force, from the suction above the wing becomes tilted backwards relative to the horizontal by the angle alpha because it acts perpendicular to the wing chord line. From this I hope it is clear that the higher the alpha, the more the suction force will be tilted aft. Since pilots have to increase alpha in order to fly more slowly, I trust you will agree that Lift Dependent Drag must increase as an aircraft in straight and level flight slows down. This is Line B on *Fig 9*. Adding the values of both Lines A and B together gives us Line C, which is the total drag of the aircraft in straight and level flight. It is also the same curve as that shown in *Fig 8* in my first short answer to the question.

The swirling vortices and wake behind an aeroplane represents a lot of energy that the aircraft has imparted to the air and as such forms a major part of the drag calculation. Such vortices are almost entirely due to the production of lift. Therefore I also feel justified in connecting these lift-related vortices to my 'aft tilt' concept of *Fig 10*.

To conclude this longer explanation regarding the backside of the drag curve, I would like to re-emphasise the piloting message that we are speed unstable when flying below the minimum drag speed. Because of this instability we need to watch the ASI like a hawk. I don't want to get into the controversial business of how you choose to control airspeed on finals here but, if you are on the backside, you must really stay on top of it, whichever technique you use. From a flight safety viewpoint I would comment that the use of stick to quickly increase airspeed can be awfully inhibited if you are at low level, which is why I always use throttle and why glider pilots pop the airbrakes in.

While being just a little below the minimum drag speed may not feel dramatically different from being a few knots above it, being a lot slower is a pretty serious business because the slope of the curve gets ever steeper. Having to fly on this steep part of the curve adds significantly to pilot workload and designers and operators may have to take steps to reduce the problem. The fix is always the same – add a lot of Zero Lift Drag – which effectively rotates the green curve anticlockwise about the origin and so reduces the minimum drag speed.

When USAF B-47s were a common sight, they always streamed their braking parachute before starting down finals as a convenient and powerful way of lowering the minimum drag speed. In those days the thrust response from jet engines at low rpm was extremely slow which

273

compounded the problems of flying 'on the backside' below the minimum drag speed. Towing the chute allowed the B-47 pilot to increase the rpm on finals as well as reducing the minimum drag speed making for a real win-win situation.

By now it should be clear that using flaps and airbrakes on any aircraft also reduces the minimum drag speed – although perhaps not quite to the same extent as a tail parachute!

Chapter 11

Wings

One glance at Concorde flying over was all that it took for anybody to appreciate its beauty. A similar brief glance at a wing by aviation insiders can enable a first assessment of its likely handling, performance and structural issues.

The wing's 'aspect ratio' (AR) as well as its general shape provide the clues for such an assessment. AR is a pure number and has no units. It is simply the wingspan divided by the average chord (wing width) or, if you are not sure what the average chord might be but know the wing area, then square the wingspan and divide that by the wing area.

If the AR is large, as it will be in the case of a typical sailplane, such a wing will be at the high end of aerodynamic efficiency as measured by the ratio of lift divided by drag when flying at modest speeds. If the AR is small, as with Concorde, then the opposite applies and the ratio of lift to drag will be much smaller at low speeds making the wing aerodynamically inefficient when taking off or landing. However while that efficiency generalisation is accurate at low speeds, it needs modification at high speeds when mach number effects come into play.

The other important aspect of a wing is its shape in plan. This can be elliptical (Spitfire), plank-like (helicopter rotor blade), tapered (Airbus), straight (Cessna 152), swept back (Hunter), delta (Vulcan) or slender delta (Concorde).

What follows is intended as an introduction to the topic of wing plan shapes with the aim of giving readers a feel for the issues involved thus enabling them to decide whether they would like to undertake more study. I am sure many pilots enjoy their hobby – even profession – much more when they have some insight into the design aspects of the aircraft that they fly, own or covet.

Wing plan shape has an effect on a surprisingly wide range of pilot handling matters. I have numbered them for ease of reference when discussing them individually later, where I refer to them as 'Issues'.

1. The amount of pitch attitude change needed to vary the lift a little (for example when cruising and holding a constant height manually)

2. The alpha (angle of attack) at the stall

3. The pitch attitude needed to achieve a normal takeoff and that necessary when landing

4. The availability of natural buffet as a stall warning

5. How the aircraft behaves at the stall

6. Aircraft maximum rate of roll

7. Amount of rudder co-ordination needed to achieve a balanced turn

8. The harmonisation of roll and pitch control forces (for example heavy in roll but light in pitch)

9. Aircraft behaviour in a spin

10. How hard the ride feels in turbulence

AR has an influence on all of the items in this list, especially if it is particularly high or low.

I stated earlier that each chapter in this book was intended to stand alone but there is inevitably some crossover, especially with the more technical chapters. Because some knowledge of lift is involved in appreciating most of the handling issues above and to avoid unnecessary repetition here, I shall assume the reader is broadly happy with the content of Chapter 10 rather than explain some of those basics again.

Fig 1 is a simple plot of the way C_L varies with alpha for three wings of very different aspect ratio: a sailplane (25), a typical general aviation (GA) aircraft (8) and the extreme slender delta (1).

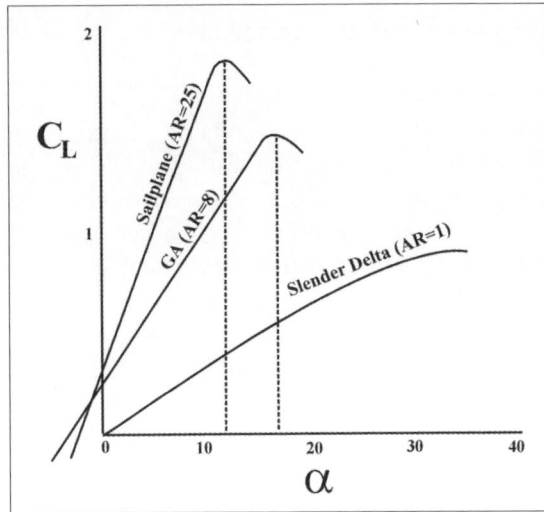

Fig 1

The marked effect of aspect ratio on stalling angle and the slope of the lift curve

Several things are clear from *Fig 1*. The line for a sailplane has a very steep slope and reaches a distinct stall at the lowest alpha of the three wings while that for the slender delta has a very shallow slope and displays no obvious stall. In between, the GA aircraft stalls rather like the glider but at a slightly higher alpha (Issue 2) and importantly has a shallower slope than the glider. The slope of this line or, as aerodynamicists refer to it, the 'lift curve slope', tells us how much we have to raise the nose (increase alpha) to get a given amount of extra lift (Issue 1). This is very little in a glider, rather more in a GA aeroplane and a lot in a slender delta. Some might feel this important handling characteristic could be described as flight path sensitivity with the glider being touchy, the GA aircraft par for the course and the slender delta very sluggish. Such a simple description would have been well frowned upon by my tutor at ETPS but is still useful in getting one's head round the topic.

Not surprisingly all this fits in with what we see at airfields where we note gliders touch down fairly flat (Issue 3), GA aircraft have the nosewheel a bit up towards a three-pointer attitude while Concorde needed such a high alpha to fly at low speed that the designers had to hinge the nose cone to improve forward view during takeoff and landing. All of this is down to aspect ratio.

The lift curve slope is also a factor in how hard the ride feels in turbulence (Issue 10). We feel gusts because they momentarily change the local alpha of the wing so the steeper the slope of the lift curve, the bigger the lift coefficient change for a given gust and therefore the more violent it seems.

Before turning to wing shape it is also worth remembering that, as the aspect ratio gets lower, the sharpness or abruptness of the stall can be expected to diminish, which is part of the Issue 5 story. However, while this generalisation is true, there are several other factors that combine with the aspect ratio to influence behaviour at the stall, examples being the aerofoil section, any wing twist, any wing 'dressings' (vortex generators, fences and the like) as well as the actual planform shape. Stall warning buffet (Issue 4) is also more likely to arise naturally as the aspect ratio reduces although again AR is but one factor among many that determine the eventual level of this useful and very desirable handling characteristic.

The effect of shape on a wing is a bit more complicated than that of aspect ratio. Let us start with the Spitfire because its elliptical wing is truly a classic. Here I am not talking about classic as in pretty or attractive (although the Spitfire is certainly both of those) but as in aerodynamically efficient. For a wing to produce lift it must have a higher pressure underneath than on top, so at the tip the higher pressure air has an opportunity to curl round into the lower pressure on top. Hence all wings have lift losses at their tips in the form of this bleed of pressure and (thanks to the swirl of air that results from the curling airflow at the tip) a vortex is formed that trails behind the tip giving an increase in drag. The elliptical wing achieves reduced tip losses because, as the wing chord reduces to nothing at the tip, the low pressure on the top and the higher pressure on the bottom also fade away together reducing the formation of wingtip vortices. The maths of establishing the spanwise distribution of lift on the wing, or 'spanwise loading' as it is termed, involves deciding how much of the wing total C_L should be attributed to each of many very narrow slices of equal width taken along the span from root to tip. These individual local lift coefficients (written as C_1) when divided by the overall C_L can be plotted from the root to the tip and naturally the result varies with different plan shapes. For the elliptical wing the value of C_1 / C_L is unity across the whole span – or as good as you can get – since the actual lift is distributed elliptically across the span because the wing area is itself so distributed.

This is far from esoteric from a piloting point of view as the spanwise loading has a very pronounced effect on where the stall starts on any wing. The optimum elliptical loading gives a gentle stall that starts along the whole length of the trailing edge and spreads evenly forward. A plank wing has a greater tendency to start its stall at the root while a very pointed tip or a swept back wing will tend to stall at the tip first. Again these general effects can be modified by varying the wing section used from root to tip and any twist built in to reduce the alpha at the tip when compared to the root and so delay a tip stall.

Since the elliptical shape is so aerodynamically good, it begs the question of why don't all wings look like those on a Spitfire? For once the answer is simple and is that they are much harder to manufacture – as the factories that produced Spitfires in WWII found out. In fact a gently tapered wing with the tip chord about half of the root chord performs nearly as well as the elliptical and is a lot more practical to make.

Going on to maximum roll rate (Issue 6), common sense applies and the lower the AR, the easier it is to achieve high roll rates while sailplanes will inevitably be sluggish in roll. With high AR wings one might be tempted to think that big ailerons would be an easy fix. This is true but only at the expense of much stronger and heavier wings to accept the large twisting forces. Again common sense rightly suggests that, if you want to roll into a turn using ailerons that are at the end of very long wings, you had better stand by to use your feet as well (Issue 7). This is because the increase of drag at the tip with the down-going aileron (remember that more lift always gives more drag) will hold back the very side that you want to move ahead. Glider pilots are well used to this of course and often use a simple piece of string that is mounted just in front of the cockpit to tell them when they have got the aircraft balanced with no sideslip.

Pilots always have strong views about the harmonisation of control forces (Issue 8) – at least when they are not how they like them! Whether the aircraft has a wheel, a control column or a side stick, it is still true to say we find it easier to apply considerable pull and push forces than we do sideways ones, while relatively high forces are easily available from our feet. Therefore everyone likes light ailerons. Reasonably powerful and light ailerons are needed in the circuit for safe and comfortable operation at low speeds, especially in turbulence. On the other hand it becomes essential when close to maximum speed to make it difficult for the pilot to apply enough control to break the aircraft. Fortunately normal V^2 effects come into play with manually operated controls making them four times as heavy when speed is doubled. As we have seen, increasing AR raises structural issues that make it harder for the designer to accommodate light aileron forces at high speeds. This really only becomes a problem if people want to use a high AR aircraft for aerobatics when some compromise in handling is inevitable.

The last item on my list of piloting issues yet to be discussed is spinning (Issue 9). Here it is hard to generalise as spinning is all about a mix of aerodynamic and inertia-based forces as I discuss in Chapter 12. The ratio of the moment of inertia in pitch (B), divided by the moment of inertia in roll (A), or 'B/A' ratio as it is called, is always significant. To reduce its magnitude by increasing A, as will happen with a high AR design, is likely to make the aircraft spin flatter and be more reluctant to stop. However that ignores aerodynamic effects which will be very type dependent and could make the aircraft more or less prone to spin. To be certain of what is going on, it is nice to be able to increase A without changing anything else, which is what happens if you have fuel in tip tanks (or outboard internal wing tanks) compared to spinning the same aerodynamic shape with those tanks empty.

However one thing about which there will never be the slightest doubt is the effect of AR on induced drag. A lower AR always involves an increase in induced drag or, in mathematical terms 'induced drag is inversely proportional to AR'. Therefore, quite apart from its effect on performance, a very low AR can mean the approach is flown well on the 'backside' of the drag curve – so you need more throttle as you slow down, not less.

Any consideration of wing plan shape must also include the use of sweepback. As a young lad in the mid-1950s, I remember flying instructors in the RAF talking darkly to each other (never to us) about swept wing handling characteristics. At that time, having just been awarded our own wings on Vampires, we were being dragged screaming and kicking (alright, I jest) towards a self-evidently swept wing thing called a Hunter 4. Although there were no two-seaters, the brief for this first trip seemed just the same as for any previous Vampire sortie except that the speeds had gone up a fair bit. There was also a lot of emphasis on fuel, touchdown speeds and how to use the brakes as well as 'false locks' (a nasty event that could afflict the power-assisted ailerons). However sweepback was not mentioned. With hindsight this was reasonable because, if we stuck to the briefed manoeuvres and flew the correct speeds, we were never going to get to high alphas, let alone the stall, which is where early swept wing aeroplanes did pose handling problems as we shall see shortly.

The use of sweepback to make it easier to fly faster, especially as the speed of sound is approached, was first proposed by a German scientist, Adolph Busemann, in an open scientific paper that he gave at the Volta Congress in Rome in 1935. Talking to the aerodynamicists who worked at the Royal Aircraft Establishment in the 1930s and during WWII, it is clear that the failure of the UK and US scientists who attended the Congress to pick up on the significance of this paper was a source of considerable professional embarrassment to them as it could have seriously affected the outcome of the air war.

Busemann's sweep angle was a way to reduce high speed drag by reducing the thickness chord ratio of a wing without reducing its maximum thickness. The reason drag depends not just on thickness but on thickness divided by the chord (wing width), is actually quite intuitive. A wing spar naturally has to have a certain depth in order to be strong enough. The greater the chord of the wing, the greater the degree of 'streamlining' that is available to ease the passage of the air past the spar. With the same depth and a smaller chord, the wing becomes more of a blunt object and so has more drag. Walk round any straight wing aircraft and look at its thickness chord ratio. Then imagine the air coming at that wing not at 90° but at 45° as it would if the wing was swept back to that angle. The air now has to cover a much greater distance in travelling from the leading edge to the trailing edge and so experiences a reduced thickness chord ratio.

At first the stressmen were delighted when the designers chose to reduce drag by using sweep rather than reducing the all important spar depth. Then it dawned that a lot of the lift produced by this swept wing was going to be applied well behind the wing spar root attachment point on the fuselage. Thus this wing was going to twist (trailing edge up) as it came under g. This was the start of aeroelastic effects and with swept wings meant an aileron going down caused the wing to twist leading edge down making it possible that the wing overall actually lost lift and thus 'aileron reversal' was born. If you like, it was the old Wright brothers' wing warping lateral control technique working in opposition to the ailerons. One of the palliatives for this was inboard ailerons which did not produce such an inappropriate wing warp but, being inboard, also had less leverage so they were not the best for twinkle rolls either.

These structural issues had to be faced if sweepback was used. However there was worse to come, namely pitch-up. Pitch-up is longitudinal static instability so, if in level flight you make a nose up control input and then let go, the nose keeps on going up. Indeed once it has started, a full nose-down control input may not be enough to stop it. Pitch-up happened to early swept wings because at high alpha the tips stalled first so the aircraft lost all the lift behind the CG but kept that ahead of it. This tendency for the tips to stall first arose from the increasing 'spanwise flow' component of airspeed that arises geometrically as the sweep angle is increased. This flow from the fuselage towards the wingtip rather naturally added to the traditional tip losses and stall problems that are inherent with any wing.

Attempts at reducing this spanwise flow resulted in many aircraft sprouting wing fences. The Russians in particular used these on their fighters from the MiG-15 onwards as well as on bombers and transports. Leading edge extensions and leading edge notches were used in the UK with some success – for example on the later marks of Hunter. The uses of 'fixes' to optimise a wing design as a result of flight test data is now commonplace. This brings me to the ubiquitous vortex generator (VG), as this is arguably the most commonly used fix of all.

While not often seen on GA aircraft, VGs are in abundance on military aircraft and airliners and their operation deserves being understood by all pilots as it involves the term 'adverse pressure gradient'. Consider the air flowing over any basic wing. We know that as the wing approaches the stalling alpha, the air flowing over the top tends to stop hugging the shape of the wing section, starts to distance itself from the skin and develops into a rather messy state. The aero guys say this is because it can no longer cope with the 'adverse pressure gradient'. This term is easy to understand if we think for a moment that air normally likes to go from high pressure to low pressure and does not naturally flow from low to high.

In order to fly a wing has to have air at a lower pressure on the top compared to that underneath. Now imagine you are in that low pressure air flowing over the top and rushing towards the trailing edge at which the air pressure is quite a lot higher. This means you are faced with an 'adverse pressure gradient' which is why the air under the wing succeeds in curling round the trailing edge and moving forward against you. It does this initially inside the upper surface boundary layer beneath you and so pushes you up and away from the skin. At this point 'separation' has started. All this takes lots of words but is easy to see in a low wing aeroplane if you attach a tuft of wool with a bit of gaffer tape to the top surface just ahead of the trailing edge and watch it turn round and face forward as you reduce speed – all well before the stall.

As a bit of an aside, I could never afford to pay for my own flying let alone that of my first wife, should she become interested. The problem was Pat naturally wanted to see what I did to earn the housekeeping. Deciding that attack was the best form of defence, I took her flying in a borrowed Tiger Moth on one of those days that looks beautiful standing on the ground but, once you are above 500 ft, there is very little to see and even less sense of which way is up. Five minutes of very gentle wingovers and rolls in these conditions turned me into a hero for doing this on a daily basis to feed the family. It also convinced her she was clearly born to stay on the ground. Some years later I took my new second wife, Adèle, up in a PA-44 and asked her to keep an eye on a wing tuft. I explained this was positioned too close to the fuselage for me to be able to see it from my side so I needed her to keep an eye on it in case it turned round and started facing forward – as flying backwards could be dangerous. Head in map, I slowed down gently and the inevitable scream meant I did not have to pay for her to learn to fly either. I suppose I am lucky that I did not finish up having to invest in a third good lady but, in the event that ever happens, I don't have a medical to fly solo any more so the problem is solved. Thank you CAA. I don't believe I wrote that. Of course the same situation might have arisen with my proof reader, Val, but as it happens she is into words not wings, so once again my luck holds.

The vortex generator (VG) works because it sticks up into the airflow just enough to generate a swirl of air behind it which induces some of the fast flowing main stream air *above* the boundary layer *downwards* to mix with the boundary layer and so 're-energises' this sluggish air thus delaying its separation when faced with the adverse pressure gradient creeping up inside the boundary layer. Although a VG clearly has drag, this may be negated if the vortex delays separation and the attendant drag rise. *Figs 2 & 3* are two pictures of a Harrier wing taken in the wind tunnel using a surface oil film to visualise where the high mach number air is still in touch with the wing and show how effective VGs can be once they are optimised. Very much more of the wing in *Fig 3* is working hard at high alpha thanks to the vortices steaming back from the VGs just behind the leading edge. This was worth nearly an extra g when manoeuvring hard at the higher mach numbers.

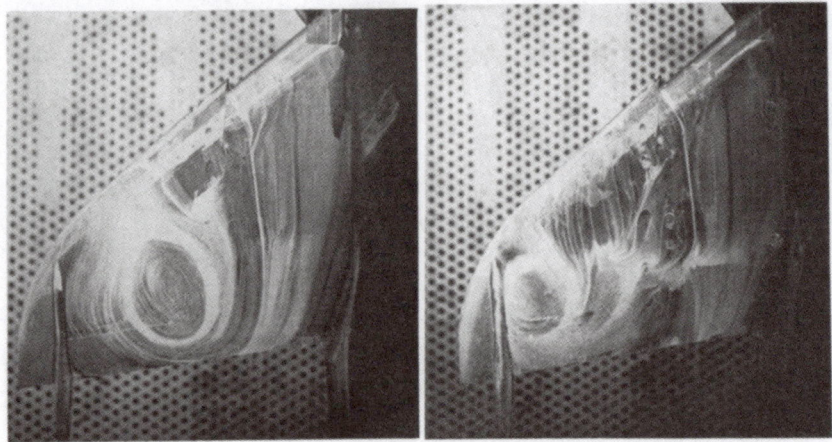

Fig 2   *Fig 3*

After a 1971 demo in Switzerland, I got a phone call on my return from Kingston designer, Robin Balmer, thanking me for providing visual evidence of his chosen wing dressing doing its stuff. I did not realise what he meant at first, until I saw a picture taken at the time. Thanks to high humidity conditions, the low pressure at the centre of each vortex, shed by the VGs and the mini outer fence, caused condensation enabling some nice flow visualisation in the form of the streaks over the port wing as in *Fig 4*.

Fig 4

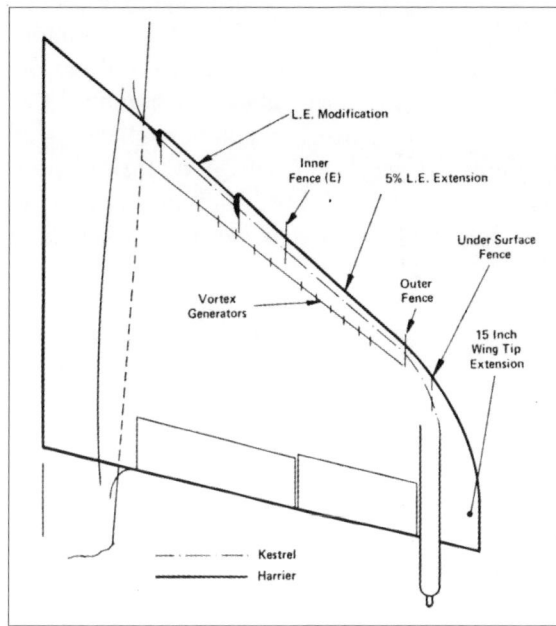

Fig 5

This diagram shows details of the wing dressing package that was developed for the original Harrier in order to meet an RAF specification point calling for 6g at 400 kt and 10,000 ft with a weight of 16,800 lb

On the other hand slender deltas, of which Concorde is the most famous example, break all the normal rules of lift generation being designed to operate in a state of continual separation when flying at higher than cruise alphas. Consider the 74° sweep HP115 shown below.

HP115

285

Here, at other than very low alphas, the air effectively makes no attempt to remain attached to the upper surface and wraps itself up along the entire length of the leading edges into a vortex above each wing. They sit there rather like a pair of ice cream cones flying point first alongside each other. The greater the alpha, the greater the energy that is imparted into these vortices and therefore the lower the pressure above the wing and the more the lift. The leading edge root extensions or 'strakes' seen at the front of so many fighter wings (e.g. F-16, F-18, MiG-29 etc) at high alphas act effectively as small HP115s just ahead of the wing proper generating large vortices that swirl towards the centreline of the aircraft from each side.

Incidentally, this inwards flow pouring down from both sides onto the upper surface centreline is what feeds the engine intake and fin of the HP115. On fighters with strakes, this inwards flow also does a good job in helping to reduce the outwards flow that would otherwise happen more markedly on the rest of the swept wing behind the strakes, improving overall high alpha handling and performance. However, such high alpha lifting capability only comes at the expense of considerable drag as mentioned in Chapter 4 where I describe the Concorde takeoff director research carried out at Bedford in the mid-1960s.

My two final points concern swept forward wings and fly-by-wire. It will not have escaped some readers that Busemann's idea of using sweep to reduce the apparent thickness chord ratio applies equally well to a forward sweep angle. What is more, such a forward swept wing has the spanwise flow component going from tip to root reducing rather than exacerbating traditional tip losses. Aerodynamic heaven? Perhaps but the structural side of a forward swept wing is extremely difficult. When a swept forward wing deflects under g, it twists leading edge up, so the tip alpha increases leading to more lift and more twist – an unstable situation. This could only be overcome with conventional metal structures by designing a very stiff and therefore heavy wing. Things are easier today as composite materials allow the designer to adjust the flexural axis more easily. Time will tell whether the aerodynamic advantages of forward sweep overcome past objections to its use.

Fly-by-wire has enabled the wing designer to concentrate on achieving optimum aerodynamic or stealth performance leaving issues associated with how the shape might handle to software writers – something that designers from the past could not have imagined in their wildest dreams.

Chapter 12

Stalling and spinning

Stalling

I think all pilots have definite ideas about stalling. The extent and form of these ideas will naturally depend on their experience and background.

So far as a pre-solo PPL student is concerned, these ideas may well be limited to a determination to stay faster than something called the 'stalling speed' unless told by their instructor to do otherwise and only then at a safe height and after some special cockpit checks that they have yet to commit to memory.

On the other hand, an experienced pilot going out to do a C of A flight test on somebody else's aeroplane and, noting some hangar rash on the leading edge of one of the wings, may well take a mental punt that when the aircraft stalls the damaged wing may drop first.

If I were to have a face to face chat with either of these pilots and the subject of stalling came up, I would naturally say quite different things to each of them and, even more importantly, would further adjust how I banged on about my own ideas depending on how I saw they were being received. Sadly, such interaction is not possible here. Therefore, please be patient in reading this because it is extremely unlikely that I shall pitch it just right for you!

One really needs to have a satisfactory grasp of the basics of lift to appreciate what is going on with stalling and spinning. While I admit I said in Chapter 1 that all the chapters in this book were intended to be stand alone, there is necessarily a degree of overlap with some topics. To avoid repeating myself, please may I ask those who may not be totally happy about the relationship between the lift coefficient (C_L) and the angle of attack (alpha) to take a look at the Lift part of Chapter 10. For convenience though I will repeat the C_L/alpha curve here to save you having to turn back.

How do we define 'the stall'? This is not actually an easy question to answer. Indeed it is one that had BAe and McDonnell Douglas (as they were then) rushing to their lawyers in the late 80s and early 90s to decide who was to blame for a possible contractual liability regarding the stall of the T-45 Goshawk trainer for the USN. Clearly in some circumstances stalling can become a very complex issue indeed. That is the bad news.

The good news is that it is not in the least a complex matter for a pilot to fly around avoiding accidental stalls and also to thoroughly enjoy the experience of deliberate stalls. That is what I want to write about here.

The normal actions to control lift no longer work when an aircraft stalls so pilots lose control of the flight path and have to take stall recovery action.

This raises the question of just how do pilots normally control lift? The answer of course is that they do it by pulling and pushing on the controls which varies the lift coefficient of the wing by varying the alpha – and nothing else. If you are not happy with this statement may I once again refer you to Chapter 10.

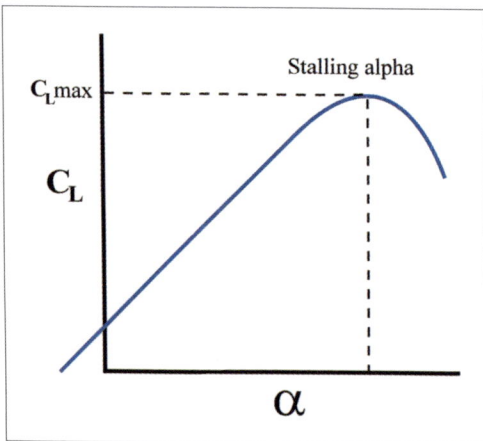

As *Fig 1* shows, there is a straight line relationship between C_L and alpha for most of the curve. This is where we are when flying clear of the stall and enjoying a linear response. That is to say moving the stick twice as far produces twice the response. Such a linear relationship is something humans prefer for any control task.

Fig 1

I have deliberately not put any values at the end of each axis of *Fig 1* as they are very type dependent. Many aircraft would be pushed to achieve a maximum lift coefficient of 2 while a few might reach 3 with full high lift devices deployed. Equally some wings will stop their linear increase of lift by 12° alpha, while others may hang in there to 20° or more. It all depends on the wing design, both the aerofoil section and the planform shape. The essence of what *Fig 1* shows is that, if you pull back and keep increasing the alpha to the right of where the line stops going up, you have stalled, although not every company lawyer might agree!

All of which is a very long-winded way of getting to the vital point that aeroplanes don't stall because of the speed at which they are flying but because of the alpha that the pilot is using. Believing and living your life by that statement is the secret of success when deliberately stalling as well as enjoying the experience as we shall see later when discussing some airborne techniques.

Before leaving *Fig 1* I should cover the term 'autorotation' as it will be needed when discussing spinning later. If one wing should drop for any reason when approaching C_{Lmax}, the subsequent way the air comes up under the down-going wing increases its alpha and could take it over the peak and into the post stall range. At the same time, the up-going wing is experiencing a slight reduction in its alpha and so is protected from stalling. Because the slope of the curve beyond the stall tends to be steeper than that approaching the stall, the down-going wing loses lift faster than the up-going one so the rolling continues. This condition is termed autorotation and if uncorrected can lead to a spin.

As I describe in Chapter 10, when considering the lift formula $L=C_L\frac{1}{2}\rho SV^2$ the only other term, after C_L, that a pilot can control in flight is of course V. As an aircraft is slowed down in straight and level flight, with more and more back stick, there will come a speed at which the ever increasing alpha causes C_{Lmax} to be reached and that is the 'stalling speed' for those circumstances.

Just what that stalling speed turns out to be for a particular aircraft will depend on the weight (because that is determining the amount of lift we need), the amount of flap used (because that can change the C_L/alpha relationship), the bank angle (because that points the lift in other than a purely upwards direction) and the amount of power in use (because that may affect the local airflow over the wing and may also include an upwards component of thrust that will reduce the amount of the weight that the wing lift has to support).

The effect of air density is not something that pilots have to consider regarding stalling speed, despite it appearing in the lift equation. This is because the V we fly is indicated airspeed (IAS) as opposed to true airspeed (TAS) and IAS includes the density effect.

The effects of weight, flap and power can be substantial. A long-haul airliner may weigh twice as much on takeoff as it does when landing and most have advanced flap systems resulting in very different C_{Lmax} values flaps up and flaps down. Also many such flap systems actually increase the wing area (S) when they are extended, further increasing the lift available for a given speed. For completeness, the stalling performance of a wing will also be affected by the mach number at which the wing finds itself. This can be of concern when flying aircraft at high weights and high altitudes. Indeed, when Walter Gibb raised the world altitude record to 63,668 ft in a Canberra in 1953 he had less than five knots between the stall and his limiting mach number (the speed above which he would have lost control due to the effects of shockwave formation).

At this point I expect you can see why I think that the 'stalling speed' of any aircraft is such a variable feast, even in straight and level flight, that it is of strictly limited value as a means of avoiding an accidental stall. Given the effects of bank (the stall speed goes up by 1.414 times the straight and level value when turning level at 60° of bank), just what number do we need to remember? What is the stall speed during a loop or a barrel roll?

Since at low mach numbers (say less than 0.4M) any given wing with flaps up always stalls at the same alpha regardless of speed, aircraft weight and bank angle and then at another constant angle flaps down, it would be really nice (understatement – see Chapter 10 again) if all aircraft were fitted with an instrument read-out of alpha. This is becoming standard in most military aircraft and on some modern airliner flight decks and with it you can see the margin you have between your present conditions and the stall. This is especially valuable if you are uncertain of your weight or have perhaps made an error with your approach speed calculations.

I was glad to have an alpha gauge one day in a CN-235 out in Indonesia. The aircraft belonged to Merpati and their training captain was in the right seat while I did some test flying for them using some instrumented controls fitted on the left. Several flights into the programme we were on our way back and found ourselves a little short of distance to do the approach and landing checks. While the super local guy in the RHS rushed round the charts and tried to work out our speeds I got on with flying the approach. I did this by simply slowing until the alpha increased to its normal approach value, then flew that speed. Working out our weight was a particularly difficult job as we had water ballast and there were imperial units and metric units all muddled up with fuel and water contents. Eventually the captain looked up from his chores. "118 kt approach speed, John". "Do you mind checking that?" I replied.

At three miles he looked up and said, "Oh dear. That was wrong, it should be 129 kt. Sorry, John." Then he noticed that I was flying 130 kt and asked with big eyes, "How did you know?" To my undying shame I tweaked the yoke a bit and said, "After a while in this business you get a feel for things, don't worry". Afterwards I felt bad for weeks because of the way I sometimes caught him looking at me.

Before going on to talk about avoiding stalls when flying without an alpha gauge, there are a couple more background matters to mention. Firstly, let us think a bit about the margin between our normal flying conditions and the stall. What is a sensible margin? It is clearly important not to stall accidentally on the approach but so is approaching as slowly as possible. Flying the approach slowly in order to reduce landing distances means using a lot of alpha but we also need to stay away from C_{Lmax}. Normal certification requirements (military as well as civil) give us speeds to fly that are based on 1.3 times the straight and level stall speed for our approach weight and configuration. This means that we are effectively prevented from using the last bit of the straight line in *Fig 1*. Normal finals control movements, plus any gusts, will momentarily nibble a little into the margin from the stall but no more than that.

Secondly (and this is a minor point that I include here only for completeness) stalling speed also depends a little on the centre of gravity position. How much it varies with CG depends on the stability of the aircraft. Longitudinal stability requires the tail to provide a downforce, the amount of which will be a maximum for any type when it is being flown at its forward CG limit and a minimum when on its rear CG limit. This downforce is in effect an apparent increase in the aircraft weight. However, just as the wing always stalls at the same alpha regardless of aircraft weight, it also stalls at the same alpha regardless of CG position.

Imagine we are airborne and cruising normally, all nicely trimmed out straight and level and we then chop the throttle and continue to hold the height constant. What does that mean is going on with regard to the lift equation? It means simply that V^2 is shrinking rapidly and we are increasing C_L in order to keep lift equal to weight. On *Fig 1* it means we are somewhere on the straight bit of the curve and moving rapidly along it towards C_{Lmax}. Please note we are doing nothing to control the rate at which we are rushing up the *Fig 1* curve since that rate is determined entirely by the imbalance of thrust and drag that we set up when we chopped the throttle.

Now imagine we have just reached the point of C_{Lmax} at the top of the curve. Did you notice that as you came off the straight part of the curve you suddenly had to pull back more quickly in an attempt to hold the height? In fact was it not the case that you did not quite compensate for this sudden non-linearity in the control response and lost a bit of height? However this is all a bit academic at this stage as the speed is still falling and we have now well and truly started on the downhill side of *Fig 1*. The aircraft has stalled, the attitude has gone to pot and the aircraft no longer responds normally to the controls.

The problem with this imaginary stall exercise was that we were not controlling the way the alpha increased, we were merely holding height instinctively with the stick. The result was that we not only reached the alpha for C_{Lmax}, but we went considerably beyond it as the speed continued to rush off.

A much better way to fly the approach to the stall is to control the rate of rise of alpha. This is done by ignoring the height during the deceleration and just using the longitudinal control to trickle the speed back at 1-2 kt per second – slower if you can manage it because the slower the better. With such a deliberately slow increase of alpha we are then in a position to evaluate any changes that may happen. The sort of changes will vary from type to type so the list can be long but the following are examples:

- The onset of vibration or buffet
- Little tugs or twitches on the ailerons
- The need to use the feet to keep the ball in the middle
- One wing getting heavier
- The nose comes up
- The nose drops

This totally controlled process can be reversed at any time by relaxing the back pressure a little, putting you back to the alpha at which you were before the symptom. To make this action easier and more natural it is important not to re-trim once you have started easing the speed back.

Before going any further, I must stress the need to watch your height above ground when doing a stall in this way. Quite considerable sink rates can be involved and the whole exercise can take minutes rather than the seconds that it takes when using the more dynamic 'hold height and let the speed rush off' technique.

If your local area does not allow you to lose more than say 1,000 feet before you have to knock it off, a full investigation of the stall using this very controlled technique should be broken down into several decelerations. For example, start the deceleration at your normal cruise speed then chop the throttle and trim into the glide holding say 10 kt below the cruise. This is your start point and from then on do not re-trim. Now pull just enough to creep the speed off. By the time you have lost perhaps 30 kt you may find you have still not reached any symptoms and you are down to your minimum safe height. No problem, note the speed you got down to and climb back up.

Next time start as before but, when you pull back to start the deceleration, pull the speed off fairly quickly until you are 5 kt above the minimum you got down to the first time at which point relax the pull and only trickle the speed back from there on. If necessary this process can be repeated again and again to ensure that you are still at a safe height when the stall eventually happens.

When examining this very basic stall (clean, idle power and wings level), the pilot can stop slowing down (increasing alpha) whenever a significant symptom appears. Then having built up confidence with coping with the first symptom, the controls can be used gently and instinctively to suppress the symptom (if it involved a bank or directional change) and speed deliberately trickled back a little more to look at the next thing. Eventually there will be an end to this, which might be the controls reaching the full back stop or perhaps a wing drop that is sufficiently abrupt to be only controllable by carrying out a proper full recovery.

This is the technique that is used for flight test purposes. It gives very repeatable results, is much easier on the nerves and can leave you very much more confident in how you feel about low speed flying in any type.

Once you are totally happy with this method of controlled approach to stalling, the way is open to do further stalls with different flap and power configurations. Finally, once you have confidence, you can look at faster rates of deceleration to see the issues associated with accidentally penetrating deep into the stall before commencing recovery action.

Any chance of an accidental spin as you slow down is reduced by keeping the ball close to centre. However, what should you do if a wing drops violently? You actually know the answer to that – get rid of the high alpha with a positive forward movement which by itself will prevent any autorotation that may be round the corner or arrest it at once if it has started, while at the same time using rudder to keep the ball in the middle or to stop the nose moving round the horizon. Never use rudder to pick the wing up since that is always the job of the ailerons once you have reduced the alpha.

I suspect the idea of using rudder to control bank angle when approaching a stall or following a stall goes back to early types where a wingtip often stalled really abruptly and in that case a dose of down aileron to pick up a wing that was starting to get heavy could actually make it stall. The wing probably started to get heavy only because the ball was not in the middle. These days wings are better designed and the ailerons are perfectly safe to use gently and with feeling quite close to the stall or even in it with some types. The 'gently and with feeling' bit is important. If a small amount of aileron does not produce the usual roll response don't persist (or even worse, add a handful) but check the ball.

When this basic wings level stalling has become easy and enjoyable, I suggest you are ready (in both head and hands) to look at stalling in turns or manoeuvres. Without an alpha gauge that is very much a matter of appreciating how the aircraft is talking back to you as you increase alpha. Just before the stall you may well find that, as well as experiencing the usual buffet or even lateral trim changes, you are pulling back more but nothing extra seems to be happening – always a sign that the wing is about to give up in my experience.

From a pilot's point of view it would be harder to pick a single bit of data that had a more tenuous connection with when a wing actually stalls than the reading that happens to be on the airspeed indicator at the time. I think the term 'stalling speed' is very meaningless. All automatics like the autopilot, the autoland system, fly-by-wire control systems and (yes!) the stall warning and recovery systems check the alpha to decide how to fulfil their functions. Only human pilots still use the idea of a stalling speed.

Spinning

Spinning is a big deal and I beg to disagree with anyone who would suggest otherwise.

It is a big deal because it involves extra risk and so deserves extra care. Unlike any other aspect of the PPL syllabus, I regard spinning as a very unsuitable subject to go and practise solo after say only a couple of dual sessions. The spin has a special ability to disorientate anyone with normal middle ear balance organs. This is particularly so in high rotation spins where the time for a turn can be a second or even less. A pilot requires special preparation to operate efficiently in such circumstances and I will return to this subject later.

If you think these are strong views, I agree but I still feel that once you have your PPL, you should give serious consideration to getting some instruction in spinning and seek to master it. Accordingly I have two aims with this section. Firstly I want to give you a taste for some of the theoretical considerations associated with spinning and secondly I want to discuss some practical piloting aspects of the manoeuvre. Make no mistake, I believe spinning can offer real enjoyment not only by the sheer nature of the physical ride but also because mastering the spin can lead to great personal satisfaction and is an unparalleled confidence builder for serious aviators.

It is a good thing to get your important points in early when trying to sell any idea. That way they have maximum impact and don't get lost in the middle or even not get read at all. However, every aspect of the subject of spinning is important and so any bit of information about the topic you can glean needs to be stored in your mental spinning file. Any bit not bothered with, or seen as a minor issue compared to others, just becomes the weakest link in an otherwise strong chain. Therefore, please do not attribute any significance to the order in which I mention things here. All of it is important.

A comprehensive coverage of the theory of spinning is way beyond the limits of this chapter (and me for that matter). Therefore I would ask that you take what follows as a selection of pointers to the topic and remember that theory is not in any way helpful to a pilot in a real cockpit spinning down towards the ground. Indeed it could actually distract such a pilot who should not be trying to 'think' his or her way out of the spin but should be concentrating on executing the optimum recovery actions established for the type during spinning flight tests.

There are three phases to a spin. The first incipient phase, the developed spin and the recovery. We need autorotation for an aircraft to enter the incipient spin and this phase can last from one or two turns to even five or six with some types before the spin can be called fully developed. As we saw earlier, autorotation is the state where the down-going wing wants to drop more while the up-going wing wants to rise more.

It follows that you cannot spin without first stalling at least one wing and getting it on that part of the lift curve where more alpha gives less C_L.

When considering the nature of a particular spin (nose down or flat, oscillatory or steady), the inertia effects of the aircraft (those forces that arise due to its mass and the distribution of that mass) are just as important as the aerodynamic effects (those forces that arise due to its external shape and direction of travel through the air). CG considerations are also very important. Just as there is an aft CG position for any aircraft that makes it a pig to handle, there is also an aft CG position that will preclude recovery from a spin. Indeed, this aft CG limit for recovering from a spin may well be further forward than that which gives rise to longitudinal control problems in normal flight.

One pointer to the likely recovery characteristics of a particular aircraft type is something called the B/A ratio. This is the ratio of the pitching and rolling inertias and, if B is greater than A, the forces that result are anti-spin and so aid recovery. If A is greater than B, these inertia-based forces will tend to keep the aircraft in a spin. If you have a lot of wing fuel or what you have can slosh outboard because of a lack of tank baffles, then your A will go right up (bad) and it will be even worse news if your aircraft is fitted with tip tanks which contain fuel. Indeed the spinning clearance for a type having tip tanks will usually say they must be empty.

Tail configuration is important. It is good if the rudder is full depth and well aft of the tailplane and elevator, whereas the other way round is bad because, spinning down at a high alpha, the fin and rudder will be in the dirty wake of the horizontal tail surfaces.

Rear fuselage cross section is significant during a spin because of the part it plays in determining the yaw damping. With high yaw damping, spins naturally tend to be slower (good). Because the airflow is up from under the aircraft in a spin, you can show that fuselages with round under surfaces but flat tops are better at producing yaw damping than say an oval section. The ultimate in these rear fuselage effects is provided by anti-spin strakes, as on a Chipmunk, which make the top of the fuselage very wide compared to the bottom. Such a shape might have five times the yaw damping of a round fuselage when in a spin. Not a minor difference.

Let us concentrate now on piloting in spins. I want to mention some specific spinning stories because my views expressed in my first line on this subject are the direct result of these and other similar ones I could quote. These stories all suggest that if you spin enough, or without proper thought, you must be prepared for an unusual spin to happen every now and then.

My first abnormal spin happened during a solo Piston Provost sortie. I had perhaps 50 hours total flying. The nose was going round only a little below the horizon as opposed to the normal nose low attitude of perhaps 45° nose down. It seemed to recover normally but a little voice said, "Go home". When I told my instructor what had happened he looked annoyed and left me in no doubt that I must have done something wrong for that to occur. I stuck to my story and eventually he walked out to my aircraft on the pan. Following a lot of staring at it from a distance he declared the fin to be leaning over to one side. This was changed to 'loose' after they got it in the hangar.

A few months later, on Vampire T11s at Swinderby, one of our course went off to do a dual spinning sortie. The weather was low cloud and rain. Some 30 minutes later we stared as the aircraft came back into dispersal without a canopy and with no left hand seat. We watched in total silence as the instructor passed through our crew room to enter the Flight Commander's office. As the door closed behind him we heard him say, "I lost my lad".

Later it became clear that a nominal four turn student spin had gone on for six more turns after recovery action was taken, that the instructor had taken over at some point and pre-occupied (as one is in those circumstances), muttered out loud, "If so and so does not work, we may have to think about ejecting". The last word of this sentence was taken as a clear and unequivocal executive order by his student. Fortunately his ejection was completely successful.

After the usual Board of Inquiry, word got back to us that the instructor was taken to task, not for losing his lad, but for spinning over total cloud cover. Quite right too, because it is hard enough to judge what is going on during a normal spin and recovery, without doing it over a featureless blur of white.

There can be no excuse for adding weather difficulties to all the others necessarily associated with deliberate spinning. Therefore if there is any cloud it must be well broken and spins entered only over a big gap (after all how else do you know you are clear of houses, etc below?). Visibility must be good with a clear horizon in all directions. If there is cloud above and the sun is obscured, you must pick a good prominent land feature to use as a mark for counting the turns and you need this feature in view as you enter. At our latitudes if you can see the sun this is likely to be the reference of choice unless you are blessed with a really good surface feature like a bit of coastline with a river estuary.

Since there is no law of aerodynamics (or aircraft design) that says, 'If the control surfaces of an aircraft can make it enter a spin, they can also make it recover', you should wear a parachute. Sure, I have sometimes spun without one but not often and never again. To spin without a chute is in the same category as flying a single-engine aircraft over water, outside gliding range of a suitable field in which to force land, without wearing a life jacket. Again I have done that a few times too but I am not proud of it and that sort of fatalistic approach to flying really has no place in a well operated cockpit.

When I was instructing on Jet Provosts at Cranwell, we had one airframe that seemed more reluctant to recover from spins than the others. It was a Mk 4 and differed from our Mk 3s in having a more powerful engine. The only external change was a very slight variation in the shape of the elevator horn balance. Because of the way it spun, we were not happy to use it for student solo exercises and the thing was generally a pain. The Boss talked Boscombe into doing an investigation of its handling and they came to take it away one Friday afternoon. The pilots did not want to chat about our experiences in the aircraft and off they went. The Boss rang me Saturday lunchtime and said that they had jumped out of it that morning because it would not recover from a spin.

A couple of years later on the course at ETPS I was allocated a two-seat Hunter for my spinning exercises. As you would expect we were told to investigate and report on the effects on the spin of a variety of non-standard entries and recoveries. On one recovery the plan called for a little outspin aileron to be applied. As I applied this combination the nose suddenly pitched down from its normal attitude and shot all the way up in a bunt to just beyond the back horizon. As it happened, I had an Army Air Corps Captain for company on the trip. He was a very loud and extrovert natural born leader of men, with a talent for drinking and mess games that left most of us floundering. He was doing the Rotary Wing course at the time and prevailed on the staff to be allowed to see what the fixed wing guys got up to. He was quite relaxed when the bunt happened and so his shins got a nasty clout as his legs flew up under the instrument panel. The phrase 'Couldn't have happened to a nicer chap' comes to mind although it did make him uncharacteristically quiet for a while afterwards. In the climb back up for the next point, he enquired whether that sort of thing happened often. I replied, "Sometimes". A sort of fixed wing guys one, rotary wing guys zero.

Back in dispersal, a member of the ground crew went up into the rear equipment bay to take out the trace recorder only to re-appear a few moments later covered in battery acid. In those days free acid was not normal as the battery cell spaces were filled with a spongy substance to stop the acid coming out of the vents in normal manoeuvres. However it later appeared this very violent bunt had a spin dryer effect that emptied the sponge.

The instrumentation traces showed the whole manoeuvre very clearly and, since the staff had not seen a spin like that before, I was sent over to Dunsfold to show the evidence to Hugh Merewether, their deputy CTP and spinning guru. He agreed it was a new variant but he was not surprised. I then listened, fascinated, as Hugh explained that, although they had done hundreds of spins on the Hunter trial, that did not mean they had experienced everything that could happen. How could you be sure that you had covered every combination of entry speed, g, turbulence, fuel state, fuel slosh, CG range, aileron, elevator and rudder handling? Clearly there were so many possible combinations of things. The same applied to recoveries. That was the nature of spinning. Until the day a type goes out of service there is always the possibility of an unusual spin.

Roger Topp (leader of the 22 Hunters that looped at Farnborough in 1958) had long been a hero of mine since I first flew with him as an observer on flight trials at RAE. Later we flew together when I was on Hunters in Germany and he was CO of the local radar unit that provided our interception control. When my ETPS course had its visit to Boscombe, Roger then CO of the fighter test squadron, took me out on to the pan saying he had something to show me.

That 'something' was a Hunter fitted with leading edge extensions. These were no more than a few inches in chord and were fitted to the last 40% or so of the span. Roger asked me to consider how it could be that something so small, that clearly could not generate much aerodynamic force at spinning airspeeds, could totally change how this great eight tons of metal responded to spin recovery control. "Think of the inertia forces when that much weight is whirling round. How come some little shape change like that can prevent recovery if there is even one degree of outspin aileron present?" He went on to say that in his view any change to the shape of an aeroplane, however small, might make it spin quite differently. I mentioned the earlier Jet Provost story. He nodded.

When I was test flying, I was quite happy to work out a plan to safely execute all but two tests without any prior knowledge of the aircraft by the simple expedient of gradually building up to the test point. (The way we talked about stalling earlier being a typical example.) However, you can't do that with spinning because you are either in a spin or not – just like your daughter is either pregnant or not. You cannot ease up to the condition of spinning, gently try a little of it and back away if you don't like the way it is turning out. There comes a point where you are simply committed to being in a spin and having to recover later.

Therefore what help did I need when doing civil spin certification testing? Basically three things: a parachute, a suitable exit and the installation of an anti-spin chute. After that I needed to do a test deployment of the anti-spin chute in normal flight followed by a jettison check. Finally I needed to be able to open the exit at say 30 kt above the stall. On one aircraft the airloads at this speed tended to hold the sliding canopy forward and I asked for bungees to be fitted pulling and holding the canopy back once the catch was released. If it is a jettisonable exit then I think it should be tested in the hangar. Whatever the exit type, I would practise my bale-out drill in the hangar until I was pretty slick at it.

However, today you are going to go spinning in a fully cleared type so no anti-spin chute is needed. You are practised and current at hangar bale-out drills. The normal sortie brief needs to be done and a plan agreed about the spinning area and what spins you will do – for example a three turn spin to the left with normal recovery. I like to stick to one direction and one type of spin (idle power flaps up say) until the exercise is going perfectly. Then you might do some in the other direction. Do not extend the number of turns or vary the configuration until you are happy with your performance in both directions.

Consider agreeing with your instructor that he will say nothing to prompt you throughout the exercise once you start your clearing turns. If you are not happy to go through it like that, then in my view there is some doubt about your mental preparation. You must aim to be totally confident about both what you have to do and your ability to execute a procedure that is a 'by numbers' application of flying controls. This confidence, allied with total concentration on taking the correct actions, is the best way to avoid motion-based confusion. That way your brain is so busy thinking about the plan that you have no capacity left to notice any off-putting sensations.

The special spinning preparations start with an in-date parachute, properly inspected. It must be too uncomfortable to stand up straight in, or the harness needs tightening. Strap in and stow any loose kit as it will be stowed for spinning later. Ensure the extra bulk does not impede you from easily applying full control. Make sure that full rudder can be applied easily, both ways, with the knee still just bent. Get airborne and go to a suitable location. Get as much height as you can, at least four or five thousand feet above bale-out height, which needs to be at least 2,000 ft agl. Mark your bale-out altitude on the altimeter with a chinagraph. The weather must be as described earlier. Pick your spinning landmark or confirm the sun is suitable. Do your aeros or spinning checks and really *look* during the clearing turns to ensure you are above open countryside as well as clear of other traffic.

Roll out pointing towards the sun or your landmark and chop the throttle. As speed reaches about 5 kt before the stall, with both hands on the stick (or wheel), simultaneously pull fully back and stamp on full left rudder trying hard to keep the ailerons central. The ailerons should be maintained neutral from now on until recovery is complete. Shout out loud "ONE" as the first turn (nearly all roll) is completed. Maintain the controls on the stops with considerable force. Do not let them move or flap about. Shout "TWO" as the second turn is finished and "THREE RECOVERING" when your mark next appears. As you shout "RECOVERING", stamp the rudder over the other way and push that pedal with all your force. As soon as the recovery rudder is on, shout "PAUSE" (this will be about half a turn later) then positively move the control to the mid-point and then (more progressively) forward, while looking for the rate of rotation to increase (due to conservation of angular momentum) and the nose to go down as you do so. When this happens, the recovery has started and you need not push any further forward but should concentrate on centralising the rudder rapidly just as the rotation stops in a steep dive. If the spin persists, try to keep shouting out the turns, move the stick on to the forward stop and hold both stick and the rudder with a lot of force. It is important to feel the mechanical stop of full control deflection, not just some high airloads.

If nothing seems to be happening, do not panic. You have thought all this through before, haven't you? Visually check you really have got the full correct recovery controls applied, the throttle is still shut and you have not accidentally got flap down and start to concentrate on the height while maintaining the recovery selections. About 500 ft before the altimeter bale-out mark, quit and get out. If you have a choice make your exit on the outside of the spin as this will keep you further from the propeller on a conventional single piston type.

Thanks to your preparation, the chances of it ending like that are very remote indeed but not impossible. Please note that unless you are very with it, very experienced and also very current in spinning, there is nothing to be gained in trying different recovery control options. Concentrate on checking you have applied and are still holding the correct recovery controls while monitoring your bale-out height.

Not a normal way to end a chapter? Correct. However, as I said at the beginning, spinning is a big deal and so deserves special treatment, even if one is only writing about it.

Chapter 13

Instrument Flying

I came home a little late one evening and mentioned something or other that had gone wrong that day while I was flying in cloud. My wife's response was, "Don't you have instruments?" followed a few minutes later by, "I'm serving up now so leave that and come and sit down". That probably sums up instrument flying from the non-pilot's point of view which is that aeroplanes are full of instruments so pilots use them to fly when they can't see out.

I have never found instrument flying that simple. It certainly was not simple when I was learning to do it before I got my wings and it was far from simple when I was trying to get back to base in bad weather on my first RAF tour. Above all, it was not simple when I was trying to sort out the awful flight instrument system that the RAF had in their early Harriers. In fact I came pretty close to throwing my toys out of the pram one day at Dunsfold over the way RAF Harrier pilots in cloud were expected to continually cross refer between their main head up display (HUD) and their standby head down instruments in order to compensate for the unreliability of the early HUDs. The result was that I wrote a paper in which I suggested that modern flight instrument displays, far from being a benefit, constituted a major flight safety hazard.

I presented this paper at a NATO Advisory Group for Aerospace Research and Development (AGARD) symposium held in 1983 to consider design lessons from operational experience. Looking at it a quarter of a century later, I was pleased to see that if I were to present it again today, I would do no more than fiddle with the punctuation and remove the odd bit of capitalisation which is considered rude these days as it implies shouting. The paper is copied at the end of this chapter in the Annexe for those who would like to read my views in more detail.

The basics of instrument flying are of course just about controlling your aircraft without the benefit of any outside visual references. Since we already use inside references to determine our speed, height and direction, what we are missing in cloud is being able to see our attitude.

Given that controlling the attitude of an aeroplane is fundamental to all flying, then finding a substitute attitude reference is vital hence the artificial horizon (or attitude indicator) instruments. As anybody who has done an instrument flying course will know, learning to use an artificial horizon is not that difficult. However, looking at it as well as the height, speed and heading information requires an organised approach to the task that is called a 'scan'. This involves looking round the instruments in turn in a very systematic and particular way and thus building up a mental picture of how the aeroplane is flying. Scanning is not that easy, especially at first.

I feel I have a fairly high resistance to panic but I also consider that I could succumb in some circumstances. Back in 1966, as part of the P1127 programme, the RAE Bedford boffins wanted a night takeoff from a hole cut in a large wood. At the planning stage I realised there were going to be absolutely no visual cues available once I rose above the tree line. I might as well have my head inside a black velvet bag for all the good the outside world was going to be. I felt I might not cope and even panic if I did not think through my actions in advance. The manoeuvre involved large and misleading acceleration cues that had to be suppressed by focusing on the instruments. I also felt it was not good enough to lurch off and just hope normal instrument flying scanning techniques would work. Therefore I decided to plan exactly what instrument information I was going to use to control the aileron, the tailplane, the rudder and the nozzle lever and my allocation of time to those tasks for the first critical half minute or so.

In other words I needed to come up with a *task* specific scan that took in only the essential sources of information and did not allow all the other information in the cockpit to intrude on these vital issues. It turned out to be easy once I realised I only had to scan three instruments. They were the artificial horizon, which needed to be kept at the pitch and roll showing before lift off by normal use of the stick; the GIV compass below the artificial horizon, which would dictate my rudder inputs because there was a need to yaw into the wind blowing above the tree tops and the vertical speed indicator. The VSI was to the right of the compass and needed to be kept between 200 and 500 ft/min climb by controlling the rate at which I pushed the nozzle lever forward.

I refused to monitor anything else. This meant ignoring speed and height, let alone alpha or sideslip (both normally very critical in mid transition), nozzle angle or even the engine instruments. Looking at any of those was not going to stop me crashing and would only serve to distract me from the best possible control of the three things that would ensure success.

I reasoned that if I kept the attitude flat the alpha had to be well away from the stall and that, once I felt the nozzle lever was fully forward, I could then mentally switch to ordinary fast jet instrument techniques because I no longer had any nozzle down. Again, why waste limited effort reading the altimeter if your rate of climb is nicely positive? As for sideslip, the normal external vane used to control this was not illuminated in those days but it could not get far out if I kept the nose pointing into the wind with my feet. The engine would just have to get on with doing its full throttle thing until I was on my wings.

I have gone into some detail about that because I feel it is a good example of how you can lower workload in brief but critical stages of flight, or emergencies for that matter, by thinking them through beforehand. The aim always being to concentrate one's limited personal resources on the essentials and by so doing avoid overloading yourself into panic mode.

How successful routine scanning will be depends not only on the skill, training and currency of the pilot but also on the individual instrument faces or displays as well as their positions in the instrument panel. In general the older the instruments the more demand they place on the pilot. Modern instruments tend to be clearer and, in the case of attitude displays, more reliable and offer better accuracy and importantly, a better range of bank and pitch attitude before they reach their limits, or 'topple' as that is called. Of course they are more expensive.

Before going into modern displays and money aspects, I would like to say that I am all for people who want to do a basic IMC rating using traditional instruments in a traditional aircraft. For obvious reasons it is a skill well worth acquiring should your carefully planned sunny day trip turn to worms because of un-forecast poor weather.

Nevertheless instrument flying is not easy for us humans, even with the best displays, because we have balance organs that are designed to work when we are walking around on our hind legs under 1g and can easily produce misleading sensations when we wave our bodies about in cloud. This raises the issue of unusual attitudes (UAs) and pilot disorientation which, although not exclusively an instrument flying issue, is certainly an important part of being confident when flying in IMC (instrument meteorological conditions, i.e. flying in cloud).

Recovering from an inadvertent UA or dealing with personal disorientation can severely test even an experienced pilot. In the case of a beginner, either issue could easily prove fatal. If you accept that the essence of aviation safety for pilots is to understand what is involved and to practice the related skills, you will never find a better example than when disorientation occurs. Accordingly, I believe the sooner the associated training process is started the better. This is because both UAs and disorientation are not checklist material. The solutions have to be instantly ready in the pilot's head.

Both can happen when flying day VMC (visual meteorological conditions i.e. flying clear of cloud) especially on those 'goldfish bowl' or hazy days when there is no obvious natural horizon although they are more likely to be associated with being in cloud. Night VMC is a close cousin to IMC but includes a potential for visual disorientation due to external lights which are not present in IMC reflecting in funny places in the canopy.

It is a simple enough procedure to recover from an UA when in good VMC. Taking the nose high case first, confirm the speed trend is rapidly reducing and select full power. At the same time level the wings by rolling towards the nearest horizon and then, and only then, use the elevator. Ease the controls forward until a nose down response starts and then hold them in that position until the nose is say 20° below the horizon, even lower if the speed is still very low as this will improve the acceleration. Once the nose passes through the horizon, your recovery is largely done and all that remains is to wait until normal flying speed is restored and to resist the temptation to pull back early.

It is good to get into the habit of checking the ASI right at the beginning because reading the ASI is not optional in night VMC or IMC. When practising this on a nice day, look again at the ASI and note what it is doing as the nose goes down through the horizon. As we shall see when discussing IMC recoveries, the behaviour of the ASI becomes a guide to judging when the nose is below the horizon. Also it is no bad thing to get into the habit of holding the controls firmly with two hands once you have added the power. This way you will stop them thrashing about should you initially slide backwards or even hammerhead out.

Some people may see no harm in putting in some nose-down elevator before the wings are levelled and that is certainly how I suspect any experienced pilot will instinctively behave. Indeed, by doing that you may even avoid the speed dropping off the clock but, as we shall see later, that would not be the best way to deal with the same circumstances when disoriented or in IMC and I think it is sensible to standardise from the beginning on techniques that will be also be correct when it comes to the harder situations.

Now consider the nose low UA where there may be much less time to spare. You see the ASI rushing towards the red line, so chop the throttle shut and level the wings. Do not pull before you have them level. If you think you are going to hit the ground, you will have no alternative but to use considerable g but hopefully that will not be the case and you can gently ease out of the dive. The higher the IAS the more careful you should be. If you are seriously above the red line, use all the available sky with a very gentle dive recovery until the IAS is below the red line so retaining the wings for landing.

As part of practising the nose low case in VMC, note how incorrectly pulling before levelling the wings just tightens the spiral, increases the g and does nothing to get the nose up. Seeing is believing.

It is clearly harder to do recoveries from similar situations while in IMC but the principle is totally unchanged. As with any IMC flying, we are just replacing external visual cues with those from instruments. The snag is that there are a fair range of instrument fits and capabilities out there. If you have a high specification artificial horizon that does not topple easily then you may be able to use it to replace the natural horizon cues. However, if the UA is extreme you have to be prepared for it to be toppled and useless. Then the only way out of a likely spiral into the ground is to have a turn and slip indicator and know how to use it because a turn and slip cannot topple. However, a turn indicator will only give you a reliable indication of wings level (zero turn) if you have about 1g applied. If you pull before the turn needle is centred the turn indicator will over read and may even become pegged at full deflection.

The other challenge when in IMC with no attitude display is deciding when your nose is just passing through the horizon during the pushing or pulling with wings level stage. I was taught to keep an eye on the VSI which is often pegged on one stop or the other at the start of the UA. Given the lag inherent in a VSI, the nose is normally close to the horizon just as the needle leaves the stop or reverses its direction of travel if it is still moving. The ASI is also very useful here as we said above. Check out the VSI and ASI indications on a sunny day in your type with some steep climb and dive recoveries flown as UAs and all will be clear.

307

I have never owned an aeroplane but if I did I would pay whatever was necessary to have it fitted with a turn and slip indicator which I could also select to run off an emergency standby battery should the aircraft electrics fail. Add a standby E type magnetic compass to the ASI and altimeter and you have a complete set of get-you-down instruments. Just those got me back from near Boscombe to Dunsfold one day in a Harrier at 2,000 ft and in cloud until on short finals. Not a relaxed way to travel but perfectly do-able if you practise 'limited panel' (as it was called in those days) and much better than attempting to fly visually below a low cloud base.

Disorientation can be a mild affair or it can be terrifying, depending on the circumstances. In the worst case, you will have to use all your will power not to panic. In any instance it is vital to get a grip on yourself and do what you know you must, rather than behave instinctively. The actions to recover from disorientation are extremely simple, namely look at the horizon (real or instrument), believe what your eyes are telling you and fly roughly straight and level or in a slight climb if you are worryingly low. Then make yourself do whatever is necessary to continue the flight to a landing. However, all that is much easier said than done if your inner ears are playing tricks.

When flying in IMC and remaining inside airliner-type pitch and bank angles, it is still possible to get mild disorientation, usually called the leans, a condition where you are totally convinced you are flying in a turn even though the aircraft is nominally straight and level. The only solution I know for this is to understand why pilots suffer from this problem and be convinced that such experiences are normal and to be expected from time to time. This leads to confidence and enables you to talk to yourself on the day (out loud if you like) and instruct yourself to do what you know is needed to sort the situation. If panic is to be avoided, you have to believe many pilots have been where you are now and have been able to recover. You can do the same.

The doctors tell us that disorientation results when our brains receive conflicting signals from the three main sources of information about how we are moving. These are our eyes, our inner ear balance organs and deep muscle sense.

Our eyes are very little affected by flying and so are to be trusted during all normal manoeuvres. The only one exception I know to this is if very rapid rolling manoeuvres make them flick in their sockets (called a nystagmus). Then you can think the aircraft is rolling the opposite way to what is actually happening. The standard preventative technique is to violently re-accelerate through a small angle (even 15° can be enough) in the opposite direction the instant after you stop the initial violent roll. There are also optical illusions, especially in poor visibility, which can lead us to misjudge our flight path but these are not really eye-related issues, more a matter of trying to fly visually when the outside cues are not good enough.

Our deep muscle sense allows us to feel what our body is doing, for example standing on our left leg or sitting in a chair. However, this sense does not lead in itself to confusion. This leaves the inner ear as the main cause of trouble. Our brain receives information on roll, pitch and yaw accelerations from the three semi-circular canals in each ear. As we said earlier, these sensors are optimised round short duration foot based accelerations applied in a normal 1g environment. It is therefore hardly surprising that these signals have the potential to become misleading and unable to cope with aircraft flight.

One simple example is what the doctors call the 'somatographic illusion'. If we accelerate forwards at 1g when sitting upright, the inner ear perceives this to mean we are lying flat on our back in a ground based 1g world. Accelerating rapidly in any vehicle does not usually make us feel we are on our backs because our eyes tell us we are not. In other words our brains tend to give priority to our eye signals and wind down the signals from the inner ear. If a pilot does the same thing in the dark with no visual external cues, he may be convinced he is climbing too steeply, push the controls forwards and dive into the ground. That is unless he looks at and believes his instruments.

The two most important words about night VMC are 'beware reflections'. The worst reflections are those from outside sources as these can suddenly streak across canopies and be extremely startling and disorientating, seeming to a pilot to be fixed external lights or on another aircraft. Reflections from cockpit lighting do not tend to move about much so are less confusing. As always, base your control on instrument indications and, if frightened by lights, revert completely to instruments at once.

An Instrument Rating (IR) is a very different matter to an IMC rating. An IR is not just about flying without external references, it is about operating your aircraft without them and at the same time meeting complex IFR (Instrument Flight Rules). If you want to fly beyond the hobby stage, for example fly yourself about on business, then an IR is essential. However, what sort of instrument display you use for this is all about money and I would therefore now like to address the issue of your aviation budget.

While making a mess of non-aviation budgets can have painful consequences for any of us, making a mistake regarding an aviation budget can get one killed. You know the mistakes I mean, things like flying home when you know you have an engine snag that needs investigating or ignoring the little voice inside your head whispering 'Neither you nor this aeroplane are equipped to fly in this weather'. Indeed I could easily fill this chapter with examples of such mistakes and still not cover the one that might immediately come to your mind. However, I hope to be a little more constructive and to use the issue of glass cockpits to offer some general thoughts on the complex decisions that lie behind our natural desire to fly safely but within our means.

Originally I intended to go on to write about my views on the pros and cons of electronic flight instrument displays which form a major part of today's glass cockpits, based on my own experiences of developing them for the military thirty-five years ago. Then I realised that the displays creeping into today's GA aircraft also raise specific private pilot problems that must be thought about if they are to be used safely. They are also expensive bits of kit hence the need to consider budgets.

Starting at one extreme, it is possible to dismiss GA glass cockpits as just rich men's toys mainly good for a bit of local posing. After all, we have flown for long enough without them to make it impossible to argue that they are essential. Hang on though, what do we mean by 'essential'? This depends on so many things. If I were to ask you whether you would take off tomorrow knowing that your airspeed indicator was not going to work, I expect the answer would be a short 'No'. However, in that case I would surely be entitled to point out that any properly trained pilot should be able to fly safely round the circuit on attitude and power settings plus feel from the controls. Indeed, if you have an open cockpit you can listen to the wind in the wires as plenty did before the ASI was invented and in aeroplanes that were much harder to handle than today's bland certificated types.

When we say something is essential for a trip (like the ASI case), I submit we have probably made a judgement based on what is normal practice and what most people in the same circumstances would see as reasonable. The decision not to get airborne without an ASI is clearly in this category and, while we should be able to cope without one, it is totally unreasonable to deliberately degrade our safety margins before the trip starts. After all, should your engine stop on climb-out, the ASI will be extremely helpful in executing the forced landing. Therefore, if you want to practise flying without an ASI, do so by putting a sticker over its face that you can remove should you have a subsequent emergency. In the hope that you will view these ASI-related comments as pretty obvious and totally uncontroversial, I want now to extend the principle behind these to the more general matter of what equipment we should have available when we taxi out on various types of sortie.

I suggest that the minimum standard of equipment that is reasonable for any sortie is creeping up all the time. To put it another way, in today's flying environment it behoves us to continually question whether what was good enough when we started in the business is still good enough. As a simple example, the topographical maps with which the RAF sent me off in 1955 only wore out when they became too creased, torn or had too many pencil lines on them. Today much of the essential information that is overprinted on the same map can become out of date very quickly and so make the map illegal, as well as dangerous to use, long before it has been worn out by physical wear and tear. Another example is having a radio. While it is legal to do certain flights non-radio, this does not make it reasonable to do so on a regular basis because it removes at a stroke many options that you would certainly be glad to invoke when your original sortie plan crumbles.

Notwithstanding the potential unreliability of a small personal GPS receiver in your pocket and, fully agreeing that a trip should never be planned or flown on the basis of needing it, I am sure that many would agree we can increase safety by having one available as a backup. In which case is it any longer reasonable to go without one when they cost less than that a couple of hours flying?

Moving on to glass cockpits, they are of course not all the same. Some are fairly basic and mainly revamp the flight instrument displays while, at the opposite end of the spectrum, others integrate several types of navigational information by overlaying them on various map options plus weather data or even the position of nearby transponder-equipped traffic. However, regardless of their degree of sophistication, they have three things in common: they display information that is not available from traditional instruments, they display traditional data in a slightly different way (often better, but not always) and, most importantly, they enable the pilot to tailor the information displayed to suit a particular stage of flight. This used to be called 'de-cluttering' in the early days and the usefulness of this cannot be overestimated in a high work load (that is to say risky) stage of flight.

I can well remember a couple of occasions when I came very close indeed to losing control of what was going on in a Harrier and would probably have goofed in a big way without the superior display format provided by the HUD. One was on a pitch black night at low level over the sea just after launch from a ship. The other was daytime after the engine stopped. The latter necessitated a steep tight spiral descent in cloud that reached from 40,000 ft down to the circuit while my mind was busy trying to work out why the relight button was having absolutely no effect. In those days, as I mentioned earlier, we were expected to continually cross-check the HUD with the head down instruments and not allowed to use it as the primary reference. I remember thinking during both occasions that I had not got the capacity to check the HUD information against the head down displays and I hoped it was correct. Taking that sort of risk is a good example of how a pilot who is in some difficulty will always go for an easier option, regardless of what the official recommendation may be.

There are two totally separate training issues (problems) with these glass cockpits. Number one is that you have to learn what information is available, how to control the displays, how to interpret some of the scales and symbols and so on. This has nothing to do with flying but is all about learning a new computer programme and new hardware facilities in just the same way as we have to learn about a PC and printer before we can use them to execute a task. Number two is that you have to learn how to use the various displays in flight to control your aircraft. This has nothing to do with computers but everything to do with developing your existing instrument flying skills or, in the case of a youngster actually learning to fly on an aircraft equipped with a glass cockpit, learning those skills from scratch.

In the US back in 1982, I was faced with a glass cockpit in an AV-8B aircraft in a flight test environment. Before getting airborne, I turned down an offer of help with how to control these displays saying that if they were to go into service then the soft key and menu driven controls should be instinctive enough to be used on a 'monkey see monkey do' basis. There was perhaps some slight merit in that approach in a test and development environment at that time but no professional evaluator would adopt such an attitude today. They would want to be totally familiar with operating the equipment before getting airborne when they could then evaluate it as a tool to help operate the aircraft.

One indisputable fact about these electronic displays is that they are much more compelling than traditional multi-instrument presentations. Whether this is good or bad from a flight safety point of view is not quite so black and white. When learning the basics of straight and level, we all know how tempting it is to try and fly the altimeter rather than look out of the window, set a pitch attitude and occasionally glance at the altimeter to check the attitude we are using is correct. Given the visual attractiveness of some of these electronic multi-coloured displays, it is all too easy to stare at them when you should be looking out. Of course the opposite is true if one is in cloud or at night because these displays make it so much easier to be aware of your situation, especially attitude. The sheer width of the horizon cue provided by many electronic displays makes it much easier to keep your wings level than having to concentrate on a tiny round artificial horizon with an even smaller aeroplane symbol inside it. As a result I am sure an inexperienced pilot who gets it wrong and finishes up in cloud or poor visibility is more likely to survive the event if occupying a good glass cockpit, rather than one offering only a turn and slip gauge and an E2 compass.

This does not mean it is unreasonable to learn to fly instruments today using traditional gauges, in fact quite the reverse. Somebody who learns to drive a car with a clutch will have no trouble converting to an automatic gearbox later but the same is not true the other way round. Indeed this is even recognised by the licensing system which will not allow you to drive a manual box if you took your test on an automatic. So it is with learning the basics of instrument flying using a collection of individual dials. The experience will serve you well, especially if the glass fails and you have to fall back on the row of traditional standby dials below.

However, just supposing your personal aviation budget for the next few years includes spending a fair amount of money on becoming an instrument pilot and then using this privilege to do some long range transit flying in your own aircraft, then I think you should give some serious thought about how a glass cockpit might fit in to these overall plans. To say that it could save your life might be a bit melodramatic but

313

there is little doubt that your safety margins will be increased by investing in one. You will also be less likely to come unstuck and kill yourself should you get out of practice, which you know happens.

Annexe

Copy of the 1983 paper

MODERN FLIGHT INSTRUMENT DISPLAYS AS A MAJOR
MILITARY AVIATION FLIGHT SAFETY WEAKNESS

by

J. F. Farley
Chief Test Pilot
British Aerospace Public Limited Company
Dunsfold Aerodrome
Godalming
GU8 4BS
England

SUMMARY

Consideration of the major causes of flying accidents over which the
airframe and engine manufacturers can exert a powerful influence shows
the following list:

1. Structural Failure

2. Engine failure

3. Flying Control Failure

4. Instrument Failure

5. Pilot Error

With the first three of these causes – Structural, Engine and Flying
Control failures – while mistakes do occur, the manufacturers have a
reasonable record, there is no evidence of complacency, and in addition
there is a large well established, government controlled, national
bureaucracy offering valuable checks and advice on testing and
airworthiness certification. Pilot error in different, but appropriate ways,
also attracts much effort aimed at its reduction. Most importantly, so far
as the purposes of this paper are concerned, the accident trends related to

315

the first three causes, as well as those due to pilot error, do not appear to have changed fundamentally during the last decade. The same cannot be said of instrument display related accidents.

Since the advent of Head Up and computed displays in general and the operator's real need to expand the non-visual manoeuvre envelope, there has been a marked increase in display related accidents/incidents in both operational and development flying.

This note suggests that attempts at curing the problem have been based on a false assumption that has ignored the reality of the piloting task in modern high performance jet aircraft. Proposals are offered to improve the situation by both engineering and organisational changes.

1.   THE SITUATION IN THE 1950s

Service aircraft used traditional mechanical and electromechanical direct reading individual instruments with well understood limitations and failure modes. Some accidents occurred due to misreading particularly of altimeters. The operators asked for a greater manoeuvre envelope while flying on instruments as well as improved display forms to reduce pilot error problems.

2.   THE SITUATION IN THE 1960s

Head down OR 946 instrument displays started to be used extensively. These were easier to read and, with the use of Master Reference Gyros, gave an improvement in manoeuvre capability. They brought some new failure problems and aircraft fitted with them were at times restricted to visual conditions while improvements were incorporated. However, the overall situation was not fundamentally changed from that existing in the 1950s.

3.   THE SITUATION IN THE 1970s

The first aircraft to be fitted with Head Up Displays as a primary instrument flying reference entered service in 1969. The head down instruments were limited in nature and number and were conceived as get you home standbys to be used in the event of HUD failure. Head Up

Displays as fitted to the aircraft in the early 1970s showed quite fundamental differences from previous flight instrument displays. These were :

(a) The symbology was very easy to use and for any given manoeuvre gave a large reduction in instrument flying pilot workload.

(b) The freedom from roll and pitch limitations given by the inertial platform attitude reference sources encouraged pilots to manoeuvre, without visual references, more violently than previously.

(c) The data displayed could be wrong without this being in the least apparent to the pilot. (For instance because the display wave form generator correctly processed an input that was itself incorrect.) Such correctly *written* information looked totally valid to the pilot.

(d) The displays could be quite compelling.

(e) The reliability of the overall display system proved to be very low. It was not unusual for individual pilots to experience some sort of failure each month.

4.   REACTIONS TO THE SITUATION IN THE 1970s

The reaction of all interested parties to this unprecedented lack of reliability was to stop considering the HUD as the primary flight instrument display and to call for the pilot to cross refer between the HUD and the standby instruments.

In the writer's view this is where we went wrong.

This solution, which called for the pilot to cross check various displays to establish which were serviceable, ignored several important facts :

(a) In conditions of high workload the pilot will abandon all but essential tasks and revert to the easiest display from which to get the information he needs. Unquestionably this will be the HUD symbology since it includes nice easy to use items such as

317

inertial vertical speed, climb dive angle, velocity vector and so forth. This leads automatically to the least reliable information being relied upon at all times of critical pilot workload.

(b) At times the head down instruments can topple, as they tend to have restrictive manoeuvre limits, leading to confusion if cross reference is used and the chance that the pilot will believe the more reliable head down displays which are this time wrong because the original manoeuvre was one that only the HUD system could cope with.

(c) Cross reference between several displays makes instrument flying harder not easier. It can force good old-fashioned mistakes associated with scan failures between various parameters because the pilot was scanning for cross reference purposes between head up and head down examples of the same parameter.

The writer firmly believes that it is unrealistic to rely on the pilot cross checking various read outs of nominally the same information in order to establish serviceability. One recent classic example of where a 3 man crew equipped with 3 attitude references did not notice that the handling pilot was following an incorrect one, was the Air India 747 that rolled inverted and crashed, shortly after a night takeoff out of Bombay.

5. GENERAL PROPOSALS TO IMPROVE THE SITUATION

(a) Engineering

Ideally the flight data should be multiplexed, the validity of data should be decided automatically in the back of the aircraft and the pilot should be presented with this reliable data through both head up and head down displays. There is no justification for treating cockpit display data as somehow less important than, say, wing spar strength or the signal to the tailplane jack in auto terrain following or auto land cases.

Since the ideal solution will require much time and cost to incorporate, an interim solution offering some level of improvement (over the present case of hoping the pilot spots which instrument or symbol is out of step with the rest) is to have duplex systems with a monitor lane that warns the pilot through an audio warning that a display disagreement exists. Leaving him to use his skills to diagnose which display is at fault.

In this connection the Royal Aircraft Establishment Farnborough have started work on how to tell the pilot visually that a flight instrument system failure has happened. Even this task has been harder than expected, for instance, writing a large cross on the display is certainly attention getting, but in some flight trials pilots have momentarily tried to use the failure indicating cross as a reference. Merely removing the invalid information from the display has been shown to be too weak. In this case too much time can pass before the pilot realises it has been removed. Time which had he been alerted, could have been used to avoid a subsequent critical situation.

(b) Organisational

Because modern displays can use several discrete black boxes in series to produce the end result, no one manufacturer/designer may be responsible for more than one element. Because each component manufacturer is in turn only interested in showing that his element meets the specification requirements placed on him, the full interactions of the total system may not be appreciated, especially the knock on effect of any changes that may be made in isolation in one box. By its nature, this sort of problem is less likely to occur in Structure, Engine and Flying Control disciplines (But watch out for fly-by wire).

The effects of limited responsibility for one link in the chain can only be mitigated by instituting an overall system co-ordination function that must itself exist in all of the interested organisations – manufacturers, airworthiness authority and customer if the full checks and balances that we have come to rely on for Structures, Engines and Controls are also to be available for Flight Instruments.

6.   CONCLUDING REMARKS

At present it is a sad fact, that with some modern aircraft, only the President of a Board of Inquiry has the motivation combined with the authority to investigate the total system operation so far as displays are concerned.

We must develop the deep infrastructure for displays that exists in other aircraft design disciplines. From the standpoint of aircraft survival, instrument displays merit at least the level of emphasis accorded to structural, engine or control factors.

No relevant authority, research establishment, licensing organisation, manufacturer or operator should be content with the present situation. It is no longer responsible to keep telling pilots to cross check better, and to imply that if they crash through a displays problem, then they are in some way not professional enough in their approach to flying.

Chapter 14

Simulation

I suspect that simulation is as old as the human race. I also suspect that one could find a significant number of people who, for various reasons, would argue that in some circumstances it is better than the real thing. The scope of simulation is truly amazing and ranges from thumb sucking, through other personal habits, right up to the operation of machines costing many millions of pounds. Indeed, if one of the top level simulators is used to train pilots on a new type, they are then licensed to carry passengers the first time they fly the actual aircraft. I apologise if that is too much information for some people.

Of course not all simulators used by today's aviators meet such zero flight time certification standards, nor is it necessary for them to do so in order to be valuable training aids. However, the use of simulators is not limited to pilot training as they have been essential tools in the aircraft research and development process since the 1960s. More recently, specialist simulators aimed at teaching undergraduate aeronautical engineers have become increasingly common tools in forward looking UK universities.

My first significant simulator experience was at RAF Chivenor in 1957 while on the Hunter operational conversion course. The device in question would not be called a simulator today but either a procedure trainer or at best a part task simulator. It was a simply a Hunter nose, sawn off just behind the cockpit, resting on the floor. This made it what is known today as a 'fixed-base' device in contrast to modern simulators that are often mounted on a 'motion-base'. The canopy was painted white so you could not see out. The six main flight instruments looked and worked like the real thing as did the stick, rudder pedals and the engine instruments and controls. There was a working oxygen regulator with its associated doll's eye that blinked when you breathed in and the hydraulic gauge and various warning lights also worked, as did the undercarriage and flap selectors. The rest was clearly dummy stuff. What more could one ask for?

Because there were no two-seat Hunters in those days, we all had to do three or four 'sorties' in this device before being launched in the real thing. The experience gave me my first lesson regarding the deficiencies of the Hunter – one being that you could not see the compass properly unless you moved the stick or your head to one side. Given that on my first actual flight I went into cloud at 2,000 ft and came out on top at 30,000, use of the compass was hardly optional. Considering the rate of roll that the Hunter produced from even a modest sideways movement of the stick, they might not have got their aeroplane back without those simulator sessions.

However that experience was as nothing compared to one a few weeks later when I had a very heavy cold. Completely bunged up, I was taken off the flying programme and told to go to the simulator for the day. There the instructor had me plan a high level triangular cross-country exercise – Chivenor, Valley, Lyneham and Chivenor. The instructor would act as ATC during the trip as well as give me various emergencies and he would turn off the problem if I took the correct actions so that I could carry on with my navigation exercise. I was sure that I would shine in such a test because, being cocky, I reckoned I knew all about the aircraft systems.

Having just done a nice relight on the third leg after he had flamed out the engine, I was smugly making my way at 40,000 ft along a true bearing from Chivenor (the normal navigational aid in those days), when I noticed that the oxygen doll's eye was no longer blinking as it should. The regulator showed that the contents and pressure were correct so I turned the emergency flow toggle to 'On'. Still no flow. At that moment the cabin altitude warning light came on. Panic. I knew I had only seconds at that height without both cabin pressure and oxygen and that I must roll over, pull through and hope that I could get below 10,000 ft before I passed out. As I started to do this, I realised that I would not be able to clear my sinuses on the way down because of my cold so I struggled with the zip on my pocket to get at a decongestant nasal spray but the zip stuck. Talk about sweat, I was drenched before I realised where I was – in the simulator and nailed to the ground.

A few years later, I was standing outside a Lightning simulator waiting my turn for an emergencies check. The game was the same as in the Hunter. If you got the drills right you flew on. The pilot was about three miles out on a GCA to land and down to one engine having successfully put out a fire in the other. Then the instructor gave him a fire in the remaining engine. The pilot made a textbook Mayday call and said he was ejecting. When you pulled the handle at this point in that simulator, the canopy slid back on rails and the seat went up a foot or so. Job done.

However, nothing happened and the canopy remained closed. Then we heard this awful scream – it was quite chilling. The pilot concerned had failed to remove the seat safety pin during his strap in checks and found he could not pull the handle. He really thought he was going to die. A bad dose of AMD (awareness of mortal danger) as the psychologists term it.

Such experiences convinced me that there are two types of pilots. The first get in a simulator and, given the right level of workload, can become so totally absorbed in the task they literally forget they are on the ground. The other group never forget where they are. I am in the first category and very grateful for that. Why? Because the training value of the experience is so very much greater when you are truly behaving as you would in the air.

Pilots who can never get away from the feeling that they are in an artificial situation in a simulator are in a very different frame of mind to when they are flying. Because of this they may not make the same mistakes in the simulator as they would in the air and thus miss out on the ultimate safe training experience.

The same point is valid when considering the use of simulators in research and aircraft development programmes. Data gathered from pilots who cannot lose themselves in simulation tasks needs treating with caution. In the world of wind tunnels, corrections need to be applied to the model results to turn them into valid full-scale estimates. Such corrections are based on the knowledge and experience of the tunnel staff. Researchers using flight simulators need similar interpretational skills regarding their subjects and the data they collect from them.

When using a simulator for either training or research, it is important to know the basis of the data that is programmed in or the old computer saying 'rubbish in, rubbish out' will apply. Some input data may be excellent, while some may be very questionable and the validity of the data may not be at all obvious to the pilot flying the machine. Indeed quite the reverse. Just as it is easy to believe the written word has to be correct because it has been printed, it is easy to assume that a simulation is valid just because it flies nicely.

Simulators are much harder to test than aeroplanes. When you find a snag is it because the simulator is correctly computing bad data or is the machine at fault and making a mess of good data? When new training machines are being accepted by the customer (possibly by an old experienced pilot who does not fly too much these days but holds the departmental budget), there is a terrible temptation for him to say something like, "It's not like the aeroplane. Make it heavier on the ailerons." It is also tempting for the manufacturer to do what the customer asks just to get it signed off and the money in the bank.

Such 'tweaking' results in a simulator being delivered that is not to drawing and nobody knowing what they have. Was it 'too light' because the feel system was wrong, the computed aileron angles too large, the roll inertia wrong, the aero damping term wrong or the basic aero law incorrect? Was it not too light at all but the pilot was getting incorrect motion cues in roll and interpreted them as a roll control problem? These questions should be answered, not brushed under the carpet. Indeed was the evaluator even correct in his view in the first place? I am glad to say that such amateur tweaking is much less prevalent these days than it used to be and, thanks to certification procedures that look after the top end equipment, probably limited to the bottom end of the market.

Before we go any further, there is one general point I feel it is important to make about the use of training simulators, especially the very expensive airliner variety. It concerns operating them outside the certificated envelope of the real aircraft. Such manoeuvres may be flown with the best possible motives – to try and experience what is just round the corner, to try to settle an argument with a colleague about some wild event in the real thing or to investigate some hearsay regarding an accident. It is a very bad practice regardless of the reason because there is no law of simulation that says the simulator is valid when you fly it beyond its own design envelope or outside the envelope of the real aircraft. Just because it is possible to dial up a weight, CG position, fuel balance etc or fly the simulator slower or faster than the real thing is cleared to, it does not mean that what you find will be representative of what you will get if you abuse the real aeroplane in the same way. The aircraft could bite and the simulator could be benign – or the other way round. The reason we can have no idea of the validity of the simulated experience is that we have no idea how the various software writers extrapolated the data they were given to use up to the boundary. However common sense suggests they did not spend sleepless nights making sure they refined the handling and performance outside of the specified limits or envelope. After all would you?

I lost a friend test flying an aeroplane because a guy who wrote a bit of autopilot software got it wrong. He programmed it to pull the nose up if the aircraft was below the selected height regardless of any change in speed this might cause. The result was that, when flying with one engine throttled back to simulate an engine failure, the programme drove the aeroplane so far below the speed at which it could remain controllable you would not believe it. I have no doubt the software guy was not an aviator and so just did not realise the significance of his simple programme in the event that insufficient thrust was set to climb to the height dialled in to the autopilot. If flight software that wrong can get into the air, what price the stuff written for simulators?

What should be done about this? If I had the power I would ensure that all training simulators flown beyond the operational envelope of the real aeroplane were required to freeze as they crossed that boundary. This would serve two purposes. Firstly, if the boundary was crossed because the crew had a mistake, it would wake them up and remind them forcibly that they had not done so well during that manoeuvre. Secondly it would prevent them having an invalid simulated experience that could lead them to believe they knew what the aircraft would be like if flown outside the usual flight envelope.

I mentioned earlier that some universities are educating tomorrow's aircraft designers with specialist simulators. There is no doubt that modern man has excelled when it comes to making complex machines and aeroplanes are one of the best examples of this. The study of how we got started designing and using such things is a dodgy occupation because different historians will always argue about points of detail. However, I suggest that the first practical and efficient powerplant – something essential for any machine – was the external combustion 'Watt Engine' of 1790. By 'practical and efficient' I mean something that stood a reasonable chance of being sold in some numbers. However James Watt was not only a good inventor and engineer, he was also a superb salesman.

Watt had an engine that he reckoned could be used to replace horses in many applications, especially ones where teams of them walked round in circles harnessed to the spokes of a huge wheel in order to turn a flour mill or whatever. Clearly if you are going to sell a device as a replacement for horses you need to say, "I have a machine that will replace X horses". Therefore Watt measured the work that an average horse could do and called this amount of work a 'horsepower'. He then applied a touch of salesman's brilliance and multiplied the number he measured by two and used this higher output to calibrate his machines. Soon the word spread: "He said his machine would do the work of three of my horses but it used to take me six to mill this much in a day." By selling something that turned out to be twice as productive as the customer was expecting, James Watt's reputation was rapidly established and hay burners as power sources were on their way out for good.

The trade of aeronautical engineer, as opposed to aeronautical pioneer, did not really start until about 90 years ago because it needed the development of the lighter and smaller internal combustion engine to become established and early flying machines to be built and crashed before we could start to use the adjectives 'practical' and 'efficient' to describe aeroplanes of those days.

Any youngster who wants to become an aeroplane designer today has a lot to get his or her head round and it is going to require much study and hard work, to say nothing of skill, to improve on the products currently coming out of the aircraft factories. As part of this study and hard work, students today have to get to grips with the basics of aerodynamics plus the stability and control of aircraft in exactly the same way as I did over 50 years ago because such matters have not changed. Fly-by-wire may make life easier and provide modern pilots with delightful handling when compared to the piloting challenges of many past designs but the designers of tomorrow will still have to fully comprehend the aerodynamic effects of their designs in order to be competent to tell the code-writers what they must achieve.

Back in 1992 Chris Neal was a simulator designer working on machines for airline use and I first met him when he needed a test pilot to gather flight test data required to build a CN-235 simulator destined for Merpati, the Indonesian internal airline. Shortly after this job was finished his parent company, as many do these days, decided to reorganise themselves. This made Chris decide to branch out on his own and establish a niche business offering specialist simulators to universities with the simple aim of improving the effectiveness of their aircraft design courses. These were not intended to help students qualify as pilots but to help them appreciate the practical results of selecting and adjusting terms in the complex mathematics of aircraft design.

As with all the best ideas the notion was simple. Start with a single-seat cockpit that is equipped with displays of instruments and the outside world. Then provide software and a control console that makes it easy for students to input their own design data for the aerodynamic model to 'fly'. The difficult bit of course was to produce a model that had the flexibility and mathematical integrity to respond *properly* to everything from the crudest dimensions of wing span and chord down to the lift curve slope of the rudder.

The key word of course is 'properly'. Today a few quid will buy you software from any computer store that will let you think that you can enter design changes into an aeroplane specification using your own PC at home but the issue is whether changing the input quantities in this data will be properly reflected in how the aeroplane then flies. In other words, is it a valid simulation? Take my word for it, you get what you pay for in these matters.

By 2006 Chris's own company, the Merlin Flight Simulation Group, had simulators installed in ten UK universities and Merlin had held six annual Aircraft Design and Handling Competitions. In these competitions students sent Merlin the data for their designs and in past years, at a suitable public forum in one of the universities, I flew each of these designs on a single day, pronounced on how they performed and selected a winner. In 2006 things were a little different. They say nothing succeeds like success and 12 teams entered designs, so I needed serious help. This was provided in the best possible form by Dave Southwood, a test flying tutor at the Empire Test Pilots' School.

The whole day was aimed at encouraging the students and helping them to learn. Therefore, whenever Dave and I found a problem, we did our best to explain what we thought might be causing it and, since a single data point never did make a flight test report, we often repeated the tests several times.

Why do I mention all this? Simply because we shall only make better aircraft in the future if we encourage the best and brightest of our youngsters into the business and educate them to the highest possible standards. They have to realise that, while aeroplanes are very complex machines, they must be designed to be easy for pilots to fly. As this competition showed, simulators are powerful tools to help the academic staff do their job and the students to understand what is expected of them – including having to deal with critical test pilots prone to telling the truth.

When Jack Henderson walked out to do the first flight of the HP115 slender delta research aircraft in 1961, he had several things to ponder. He was undoubtedly pleased that, as a serving RAF Squadron Leader and CO of the RAE Aerodynamics Research Flight at Bedford, he was considered better qualified to do the first flight than any of the company test pilots of that period. At the same time, however, he knew that the whole reason the aircraft had been built was because theory suggested such a planform would be difficult to control at low speeds. Indeed the aircraft had been built just to establish whether pilots could cope. He had also flown the RAE HP115 simulator and found it terrible. Seeing him struggle with controlling the simulator in roll, some of the boffins had real reservations about whether it was safe to go ahead with the flight trials. After all, what if the aeroplane turned out to be harder to control than the simulator?

However Jack was exceptional when it came to aeroplanes. He had his reasons for thinking that the aeroplane would be easier to control than the simulator and he was right. This was just as well, because the Supersonic Transport Aircraft Committee decided in 1959 that if an airliner flying at Mach 2 was to be successful, performance considerations required it to be a slender delta. Hence the decision to build the HP115 research prototype and find out if the handling could be made acceptable for the shape that would eventually become Concorde.

The message from that story is that Jack knew simulator results must be treated with caution. Even today it is still necessary to think about and interpret R&D simulations, not just take them at face value.

At the heart of the matter is that when we fly, we use a very wide variety of cues to help us control the aircraft. Should any of them not be correctly reproduced (modelled) in the simulator, then clearly the two experiences start to diverge. Of course, how much such divergence matters depends on the details of each case. It is also possible to have cues in a simulation that are not present in flight, in which case it may be that pilots will use them to help their control of the simulator without even realising it, as we shall see later.

However, despite the devil being in the detail, it is still possible to come up with some reasonable generalisations. Let us start with motion. The simulator available to look at the HP115 in those early days had no motion, so was fixed-base. The aircraft was expected to have a very high rate of roll because its very small span meant there would be little to aerodynamically damp such a motion (roll damping derives from the increase in alpha experienced by the down-going wing and a similar reduction on the up-going side). When applying and holding any amount of aileron in a conventional aircraft, the pilot is rewarded by an initial acceleration in roll but the aerodynamic damping quickly kicks in as the roll rate builds up and therefore you finish up with a steady rate of roll where the damping and aileron effects have become equal and opposite. We are all used to this – the boffins call it a rate control and humans are very good at using such a system.

Since the HP115 shape had so little roll damping, the researchers saw the lateral control as behaving more like an acceleration control system which they felt would lead to over-control and pilot induced roll oscillations. Certainly this was very much the case in the fixed-base simulator. However, Jack correctly predicted that the roll acceleration when airborne would provide a marked cue that would make him instinctively back off the aileron before things got out of hand.

Since Jack's day it is now widely accepted that fixed-base R&D simulators are normally harder to fly than the real thing. However this may not be the case with some fixed-base training simulators where the model could have been tailored to respond a little more slowly than the aeroplane just to make the simulator seem more like the aircraft.

Valid motion systems for simulators are not easy to design or manufacture. While anybody can wobble the cab about to create some illusion of motion, making the simulated sensations identical to what one would feel in flight is not just difficult, it is actually impossible. A moment's thought explains why – an aeroplane has freedom to move in all six axes: roll, pitch, yaw, heave (up and down), sway (side to side) and surge (fore and aft). Even if the simulator motion system has freedom in all six axes like an aeroplane, it necessarily has pretty small limits on the physical range of these movements.

However as we saw with the HP115, it is the initial acceleration cue that triggers a pilot into doing something with the controls and motion bases can certainly provide such a cue for a brief period before they have to then gradually reduce it to zero ('wash it out') in order to stop the simulator banging into the limit of the available motion travel.

If, in theory, it is easy to provide the acceleration cues, in practice there are engineering problems. This acceleration cue must be immediate. If it comes with lag, forget it as it will be worse than useless. Time lags injected into control tasks or cues have exactly the same effect on messing up a pilot as rubber control runs would have in an aeroplane. In addition, motion systems need real horsepower to get on with their act, especially with a big multi-crew cockpit, which will not be a light device. This horsepower, whatever the weight of the cab, must be applied very smoothly as any jerking or vibration completely destroys the value of the cue.

The vast majority of training simulators are used in the airline business, which is just as well because that job requires only modest manoeuvres without huge displacements and so some very valid motion bases can be provided for this important training.

It is clearly not so easy to simulate the motion of an agile military aircraft. To this end back in the 1970s McDonnell Douglas had a very powerful motion base which they used for fighter aircraft research. Their aim was to provide very large and rapid motion cues closer to the reality of a fighter pilot's experience. To achieve these, the cockpit was mounted on the end of a long arm that could be moved very violently by a large hydraulic system. Because of the forces it could impart to the pilot the simulator was restricted to fast jet aircrew.

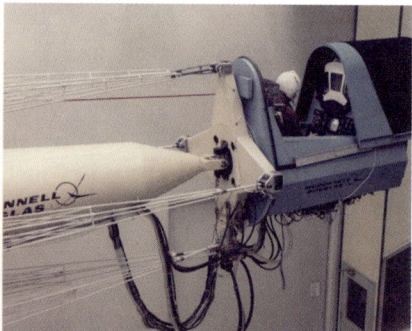

The McDonnell Douglas motion base used for research

These forces on the pilot could arise in two ways, firstly when you put in a big control input and secondly – and much more worryingly – if the subsequent manoeuvre caused the motion base to hit its stops while it was moving fast. The resulting jolt was not pleasant to put it mildly and you had no warning it was coming because you could not see out and appreciate your position in the building with the canopy closed. A lot of test flying involves putting in an abrupt control movement and then leaving the aircraft to its own devices to see how it responds. In an aircraft well away from the ground, such manoeuvres are a total non-event but in this simulator they were something else again, in case it hit the stops. During certain tests this was the only simulator which made me more apprehensive than doing the same thing in the real aeroplane.

Staying with motion, the business of simulating hovering flight is another interesting area because holding a steady hover is a remarkably acceleration free experience. Therefore what motion cues does a pilot use (if any) to help control the hover? Back in the early days of VSTOL, NASA were not sure of the answer to this question but their boffins had a feeling that it was possible that quite gentle translational movements might be detected and used by the pilot to help him decide what to do. If you like, they thought pilots might use subtle seat of the pants cues, especially in height control. Clearly this would require a simulator that would need relatively huge up and down, sideways and fore and aft movement because washing out such limited cues just after they arose was clearly not going to be like real hovering, where you can slide about all over the place as you try to get a hover under control.

Accordingly NASA built an enormous motion base. It literally filled a hangar. There was a small open cockpit cab mounted on the end of a long horizontal arm via a universal joint. Thus the cab could roll, pitch and yaw to its heart's content at this joint. To get heave they tilted the arm upwards and at the same time arranged for the cab to pitch nose down with respect to the arm and thus hold a level pitch attitude. Sway was done the same way with a combination of sideways arm travel and yawing of the cab to hold its heading steady. The support for the arm at the opposite end to the cockpit was another great structure that could run about on rails and so provide even greater travel as you charged about this huge hangar. For a visual display they opened the hangar doors and you used the car park outside, which was of course a perfect set of visual cues – nothing synthetic about them.

By using this simulator, NASA investigated a whole host of hover control issues over many years using a large number of pilots. They then published what was to become the free world's standard reference work on the subject of the control forces, displacements and sensitivities needed for easy to handle hovering vehicles. It was just as well that this work was started after Hawkers decided to design a fighter that could hover, otherwise the Kingston guys might have thought it all too difficult.

As an RAF test pilot flying the P1127 in the mid-1960s, I was asked to go and try this NASA goodie as they had a model of the P1127 installed and wanted to know how it compared with the aeroplane. This motion system really annoyed me right from the off. It made such a noise. Going sideways it sounded like an underground train leaving the station. Aeroplanes just don't make noises like that. Therefore over the course of a day or two while carrying out their hovering tests, I taught myself to set up a hover by zeroing any noise (no noise meaning no movement!) which I then tested by flying briefly with my eyes shut. When it came to the last day I quietly asked if I could fly it with the doors shut. I was told that had been tried and it was impossible, as one was driven to violent over-control as the hangar doors flashed about just in front of your nose so the only way to hover it was to look outside at the car park.

You can guess the rest. I prevailed upon my hosts to humour me and I was launched with the doors shut. After a brief period of acceptable hover, I thanked them on the intercom and asked to get out. At the debrief there was some disbelief at my view that the doors did not matter and a lot of asking what technique I used. When I explained that I had my eyes shut, that only produced more disbelief. At which point I suggested they listen to their motion base and bin all their programme results because how could they know whether their past test subjects had been helped by zeroing these false audio cues when setting up their hovers? I was not asked back.

Years later when considering the initial design of the Sea Harrier, I wanted to increase the sensitivity of the lateral control to make life easier when landing on a small moving deck. I felt that the time taken in moving the hand across the cockpit to apply control was time wasted as it allowed any situation to get away from you even further. Therefore I suggested doubling the sensitivity to the controls designer, whereupon he reached for his NASA hovering reference, looked up the appropriate page and explained that such a change would put the aircraft outside of acceptable handling criteria.

I gave him my views on the reference and said I wanted to try out my idea that afternoon. He explained it would take a long time to modify an aeroplane and that it would only be safe to modify one cockpit of a two-seater in case the pilot with the more sensitive stick induced a lateral oscillation and lost control. I insisted I was going to try it that afternoon in an instrumented single-seater at Dunsfold. I think he was on the point of phoning for the nurse but actually asked how I was going to do that. "By moving my hand halfway down the stick," I replied.

That afternoon I gave it a go and thought it made life much easier and during the following week I got the other Dunsfold pilots to do the same. They loved it as well so the change to the controls was made before the first Sea Harrier was flown, despite a certain simulator-based reference book of hovering criteria.

Chapter 15

Material and other thoughts
(plus a personal selection of best aeroplanes)

You probably don't think I have much in common with Madonna. However you could be wrong because some years ago the singer announced to the world that she was 'a material girl' and right now I am going to try and explain why I am 'a materials man'.

What do I mean by that statement? It means that while I have little materials expertise myself, I very much admire specialists in this field, as well as those who develop the methods that are needed to turn new materials into manufactured parts.

I have this admiration because it became clear to me in the 1970s that it was getting harder and harder to make better flying machines without improved materials and new ways of using them. To test that view, I ask you to travel back with me and consider how things were when I joined the industry over half a century ago.

The Brabazon coming in to land at Farnborough over Cody's tree in 1950

I was just starting my apprenticeship when this picture of the Brabazon was taken. Looking back on the 1950s and also the 1960s, it is apparent that aerodynamicists were still developing their science. New aeroplanes abounded of all shapes and sizes and different ideas were constantly being tried out.

As an example of this, consider the huge difference between the wings of the Vulcan and the Victor even though both aircraft were designed to the same specification (B35/46 issued in 1946 for a bomber to replace the Avro Lincoln). Compare the totally different shapes of two successful early Mach 2 (twice the speed of sound) fighters, the Lightning and the Starfighter. What about the different approach to jet lift aircraft demonstrated by the five engines in the Short SC1 or the nine engines of the Mirage IIIV and the single engine in the Harrier? I could list plenty more examples but I am sure you get my point. In those days aerodynamicists and aircraft designers were still exploring a whole variety of possibilities.

However, all that was a thing of the past by the 1970s. The job of expanding the performance envelope of aircraft (that is to say how high, how fast and how slow they could go) was essentially complete. By then designers had already provided safe and efficient subsonic airliners that would cruise at 36,000 ft and .85 Mach (85% of the speed of sound). All they did was put a pair of swept wings onto the sides of a tube, add a tailplane and fin on the back, attach two, three or four jet engines and bingo the job was done.

Of course, when you look in detail at airliners that were around at any particular date, some designs were a little better than others, in that they were cheaper to buy, cheaper to operate and safer to fly. However, did that variation exceed say 5 or 10%? I very much doubt it.

Staying with airliners, again by the 1970s research had produced a safe airliner that would fly at 60,000 ft and Mach 2 by using a slender delta and dispensing with the tailplane. The big snag was a vehicle of that size flying supersonically made a bang that populated areas would not tolerate so it could only be flown supersonically over the sea. Clearly the world was not going to need many of those then. However from an envelope expansion point of view, it was job done once again.

It was a similar story with military aviation. Using the same criteria of how high, how fast and how slow they flew, flight envelopes stopped expanding after the 1970s.

When the Hawk flew in 1974, it offered sustained g capabilities to levels where the pilot could not remain conscious (sustained g meaning you have enough thrust to keep your speed up during the manoeuvre and so can continue at that g until you run out of fuel). No point in designing for even more g then. Certainly aerodynamicists were still improving low speed turning and combat pointing performance by design refinement but that was hardly revolutionary stuff.

The Harrier family of VSTOL aircraft showed considerable progress in payload and range but that was mainly thanks to engine developments and, as we shall see in a moment, such jet engine improvements are extremely materials dependent.

The only exception to all this was in the rotary wing world. Helicopter envelope expansion did take a few years longer to stagnate but by 1986 the UK had raised the helicopter airspeed record to 249.09 mph (or 400.22 kph as the team would prefer you to remember it) using a modified Lynx fitted with a special experimental rotor developed under the British Experimental Rotorcraft Programme.

Lynx Helicopter World Speed Record Holder

That record still stands. Even more significantly, no helicopter design organisation is even trying to build a helicopter that will go as fast let alone faster. Envelope expansion job completed once again.

Therefore what about the future? Given the maturity of aerodynamics today, the scope for significant improvement in that field is pretty limited. The efficiency of the modern Airbus and Boeing wing is such that any increase will only be marginal. However, the rest of the aeroplane, namely the fuselage and tail, does provide significant quantities of weight and drag without contributing to the lift in any way.

This leads me to the only real prospect for better airliner aerodynamics that is on the horizon. The School of Engineering at Cranfield University, as well as several other organisations, is working on a new design of blended wing and body (BWB) to improve on the efficiency of the standard tube, wings and tail that is today's fully optimised airliner.

The BWB concept changes the various design compromises that have become the norm with airliners. It offers advantages of greatly increased aerodynamic efficiency and usable internal volume, which in turn will provide serious reductions in fuel burn and atmospheric pollution. Indeed improvements of 25% are confidently predicted. However, this is only going to happen if the researchers can find solutions to several potential downsides, at least so far as passenger carriage is concerned.

Cranfield Blended Wing Model

Passengers today sit very close to the roll axis and so are happy to have their airliner change bank from 30° left to 30° right but they will be subjected to quite another ride if they are sitting well out towards the wingtip and so go up and down a great deal whenever the bank angle changes. Other people issues relate to what this configuration means regarding windows and evacuation routes.

This new BWB shape is much less problematic for freight carriage and there are many who believe the demand for air freight will rise inexorably. They say this because the world as a whole is getting richer and so the demand for trade and the transport of associated goods will continue to increase as a result. In these circumstances, the advantages of using the air are immediately apparent to anybody who considers the fundamental limits on moving goods round the world by land or sea.

If those who predict this growth of air freight are right, then the market might be forced to fund a dedicated and efficient BWB freighter in order to address pollution limits. Remember anything we dump into the stratosphere stays there, whereas stuff we put out into the troposphere does at least mix and is subject to atmospheric washing effects. Indeed, the word troposphere stems from the Greek 'tropos' meaning 'mixing'. The advantages of limiting freighters to fly just below the tropopause are therefore very real. The aerodynamic efficiency that the BWB offers will assist these freighters to fly economically at these slightly lower levels.

That still leaves the conventional airliner full of people up in the stratosphere searching for ever better performance in payload and range, if not in height and speed. Until somebody starts selling large tins of anti-gravity paint or material for lighter airframes, we will need better engines that will deliver more thrust but will use less fuel and engines that weigh less, last longer, produce fewer of the bad emissions and make less noise.

We are back again to the need for better materials. While the airframe designer craves materials that are lighter, stiffer and less prone to fatigue or corrosion, the engine designer wants materials that can be used at ever higher temperatures.

In my view, the hot end of jet engines today represents the pinnacle of the mechanical engineer's art to date. Therefore if the experts among you will forgive me, I would like to mention some of the mechanical engineering facts that apply to the airliner powerplants that we all take for granted today but by using everyday comparisons rather than engineering units.

The Rolls-Royce Trent 500 is in widespread use with airlines. The high pressure turbine (HPT) wheel at the back of that engine has blades that extract energy from the gas stream in order to drive the high pressure compressor up the front. Each of those blades is about the size of a credit card and extracts rather more horsepower from the gas stream than is installed in the average Formula 1 racing car. The HPT on the Trent 500 has 90 such blades.

Because the HPT is going round at about 10,000 rpm, each of its blades is trying to fly off with a force that would lift a double-decker bus. If that does not impress you, please note that the temperature of the gas stream in which these blades are working is 200°C above the melting point of the material used to make them. To cope with this the blades have to have a ceramic coating and be cooled internally using air that is already at 700°C.

They also need to demonstrate a safe service life quoted in years of operation which means considering the possibility of fault lines developing between the individual crystals that make up the material. To prevent these the blades, complete with their cooling passages, are cast as finished products by growing, yes growing, a single crystal of the material to fill the mould.

In my view achievements like these represent remarkable mechanical engineering expertise but there is even more to the story. If you move to the front of the same Trent engine and look at the big fan blades they too incorporate amazing materials technology. Each fan blade is made by taking three sheets of titanium and diffusion bonding them together in a specific pattern of joins. If diffusion bonding is an unfamiliar term, think of it as a superior welding process that does not reduce the characteristics of the material. The flat bonded sheets are then inserted into a mould where they are heated and an inert gas is pumped in between the layers to inflate them so that the outer layers form the required twisted aerofoil shape while the middle layer becomes stretched to form a honeycomb to give great strength to the hollow blade. This process is called super plastic forming.

By now you are either in awe of materials technology as I am or fast asleep so I had better move on to the other thoughts mentioned in the title to this chapter.

If we split the first century of powered flight into four quarter centuries it is easy to see how aviation progress has varied. From 1903 to 1928 it went from the Wright brothers' first fixed wing powered flights to a point where flying was established. Many aeroplanes were in use, they did not go particularly high, fast or far but they were clearly here to stay.

The second quarter century from 1928 to 1953 included WWII. This period produced huge advances in aircraft performance and by 1953 jet aircraft were commonplace.

The third quarter century to 1978 included the first landings of the US Space Shuttle and the USAF deploying the Lockheed SR-71 world wide. Both of these aircraft set new standards of faster and higher. In the same period, helicopters and jet VSTOL aircraft made routine and widespread use of flying at zero speed.

However, using my simplistic criteria, the last twenty-five years have produced nothing new, neither military nor civil. Indeed, given the retirement of Concorde, commercial aviation has stepped backwards with what is on offer to the airline passenger. Therefore the evidence is that commercial aviation has become a commodity where the market wants aircraft that are cheaper, quieter and safer. Because of this military aviation has become a separate and very different type of specialised activity that no longer indicates future trends in civil aviation as it used to when I joined the industry.

That said never forget the materials bit. Better materials will allow improved military and civil aircraft, regardless of any other developments. Thus I suggest that anyone who stands in the way of materials research is sadly lacking in vision. When doing my reading to establish that aeroplanes had not gone faster, higher or slower during the last quarter century, I frequently got sidetracked – often for hours – looking at the details of various aircraft development programmes. As a result I found myself wondering more and more about which aircraft I felt were the best, not just in their day but in the overall context of aviation so far. This led me to what is obviously a very subjective selection of aeroplanes!

First up I produced a shortlist for the title of the World's First Great Aeroplane. I decided very quickly that several of the well known aircraft used to set records (at least pre-WWII) were not necessarily great aeroplanes at all. I feel that these spectacular flights invariably said more about the courage, skill and determination of the pilots than the quality of their various mounts.

Therefore out went the Wright Flyer, the cross-Channel Bleriot monoplane, the Ryan NYP, the Vickers Vimy and all WWI types. "What, no Great Aeroplanes from WWI?" I hear you cry. Well that would be my view. Some aeroplanes during WWI were clearly more effective than others and were very successful when flown by 'aces' but on balance I suggest that was again down to special pilots rather than special aeroplanes.

My shortlist started with the de Havilland Tiger Moth which first flew in 1927. Second was the Taylorcraft Cub of 1930, which went on to become the Piper Cub. Both the Tiger and the Cub established careers that are still going strong today. Given how relatively immature aircraft design was all those years ago, it is clear that for these two to be so loved and still flown in large numbers today, they have to be serious candidates for 'The World's First Great Aeroplane' until that is you consider the Douglas DC3 of 1935.

The DC3 was the first really successful airliner design which slept 14 passengers in bunks as the Douglas Sleeper Transport (DST) and later carried 21 in seats as the standard DC3. Using a fleet of these, American Airlines became a real force in the air passenger transport business. Given the more modest role of the Tiger Moth and Cub pair, there really is no contest even though the DC3 was eight years behind the Tiger. Toss in the part played by the DC3 in operations during WWII to say nothing of the Berlin airlift and the case for it builds further.

To all of this I added some personal experience. Back in 1997 the new version of the Nimrod for the RAF was slipping and slipping due to airframe issues. The radar subcontractor, Racal, later to become Thales, decided it really did need to crack on and do some airborne development of its new equipment and not sit on its hands pending the Nimrod. They decided to fly it in an Air Atlantique DC3. I was lucky enough to get the job of clearing the modification to the satisfaction of the CAA. It was quite a big mod. Not only was there the matter of a large radome under the nose, the basic electrics of the DC3 were designed to run little more than a radio and the navigation lights plus provide a modest level of illumination in the cabin and cockpit. Therefore a seriously large auxiliary power unit with its own air intake and exhaust plus a tank of jet fuel had to be installed in the rear of the fuselage just to generate the required amount of electrical power.

Air Atlantique DC3 modified as a radar test bed

During the flights needed to clear this mod, including in the way of such trials a lot of flying on one engine, I developed a tremendous admiration for the team that designed the DC3 sixty-two years earlier. During every pre-flight I reflected on the simplicity of the structure and the incredible longevity of the whole machine to say nothing of its utility and ladylike handling. The DC3 was truly a great design and my choice for The World's First Great Aeroplane.

I next considered what I felt was the Greatest Ever Aeroplane Programme where the aircraft was designed from the beginning for service use. No shortlist needed this time as for me nothing comes close to the technical challenges that faced Clarence 'Kelly' Johnson when in 1957 he was asked to come up with the highest flying, fastest and lowest radar cross section aircraft that he felt was possible. The result was the A-12, YF-12 and SR-71 family from the Lockheed Skunk Works. The 21 years of continual operational use of the Mach 3 SR-71 Blackbird between 1968 and 1989 represented a pinnacle of achievement and operational capability that will never be surpassed now that we can rely on ever more sophisticated military satellites.

Until the 1990s, all worthwhile details of the Blackbird and its ancestors were buried deep in the black world. I had my first glimpse of the A-12 on a visit to Edwards as a guest of Lockheed and their SST slender delta team back in 1966. I had been sent to the USA by RAE Bedford to liaise about our joint interest in the slender delta configuration that was emerging for Concorde following RAE flying of the HP115. By then the A-12 had been to Mach 3.56 and 96,200 ft. This single-seat predecessor to the Blackbird first flew in April 1962 and did its first operational overflight with a CIA pilot out of Okinawa a mere five years and one month later in May 1967.

In case anybody thinks all you need to cruise as fast and as high as the A-12 or SR-71 is a pair of very big engines and a nice sexy shape, then they should do some reading and preferably go to Duxford and study the SR-71 example there, especially the engine diagrams. Without banging on too much, we are talking about a unique engine cycle, a unique type of fuel, a fleet of specially modified AAR tankers to deal with the fuel and a unique type of titanium airframe construction.

Initially the workers on the shop floor used tap-water to wash components, Pentel pens to mark them and chrome vanadium spanners to tighten nuts. They soon learned that all of these hitherto normal workshop practices produced scrap if the material you were working on was titanium. The problems the Skunk Works uncovered and had to deal with in the course of trying to design and build this family of aircraft were literally amazing.

As for the flight development task, it took a month under six years from the first flight of the SR-71 (at Groom Lake Area 51) to the day the two-man USAF crew flew an operational over-flight out of Okinawa. Just comparing those timescales of 61 months (A-12) and 71 months (SR-71) with the interminable progress seen on relatively mundane military development programmes of today is I hope enough to explain my choice of the Greatest Ever Aeroplane Programme – plus why I am in awe of the chaps who did it.

Next I thought about some of the world's outstanding research aeroplanes and how they have advanced our knowledge. There have been many notable examples around the world in Russia, the US, Europe and the UK that have all opened doors to the future and have a claim to compete in this category. The problem with even listing them is that one does not know where to start and stop. As it happens I know in my heart what I think leads any list by a runaway margin. The visit to Edwards that I mentioned earlier also gave me my first look at an X-15. This 'monster' sat in the hangar with its nose cone various shades of blue thanks to the heat generated at high speed. My apprentice master would have said they were the perfect colours to achieve when hardening the tip of my file by heating and quenching. The X-15 led the aeronautical way from so many points of view – structural temperatures, speed, altitude, stability and control, propulsion, you name it. Delete the X-15 from history and you delete the basis for designing much of the Space Shuttle. Therefore in my view, the X-15 is king of the heap for making it all the way to Mach 7 and so becomes my choice for the Greatest Ever Research Aircraft.

When considering WWII, unlike WW1, there were unquestionably many aeroplanes that have stood the test of time and hindsight. I have no doubt that your list, like mine, will have all the usual suspects. Thanks to their operational records, the Lancaster and the B-17 have to be the Great Bombers, the FW190, the Mustang and the Spitfire the Great Fighters. The Me109 is not in my list of great fighters because Adolph Galland convinced me one night in a bar in Hamburg that it was too tricky to land and that constitutes a fundamental flaw for a service type. Not for me the Hurricane either because, unlike the Spitfire, it was not developed to its full potential.

Post WWII, the B-52 record of achievement and longevity must make it a Great Aeroplane. The Vulcan has to be the Best High Level Turner (if you doubt that, you should have tried to creep up behind one in a Hunter) plus also the Biggest, Tightest, Noisiest and All-round Spectacular Air Show Performer. I suspect it is very fair to call it a great aeroplane, given its deterrent abilities throughout the Cold War.

It is widely accepted that no aircraft has ever given a better ride and better handling to a crew flying at low level, right down on the deck, than the Buccaneer but to call it a Great Aeroplane (given its warts) would I feel be a tad OTT. On the other hand, the F-15, although a bit too heavy on the controls for my taste, is without doubt a Great Aeroplane, as is the F-16. In different ways both offered capabilities that had only been dreamed about before they arrived on the scene and both were developed to their full potential, a sure sign of a great aeroplane.

The Harrier family was a remarkable achievement when it came to giving the fast jet world a genuine operating site flexibility but it was not until the Sea Harrier was given a beyond-visual range air to air capability with the AMRAAM (a full 15 years before any other European aircraft), that it became a great aeroplane in my judgement. Likewise it took development to the GR7A and 9A standard as a day/night low level attack aircraft before the land-based versions really qualified for the same title.

One night in the 1970s a USMC test pilot, if not *the* USMC test pilot, took me to a night club down town Los Angeles and talked of flying Russian fighters from Groom Lake. What he said left me in no doubt that in those days the MiG-21 was a Great Aeroplane. Today the high alpha aerodynamic capabilities of the latest variants of the MiG-29 and Su-27 families are quite simply in a class of their own. Keeping the airframe under control (let alone the engines running) while the angle of attack increases to 180° and then back to zero via *minus* 90 is a truly remarkable achievement. Not that long ago I showed a film of this to three of the UK's most experienced test pilots and their mouths hung open. To see the Cobra taken to about 120 alpha before recovery at airshows was spectacular but to see the pitch rate of the Cobra continued all the way round (as in a zero diameter loop) was mind blowing. Please don't tell me it has no operational significance because that is what those who cannot do something always say. For me it is not that it demonstrates a useful operational manoeuvre but rather one that shows a degree of aerodynamic and engine refinement that means the margins surrounding normal low speed manoeuvres are literally unlimited. That has to give a squadron pilot confidence in his mount that goes far beyond that provided by a clever helmet and an autopilot designed to take over if the minimum controllable speed is approached. For me the Su-27 is another Great Aeroplane.

When it comes to airliners and transports, so many are similar in performance and capability that any attempt at an order of merit, or calling some and not others great aeroplanes, is bound to be very controversial. How can you not give the title to the 747 as the fully developed 707? Or the Hercules and the An-124? Or even the Trident which could cruise at Mach 0.9 and was the very first airliner to be cleared for autoland?

When thinking about helicopters, thanks to its Vietnam War record for availability and ruggedness throughout years of combat, was not the Huey the World's First Great Helicopter?

My last suggestion is for the title of Everyone's Favourite Great Aeroplane. Not just mine, not just yours but everyone's. Concorde.

345

Chapter 16

General Aviation thoughts

For ease of reference I have divided this lengthy chapter into topics

1. Learning to land

2. Approaching without power

3. Powered approaches

4. Crosswind approaches and landings

5. Staying current

6. Making mistakes

7. Showing off safely

8. Pilot types

9. Pushing your boundaries

10. Stability and control

11. Climbing speeds

12. The theory and practice of flying

13. Maintenance time

14. Very serious failures

15. Evaluation tips

16. Being your own test pilot

17. The PPL syllabus

1. Learning to land

My problem for the first eight years of my flying career was that I could not land. The fact that I had such a problem is not meant as a criticism of the formidable WWII Master Pilot who sent me solo in a Piston Provost in 1955 (or indeed any of my other RAF instructors) but rather a simple statement of how I saw things. In a nutshell I was never sure how any landing was going to turn out until I had done it. There was of course the point at the end of the approach where I felt everything looked good enough to land (or not, as the case may be) but could I reliably predict the quality and precise position of touchdown? No way.

I can actually remember the day it dawned on me that I could land. It was a distinct surprise. I was a student on the course at ETPS in 1963 and we were being taught how to evaluate handling characteristics during takeoff and landing. I was given a Piston Provost for this job and did not relish it because of my training experiences. On the ground I went through the exercise brief and made up the necessary test cards listing all the things I had to do and the data I had to record – landing fast, slow, heavy, gently, one wheel first, three points, tailwheel first, crosswind, flapless, glide and so on. Then off I went. Surprise, surprise I did what was on the cards. No problem, except why was it no problem?

I came to the conclusion that, while good landings are obviously about all the things we are taught (controlling the aeroplane properly on the approach, having the correct speed and rate of descent with everything nicely stabilised as you cross the threshold), they additionally require you to be able to 'see' very accurately your height above the ground and your flight path relative to the surface. If you can do this well you will know before the touchdown when it is going to happen and also the quality and type of the landing that will result. If you wonder what exactly I mean by 'see' try substituting it with 'instinctively appreciate'.

While there is nothing very profound in that, how I wish that somebody had said to me when I was having trouble, "Don't worry, Farley, you can see what is going on well enough to do safe landings and not everyone can see it well enough to be an ace". Being able to 'see' what is happening at the end of an approach is a skill that comes and goes. It comes with a lot of experience and very good currency and it goes away again, regardless of experience, when you are out of practice. If you have not flown for a while how should you make that eventual decision to continue with the landing or to go around? What should be the basis of telling yourself it is safe to carry on? Without doubt it is the quality of the approach.

With the best approaches very little is changing. Indeed, in still air (if there is such stuff) and with the perfect approach, the only thing that would change would be the height – not the power, the speed, the bank, the pitch, the yaw nor the rate of descent. The constant track would also be pointing down the runway.

One of the hardest things to measure in flight test is the ground effect when landing (n.b. this is neither a digression nor a printing error and hopefully the connection will become clear shortly). What happens to an aeroplane when the presence of the ever closer ground starts modifying the way the air flows round the aeroplane? Does it want to sink, to balloon or to pitch nose up or down? Or is it just a non-event? One way of trying to measure this is to look at the average control surface positions needed to hold the aircraft steady just before it enters ground effect (say about a wingspan above the ground) and compare those with the later positions going on inside ground effect.

The rub of course is trying to separate out ground effects from pilot effects, especially when a flare is being carried out. Because of doubt about this data, simulating ground effect correctly is notoriously hard and the results may not fully reflect real life even with the most expensive simulators.

In 1991 I was hired to measure (amongst other things) the ground effect on a CN-235 twin turboprop transport aircraft so that it could be properly simulated. The boffins asked me not to move the controls during the final stages of the approach so that the angle of attack sensor would only be showing the effects of the ground and not my inputs. When I enquired how long before ground effect they wanted everything steady, they said, "The last minute before touchdown".

Therefore in the terms that we are talking about here, namely landing, they wanted a hands off approach to a touchdown from about two miles out. May I suggest that sort of requirement makes you take serious stock of just how you set up a steady approach. If the last two miles and the touchdown were to be essentially hands off, then a long straight in and shallow approach at a light weight was needed so that a no flare impact could be accepted by the gear. They wanted two sets of good traces as a minimum and to even stand a chance of achieving this, we had to accept a touchdown anywhere on the runway that could result in an immediate safe rolling takeoff. Still air would be essential. That all added up to just post dawn on a foggy morning. In those circumstances with visibility poor, the initial approach had to be based on the ILS.

My point? May I suggest that, if you can't let go of the controls for even a few seconds on any ordinary approach to land, then you ought to be paying more attention to how you are setting up the approach, your power and flap usage and how well you are trimming the aircraft.

If you were expecting a few magic words that would make every landing you do in future a greaser I am afraid I do not have those. However, I do feel that if you work at this notion of the stabilised approach and what is involved in that, you will be well on the way to a safe landing from every approach. Your share of greasers will then follow. While it is impossible to learn some of the hand/eye co-ordination skills associated with various flying exercises without getting airborne in a real aeroplane, once you have a few solo hours under your belt you can learn a tremendous amount about flying while on the ground.

Something I learned on the ground during my pre-wings training has stayed with me all my life. It was a dirty rotten day at Swinderby and our Vampires were clearly going to have the day off. In the crewroom were all the usual out of date magazines as well as the latest issue of the RAF Fighter Command monthly accident summary and flight safety bulletin. In the latter was an account of a young junior pilot's evidence to a Meteor fatal accident board. He had recently joined his first squadron and was taken on a tour of the local area by his Flight Commander. The RAF was a very hard school in those days and wingmen were supposed to stay tucked in and ask no questions. Maybe our JP had been tipped off that his leader liked to demonstrate his low flying prowess but for whatever reason as his leader got lower and lower he decided to ease up to 100 ft or so. In his evidence he said, "From this position of advantage I watched my leader leaving a trail across a field of standing corn". Unknown to his leader in the middle of that field was an old potato bund just below the corn tops – predictably the leader died when his ventral tank hit this obstruction.

'From this position of advantage' – what a wonderful phrase. Thirty-five years later was the last time I eased up just a little on a leader because of what that young lad said. I was in a Spitfire, my leader was in a Me109 (and before you wonder, Mark was not flying it) and there were a couple of other warbirds in the formation which was returning to base at dusk after a display. As I got out my leader came up to me with a smile and said, "Don't worry, John I wouldn't wipe you off on the hangar". I smiled back and said, "No, you won't". Now don't get me wrong, I did not think my leader would hit the hangar but I was not certain enough of my own ability to avoid getting low on him momentarily and so leave myself poorly placed. You must know your limits and always bear them in mind. Easier said than done in one's early days of learning to fly.

Trying to enhance a reputation by showing off outside your capabilities (and those of your aircraft) is a pretty well trodden path to hurting yourself. However, not everyone sees it like that. For example back in 1972 in the US, I tore a strip off a Marine squadron commander after the way he joined the circuit in a Harrier. I finished my outburst by suggesting that he would kill himself if he carried on like that. "I'd sooner be dead than look bad," he replied.

My first flying lesson was in an RAF Piston Provost in December 1955 and my most recent was my last working flight because you can learn something about flying and yourself every time you get airborne. In between those two lessons there were a lot of flights, a lot of types and some fifty years.

What did I learn on that last flight? I learned that, if you are flying at the correct height but your height encoding transponder has a fault and over reads by 1,000 ft, you will scatter airliners all over the place when your blip pops up near Birmingham. However what if our transponder error happened to be one of under-reading and we had been accidentally flying too high? Clearly the lesson is that if you are going to go about your lawful business near controlled airspace, it makes sense to get the controlling ATC for the airspace to check your transponder readout against your altimeter reading, even if you are planning to stay under their patch. Learning to fly never stops, both on the ground and in the air.

2. Approaching without power

The handling and judgement involved in flying an approach and landing without the benefit of power is a subject which has always interested me. Sometimes the manoeuvre can be quite straightforward while at other times it can require considerable piloting skill if the aeroplane is going to be used again.

This is not intended as a discussion about forced landings which I view as an altogether bigger and more complicated topic. Forced landings necessarily start with an unexpected engine problem that will require a variety of aircraft type specific actions to be carried out post haste. These could range from selecting a tank that has fuel in it (after you forgot what you were doing) and simply restarting the engine, through to dealing with a fire after your engine has elected to spontaneously destroy itself. Forced landings raise ATC and radio procedure issues to say nothing of decisions that will be affected by aircraft position, the type of terrain or water you are flying over, your experience and of course the weather conditions.

On the other hand, I do feel it reasonable to discuss here the last bit of a forced landing – the handling of an approach and landing without power. As with any handling issue, pilots gradually gain more competence in glide approaches as their general flying experience increases and may also change their views as time goes by. What follows is how the subject developed for me.

Like most students, I was introduced to glide approaches pre-solo and while I still had problems with an ordinary powered circuit. I was exhorted to aim the glide approach about a third of the way into the field, not to put down flap until I was sure I was going to get to that point and then to bring the touchdown point forward by the progressive use of flap. Pretty standard stuff as I am sure you will agree.

Such glide approaches started with an ordinary powered circuit with the usual base leg power and height reduction being delayed until much later. When it was decided the whole thing looked adequately high and close, the throttle was chopped, the nose was lowered and the glide approach was commenced. Clearly success depended totally on waiting long enough (but not too long) before chopping the throttle. Pre-solo was not the time to teach techniques such as 's' turns or sideslipping which can give some degree of control over the eventual outcome. As a student that vital throttle chop point was established by looking out of the window at local ground features and doing a plus or minus bit for the wind. Hardly a basis for a general ability to set up a forced landing approach into the nearest available airfield or strip but we all have to start somewhere.

As we progressed through the training, things gradually changed. When circuit conditions allowed, the throttle would be chopped by 'Sir' well

351

short of the academic point described earlier – perhaps even on the downwind leg – and Bloggs would turn towards the airfield and try and set up an approach onto a cross runway or onto the grass. Clearly some judgement was starting to develop of where the aircraft could reach in a glide. Then we started to learn the full forced landing techniques of picking a field and so on. In those days, I did not have much confidence in my ability to judge the likely touchdown point until pretty late in any glide, by which time it was often too late to do much about it if it was wrong. This remained the situation throughout my Piston Provost time and, since I was not chopped from the course, I presume I was not alone in having this problem.

Jets came next, dual Vampire T11s and single-seat FB5s for our solo exercises. Glide approaches were still taught as a circuit variation, just as before, but there was also the new flamed out 'controlled descent through cloud' or CDTC. Here, you set off on a steer for base at the best gliding speed until the manual direction finder operator got an R/T transmission from you that showed you had just passed through the overhead. This was your cue to lower the nose to increase speed and start a spiral descent round base. The high speed was to build your kinetic energy thus allowing you to level off once you had popped out below cloud and fly round with a decaying airspeed as you endeavoured to set up a glide approach on an appropriate runway.

On days when there was no cloud, such a spiralling descent could be flown with rather more certainty that the last bit would work out because the centre of the spiral could be adjusted visually. Naturally this procedure relied on you having height in hand once you had reached the overhead but this was usually the case as we flew at medium or high level for the majority of our exercises in those days.

Any good emergency procedure should aim to minimise the skill needed to carry it out and so enhance the chance of a successful outcome. The spiralling CDTC was a start as it gave you an energy surplus with which to adjust the final visual approach. The next stage in RAF development of glide approaches for operational types was something called a 'one to one' (written 1:1). This was a cracking idea and used the approach radar that was by now the norm at operational airfields to assist the pilot and reduce the need for the final visual judgement of the CDTC spiral.

It was based on the fact that the standard Hunter of those days would glide about 1 mile per 1,000 ft loss of height when flown with the gear down at the appropriate speed but two miles per 1,000 ft when clean. For a 1:1 the controller would home you to the overhead, then send you outbound for a later inbound turn that would have you ending up gliding straight in towards the runway in use.

Clearly the controller was vital to the success of this manoeuvre as he had the radar range information. Once he knew your height in the overhead, he had to subtract an allowance for the inbound turn and the last couple of miles with the gear down, divide the new number by two and send you that many miles outbound on the appropriate heading. You steered his headings at the correct glide speed and kept him informed of your height. He then talked you through the procedure while he assessed how the range/height combination was working out. Towards the end he would announce when you were 'approaching the groove' then 'in the groove' when your height in thousands of feet equalled your range in miles and so you could lower your gear and push the nose down to hold speed. When you popped out of cloud, there was the runway ahead of you and all you had to do was dump the flap as you saw fit.

These 1:1 glide approaches were actually quite easy to do given the necessary currency on the part of the pilot and controller. However such currency was vital so practices were frequent. Clearly such a procedure works best with a stack of height remaining when you first arrive overhead. If cloud did not require such radar assistance, we had what were called high key and low key positions for use in a visual circuit.

High key was usually set at the upwind end of the runway and low key halfway round finals. If you went through the high key position clean and at the right speed at the correct height for your type, then you would be able to glide to low key at the correct height to lower gear and flaps and arrive on the numbers.

Obviously there was still considerable skill needed to try and hit the two key points depending on your weight, configuration, the surface windspeed and initial position. Cutting the corner was very likely to be needed if you started with rather less height than desired and the whole thing was no piece of cake, especially as in those days you needed most, if not all, of the runway in order to stop. Clearly low key was the vital point. High key was just an aid to reaching low key.

When I left my Hunter squadron I would not say I could guarantee to pull off every glide approach that should have been possible. My judgement problem was that I found it difficult to look ahead and appreciate where the flight path would take me. The glide angle clean was relatively flat and so hard to judge. Toss in a bit of wind and failure was always a real possibility.

A few years later I found myself on Aero Flight at Bedford where we operated several very valuable single engine prototype research aircraft. The boffins were naturally very keen not to lose one of these just because the engine stopped. Without exception, the aircraft were all the aerodynamic opposite of a good glider. In the jargon they were low lift over drag devices (low L/D) which meant that they all had very steep glide angles.

We have now arrived at one of the enduring myths of aviation. Aircraft that glide down at a 30 or 40° angle must be awful to land. Wrong. Totally wrong. They are the easiest of them all so far as the final approach and landing goes. Only when I started practising glide approach and landings for aircraft of that type did I start to get a 100% success rate with smooth touchdowns, just after the runway numbers and at the correct speed.

Because of the steep glide angles, it is necessary to be pretty close to a suitable runway when the engine stops. The difficulty that had previously dogged me of looking out the window in order to judge the shallow glidepath and so how to fly round the circuit, just vanished. With the nose apparently pointing straight down at the ground you can see exactly where you will impact if you do nothing. Wind is not an issue and there is nothing to judge. All you do is throw down the gear and flaps, dive at the flap limit speed and point the thing at the beginning of the lead in lights (or just short of the runway if there are no lead in lights). Then pull out of the dive at the last moment and fly level, as low as you dare, until the speed bleeds to the one you want for touchdown.

This way you impress those who do not realise how easy it all is by plopping it on the numbers. If there are any Hunter pilots out there who read this, try gliding it with gear and full flap at 250 kt and you will see how well it handles – except in manual. Handling is excellent during the flare because of all the speed. What you must not do is try to land a low L/D device from a descent at its best glide speed as you will be very disappointed when you try to flare from the steep approach.

In 1982, doing AV-8B engine work at Edwards over the lake bed, I had over two hours of gliding in 40-odd episodes with never a concern should the relight fail. I started each sortie with a practice engine chop climbing through 15,000 ft or so and then, with wheels and flaps down, did the practice 'dirty dart and flare' over the lake bed as a bit of very enjoyable legalised hooliganism. High risk stuff so far as some onlookers were concerned. But you know better.

Of course glider pilots know all about the use of drag to make approach and landing easier. That is why they set up the approach with airbrakes out and pop them in at the first sign they are going to land a bit short.

If you are a power pilot who has trouble with doing the occasional glide approach you may (secretly) wonder how glider pilots have the skill and judgement necessary to do it every time. May I suggest a reason for their success? Currency.

3. Powered approaches

Having written my thoughts on approaching without power I suppose I can hardly avoid discussing the more normal case of approaching with power. When the spacecraft taking the Apollo 13 crew to the moon suffered an explosion, they made the legendary call, "Houston, we have a problem". If I may be so bold as to paraphrase this, my message is, "GA, you have a problem" the problem being that you teach speed control with the stick not the throttle.

This topic is not something I write about lightly as I am well aware that the vast majority of experienced instructors think GA pilots should be taught to control the speed on finals with the stick. To make things worse, my time in GA was limited to the final decade or so of my flying career so my credentials hardly compare with the experienced GA guys who have been at it three or four times as long. Therefore if I am to make this case it will have to be with words alone.

These thoughts were triggered by a thread on the web where the topic starter was looking for tips to deal with a very strong headwind on the approach and the associated risk of windshear in the final stages, leading to a sudden loss of airspeed. One reply was from a chap who proceeded to spell out his solution in a single sentence: stick for airspeed, throttle for rate of descent.

355

This took me back to an event in 1960 when I was training as a QFI on number 206 Course at the RAF Central Flying School. My 'Sir' on this course preached speed with the stick and would not have me patter an approach any other way. Recognising that he had many thousand hours of staying alive in the business, including WWII, I did not try and rubbish his ideas and attempted to debate the issue with him during briefing but with no success.

Then one day when I was playing the part of an ab-initio student and he was pattering an approach, I let our Jet Provost Mk 3 get quite a few knots slow. I then looked across at him and said, "Sir, could you please show me again how you control speed with the stick?" We were low over the lead in lights at the time so he very sensibly did nothing of the kind but slammed open the throttle. He refused to speak to me again and I was given an instructor change. Additionally they decided I should complete my training as an advanced instructor on the Vampire. My new 'Sir' on the advanced course was a fair bit younger and believed in pattering speed with throttle. With hindsight, I suspect that at the end of 1960 and during early 1961 RAF training policy on this issue was in the midst of changing. On completing the advanced course, they posted me as an ab-initio instructor on the JP to Cranwell – the RAF could be quaint in those days but I digress.

I expect you have realised what I have against the speed with the stick notion. However, just in case anyone is in any doubt, please bear with me while I take it from the top.

Speed with the stick can be shown to work really well when up and away or, for that matter, on finals above 500 feet. However, once you get closer to the ground, it starts to become less than ideal because of the ever smaller space beneath you. Indeed, given a sudden low level and really nasty loss of airspeed due to windshear (which started the web thread that got me going), lowering the nose would reduce the alpha and dump lift as well as dive you into the ground.

I suspect that at this moment some very experienced hands will be screaming out that speed with stick is not taught in isolation as I have described it but that the teaching includes co-ordinated use of throttle and stick to control glidepath and speed. I accept that. However, we all know that pre-solo students are encouraged (if not actively taught) to do things a bit by numbers – indeed were this not so then no doubt many would never succeed in going solo as they would be too confused by the whole interacting dynamic problem that is flying.

I am therefore uneasy about the early indoctrination of students with an idea that they will find later has real limits on its use. If GA people were taught speed with the throttle and point the nose where they want to go with the stick then there would be no change-over point during the approach because the technique is useable all the way to touchdown. What is more it needs no modification for the effects of a disastrous windshear or on overshoot (or go-around if that is your lingo) or anything. For once a genuine one size fits all.

Although I have stuck my nose into GA business, there is one other group who also use – indeed blindly swear by would be a more accurate description – the same speed with stick idea. They are the Top Guns of the US Navy. In my view they get away with it because of the tremendous approach accuracy that is needed to arrive in the wires. This precision demands various aids, from a special 'on speed indexer' in the cockpit, to the 'mirror landing sight' and a Landing Safety Officer (LSO) on deck. As I have described in Chapter 7, the LSO looks up the approach and gives advice on the R/T. He can even see what the cockpit indexer is telling the pilot through a series of lights on the nose leg! His advice can also culminate in the all important wave-off order and, should the pilot become fixated with the mirror and go deaf (literally) to the R/T, then the LSO can and does switch on a bunch of wave-off reds on the mirror. Thus in my view they require such a stabilised and accurate approach that major corrections are not required (or tolerated) during the last part of the approach. Therefore, although they use a technique that will not work at low level, they insist that the whole thing is stabilised and on rails long before then, which is not likely to be the case with trainee GA pilots.

At this point I could conjecture about how GA and the USN got so set in their ways, as opposed to the very different business of how they got started in those ways. However, I will not indulge in that rather unproductive luxury as there are still things to mention which may actually help the debate.

The RAF Central Flying School was established at Upavon in May 1912 and led the way in trying to structure and then standardise the whole process of learning to fly. Since early engines were unreliable beasts, what was more natural than to adopt the glide approach as standard, slip off any excess height once you were sure of reaching the field and use a blip of power if you misjudged things and finished up low. Looking back, this seems totally reasonable and in all probability is how speed on stick and throttle for glidepath became the established norm. Many years later the early jets came along and had a very sluggish response to throttle. People getting to grips with these new aircraft on squadrons quickly learned that control of the glidepath with power was now a very hard thing to do.

As approach speeds were still determined using the traditional 1.3Vs, it was also clear that these early jets offered, by comparison, quite an immediate and positive glidepath response if you used the stick. Of course the downside was that you were left trying to control speed with a sluggish throttle. However, on balance that seemed the lesser of the two evils and anyway, provided you put your mind to it, you could get the speed roughly right fairly early on. Certainly at these new very high approach speeds, the most important thing seemed to be having a good control over one's flight path – which the stick provided.

As a Hunter pilot on my first squadron and having been very influenced by the RAE boffins during my five year apprenticeship at Farnborough, I took a particular interest in the comments of one Wing Commander Spry (a pseudonym for a senior staff officer in the Flight Safety HQ) that were published every month in the RAF magazine Air Clues. This led to the April 1960 issue of Air Clues containing a letter from Fg Off J F Farley about some earlier Spry criticism of a V-Bomber pilot who had touched a little short in the undershoot. I considered this criticism was unfair because it categorically stated that, when flying on the backside of the drag curve, you could not pull the stick back to control the glidepath. It said this was because if you did, you would just lose speed and so lift and thus make the aircraft sink even more. I took two whole pages to explain with some simple maths why this was factually incorrect and that in the short term there was a near instantaneous increase in lift, whereas the drag took longer to reduce the speed of the aeroplane and so reduce the lift.

Coincidentally, in the same issue as my letter there was an article by a Flight Lieutenant A J Camp of the Blind Landing Experimental Unit at Bedford expounding on just why the stick should be used to control lift and the throttle to control speed when on the approach and not as the RAF then taught. Camp produced a lot of analytical data from RAE trials that were done in order to measure which technique actually kept the aircraft more accurately on an ILS and, importantly, which method got the aircraft back on to the glidepath sooner when starting with a known error. This work was aimed at helping the boffins design the first auto land systems. The RAE data was quite clear – the best approaches resulted from controlling speed with throttle and flight path with stick – even with one slow prop-driven type that was included in the trial. At the time Camp's article amounted to heresy in the RAF but, as I mentioned earlier, a few years later it was being reflected by at least some of the CFS instructors.

Be that as it may and, even if you totally reject the idea of controlling the airspeed with the throttle, please read this next bit. Regardless of the control technique you used to get on short finals, if you suddenly find yourself with the ASI reading much less than you want then please use the stick to set up the normal flare attitude for your type and slam full throttle. That way you will have done what you can to maximise the alpha without inducing a stall and at the same time ensured the gear will be available to cushion things as well as it can should you hit. If it misses the ground and climbs away – enjoy. This is the best a GA pilot can do to mimic what every airliner pilot is taught to do in similar circumstances, namely pull to the stick shaker and slam full power. (Shakers are driven by alpha and set to fire at a small margin below the stalling alpha.)

Funnily enough, I met a trials officer from the USN Flight Test Centre at Patuxent River a few years ago. He was designing the flight control laws for the USN version of the JSF (the one with the hook). He said all their simulations showed that speed on throttle was better for a carrier approach for any aircraft and could I explain from the pilot's point of view why the USN pilots did it differently. I said I could not help with that as the RAE boffins had brainwashed me years earlier! A while later he sent me a super PowerPoint presentation of the case he was going to put to the Navy insisting that it all had to change because scientists today could demonstrate that it was better. I wished him well with his crusade some 40-plus years after the RAF finally got the message and nearly 50 years since the RAE got on top of the problem. Therefore, GA, who is going to be the last to give in – you or the USN? Please tell me it is the USN because they are, as the saying goes, big enough and ugly enough to look after themselves.

4. Crosswind approaches and landings

All pilots are aware that there are two options when it comes to doing a crosswind approach – wing down or crabbing. I was a crabbing man for reasons I will try and explain. For all aircraft types there is literally no limit to the crosswind in which it is perfectly safe to carry out a crabbed approach. Neither is there any problem during the crabbed approach should you be hit by a huge gust – at least no more than there would be with the same gust during an into-wind approach on the same type.

In contrast there is a type dependent limit for the wing down approach because of the way it requires crossed controls. The crossed control technique has implications about stall margin and even, in extreme circumstances, for loss of lateral and directional control by flicking. It is not possible to progressively establish (and therefore be sure of) the control margin that surrounds a crossed control approach without installing special flight test instrumentation. Of course there is pilot feel and experience but this can be fallible. There may be a temptation to use stick position to judge control margin but this in itself presumes a linearity of control response that may not exist at large deflections. However, my main concern regarding a crossed control approach is the effect of a big gust that could lead instantly to going outside the boundaries of control.

Before I upset those pilots who prefer the wing down technique, may I make it clear that I agree the wing down way is not in the least bit hazardous in moderate crosswinds and moderate turbulence. However, as the strength of the crosswind component increases, it does eventually have it own limits whereas the crabbed approach does not. Anyhow what is moderate?

Now to the landing. Some aircraft configurations are prone to damage on touchdown if the gust level is high – even without a crosswind. For example, low wing airliners with podded engines can tolerate only a small bank angle at touchdown or they will scrape a pod. Any tricycle undercarriage aircraft will be very happy to land mainwheels first with some crab still present because the drag from the gear acting behind the CG will smoothly remove the crab. This is not the case of course with a tailwheel aircraft.

Regardless of what technique is used for the approach, the biggest problem is the nasty area between the stabilised approach and the aircraft running along the ground under full control. Full control requires considerable weight on the wheels if the friction between them and the runway is to be able to resist the across-runway force from the wind. Until that state has been reached, some downwind drift will occur as soon as the approach crab or wing down angles are reduced. There can be no valid generalisations about how many seconds this difficult control of track lasts as it is very type and pilot technique dependent.

On a personal note, I have only flown on one occasion in a very strong gusty crosswind where I was greatly concerned about my ability to avoid a crash. At a guess, the wind was probably twice the sensible crosswind 'limit' for the type. This happened at an airshow at a large US base in the UK and involved three different WWII open cockpit, single engine US tailwheel training types with which we had agreed to do a formation display routine.

Following a pre-flight discussion, we eventually agreed not to cancel. We obviously binned our normal formation takeoff and landing and replaced these with streams at very conservative intervals. However, we all felt the landing was going to be the worst part of the trip.

We were wrong and our landings turned out to be quite straightforward. We briefed that we would just keep flying the aircraft smoothly and gently until they were down to taxi speed. We felt it important to do nothing suddenly and in that context to 'kick off' drift is doing something suddenly. Therefore we all used the crabbed technique for the approach and then flew low along the runway, gradually reducing the crab with wing down until we felt we could ease one wheel gently on to the ground still with some wing down. Of course we had the luxury that runway length was never going to be an issue so, after a wheel was on, we very carefully increased the weight on the wheel, then wheels, by carefully reducing power and speed, watching like hawks for the slightest tendency to swing. In the event none of us had a problem.

On the other hand, the takeoff was another matter. When you are using full into-wind aileron on a ground roll and the up-wind wing starts to rise, you have no alternative but to snatch the aircraft off the ground and let it weathercock. We all experienced this and we had not briefed for it. A most unpleasant feeling.

That experience taught me that the safe crosswind limit could be lower for takeoff than landing, something which had not previously occurred

361

to me. At the risk of stating the obvious, if possible start a crosswind takeoff near the downwind side of the runway so that you will at least veer towards the centre if you fail to prevent the aircraft weather-cocking into wind. The perhaps intuitive (but wrong) thing is to start close to the upwind edge on the basis that you might be blown sideways and so will end up going towards the centre line.

With so many variables that can affect the outcome of a crosswind landing, it is not surprising that the crosswind limit in the aircraft manual is often the maximum that was demonstrated during certification rather than a definitive statement of a hard limit.

5. Staying current

Let us dream. You have a day off, a licence, access to an aeroplane, cash to spare and the weather is perfect so there is only one thing to do – get airborne. If the next thing that comes into your mind is, "Where shall we go?" please give yourself 0/10 because, if you are serious about your aviation, the question you should be asking is, "What do I need to do on this trip?" Furthermore, you will establish just what exercises you need to do by looking at your currency chart which is hanging on the wall in your bedroom.

Most GA pilots have no delusions about their abilities, they have no obsessive ambition to become aces, they just want to fly safely and enjoy flying as a hobby. The problem with that very reasonable stance is that aviation has to be worked at all the time and on every flight for it to remain accident free. To complicate things, the demands of any trip can vary enormously and be outside the control of the pilot. A routine circuit on a nice day is hardly the same as one where a fuel pipe lets go at 300 ft after takeoff and the engine cuts, although for the first 40 seconds they were identical.

There are two ways to deal with such serious emergencies. You can just put your faith in others, from the CAA to the engineer in the hangar, hoping they will protect you from a situation you cannot handle. Alternatively, you can be a little less fatalistic and do more training to reduce the odds stacked against you. Even without emergencies there are plenty of ways for pilots to finish up in charge of a bent aeroplane. If we are honest with ourselves, we also know that such events are avoidable if we plan properly and *only operate inside our current levels of skill.*

Those last eight words are at the heart of the issue I want to discuss here. If you accept this notion, which is hardly controversial, then we do need to try and be objective about our currency. Such objectivity requires a lot more information than traditionally appears in accident reports where currency is usually expressed simply as hours flown on type in the last 30 or 90 days. I am deeply suspicious of flying hours as a measure of currency or even of experience for that matter. What should matter is what the pilot did when airborne, not how long it all took.

When I was a civilian testing Harriers, the MOD Flying Orders for Contractors under which I operated required me to fly 20 hours a month on type to retain my Ministry Type Approval. Although I started on the vectored thrust family in 1964, it was not until 1982 that I managed to log 50 hours on type in any one year. That's right, I flew less than 50 hours each year. Because of this I had to argue and debate with various bureaucrats that such a simple measure as hours was meaningless. At the very least we needed to count sorties.

Take August 1977 as an example. At that time we were just starting on the ski-jump takeoff experiments at RAE Bedford. Once the aircraft had left the ramp and the nozzles had been moved to the conventional flight position, the whole test was over and all that was needed was to leave the gear and flaps down, do a quick 180 and land from a slow approach downwind on the main runway. Airborne time was less than 90 seconds. Then it was off to the boffins to debrief, look at the film etc and decide what to vary on the next launch. We did ten jumps a day at the most. Say 15 minutes for your logbook. About 1.5 hours for a six day week. On the other hand, I was certainly in practice at getting in, starting up, taking off, landing and shutting down because I had done it 60 times in the last week.

Specialising as I did in VSTOL handling trials may be a pretty extreme example of doing a lot in a short time but the principle is still sound. Currency depends on what you do, not how long you take to do it. If you accept this, how should you decide what you need to do on this next trip? You get out your chart and look at where the biggest holes are in your currency. Doubtless you are asking yourself questions like how do you draw up the chart in the first place? Just what should go in it? How should you use the chart to reduce risk?

Let us split flying into pure and applied categories. Pure flying is about handling the aeroplane, making it go up and down, right and left and slower and faster. It is about taking off and landing in good weather conditions from an ample strip or runway. It is also about not stalling when we do this. However, every time we do such pure flying we cannot avoid certain risks that are inherent in being airborne.

On the other hand, applied flying is about what we choose to do with the aeroplane when we are airborne. This might be anything from a simple land away cross country to an instrument approach into Heathrow, from low level display flying to deliberately waiting until it is dark to do some circuits at night. All of this applied flying carries extra risks but my point is that such risks can be totally eliminated at a stroke for the amateur pilot by choosing not to do such stuff. However, the pure flying risks remain. They are inevitable and can only be eliminated by not flying, something which by definition pilots find unacceptable. Therefore I want your chart to be the tool whereby you assess whether you are as skilled and current as you can be at pure flying and so as well placed as possible to minimise these risks.

There are three distinct things to do in constructing your own personal currency chart. Firstly you must make a list of exercises that you feel (know) you should practise. In the early days of your flying careers that list may include most of the PPL syllabus headings. Later, as you become more experienced, some items can be binned, although probably not that many if you are honest with yourself. Another way to look at the list is to ask yourself what things you would want to go and practise today if you were going to re-take your PPL skills test tomorrow. You should certainly include any exercise that you pray would not come up on your skills test!

The next thing is to decide just what maximum period there should be between the practices of all items on the list – 1 month, 2 months or whatever and note that interval in the second column. Then you want a column for each month, where you will fill in the date on which you carry out the actual practice. In no time at all, you will build up a very useful picture of just what you did with your recent time airborne. An example of what I am suggesting is shown at *Fig 1*. It is not intended to be definitive and it is up to you to tailor the concept to your needs.

Just boring holes in the sky is a terrible waste of flying time, whatever your type of aircraft or level of flying experience. Whether you are an amateur or a professional, planning your currency training is very important and needs to reflect the tasks and emergencies you currently face with your normal sort of flying.

My Currency

	INTERVAL	January	February	March	April
CIRCUIT WORK					
Runway landing	1 month				
Grass landing	1 month				
Glide landing	2 month				
Flapless landing	2 month				
X-wind landing	1 month				
Landing from slideslip	3 month				
Fan stop	1 month				
Go-around	1 month				
STALLING					
Clean idle					
Approach idle					
Approach power					
Go-around power					
Turning idle					
Turning cruise					
UNSUAL ATTITUDES					
Nose high					
Nose low					
FORCED LANDINGS					
Field selection					
Sideslipping					
PFL and go-around					

Fig 1

During my time as a pilot at RAE Bedford, we had several experimental prototypes and some hack aircraft for communications work and continuation training or 'CT' as the RAF called currency flying. In those days a test pilot was still expected to write data down on knee pads and observe important test instruments often during busy manoeuvres. Since it was the height of professional shame to fly a rare prototype and not bring back the information the boffins needed, it behove a young wannabe test ace to make good use of his CT. We had three Meteors on the flight that could be used for this but what would constitute useful exercises on such a flight?

The Meteor was pretty benign to handle compared to most of the test aircraft so you had to think how to stretch yourself. One thing that I found useful was to fly inverted with one engine at high power and the other near idle, keep it straight and use a stopwatch to time how long the high power engine took to flame out given the small amount of inverted flight fuel available to each engine. With a few of these points at different high rpm values one could plot a nice curve of inverted capability against altitude and rpm. Such data was not of much interest to the world but recording it was a useful exercise to keep a young lad up to speed and ready to tackle jobs that did matter.

The bottom line of all this is that currency training is important. If you don't make time for such training and plan it in a systematic and thoughtful way, then you are letting yourself down and certainly increasing your chances of bending an aeroplane (or worse) when doing even the most basic pure flying, let alone the complex applied stuff.

Truth has a habit of coming out, however much some people try to hide it. The bit of truth I have in mind here is that today it is the light aircraft category that makes the greatest demands on piloting handling skills. Forget most modern military fast jets or modern airliners because they are all much easier to handle. I expect a lot of professional pilots will see red at that remark so I had better justify myself.

The operative word above is 'handling'. Handling is about steering the aircraft through the sky which is quite a different thing from operating it. Modern fast jets and airliners are extremely complex devices to operate which is why their pilots have to undergo so much training and are then faced with never ending currency and rating checks throughout their careers. This operation of airliners involves navigating extremely complex air traffic environments, coping day in and day out with weather that would ground any light aircraft pilot and dealing with command pressures from a wide variety of sources. The operation of a modern military fast jet is again very demanding, indeed so demanding that it is beyond the abilities of the majority of the general population.

Despite how demanding the operational work of military and airline pilots may be, that does not mean the aircraft they fly are hard to handle. Indeed the opposite is true because quite properly the civil and military airworthiness authorities will only accept benign handling qualities precisely because they know their pilots will have their hands full operating the aircraft. There are exceptions to such generalisations, particularly among the older types still in service. Harriers and some helicopters for example. Those aside, I maintain that light aircraft as a breed do call for more stick and rudder handling skills than most modern heavy metal. It bothers me that some GA pilots may underestimate the challenges they face every time they get airborne because they assume they are at the bottom of the aviation ladder. In fact they are at the top when it comes to handling which is another reason why currency is important for GA pilots.

6. Making mistakes

We all make mistakes every day and some days more than others. The problem with aviation is that mistakes made in the air have the potential to produce very serious results. The good news is that aviators as a group are very aware of all this and go to considerable lengths to learn from each other's mistakes. This is epitomised at the institutional level by the remarkable efforts of professional accident investigators to find out what happened and then publish the word, as well as the existence of several very valuable confidential reporting systems. On a personal level, most of us who have had a bad fright tell another pilot – or even a room full of pilots – after we are back on the ground.

These days the internet is a tremendous tool for communication. On it I found an interesting safety thread started by a US medical doctor doing research. He wanted to try and establish what procedural thing it was in a pilot's education that made him so safety conscious and why, as a group, pilots stuck to the rules better than doctors. As you can imagine there were several replies on the lines of: pilot breaks rules so pilot dies, doctor breaks rules so patient dies. However without getting sidetracked, it is good that the aviation safety system, imperfect though it is, is looked up to by professionals outside aviation.

In fact, regardless of where and how you started to learn to fly, I would bet that right from day one you became aware of the safety culture that pervades aviation. I do a lot of driving and wish the road was as safe a place as the sky. I really mean that. I mean it so much that I spent a considerable amount of my money, at about twice the rate it costs to rent a club aeroplane, in order to be taught how to drive a new car I bought some ten years ago.

It was far from being a supercar but it was light and small, had 220 hp and so would reach the national speed limit in second gear and do 100 in third, at which point it still had three gears left. The purpose of this driving instruction was simply to reduce the chance of me having an accident. It started with a day on the roads and progressed to track work later. The bottom line for staying safe on the public roads was what they called COD. Concentration, observation and distance.

The concentration and observation bit took me back to 1957 and my days with Vampires at Swinderby and Valley. The side by side two-seat T11 seemed pretty reasonable because you sat fairly well down in the cockpit, often had a mate for company and there was a nose in front of you. However the single-seat FB5 cockpit was a very different kettle of fish as you were perched out in the very front with no reassuring nose in view. Rather like riding a witch's broomstick fitted with a windscreen. I don't know whether it was because of that sense of isolation or for some other reason but I do remember feeling the need to keep concentrating and not daring to stop checking everything all the time. Looking out, checking the instruments and the systems, checking where I was, checking the generator charging light down by the floor had not come on, checking the fuel pressure and quantity were okay and what about the engine oil pressure? While the list was not terribly long, it was totally time consuming because of a perceived need never to stop. I remember my instructor telling me that, if I found myself enjoying the view, then I was not concentrating enough on my flying.

Of course it does not necessarily mean you will have an accident if you do not concentrate, whether on the road or in the air, however the probability must increase. What you choose to concentrate on and continually observe in the air is obviously down to you and will also vary with circumstances. Being several thousand feet above the ground, cruising in the open FIR on a nice day is clearly not so attention grabbing as being short of fuel at low level in grotty weather. However, after landing you may well ponder just how your lack of concentration allowed you to get from the first state to the second.

One day I shut down the engine of a Harrier when descending into the circuit instead of selecting full reverse nozzle angle to slow down. Another day I started the engine with the undercarriage selected up during a last minute check of the aircraft before a demonstration for the Queen. Yet another time I landed a Vulcan without a flare. I hope that by looking back at these events I might provide some food for thought about your own flying. Please don't think the incidents were type related, because they were not. They were all classic piloting mistakes.

My inadvertent shut down was at the end of a trip from Switzerland to Dunsfold. I had been away several days and had done a stack of demos at Lugano and Grenchen so I was not out of practice, in fact quite the reverse, something which most of us would consider good news. However lots of trips in a few days in unfamiliar surroundings can make you pretty tired. Toss in a return journey that involved an hour and more of struggling along a very unfamiliar civil airways system in an aeroplane singularly poorly equipped to play at being an airliner and you can imagine I was extremely relieved to be released below the airway, almost overhead base on a lovely summer evening. Job done in fact.

Of course the job was certainly not done, the altimeter still said 1,500 ft for one thing. However, in my head the flight was very much over because there was nothing left to worry about. Indeed, the thinks bubble over my head said, "Look, there are the chaps playing the local Kingston vs Dunsfold cricket match. I wonder who's winning? I'll give them a wiz. A nice steep, full reverse thrust, decelerating transition pointing straight down at them should get their attention and make them realise some of us are still working."

You can guess the rest. I had to stuff the map down the left hand side of the seat, then put my left hand on the nozzle lever, select it all the way back to the reverse thrust position, before opening the throttle to nearly max power and standing the aircraft on its nose in a nice, slow, noisy descent. Instead I went from the map to the throttle, moved it all the way back and so shut the engine down because all the way back on the throttle was fuel off. Fortunately the dying whine got my attention so I relit the thing, did a rather lame circuit of the field and a normal vertical landing at the eastern end.

Talking about it afterwards, while most people understood how I could grab the throttle by mistake, they did not see how I could possibly shut the fuel off because it required a deliberate selection of a finger catch at the base of the throttle to get it further back than the idle position. This was a totally different action to pulling the nozzle lever back into reverse, which required the whole lever to be lifted up and over a stop set at the hover angle. The more I thought about it afterwards, the more I reckoned that it did not matter that the operation of the two protecting gates was so different. Once I had made the mistake of putting my hand on the wrong control, the trained monkey inside that hand and arm took over and instinctively did whatever it normally did to move that control all the way.

369

My mistake was relaxing before the trip was over and so making a stupid incorrect selection. Cause: Lack of concentration.

As for partially collapsing the gear on the ground, starting the engine with gear up selected will do it every time. My job was to take Dunsfold's civil registered Harrier demonstrator, G-VTOL, and do a hover alongside HMS Invincible as soon as it came to a stop after being launched by the Queen at Barrow in Furness.

Barrow was a tidy step from Dunsfold and letting down at a shipyard might be affected on the day by the weather. On the other hand, a hover could be done almost regardless of the conditions. Clearly we needed to pre-position the day before to an operating site close to Barrow, thus virtually guaranteeing our appearance on time. There was a semi-disused airfield which looked just perfect on Walney Island, just a few miles from the launch site. There was no possibility of arranging fuel on the island so we had to arrive with sufficient for the demo the next day and have enough left afterwards to go home or at least to Warton. However, G-VTOL was a heavy old two-seater lady which meant one needed a low fuel state for a hover demo, too low to be sure of getting to Warton afterwards, especially if the weather was grotty.

The solution was to fit 100 gal drop tanks, not use them en-route, lower them off full at Walney, do the demo on residual internals, go back to Walney, winch up the drops and go home. Easy, just transport some rope and tackle plus a few ground crew to Walney in the Dunsfold Dove. The plan started to go wrong after takeoff from Dunsfold when the gear up button would not go in. It had to be a stuck weight on wheels switch. I tried to shake it loose with a touch and go but it was still stuck. I tried again and again by which time the fuel was now nearly too low to get to Walney and still have enough internals left for the demo. At the last go, up came the gear. I landed at Walney and whinged to the crew that I didn't want the gear stuck down after takeoff for the demo. They said they would look at the problem and I went off to find a phone (as one did in 1977).

I got back to find that they had done lots of checks by operating the weight on wheels switch with a screwdriver and the up button went in every time. I decided I had sufficient internal fuel for a quick lift into the hover to prove the gear cycled correctly. Afterwards it turned out that the weight on wheels switch still had the screwdriver stuck in it, inhibiting the normal protection system and I must have kicked the UP button in as

I got in (it was right by the side of the left hand foot well and always had the paint worn off it from people's boots knocking it on the way by) or perhaps the crew had left it in. None of this would have mattered if I had done my checks properly of course. However I had other things on my mind and didn't. Lack of concentration again.

G-VTOL at Walney Island

We were lucky to find a farmer with a fork-lift who took some of the weight while the hydraulic hand pump had a work out and bingo it stood up on its wheels again. The main leg gear doors were all mangled so off with them. Now we needed a proper airtest to check everything was fine at high IAS with no main gear doors fitted to cover the case of the initial demo flash by. If this airtest went alright I would land at Warton, refuel the internals, then charge back to Walney all ready to go. At Warton I asked them if they could do the same with three blokes, a farmer and a Tornado sitting on the ground. No answer.

The Vulcan non-flare arrival was on a 150 ft wide runway. I had just been bashing the circuit on the long main 300 ft wide runway and moved to a smaller cross one for the final landing. I was still waiting for the sides of the narrow one to come up either side of the nose when we hit. You must think about those sort of perspective changes downwind. As it happens no damage was done but clearly no thanks to me. Dare I mention concentration again?

When cars had manual chokes they were a big help in determining one's concentration on any particular day because if you forgot to push it in after the engine had warmed up you should find an excuse not to fly! Indeed Tom Brooke-Smith who did the early testing of the Short SC1 in the 1960s always said he gave up test flying when he found he kept forgetting to do this. He may have been joking but, then again, perhaps not. The bottom line has to be that, if you ever find yourself in the air and realise you are not concentrating, then pull yourself together and give yourself a real talking to or find another hobby.

7. Showing off safely

Showing off is something we all like to do which is doubtless why most pilots I know like to demonstrate their flying skills. Such demonstrations can vary from a new PPL holder taking their favourite friend or relative as a passenger, through to the experienced airshow pilot trying hard to be chosen as man of the match. Both activities involve special risks over and above those of normal flying. While the extra risks of flying passengers for the first time are modest, they are still worth thinking about because with care they can be managed so that the trip becomes as safe as routine flying.

The extra risk to the new PPL holder flying a passenger is one of distraction – not necessarily from inappropriate passenger behaviour although that is an issue any pilot is wise to consider – but something potentially more troublesome. I am thinking of the social aspects of having a guest along for the trip. These mean it will probably be the first time the pilot has had anything on his or her mind during the various pre-flight preparations other than the processes of aviation.

Flying is an exercise in risk management. If you think about it, the total pre-flight period is all about minimising the risk associated with getting airborne. Weather, ATC and NOTAM checks, flight planning procedures, aircraft external and cockpit checks are all about reducing the inherent risks of flying and we have not even started the engine yet. I am sure you get the point – aviators do everything extremely carefully. It is for very good reasons that they are extensively trained, licensed at many different levels, subject to currency checks, frequently supervised by their more experienced peers, often specially trained to work together as crews and generally standardised – probably more so than people in any other profession or hobby.

Therefore my advice to those contemplating taking up a passenger for the first time is to recognise that the trip will not be a normal one for you. Be aware of the need to concentrate and take extra care not to deviate from your usual routines. If at some point your passenger disturbs your pre-flight concentration, which is quite likely to happen, start whatever it was you were doing all over again – or from some point that you are quite certain you reached before the distraction. For example, if you were in the middle of checking the engine oil, shut the cowling, then open it again and repeat your complete engine bay routine.

When distracted during the process of using a checklist, even the best people can boob by returning to it at the wrong place. For example, when I was a civilian flying military aircraft, I had to go to Boscombe once a year to renew my military instrument rating by flying with an ETPS instrument rating examiner. On one occasion the Hunter allocated to us happened to have a very non-standard cockpit layout and so my examiner (I'll call him Sid to protect the innocent) kindly agreed to sort out all the checks so that all I had to do was taxi, line up and do the required head down instrument takeoff. All very reasonable as he was checking my jet instrument flying capability and not how I coped with operating this particular one-off cockpit.

The Flight Reference Cards for our aircraft were those for a standard Hunter 7 but with a couple of extra Normal Operating Drill pages added on the back after the Emergency Drill sheets. The need for Sid to refer to these extra out-of-sequence pages was indicated by manuscript asterisks at various places. When we were at the holding point and he was doing the pre-takeoff checks, Sid was greatly exercised going backwards and forwards through these extra cards before he eventually announced the checks were complete and I could line up and take off. I replied, "I have control" and pointed upwards to the clear blue sky above us which was unsullied by the canopy. Sid uttered a very impressive sentence-long oath, stowed the offending checklist with a flourish, brought the canopy down and remarked, "From now on I propose we rely heavily on experience".

Back to flying passengers. When airborne, passenger-related distractions can vary from airsickness to interfering with the controls and talking just as you are trying to sort out something on the radio. As always a bit of planning works wonders at reducing the problem. This starts with a good brief once you are both strapped in and before you do the engine start checks. Show them where the controls go to at full travel so that they are not surprised by this later. Ask them not to touch anything and to ensure nobody is talking on the radio when they want to say something. Enlist their help in keeping an eye open for any other aeroplanes and suggest they point at any they see. If they want to say something important when the radio is busy, let them know what you would like them to do to attract your attention. Touching your arm is the obvious solution when side by side. If you are in tandem cockpits and can only communicate by intercom, you must consider what you are going to do if the intercom fails (or their lead comes out). Many tandem aircraft have mirrors so brief to use these if they enable eye contact. I am not going to insult your intelligence by going on any more. You must do the thinking appropriate to your aircraft and your passenger, make a list of things to brief well in advance of the day and don't forget the airsickness bit. The whole thing is meant to be fun not an ordeal so, if your passengers seem to lose interest in what is happening they may well be starting to feel queasy – in which case think about getting them on the ground sooner rather than later.

Finally, don't plan a trip that is at the limits of (let alone beyond) what you have done solo. Why not plan to keep it down to 15 minutes round the local area and a couple of circuits? If they love it you can always do more the next time. You built up gently to everything in your flying training to date so don't change those habits the first time you up take a passenger. You are the 'expert' who is showing off and you will be able to do a much better job at impressing your passenger at what a cool aviator you are if you have a simple plan that stays well inside your current capabilities.

Now for the harder topic of how to be chosen as 'Man of the Match' at an airshow. In my view there are no new ways to kill yourself when flying a display as they have all been thoroughly tried and tested. Therefore short of a major technical failure, if you fly into the ground during a display or rehearsal, do not expect much sympathy from the other display aviators you have left behind. More than anybody they will be only too well aware that you have just killed yourself and the accident was avoidable. Harsh? Well the truth is not always soft and cuddly.

I started in the fast jet display business in the mid-1960s. Youngsters today will think I exaggerate when I say that in those days there were no minimum height rules. I can well remember a few years later, when an amendment to MOD Flying Orders for Contractors specified minimum demonstration heights, how personally offended I felt that somebody who knew nothing about my aircraft – and especially how to fly it – should question my judgement over such matters. As I saw it, they had no option but to trust me to do the difficult stuff without guidance but they then had the gall to specify minimum fly-by heights. So much for the arrogance of youth that I have mentioned more than once before.

Therefore was I lucky to survive that period? Possibly, but I do feel there was more to it than luck. I was only too conscious of the handling problems that some of those early prototypes possessed and I was far from cavalier about them. I went to great trouble to build in margins of safety between my capabilities and the demands of the aeroplane when in powered lift flight. Perhaps it was that very consciousness of the true problems involved in showing off jet VSTOL as something ready for the customer which made me so upset at those conventional flight height limits. In those days I saw a wing-borne pass as very low risk when compared to the jet-borne elements of the display.

I talk about Harrier display issues in Chapter 8 but there is a non type related issue I would like to mention here. I never frightened myself doing a barrel roll or wing over. Perhaps that was because I always thought they were two of the most dangerous low level manoeuvres you can do in any aircraft. They have no recognisable height and speed gates at the top to ensure you can successfully complete the second half – unlike say a loop or a pull through – so they need special care and must be done gently leaving a lot of performance in hand. When I used to check out pilots for CAA light aircraft display authorisations, I objected to any pilot who started a barrel roll by rolling away from the crowd. In my view you should always initiate such a roll by moving the stick towards the crowd. This is because if the manoeuvre goes wrong it will be in the second half and by rolling towards the crowd at the beginning, you have ensured you will be pulling away from the people should it all go pear shaped towards the end.

These days I am glad to say that pilots will not get a display authorisation for formation work without evidence of suitable training and experience. Even then, careful preparation is needed for flying in a dissimilar type formation involving hard manoeuvring or aerobatics. With similar aircraft and a good leader using less than full power, nobody in the formation should lack the aircraft performance needed to stay in position, for example when pulling out of a loop. However, with dissimilar types the wing men must check to ensure they are not being led into something their aircraft cannot complete at the speeds and heights the leader is flying. This is an advanced task and not something to be undertaken lightly – as in, "Come and tag along on the back of our tailchase. Start up is in five minutes."

8. Pilot types

Are some people better suited to being pilots or are we all the same? I think we all know the truth about that. Yes, some people are better suited and no, we are not all the same. Of course common sense suggests the same thing applies to many groupings from athletes to brain surgeons and car drivers. However, that does not mean there is not a lot of useful stuff to consider regarding pilots.

Top of the list is the need for pilots to pass a medical, not once but regularly. How much of a problem that is will depend on the individual and the type of piloting they are considering. I have had a stack of problems in this area throughout my flying career and, while most of us are agog with indifference at the health problems of others, two of the things that happened to me might be of interest to other pilots or wannabe pilots. As I have described in Chapter 2, I intended to become an RAF pilot when I left school and was initially put off because I believed I would not meet the medical standards. It was to be five years before I risked presenting myself for an RAF medical. I passed. The message is not to assume you have a problem without first asking somebody who is competent to know. My other point is that I do not see the case for volunteering any information about medical conditions unless you feel they affect your performance. In my view it is up to the system to screen you. Why should you do their job for them? I was about 10 the first time my heart started leaping about and behaving erratically yet it was 53 years and dozens of normal ECGs later before I actually felt poorly during one of these episodes and so took myself to the doctor.

Let us now turn to the much more interesting and totally normal variation in people's physical and mental makeup which could affect their suitability and aptitude for piloting. By this I mean such things as:

- Resistance to panic
- Ease of clearing ears and sinuses
- Susceptibility to motion sickness
- Hand, foot and eye co-ordination

- Ability to concentrate
- Ability to do more than one thing at a time
- Short and long term memory
- Reaction to increased g
- Reaction to reduced oxygen levels

This list and my comments from now on are intended only as food for thought. I happen to think that pilots should try and take an objective view of their suitability for the job and such a list can help one do that. Trying to be realistic about your own strengths and weaknesses is a good starting point for progress in any endeavour but it can be critically important when it comes to piloting and flight safety.

Naturally the significance of the items in the list varies with the sort of piloting you have in mind. If your aim is just to fly a light aircraft solo round your home circuit on nice days, then probably the only one that has real relevance for you is the first one about panic. I view panic as a reaction to stress and it comes in various strengths. The effects of panic can range from a step reduction in performance when doing a task that normally you would gobble, through to a total breakdown of any ability to act logically. Experienced pilots will be able to look back on events that indicate how they stand with respect to the onset of panic. With luck, they will remember those moments as a blast of adrenalin and a bunch of slow motion images seared forever onto the hard disc of their memory, rather than as the day they lost it and panicked.

If you are inexperienced you will probably have no such memories to recall. In this case it may be helpful to imagine yourself in a situation where panic could occur and then logically try to think your way out of the problem. In other words, do some planning and decide in advance how you are going to deal with a tricky situation and by so doing prevent panic. You could imagine the engine going bang just as you lift off or at 300 ft or even later on the downwind leg and so on. None of these very nasty possibilities and many others that aviation has to offer are necessarily beyond your ability to cope, provided you have rehearsed your instant reactions to them in your head many times before.

Indeed your instructor will have been quite specific about all of these things and many other possible emergencies and will have taught you the necessary handling skills. However, ask yourself have you thought about any tendency you might have to negate all that training by panicking on the day? If you can accept that you might panic then I believe you are well on the way to ensuring that you actually do not. As ever, planning is a powerful aid to increasing your chances of doing anything.

I once read a most thought provoking article that quoted medical sources who considered that as many as 10 percent of pilots fall into a mental category termed Field Independent. This has to do with the way their brains are hard wired and predisposes them to locking on to one task and losing the big picture when the going gets unexpectedly tough. I will not insult your intelligence by commenting on most of the other items on my list, except to suggest that, if you do not see the relevance of any of them, perhaps you should seek out a more experienced aviator and buy him or her a beer.

Talking of 'her', now that many air forces screen pilot applicants for their reaction to increased g levels, there is no more hiding the fact that women have a higher g tolerance than men – about half to one g more on average. Given that most women when pushed, even the fluffy ones, are also more ruthless and vicious than men, perhaps we should note that men are inherently less suited to piloting fighter aircraft.

Although I am not aware of any air force that screens potential pilots for their reaction to reduced oxygen levels, there are definite piloting advantages to being abnormal in this context. The classic response of most people to reduced blood oxygen levels is euphoria. However a few actually feel unwell and sweat when you turn off their oxygen. I always counted myself lucky to be one such. Another was Andy Jones who later became Mr Hawk.

In the early 70s, Andy was doing a performance climb on an export Hunter at Dunsfold. That aircraft had a cabin altitude of about 22,000 ft when the aircraft was at 45,000 ft (a low level of pressurisation by today's standards I know – but that is how it was then). By 30,000 ft he felt unwell so checked all his oxygen indications. All fine, both flow and pressure. By 40 he felt rotten and decided he was ill. He checked the oxygen system again but no problems showed up. He decided he needed to land asap before whatever was wrong with him got worse. He remembered putting the aircraft into a rapid descent but the next thing he recalled was waking up to find himself supersonic and going through 10,000 ft very quickly. He sorted things out and landed. When we checked his oxygen cylinders, they had been filled with air. Now that is what I call a gotcha. When he had selected 100% oxygen and emergency flow, it blew out nicely all round his mask so everything about the system seemed normal. In those circumstances what is a guy to think? Just imagine if he had tent-pegged. Would they have ever dug deep enough to find the bottles? Probably not and it would have been put down to just another unexplained pilot problem. In the event an accident was avoided because of the pilot's physical characteristics.

There is one final point about pilot types that I should mention and that is whether a person is particularly susceptible to pilot induced oscillations (PIOs). These are just an extreme example of the pilot over-controlling a situation. They are not common events in certificated and serviceable aeroplanes as good design and development can go a long way to preventing the phenomenon from occurring. However there are some simple aircraft faults – as distinct from design defects – which can lead to a pilot finishing up with a PIO in a certificated aeroplane and I will return to those later.

First however, I would like to start with the more general case of pilot control. When my initial instructor had his first real go at me, it was about control technique. I can see us now. We were climbing up in a left hand turn towards the downwind leg in our Piston Provost and he wanted to know what on earth I thought I was up to. "Climbing up to the downwind leg, Sir," was not what he wanted to hear. His head whipped round towards me for a very long silent stare, while I suspect he seriously considered whether I was a smartarse or just thick. Fortunately he must have concluded that I was thick. "Why are you waving the pole about like that?" was his next question. I made no reply because I had not realised I was. Then his right hand (which had no thumb) came down on top of the right hand stick and locked it in position – a position I should point out that made the aeroplane do exactly what was required. He often did that in those days and how demoralising it is when you are struggling with a task.

Later, in the crew room, he used a vivid selection of words to make his point that it was stupid for me to move the pole around at such a rate that the aeroplane did not have time to respond. I remember suggesting that moving the pole a little all the time enabled me to feel what was going on. "Well don't do it," he said and left the room.

Thirty-two years later I found myself in a two-seater Hunter T8M that was used at Dunsfold to help develop the Blue Fox radar for the Sea Harrier-to-be. The aircraft was turning finals and being flown by a Royal

Navy Lieutenant Commander. The instruments were nailed exactly where they needed to be, the approach was perfect but the stick top was flashing about all over the place. At the time the RN had just decommissioned their last conventional carrier, HMS Ark Royal, which had been operating Buccaneers and Phantoms. I was becoming increasingly bothered at Dunsfold that nobody on my team had any first hand experience of Fleet Air Arm operations, yet it looked as if we would be designing and developing a cockpit for that role. I therefore asked the RN to let us have one of their best squadron pilots from Ark to act as a liaison officer with the Dunsfold pilot team and be our day to day advisor. I mention this background because anybody with the slightest bit of imagination must realise that to land a Phantom at night on the undersized deck of Ark in the 1970s had to be one of the most difficult fast jet handling tasks of that time. The guys that did it were good, in fact very good.

The chap flying me round finals in the Hunter T8M was that RN liaison officer. Taylor Scott was his name. Since his name may ring bells with some people, let me confirm that he later left the RN and joined the Dunsfold team as a test pilot. No, he did not go to ETPS but as a result had more recent squadron experience and brought a very valuable and refreshingly new approach to our Dunsfold tasks. Eventually I was able to get the Ministry to allow him to test fly Harriers although not without some pretty hard things being said about me being anti-ETPS and Boscombe Down. I was not anti them of course, I was just a bit before my time in wanting a test team made up of pilots with a variety of experience, not just experts in test techniques.

Today such 'Joint Test Force' teams are common-place in the US and the basic notion is creeping over here under several acronyms. However I am not sure I did Taylor any favours as he was to be killed during a Harrier GR5 production test when he was dragged from the cockpit, at high speed and high altitude, by a malfunctioning parachute. The aeroplane, with the seat still inside it, went on towards the US until it ran out of fuel some 90 minutes later. Taylor clearly had it well trimmed.

Pilots vary from low gain to high gain in their flying technique. My 'Sir' in the Piston Provost was trying to bring me up as a low gain one, while Taylor was the highest gain chap I ever flew with. However, as I stressed earlier, Taylor was a pilot who had a track record that clearly showed him to be at the top of his profession as a deck landing pilot. You cannot fake coming aboard a small ship with a fast heavy jet so clearly his technique worked even if my Master Pilot instructor might not have approved of such rapid continuous inputs.

Looked at simply, a high gain technique seems to imply such pilots are closer to starting a PIO but I am not sure that is actually the case. If their genes have equipped them with an instinctive appreciation of when their high gain is making things worse, not better, then it could be that they are no more vulnerable to initiating a PIO than low gain people. My experience suggests any of us can over-control in some circumstances. If you feel you are so ace and super smooth that you would never do that, take my tip and try to hover an R22 chopper – just so long as you are ready to buy the beer afterwards.

I mentioned earlier that some simple aircraft faults can lead people to over-control. The two most common are both mechanical control run issues: lost motion (sometimes called backlash) and any spot of lumpy friction where normally things would be smooth. With backlash, you make a modest input at 'your end' of the control system but nothing moves at the far end. Getting no response, you put in a bigger input. This makes the far end move much further than you wanted in the first place. Because the aircraft now does more than you want, you go in with a small opposite input which gets lost again so you make the bigger one which suddenly bites and off we go again.

In the old days before MOTs woe betide any prospective purchaser of a second hand car who did not wind down the driver's window, reach in to the steering wheel and give it a wobble while standing and watching the front wheel for a reaction. If the steering wheel moved very far without anything happening, it was not going to be easy to drive the thing in a straight line. Because the front wheel was held nice and steady by friction, any lost motion caused by wear in the various steering joints was very easy to see. With an aircraft control run you really need an assistant during the pre-flight to hold the surface and provide the equivalent degree of rigidity so that you can detect any lost motion at the control wheel or stick. As ever such checks should use gentle finger tip inputs so that you can really feel what is happening. They are not achieved by a quick dash round the outside accompanied by much thumping and waggling of everything in sight. Not that any pilots behave like that of course.

In the stability and control section of this chapter I discuss the importance of having low friction in control runs and give a specific example of how it can cause a PIO in the flare with a PA-44 Seminole. This just underlines the importance of always doing full and free checks in a very gentle and finger tip feeling way if you intend to detect friction problems. Just quickly bashing each control in turn to the stops is not best practice.

The classic way that test pilots check for any design-related tendency to PIO is by doing a very 'tight' control task. Tight in this sense means an extremely demanding need for accuracy, such as prodding a flight refuelling probe into a drogue basket. Another good and more generally available way is holding a fixed aiming mark exactly on a spot on the ground as you dive towards it. The aiming mark in question can be a fly on the windscreen or a chinagraph cross you have marked in the middle of your field of view, it does not have to be generated by an expensive bit of gun-sight technology. The wide variation in pilots' gain (Taylor versus my 'Sir') provides fly-by-wire (FBW) control law software writers with a real challenge in accommodating all pilots that are out there. The SAAB Grippen and the YF-22 were two famous cases where PIOs rose up and bit the teams in the early days of their testing even though neither of them were designed or operated by beginners.

As I mentioned in Chapter 7 I was asked to evaluate the Israeli Lavi. I understood I had to do a sharp right turn at the end of the runway to avoid a no go military area. As I started turning, the voice in the back shouted, "No – left, left," so I stuck on full left aileron to go the other way. As I tried to stop the rapid left roll at the bank angle I wanted, I set off a violent lateral PIO. Before Menachem Shmul, their CTP in the back, had a chance to say or do anything I had let go of the stick, the oscillation stopped dead and we went on our way. At the debrief Menachem remarked that "I realised you were an experienced pilot by the way you reacted after takeoff". I was well chuffed of course but, as I pointed out at the beginning, such a reaction on my part probably had more to do with genes than experience.

9. Pushing your boundaries

"What comes next?" is a question many new PPL holders are likely to ask themselves sooner or later. Rather naturally the answer will vary. A lot will depend on why the person wanted to get the licence in the first place. Some may well be happy just to keep it valid, use it occasionally with family or friends, go for day trips and so on and good luck to them because it is their licence.

My only comment to such pilots is please don't forget the continual need to practise handling and emergencies in order to maintain the level of ability you demonstrated when you passed your skills test, as I discussed under the continuation training section earlier in this chapter.

However, for those who want to move on and find a challenge to replace the original one of getting the licence, I would like to suggest an alternative to the more conventional things such as IMC, night, twin ratings and so on. This alternative might be useful if you are not sure you can afford further expensive dual instruction for a while but still want to give your flying a bit of direction and purpose.

My suggestion is to push the boundaries of your handling experience by going further into the flight envelope of your aircraft than you have done before. If you think that sounds far too way out and risky, please read on because I think I can get you to change your mind. Working through such a programme is likely in my view to be considerably safer than flying with no particular purpose or plan in mind. First however a health warning. There is a potential problem if you are a low hours pilot with only one solo type in your logbook. You will need to really concentrate on what you are doing, not because it will be difficult, but just because you will not have done it before. This means that lookout and navigation could suffer.

In order for this not to pose a significant risk, it is important that you set yourself up properly before starting. This means good weather, well away from the ground and in an area that has the necessary ATC freedom for what you intend to do. You need good, clear ground features for easy navigation and must carry out some thorough clearing turns to make sure you are on your own, looking up above you as well as below. It is all too easy to have clearing turns on a checklist but only execute them in a nominal manner. That is never adequate. Overall, such preparations are what an experienced pilot would do before, say, practising an aerobatic display sequence.

Back to the programme. There are essentially three aspects of non-aerobatic category aircraft envelope exploration that I would like to discuss here: going slower, going faster and using more attitude in both roll and pitch. You are going to do some test flying.

If that brings on an attack of "He has to be joking!" just consider the following. Test flying is normally used to describe the process where an experienced pilot gets airborne to test an aeroplane that may be in good shape or may be full of problems. Because of the doubts inherent in this situation, each such flight is specially planned and flown. One could write a thick book and still not cover all the things that might be taken into account depending on the circumstances but there are two major factors at the heart of such planning. The first is to take an iterative approach or, if you prefer, take one step at a time rather than a huge leap into the unknown.

For example, the first takeoff on a new type would be preceded by taxying, fast taxying and accel/stops on a suitably long runway, finding out what it was like to raise the nose (or tail) and put it down again and so on, perhaps culminating in a short hop. If on the other hand it was the first takeoff of your favourite club aircraft after some serious engine overhaul work, then checks before flying would include a series of ground runs on the engine followed by removing all the cowlings and looking for leaks or other signs of problems. I am sure you get the point.

The second of the two things at the heart of flight test planning would be to make sure all the peripheral issues have been optimised. That would mean using only a suitable runway and defining sensible weather limits for the takeoff tasks as well as making sure that the pilot was suitably qualified and current.

Test flying usually means an untried aeroplane with a tried pilot. What I am suggesting here is test flying using a tried aeroplane but an untried pilot. We are going to extend the pilot's envelope, not that of the aeroplane. However, we are going to bring to this flying the same detailed planning and gradual airborne steps as one would for the more traditional type of test flying.

The essential thing that makes such DIY personal envelope expansion safe is that you realise you are in charge throughout. You plan the preparation, you decide the size of the steps and you execute them in the air or perhaps change your mind and do not execute them, according to how the flight goes. This is just like a company test pilot who, half way through a sortie, does not like what has just happened and wants to talk it over with somebody on the ground before taking the next previously planned step. If all this seems hugely dull, conservative and making altogether too much drama about trying something new, I have made my point because that is how I think test flying should be, whether testing aeroplanes or testing ourselves. That way experimental prototype aeroplanes finish up in museums and junior inexperienced pilots become senior experienced ones.

I suggest you start with flying slower because this will involve stalling and stalling is something that might occur with some of the attitude stuff later. Therefore you need to be totally happy with all aspects of deliberate stalling before you risk tripping over a non-deliberate one during a later manoeuvre.

Stalling is also a very good confidence building exercise. Ways of teaching the stall vary between instructors so start with a few clean stalls using whatever method you have used to date. Keep a record of what you do, including type of stall (clean, power off or whatever), the approximate height band the exercise used, fuel state, minimum speed reached and wing or nose drop behaviour.

Then, when thoroughly refreshed on stalling as you currently do it, consider planning a series of clean idle power stalls using the technique flown by development pilots when obtaining flight test data. You may well find this technique easier than the one you used for your previous stalls. You will certainly find it more repeatable and you will not find it harder. Start your deceleration as usual but, when you get to about 1.3 times the speed at which you expect to stall (i.e. about 80 kt), lower the nose as required to hold that speed. Trim the aircraft in this shallow descent. From now on do not re-trim until climbing away again under power. Then tickle the speed back at about 1 knot per second using a very gentle back pressure. Once you have it coming back like that, ease forward and hold the speed then ease back again and continue the slow speed reduction as before. Notice how easy it is to stop and start this speed reduction. Note you are only controlling speed, not height.

Because you are descending, you must continually check that your height is still sensible from a ground clearance point of view and therefore set yourself a lower limit in your planning. This should be about 300 feet above the height at which you would be happy to complete a stall recovery. If you reach that, stop the deceleration and climb back up. Start again but this time, after reaching your trim speed and trimming out, feel free to do a faster deceleration to some 5 kt above the speed at which you broke off last time, before picking up the 1 kt per second deceleration again. Eventually you will get to a speed at which you detect something has happened. It may be the onset of buffet, it may be an abnormal need to put in rudder to keep the ball in the middle, it may be a tug on the ailerons or it may be a nose down trim change. Whatever it is, that is where you relax to stop any further speed reduction, add power and gently climb away.

After you are completely at home with this technique, you can plan to reduce the speed a knot at a time beyond the first onset of symptoms and so gradually penetrate deeper towards the full stall. This way you are exploring the feel of the aircraft as it flies slower without any tendency to suddenly get pitched deep into a violent stall. You are always in control and deciding what to do next. From there on it is a natural progression. Repeat some stalls with a trickle of power, then more power, then try some in a gentle turn, then a steeper turn, then start all over again but with flap down. Always keep notes of what you have done. Plan each sortie to start with a recap of your last test.

You will now be happier with stalling than you ever thought possible so it is time to plan a high speed sortie. You want fairly calm air for this, certainly no big bumps. With cruise power set, preparations and clearing turns done, ease into a dive aiming to go to Vne minus 20 kt. Trim normally. Watch the prop rpm like a hawk and be ready to throttle back if it approaches the limit. If you have a constant speed prop – enjoy. As you very gently – not suddenly nor roughly – approach your chosen speed, ease out of the dive. If you exceeded the speed you planned, give yourself a talking to and repeat the exercise until you anticipate the pull out correctly and hit your chosen speed. When really happy, go to Vne minus 10 kt, get that right and then go to Vne. The height loss will be reduced using higher power but never forget the rpm limit. Later plan a series of similar speed dives and check aileron response and the forces needed to go to 10° of bank each way. You will already have learned what the pitch response is like as you control the dive and pull out.

Once you are happy to fly to Vne and back away from it under perfect control, plan to do some separate dive recoveries to experiment with steeper climbing attitudes. Do this very carefully as the speed will reduce rapidly once the nose is up above the normal climb attitude and you do not want to finish up with an inadvertent stall. Recovery from a steeper than normal climbing attitude may be more comfortable if you roll on some bank and let the nose lower itself naturally, rather than pulling back as you would if trying to turn level at that bank. Again, when you have speed control and pitch attitude excursions confidently nailed, try rolling to some momentary large bank angles and back to 30°. However, do this only when the nose is well up, you are nowhere near the stall and never pull when you have a big bank angle or the speed will rush off.

If all this cautious stuff bores you, then it is your call should you prefer to take a deep breath, point the thing at the ground and, when it is going faster than you have ever seen before, yank back with two hands to check if those stories that it will loop are true. However, not over my house please.

10. Stability and Control

Stability

Given what the Wright brothers were trying to do all those years ago, it was quite simply a masterstroke not to incorporate dihedral in their aircraft. The importance of this only hit me in the mid-1960s when I tried to cope with an aircraft that had much too much dihedral effect.

It is not necessary to know anything about stability and control in order to fly a certificated aircraft. Indeed such a state of blissful ignorance is arguably the condition that most of us are in when we first go solo. However, as one progresses beyond flying by numbers, knowledge can be a significant factor in enjoying the flying experience as well as being at the heart of developing the confidence necessary to deal with any unexpected situation.

I will not pretend that reading these next few pages is going to be painless but neither should it be excruciating. Please give them a go because it is clear from the internet that there are pilots out there who are confused about stability terms – which is a polite way of saying they have got them wrong.

The terms used in discussing stability can just be listed and defined but that is a very boring and hard to remember approach so I am going to try and make some converts to the topic by setting the terms in an appropriate context. I will also put all the terms in italics the first time I use them.

We say something is *stable* or has *stability* when, following a disturbance, it tries to return to what it was doing. It does not matter whether the something is a bottle of milk on the breakfast table, a weight hanging on the end of a spring or an aircraft in the cruise. However it is worth comparing those three things for starters because the differences in how they behave can nicely introduce us to some of the terms used in discussing stability.

If the bottle of milk is knocked so that it is tilted only a degree or so it will just flop back upright and no harm is done. If you knock it harder, it will continue to tilt and topple over. Such a bottle is said to be stable to a certain angle but *unstable* beyond that. The weight on the spring is simpler. No matter how far down we pull it (short of breaking the spring), it will always go back towards its starting point when we let it go. However, we can certainly expect it to bob up and down for a long time after we release it. The milk bottle did not do that, although there would be a small range of initial tilt where it might have wobbled once or twice before it settled back on its base.

It is the initial response of something following removal of a disturbance that decides its *static stability*. Thus in the case of the bottle, we should say it is *statically stable* to small angles and *statically unstable* to large angles, while the weight on the spring is statically stable to all deflections. The way the weight behaves over time after release defines its *dynamic stability* as does any wobble of the milk bottle. We would say the weight exhibits *poorly damped* dynamic stability while the wobbling bottle is *heavily damped*. In other words, damping is about how many oscillations go on before a system becomes steady again. Boffins talk about either the time or cycles to half amplitude – or how long before the weight is only bouncing up and down half as much as it was at the beginning. If something does not oscillate but exactly returns to its starting point, it is said to possess *dead beat* damping or simply to *be dead beat,* as in 'the aircraft was dead beat in yaw'.

Pilots are very much affected by the static stability of their aeroplanes, especially in pitch and yaw, where having the right amount and type of stability is pretty much taken for granted. Imagine a nicely trimmed cruise with your hands and feet off. If you then give the stick a nudge forward and continue hands off, you would expect the nose to initially drop because of your nudge then start back up of its own accord. Ditto if you gave the rudder a brief kick, the nose would go out one side and then start to return. I realise that there might also be a bank angle change as this happened but please ignore that for the moment as it will be easier to deal with later. It is extremely unlikely with a certificated aeroplane that static instability would apply in either axis however if it did then the nose would continue going down or sideways unless you applied control to make it come back.

Whether the nose bobbed up and down several times before settling would depend on the *longitudinal dynamic stability*. If it went through several cycles before settling back to trim (and it well might if your initial input was large enough), then the motion would be called a *phugoid* and described as stable. On the other hand, if the phugoid slowly got bigger and bigger until you once more intervened with the controls, then the aircraft would be said to be *longitudinally dynamically unstable* or to have a *divergent phugoid*. In the yaw case, if the nose swung from side to side after your brief kick on the rudder then the motion is described as *snaking*.

To complete this one axis at a time idea, let us finally give the aileron a nudge to investigate the lateral stability. One wing will go down a little (the amount clearly depending on the size of the nudge) but it may not immediately and obviously bounce back towards the starting position as the nose did after the pitch and yaw disturbances. The operative words here are 'immediately' and 'obviously'. If the aircraft has a positive *dihedral effect*, it may well ease back up over a few seconds.

At this point let us return to any roll that developed when you gave the rudder a kick earlier while we were looking at the directional stability. This roll with use of rudder, which we experience with most aircraft, results from any dihedral effect possessed by the aircraft. Instructors are likely to refer to it as the secondary effect of rudder. My use of the term dihedral effect (not dihedral *angle*) is quite deliberate and not a nit-pick because there are several design features that can result in roll happening when rudder is applied. Certainly any dihedral angle is a big factor in producing this but so are such things as sweepback, a high wing with a low centre of gravity and even a high fin and rudder. Apart from the high fin and rudder, all are likely to produce right roll if right rudder is used. However, any roll produced by the aerodynamic side force from the rudder being applied well above the centre of gravity will (if you think about it) be in the opposite sense and so will actually reduce the effect of the other features a little. The dihedral effect or, as aerodynamicists call it, *rolling moment due to sideslip,* is the sum of the various components taking into account whether they are positive (right roll following right rudder) or negative (left roll following right rudder) as they are added up.

389

This interaction between the yaw and roll axes is very important and arguably one of the most important things to get right with a design if you want pilots to say it is a good handling aeroplane. The combined motion of yawing and rolling that so often results from just kicking the rudder is termed *dutch roll.*

Now for a most important point: the response of the aeroplane to the single inputs we considered earlier is also what the aeroplane will do if you do not move the controls after the aircraft encounters turbulence. A gust that blows down on top of the aircraft reduces the angle of attack and has the same result as the forward stick nudge, while one from the right will make the aeroplane behave as if you had kicked in right rudder. The latter sets off the dutch roll mode and is disliked by such diverse groups as passengers, those trying to aim weapons and all of us when we are trying to show what consummate smooth flying aces we are. Fitting a *yaw autostabiliser* is the usual way to ensure the dutch roll mode is well damped and less of a bother.

The last thing the Wrights wanted when flying so close to the ground was to have their aircraft roll if hit by a gust. Therefore no dihedral, thank you. Very smart. The Wrights were not expecting to want to take their hands off in order to fold maps, use the GPS, open a sandwich or whatever so they did not want lateral stability, they just wanted lateral control. Indeed they eschewed stability in pitch for the same reason, which is that they did not want the aircraft disturbed by anything except their control inputs. Of course, the lack of stability of their Flyer meant they could not trim it hands off in the cruise but they did not plan to do that, at least not to start with!

The bad news is that, if an aircraft has lateral stability, it will roll when hit by a side gust, if it has longitudinal stability, it will pitch when hit by a vertical gust and, if it has directional stability, it will yaw when hit by a side gust. The good news is that these very same stabilities will tend to restore the aircraft after it has passed through the gust, even if the pilot does nothing.

If you have read this far you may feel like checking out some of this stuff in the air. Try and find some pretty smooth air or the things that take a while to do, such as finding out how long the phugoid takes to damp out, will be well muddied by any turbulence you hit during such hands off tests.

One type of stability I have not mentioned so far is *spiral stability*. This is about what happens if the controls are released in a turn. Does the aircraft then wind up into the turn until it hits the surface (negative spiral stability or spiral instability) or does it oblige by tending to come out of the turn by itself (positive spiral stability or spirally stable)? This is probably the only area where you will often find instability in a certificated aeroplane. It does not bother us really because it all takes so long to go wrong that we have ample time to intervene with the ailerons or, if our hands are busy, push on the top rudder a bit.

That has covered a fair bit of the language of stability. Basically, directional stability comes from fins, longitudinal stability from tailplanes and lateral stability from dihedral. *Pitch up* says you have longitudinal static instability and *wing rock* says you have a bad dutch roll mode that is primarily in *roll* with not much yaw. If the motion was mainly *yaw* and not much roll it would be called *snaking* – but you already knew that.

It is important to note that aircraft stability resists pilot control. It's a war, folks – stability versus control (unless the aircraft has FBW).

Control

Control is everything to a pilot all of the time. If you doubt this, ask yourself who controls the flare, the touchdown, the loop entry speed, the bank angle or the height in the cruise? Who is it that controls the distance in close line astern, the speed and direction when taxying, the aiming point of fixed guns or the position of touchdown on the back of a frigate? It makes no difference whether the pilot is a pre-solo student, an airline captain or a combat aviator over the target nor does it matter what type of aircraft the pilot is in charge of, from balloon to Space Shuttle, the need for control is always paramount.

There are many books about 'The stability and control of aircraft' but I have never seen one that refers to 'The control and stability of aircraft'. This is surprising because control is essential whereas stability is not. Pilots can cope without stability but they must have control. The right amount and type of stability can certainly help a control task but it is only one of the factors that determine whether the pilot can cope.

As I said in Chapter 8 the best lateral control I have ever experienced during those critical final stages of an approach and landing was in a

Spitfire IX. While it is one thing to assert this, it is quite another to explain why. It was great because it was easy to use, it remained precise regardless of the reducing speed, it did not require a lot of training or acclimatisation, it enabled a turning approach all the way and never left me in doubt that I would be able to roll wings level in the flare. In short, it was the sort of control that makes everyone look and feel a current ace. However, that still says nothing about the physical design features behind such desirable handling.

To start to get a feel for these consider what we do when we control aircraft. We use a force combined with a displacement and we vary both according to the aircraft response we detect, very often as a continuous activity, as in the case of lateral control on short finals. The need for constant adjustments may be less at other times, for example the use of the elevator to control cruise height where activity is reduced because the aircraft, if stable and carefully trimmed, may well fly itself for considerable periods of time. Very importantly in this case, the height holding task is not terribly onerous because holding 3,000 ft plus or minus 50 ft is likely to be considered good enough.

Therefore the nature of the piloting task has to be taken into account before we can say a control is good or bad. In the jargon of the control business a *tight* task is one where great accuracy is essential to success, like an ILS in low cloud and poor visibility. Pilots need better controls to be successful at tight tasks than they do with those that are less demanding. Therefore it is essential to include a tight task if you are to fully evaluate a control because it may show up over-control tendencies about the desired datum.

Over-control is a common problem when learning to fly, almost regardless of the task but with experience we get better at relaxing, better at trimming, better at letting it fly itself for a bit and then coaxing it back to the desired state. In fact better at becoming a low gain (relaxed) pilot rather than being a high gain (overactive) one. Aeroplanes take time to respond and it is a waste of time to oscillate controls. If you doubt this, fly straight and level then move the ailerons quickly left/right/left/right and observe how the wings stay level.

Back to tight tasks. The directional control task is tight during a Harrier short takeoff from a ship. Too much to the left and your outrigger wheel is off the edge, while too much to the right and your wingtip hits all sorts of expensive parked kit. In these circumstances it is very easy to start over-controlling either side of the centreline. As described in Chapter 8, I once found myself needing to fly for a while from an Indian ship that had less width to spare than I had been expecting. Worried that I would make a mess of things, I selected a line on the deck that showed the safe left limit and the edge of another that showed the safe right limit. The lines turned out to be seven feet apart. I then found it a nice relaxing experience running between these two lines simply because I knew anywhere in that bracket was fine and so I could reduce my inputs. That was how tramlines were born on ships designed for Harriers.

The list of things involved in giving us a control we like or dislike is long. For the lateral case during the approach it would include at least the following:

- The forces and displacements needed to achieve the task
- The aircraft response to a given aileron deflection
- The friction characteristics of the control runs
- The elasticity of the control runs
- Any backlash or lost motion in the control runs
- The aircraft's roll damping
- The aircraft's lateral stability
- Any aileron induced yaw
- The lateral trim system
- Cockpit layout issues – like the position of the stick with respect to your body at full aileron deflection as you pull back in the flare

Let us get practical and consider some items on that list that can vary between aircraft of the same type due to maintenance or lack of it and which we might be able to improve if we know what we are looking for. The control linkages play a vital part. To avoid confusion, let us call the things in the cockpit 'controls' and the things outside 'surfaces'. We are in the hangar (or if in the open there must be no wind) and we have a helper outside the aircraft. Move the controls slowly and carefully using just a finger or two so that you are really sensitive to the forces involved. Friction is bad although any linkage must have some.

Breakout is very bad and is where you have to apply a significant force before the control starts to leave the central position. If there is much breakout, the force you use to overcome it in flight may make your subsequent control movement too big and cause you to overshoot what you wanted to do. However, if you apply half control, stop and then try to increase the angle some more and find another breakout then that would be evidence of a dose of friction or 'stiction', not classic breakout.

Stickiness can be very bad news indeed so far as handling is concerned. With a PA-44 Piper Seminole that I once used to fly (which uses an all moving tailplane instead of elevators and a large anti-balance tab to stop it being too light), if you did not lubricate the control tube where it slid in and out of the panel, so enabling smooth pitch control adjustments, then you could forget about doing a greaser as the fore and aft stiction would make you overcontrol in ground effect. A touch of silicone spray (or furniture polish!) and you were back to being an ace again.

It is also well worthwhile to have your helper hold the surfaces central while you very gently check (real fingertip stuff) for free play or lost motion. If you are not sure whether the surface is being held rigidly enough then get the helper to hold it at full deflection. This will also be necessary to check for any elasticity or 'cable stretch' as it is termed. In fact it may not be cable stretch, it may be a bracket holding a cable pulley that is flexing or loose and so absorbing your control input. All such things spoil handling, especially at low speed on finals on a gusty day when very large doses of aileron both ways may be needed. The DH Dove was always a bad example of the 'cable stretch' syndrome and on a gusty day you could think the ailerons had stopped working.

Going back to design matters, it is accepted that pilots usually prefer controls to be linear in their response (i.e. double the force or displacement gives double the response, or half the force or displacement gives half the response). There are exceptions here, nosewheel steering for one, where it is often nice if it is linear around centre where you need to use it carefully to keep straight but then has the sensitivity increase rapidly so that you can easily select full lock to help with parking tasks. How far a control has to be moved to get a desired effect, called sensitivity or gearing, is a big design issue.

If the aircraft has good stability then gearing may be less important. However, if the aircraft is lacking in stability then the pilot will need a very sensitive and powerful control that can be applied quickly without wasting the time needed to move the hand a long way. Imagine balancing a snooker cue in the vertical with its tip on the end of your finger. The cue is statically unstable and wants to fall over. As it does, providing you are quick, you will move your hand a small way and so return it to upright. Indeed you may well be successful at this for some time but, if any input you make is only briefly delayed, the cue will tilt further before your correction and you will have to start moving your hand further and further in an attempt at control. This is the beginning of the end because it starts taking you too long to apply the necessary correction so you lose control and the cue falls down.

The original Harriers in the hover had no stability and, with little roll inertia to provide any quasi damping, you needed lateral controls that were both powerful and sensitive to do the balancing task reliably. With the Sea Harrier on the horizon and the need to routinely deal with a rolling platform and not a stationary pad, I fancied doubling the lateral stick sensitivity in order to be able to apply the available control power more quickly. As I mentioned in Chapter 14, we checked this out by hovering the original Harrier holding the stick halfway down (think about it) which showed it was easier with this increased sensitivity so the change was incorporated into the design before first flight.

If controls are too light then arranging a higher force for any given control deflection may prevent a pilot induced oscillation. Such force may be applied by aerodynamic means, as with the PA-44 anti-balance tab, or mechanically with centring springs.

The stick force per g criteria that stops the heavy handed pilot from breaking the wings may be increased by a positive bob weight. Positive in this sense means a weight that will move the stick forward as g is increased. Imagine a rigid rod, with a lump of lead on the end of it that is attached to the top of a control column and sticks forward in front of your hand. Even at 1g this would make the stick try to topple forwards but, as g increased, you would have to pull harder and harder to keep the stick where it was. Such a device is normally fitted down at floor level and takes the form of a lever attached to the linkage at any convenient point where there is a cross tube which rotates with all fore and aft control selections.

During our training on Vampires a friend of mine had one of these positive bob weights break off his Vampire 5 during a pre-wings solo sortie. After he had been coaxed back down by an instructor in the tower (the weight was loose and sliding about the cockpit floor) he talked for a long time about how light and sensitive the aircraft had become and then left the RAF.

11. Climbing speeds

There are more exciting things to read about than the theory and practice of what speed should be flown on the climb. However one question I have been asked more than once is why Concorde had a climbing speed that started as a constant indicated airspeed (IAS) but later became a constant indicated mach number (IMN). This changeover is not unique to Concorde. It is something that affects all aircraft capable of flying high as well as those with a supersonic capability in level flight. As ever the explanation of this phenomenon comes in two sizes – short and long.

The short explanation is that, as you climb at a constant IAS, regardless of your aircraft type, your mach number is actually steadily increasing thanks to the reducing air temperature and density. If your aircraft has sufficient power to climb high enough, the mach number will eventually reach that at which a pretty steep drag rise starts to happen, even if your climbing speed is only 80 kt IAS. This mach-related drag rise would probably start in the range of say 0.60 to 0.90 IMN depending on the shape of the aircraft and, in particular, the thickness chord ratio of the wing. Naturally such a drag increase will quickly put a stop to any climb rate. It is therefore necessary to hold an IMN a little below the one where the steep drag rise happens in order to keep the best climb going. Eventually of course full power will be needed to hold height at that speed. Once at this point, you have reached the absolute ceiling of the aircraft. To summarise, all aircraft climb initially at constant IAS and increasing IMN and then change over to a constant IMN and a reducing IAS. Therefore, if your aircraft is a Cessna 152 modified with a huge engine, take care that you don't stall while you are staring at the mach meter to hold your IMN climb speed, especially if you are distracted by noticing that the sky above is getting dark.

The longer explanation has to do with how climbing speeds are chosen and the theory that lies behind them. Here some differences start to emerge both between the theoretical optimum and what it is sensible to expect pilots to fly and also between piston-powered and jet aircraft. Any reasonable textbook on the subject is likely to cover the topic of climbing in a few equations but I have always found it more useful to understand the words behind the equations.

Understanding the words behind the maths when you are flying can rid you of that niggle in your head which says 'I'm not really sure why I am doing all this'. Such niggles have more than once spoiled trips for me in the past and probably reached their peak when I was sent off to do my first solo hovers in a chopper away from the airfield at Farnborough. Over 40 years later, I still cannot drive past that farmer's field without being instantly back in that Dragonfly remembering how unsure I felt about what was going on around me.

Enough of my personal problems and back to climbing speeds. There are three things going on in any climb at a constant IAS. First the engine is having to overcome the drag that would be present at the same speed in level flight, second it has to provide the energy necessary to 'winch' the weight up vertically at a speed equal to the rate of climb and finally it has to accelerate the aircraft because at constant IAS the true airspeed (TAS) is steadily increasing as height is increased. I do accept that the latter term is small enough to be ignored in low performance aircraft but it is not insignificant with jets that have high rates of climb.

Sticking with words not formulae, the *rate* of climb is dependent on the amount of excess *power* that remains when in level flight at the climb speed. It is easy to get a feel for the power that remains to generate a climb by seeing how much the throttle is back from fully forward. On the other hand, the *angle* of climb depends on the excess *thrust* left over when in level flight at the climb speed. This is of course also related to the throttle position but not as intuitively as power. Thinking about the practicalities of takeoff and climb in a piston aircraft, the steepest angle will normally be sacrificed a little to improve engine cooling or even the need to preserve forward view. This means using a higher IAS than that for the best angle of climb. The speed for best angle will be lower than the minimum drag speed (i.e. on the backside of the drag curve) because the thrust available starts to fall from the moment speed builds and what you are looking for is the speed for maximum excess thrust over drag as in *Fig 1*.

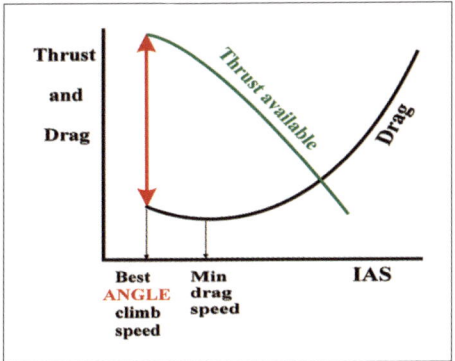

Fig 1

Best climb ANGLE speed

This shows why the airborne speed for maximum excess thrust over drag in a piston is so very low – indeed the slowest speed you can fly. Therefore, if you consider after takeoff that you may not get over the obstacle ahead, raise the nose and hold the lowest unstick speed you would be happy to use.

Should the engine fail at this nose high attitude, you have some serious de-rotation to do very quickly and almost instant full forward stick is likely to be required until the nose is below the horizon. If you plan to do something regularly (in this case going for maximum angle of climb immediately after unstick) then the thinking pilot's reaction is to practice any related emergency cases at a safe height beforehand.

The speed for maximum *rate* of climb is the speed at which you have maximum excess power when related to the power required curve which is no more than our familiar drag curve after it has been increased by multiplying by the TAS. *Fig 2* shows the shape of the power available and power required curves for a typical piston aircraft.

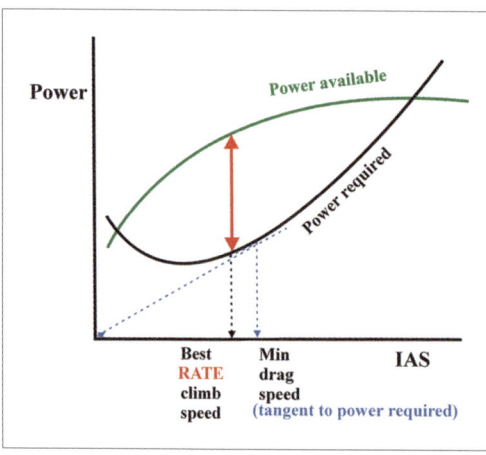

Fig 2

Best RATE of climb speed

I have not put numbers to the axes in order not to lose sight of the generalities. The speed for maximum rate of climb is again likely to be below that for minimum drag but not by as much as the speed for maximum angle of climb.

When I talked this subject though with a friend of mine who used to write operating data manuals for a living, it became clear that when pilots fly a constant climb speed we are only approximating the true optimum. If climbing theory were applied precisely then, as altitude changed during the climb, the two curves would move because of mach effects on the airframe and pressure and temperature effects on the engine output. In reality such changes in their relative position to each other are not great up to normal piston heights so we can (thankfully) achieve enough accuracy by flying the constant speeds that we naturally find easier.

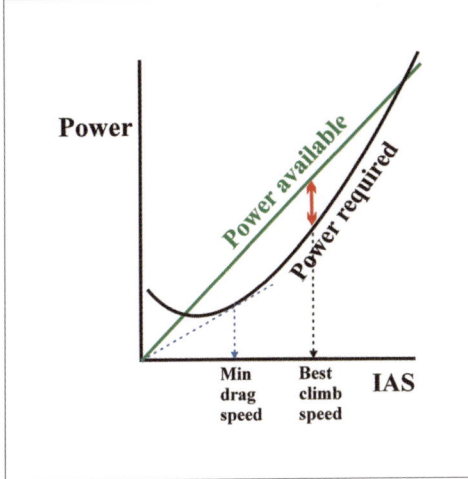

Fig 3

Having got this far, it is probably worth mentioning that the basic shape of the power available curve for a jet engine is quite different from the curve for a piston. With a jet it increases virtually in a straight line as in *Fig 3* and does not fall away at high speed due to reduced propeller efficiency.

Quite early on during my course at ETPS in 1963, the staff promised us a flight in a Scimitar. This was not to do any specific test exercises but just as a speciality type to broaden our general experience. Accordingly the whole course was briefed for this ride. The briefing took place in March but the aeroplane did not become serviceable and emerge out of the hangar until October by which time any recollection of the brief had long faded. Quite out of the blue when we arrived at work that morning, we were told the Scimitar was ready and that Jerry Skyrud, a USN Lt Cdr exchange student and our course leader was to be first up. Farley was to be second. Skyrud was expected to go as soon as he had changed while I was to go and collect a sandwich lunch from the mess and walk out as Skyrud walked in to maximise the number of trips that day.

Naturally while Jerry was airborne I got out a set of Scimitar Pilot's Notes and did what I could to refresh my memory on the fuel and control systems (as one does). It is worth bearing in mind that the most powerful thing most of us had flown up to that point was a Hunter with a single Avon engine. The Scimitar had two Avons in only a slightly heavier airframe. Clearly it was going to go. As per our instructions, I walked out to fly it as Jerry was coming in. He stopped me on the pan and quietly enquired whether I knew the correct climbing speed for the aircraft. When I admitted that I did not, he shook his head and walked off, calling over his shoulder, "Well take a tip from me and you hang on to the first one you get".

As well as being a great one-liner in the light of what a clean Scimitar had to offer, it was also not as far from technical correctness as you might think. As *Fig 3* indicates, the straight line power available curve for a jet almost parallels the power required curve for a typical jet airframe over perhaps as much as a hundred knots. All of which means that if you wander away from the best climb speed with a jet, you will not affect the performance anything like as much as you would do with a piston aircraft.

12. The theory and practice of flying

While this title could well be used for a book running to several volumes, what I have in mind here is very short and simple and concerns just one question – need a pilot's theory of flying fit his or her practice of flying? My experience says that the answer is no. I suggest it does not matter if the theories which pilots have in their heads are less than perfect providing their actions in flight are correct. After all it is incorrect pilot actions that cause accidents, not incorrect pilot theories.

It is impossible to be around aviation for long without realising that many pilots hold different theoretical views from your own. Indeed, some individuals occasionally push their theories with a conviction that allows no other possible view of the topic being discussed. Both sides cannot be right and yet both sides clearly manage to fly safely. I suspect all these debates and arguments in the club house and on the web may surprise non-pilots when they realise people are flying around with so many diverse ideas about how they do it.

When people are learning to fly I believe that what matters is that they have a theory which assists them to do the right things in the sky. If it works for them then the theory is fine for that stage of their flying career.

Should you happen to be an inexperienced and under-confident student, may I suggest you don't worry too much about theories until later. At the beginning you are very much in the hands of your instructor and, unless you have some reason to ask for an instructor change, it is your instructor's view and practice of aviation that you should try to emulate. Your instructor will doubtless include technical explanations aimed at helping you overcome your current batch of problems. Try to take these explanations at face value and use them to get better. You can join the crew room debate about whether the theories are the best available or even correct, after you have learned how to fly.

On the other hand, should you be inexperienced but feel superior because you have reason to believe your theories are right and your instructors are wrong, please take care. I say this because there are no new ways to come unstuck in flying – they have all been very well tried and tested. It won't matter if your theory was right if your inexperience (and over-confidence) leads you to do the wrong thing in the air.

Debating the questions about theories of flight is an intellectual exercise that may be very important to some and I don't dispute the fascination of studying aerodynamics, theory of flight and whatever else about aeroplanes and engines turns you on. We must also not forget the need to pass the ground exams for your licence. However, I would hate it if any youngster thought that such knowledge *necessarily* made them a safer pilot in the sky. Only one thing does that, namely properly executing and keeping current your skills test exercises. Being above the ground in an aeroplane is an intensely practical thing. It is not a theoretical situation at all and you should not feel you are any worse as a pilot just because you can't give a talk about the factors that influence induced drag.

Talking about induced drag reminds me that one day a senior USAF general pitched up at Dunsfold. The red carpet was out and the directors were everywhere. From the moment the General got out of his car he was in continuous transmit. He insisted he could not fight an air war from an airfield that was too small to accept the C-5. He would not listen to any case for STOVL.

I found a phone and told the hangar to put our two-seat G-VTOL demonstrator back in the shed and asked Andy Jones to get him airborne in G-HAWK, go to 450 kt, pull 6g and hold it until they ran out of fuel. This little Hawk party trick of sustained high g was courtesy of the low induced drag of its wing. It always got the attention of older aviators used to the inefficient early swept wings where their enormous induced drag could rein in even the biggest engines during a single 360. After his trip and over the lunch table the general shouted across to me, "Why has the Hawk got no induced drag?" I replied, "It was a fixed price contract,

401

Sir and we ran out of money." At this my MD coughed up a prawn but the good general ignored me because he was already transmitting again about something else.

I did say this section would be short.

13. Maintenance time

Let us imagine you own your own GA aeroplane and it is due a major airframe check, engine overhaul or both. Clearly you will have to organise a load of cash but what other part do you have to play in this process? The answer to that question is nothing. A whole regulatory and licensing process exists to ensure that the appropriate work will be done properly with no input from you.

While there is nothing wrong in adopting this attitude – and I am sure plenty of pilots do – I submit they are missing out on an opportunity to understand more about the flying business in general, as well as their aeroplane in particular. I say this because I believe any routine maintenance activity provides opportunities to improve our knowledge of our aeroplane and better appreciate those things that affect the way it handles and performs. Also, since mistakes can be made in the hangar as well as in the sky, having a proper appreciation of what work has been carried out helps us plan the first few flights after servicing in order to maximise safety.

It all starts with establishing exactly what work will be done on your aeroplane. What will be inspected, what will be measured, what will be changed and so on? Clearly the people to whom you are entrusting your aeroplane will be able to help with that and also the manufacturers' schedules are hardly dark secrets these days, given the power of the internet. The earlier you can establish this information the better because, without attempting in any way to infringe the world of the licensed engineer, when you have it you can – and should – have a more informed look round your aeroplane before it goes in. The essential tools of this look-see inspection are a very good torch and a proper mirror mounted on a universal joint at the end of a telescopic rod that may even have another joint along its length.

With all the normal inspection covers and cowlings removed and placed in a suitably clean area – which is unlikely to be under the aeroplane you are working on – you are ready to start. What follows will not be a quick process and you need a decent notebook and pen to record your findings. If you have to work outside you will need reasonable weather although a clear sun (if it is in the wrong place) can also play havoc with your ability to see up and into dark areas – so a hangar is certainly favourite for the job.

There is no magic or mystery to what follows. You are merely going to have the most detailed look possible at the entire aeroplane. You are looking for any everyday dirt and debris as well as more obvious foreign objects from washers to old wire locking remains. When you find something that needs cleaning and you can get at it, then go ahead and clean it. Therefore make sure you have plenty of suitable cleaning rags and paraffin or similar. The cleaning process is not just cleaning for cleaning's sake but part of the minute examination of every part of the aeroplane that will help you notice everything from oil leaks to cracks to loose rivets and wire locking problems. Make a proper note of anything about which you are not sure.

If you can only afford an hour on your first session, you might consider leaving all the panels on and just dealing with the cockpit so that, when you run out of time, you have nothing to replace and can cut and run. It may be some time since you removed all loose kit (cushions, contents of map pockets etc) so be prepared to make the odd find! Make sure you are properly dressed before you get upside down and look up behind the instrument panel. An overall with nothing in any pocket would be a good start as you do not want your inspection to leave the aeroplane in a worse state than before you started. You do not need to be an engineer to realise when electrical cables or pipe work are not looking as young as they once were or are not properly clipped in place. You will get nowhere when doing any of this without your trusty torch and mirror but don't forget that any tools or cleaning aids you take into the cockpit are going to leave with you. They do not stay there for the next time – nor anywhere else in the aeroplane when you are checking those other areas.

Rust or other types of corrosion are unlikely to be within your ability to sort out so make another careful note for when you brief your servicing organisation. Remember that absolutely nobody has as much interest in the state of your aeroplane as you do. Only you have the real motivation to look everywhere and beyond the bare schedule of checks. For the purposes of this examination treat the aeroplane as you would your family jewels.

When checking the outside of the aeroplane, pay particular attention to the control surfaces, their linkages, the end float of the hinges and their freedom of movement – there should be no rubbing or lumpy friction. If you can find a helper, get that person to hold the cockpit controls firmly so that you can then check carefully for backlash by gently trying to move the surfaces both ways – this is fingertip stuff so that you can feel any slack in the linkage and no force is called for at your end.

Lie on the ground and look up at the whole underside as carefully as you did the inside of the cockpit. The cleaning kit will almost certainly need to be pressed into service here before you can notice any faults but make sure you have properly noted any evidence of the sources of oil leaks before cleaning. Don't neglect the gear and tyres plus any brake connections and pipes. You will have to move the aeroplane to check the tyre patch that is on the ground.

I will not go on any more in this vein as my intention here is not to insult your intelligence with a long rigmarole about the obvious things to look for when checking your aeroplane but to show how much one can do without even getting into any type or maintenance specific aspects.

I have stressed the need to make notes so that you can provide your maintainer with a decent written brief about what you have found, things that you are sure they need to look at and also things about which you would like to be reassured because you are not sure if they are significant. If you possess a camera remember a dozen photos must be worth a million words!

If the maintenance involves serious dismantling such as engine out, then a photo album of the condition of the engine bay and its contents from every possible direction, including close ups, will be a very useful check for you when you carry out your pre-flight inspection after maintenance. I do not wish to imply that there is any organisation out there that would not do a proper job but it is your neck when you rely on the work of others. I cannot imagine that any professional maintenance organisation is going to feel other than delighted that they have a customer who takes aviation seriously so, if things appear different under the bonnet after they have done, I am sure they would be happy to discuss the reason for any changes.

However, most importantly of all, well before your aircraft goes in for any work, you need to decide and agree with your licensed engineers the detailed content of whatever post-maintenance air test is prudent or necessary. You should then fly this flight in every detail *before* the maintenance is done. This way you will have practised the routine and you will have a set of data to compare with that recorded on the first post-maintenance flight. I cannot stress too much how helpful this can be after engine work has been done. If you wonder what to record, the golden rule is if you can measure it or record it then do so – especially engine pressures and temperatures plus max rpm and mag drops before takeoff as well as climb and cruise data in flight.

If all this leads to you finding nothing worth reporting then your aircraft is in great shape! On the other hand, if you do come up with a point or two (or even more) then I believe you will earn the respect of your engineers, as well as getting a warm feeling that you really know about your aircraft.

14. Very serious failures

Within a few days of the Ryan NYP replica losing its right wing just after takeoff at Coventry in 2003, the Air Accident Investigation Branch posted a bulletin giving the cause as fatigue of the wing strut and undercarriage leg attachment system.

Please note that nothing that follows should be interpreted in any way as a comment on the Ryan accident. My aim is to look at the general case of severe failures that this sad event brought into focus for us all. No business has a better track record of learning from experience than aviation and long may that remain the case.

What I want to discuss here is whether there is such a thing as a list of very serious failures over which pilots can have no influence unless they have a personal or aircraft recovery parachute available. Events, if you like, about which we just have to be fatalistic and say, "If that happens, tough". In my view there is no such list. I believe pilots can always reduce the chances of such failures happening and, if the worst does occur, there may be things they can do to increase the possibility of a survivable landing. Fatalism should never enter into aviation, whether in the cockpit or the passenger cabin.

One night I was coming home from New York and got pleasantly bumped up into first class on a 747. Sitting next to me was a very distinguished looking gentleman who kept his head buried in the New

York Times throughout the safety brief. Nothing infuriates me more than having to share a cabin with people who do not take the trip seriously so I decided to have this bloke. As we taxied I very diffidently muttered, "Excuse me" until I got his reluctant attention, then I asked, "Did you catch what she said we have to do to turn the oxygen on?" He looked at me as if I was from another planet and eventually said, "It comes down from the ceiling". I explained I was happy with that but asked again, "How do we turn it on?" Of course he didn't know and neither did he want to know so I ostentatiously fiddled with the safety card pretending to try and find out. With him now back inside his paper, I did the "Excuse me" bit again and burdened him with my pleasure at 'finding' the solution. I was rewarded with a blank stare and another withdrawal behind the newspaper.

Deciding he was fairly well wound up by now and seeing he had made himself comfortable by removing his shoes and donning the courtesy socks, I did the decent thing and advised him why he would be better off putting his shoes back on until we had got airborne. He was so surprised at yet another interruption from me he lost the place and just said, "Why?" "Because they will make it easier to run away over the jagged metal and burning fuel if we crash on takeoff," I replied. "If that happens, we have all had it," was his response.

Having finally got his attention, we then had a sensible conversation during which I put the view that modern large aircraft had a considerable amount of crushable material around their passengers and some people would very likely survive any late aborted takeoff and overrun. Whether they went on to escape depended very much on them and how mentally prepared they were to act at the start of the takeoff. My fellow passenger turned out to be the chairman of an international bank but prior to our chat, all his intelligence, education and intellectual horsepower counted for nothing. Once he entered an airliner cabin, he simply gave himself up to fate.

In my view, there is much safety planning and personal preparation that passengers can do between boarding an airliner and getting safely airborne but this requires them to take their situation seriously, use their heads and not be fatalistic. It centres round planning your route to the nearest exit (which may be behind you) and never forget you need one planned for both sides in case only one side is available. When we used to fly on holiday as a family (with two to four children), we always held a briefing after taking our seats. In principle they had to follow me.

Women and children first may be an admirable concept but common sense dictated that I stood most chance of making the right decisions and getting us moving while many around us were still sitting in the sort of shock that comes from not thinking about a problem before it arises.

Back to piloting and coping with the really serious failures for which there is no checklist. Two well known examples of aircrew saving apparently impossible situations come to mind. First, the Sioux City DC10 that was crash landed in 1989 without the use of elevator or ailerons, saving 185 out of the 296 people on board. The other was back in 1970 when the late Neil Williams realised that one wing attachment of his Zlin Akrobat had failed under positive g so he inverted his aircraft and only rolled erect for the flare and touchdown. Neil's case may not have much general relevance as very few people fly aircraft which have engine oil and fuel systems designed for prolonged inverted flight. Neither of course do many pilots have his legendary aerobatic handling skills. However, the same cannot be said of the Sioux City incident which provides valid food for thought for us all.

Right at the start of our flying training we are all taught the effects of controls including the secondary effects. At the time we are trying to get a handle on how to use the primary effects well enough to be sent solo and so don't give the secondary stuff much serious attention. However, once you have your licence, perhaps it is a good time for a rethink. The use of rudder to make an aircraft roll and the use of power to raise or lower the nose could literally save your life following a control jam or linkage disconnect.

Such techniques require practice and currency if they are to be done well. Whatever some individuals may think, nobody is born a pilot, we all have to work at it. Yes, as I discussed in Section 8, some people may have a bit more natural aptitude than others but they should never allow such natural talent to let them think they don't have to work at some things. This is especially so when it comes to landing an aircraft without all the usual controls.

When the USMC decided that they were interested in Harriers back in 1969, they started asking questions about the effects of combat damage. One of their concerns was recovering to base without ailerons. I was happy to be able to demonstrate to them that, not only could we use rudder instead of ailerons (as with many jets of the day), but we could bring a Harrier back without any use of the stick at all because pulling the nozzle lever back a few degrees gave a nose up trim change. Similarly pushing it forward lowered the nose. Since the control of bank with rudder was crisper and easier if the speed was kept some 30 kt faster than a normal conventional approach, I never took the risk of actually touching down as it would have been nosewheel first. Instead I did some pretty low overshoots which were enough to make the point about the usability of the secondary effects of controls.

Later I was asked to get data on a CN-235 in Indonesia using only one aileron and one elevator. Like many recent non fly-by-wire airliners, the design made provision for landing following a control jam. To achieve this the left wheel controls the left aileron and left elevator, while the right wheel is connected to the right hand surfaces. In normal operations the two systems are joined under the cockpit floor by a link, thus giving both pilots control over all the surfaces. Come the day there is a jam somewhere you use a lever in the cockpit to disconnect this link and the pilot who no longer has the jam flies the rest of the trip.

Training for control disconnects or testing them is not fully realistic unless you hold the simulated jammed half of the system rigid. Therefore in flight after pulling the disconnect we fitted suitable chunks of wood to the 'jammed' side wheel to provide a real jam. Without this the control surfaces not in use were free to float about and affect how the aircraft handled on half controls.

If you normally fly a GA aircraft and would like to experience what it would be like to control it following an aileron jam, you will need to use the rudder for roll control. The only practical way to do this is to let go of the wheel completely, use the trimmer for pitch control and steer the aircraft left or right with your feet. This will clearly be harder than being able to use the normal longitudinal control so don't get too disheartened as you try to fly a particular heading and height. Practice may not make perfect but it will make much better.

If your elevator jams, then you can still fly on the trimmer but this time it will work in reverse because you are actually using it as a small elevator. Please remember it may not have all the authority you need because it is very small so you may have to use other trim change producing effects like power or perhaps flaps to help with longitudinal control. In the case of a dual control aircraft, it may be possible to get a mate to hold their side of the controls fixed while you try out the reversed tab but I suspect your helper might need a bit of wood or a string as a stop or reference to help them hold their side truly steady. Providing they use one hand on the wheel and the other to hold the 'stop' in position, there should be no risk that you finish up with an unintentional real jam. As ever, the hangar is the place to develop such ideas and to practise them, prior to any possible airborne use.

We have now dealt with how one copes with some serious failures in the sky and I think you will know what is coming next – prevention is better than cure. Many nasty airborne problems can be prevented by doing a meaningful pre-flight inspection. The operative word is 'meaningful'. Everybody does pre-flight inspections but not all are meaningful. The most extensive visual check of everything that it is possible to see, feel and move is not a quick matter. Indeed establishing the content of a sensible in-depth check will probably require the services of a licensed aircraft engineer (LAE) familiar with the type. On the other hand, you don't need an LAE to tell you it is advisable to look carefully for any cracks that might be starting at the attachment points of your wing struts.

Putting together such a check will be very worthwhile if you own an aircraft. Even if you don't use it before every sortie, there will be days when you are waiting for a passenger or the weather to clear in which case what could be a better way to spend your time?

How many times have I found something critical in a pre-flight during a lifetime in the business? Only twice. In the end you must decide whether it is all worth the bother. Should you tend towards fatalism regarding serious failures I hope I have at least offered some food for thought.

15. Evaluation tips

If you are fortunate enough to be able to think of buying your own aeroplane then you may wonder how to go about the selection process. On the other hand, perhaps you already have a specific aircraft in mind but need to feel a little more certain that you are doing the right thing before you take the plunge. Either way I would like to suggest some points for you to consider regarding any flying you carry out as part of your decision making process. Please note I shall be covering only handling and performance issues rather than engineering or paperwork matters. At the risk of stating the blindingly obvious, there is only one question you are trying to answer namely – Does it meet my needs?

Simple though that question seems, you will probably need to check a lot of things to be sure of the answer. Of course it could be that the thing has a shape and colour that makes it just perfect in your eyes and so nothing else matters. In this case I can only say, "Good luck!" In fact I can remember making a decision on such a basis many years ago – although not about choosing an aeroplane. That did not work out either but how else do we gain experience?

Does it meet your needs? I know the question is obvious but during your evaluation of a type it will be surprisingly easy to lose your concentration on these five words – so don't be surprised if I keep repeating them. Test pilots are taught to evaluate aircraft for a living and, if you speak to the staff at any test pilot school, they will tell you that their biggest task when faced with a new bunch of students is getting them into the right frame of mind regarding evaluation. I am not for one moment suggesting you need to be trained as a test pilot to evaluate an aircraft for your own use because of course you do not. However, there are aspects of the frame of mind of a professional test pilot that are worth thinking about.

What is it that test flying instructors have to sort out in the heads of their new students? Notice my use of the word 'heads'. This is because in the main such students have been through enough filters before the course to ensure their hands and feet are up to the job. The problem is that most of the students come from the top end of the military pilot population and so exhibit in spades a typical military 'can do' culture. Such people did not get where they are today by telling everyone in the bar that they found something difficult to fly. On the contrary, they kept it to themselves, did their best to compensate for their aircraft's deficiencies and treated the whole thing as a personal problem. Such people now have to realise that in future what they find difficult must become the subject of their report.

The message from this for the amateur evaluator is that you must be honest with yourself throughout your evaluation. If you find something about an aeroplane that is knocking on the limits of your ability to cope then it is time for some reflection. If everything else about the type is just perfect then probably this issue can be treated in isolation. For example, can you get some instruction in improving your relevant skills before making your decision to buy? If there are several things about a type that you find tricky then perhaps this is not the right aircraft for you at this stage although it could well come back into the frame later on in your flying career.

Let us imagine that you, as a nosewheel person, hanker after buying a tailwheel type. Should you get somebody to teach you once it is yours or should you go and get taught to fly tailwheels first? Clearly only you can make this decision which brings us back to that question again – Does it meet your needs? Your first task is therefore to decide just what your needs are and this must be done before you can even start to plan the evaluation.

The professional test pilot embarking on a programme will likely have very many documents that spell out the development, certification or service use needs of the type. This is not so with you and your 'needs list' becomes your 'certification' standard against which you will be evaluating the aircraft.

If you think I am banging on too much about the obvious then think again because I don't agree. Anything that you overlook that should be on your needs list will certainly have the potential to take the shine off your experience with your new toy. Therefore you must do everything possible to make it complete. On the other hand, do not just put everything you can think of into the list. It should not include things that really don't matter or you will unnecessarily complicate your plan and as a result fail to pick up in flight something of real concern because of the time you spent on trivia.

My problem here is that so much of the contents of your needs list will depend on your experience and ability as well as your planned use of the aircraft. Because of this I either run the risk of teaching my granny to suck eggs or (an even worse sin in the aviation business) assume knowledge that you do not possess. Before I make suggestions for your list here is a little background about the gentle art of being a test pilot.

When I was a lad at test pilots' school, they taught us a large range of flight test techniques about aircraft handling. The main ones concerned stick free stability and control measurements about all three axes and involved both static stability and dynamic stability. I have addressed stability in more detail earlier in this chapter but basically with static stability, you trim the aircraft out in whatever circumstances are being examined then give a control a nudge to disturb things and observe whether the aircraft immediately tries to recover from the nudge (stable) or goes on wandering away from trim (unstable). Dynamic stability checks involve watching the behaviour following the nudge over some period of time and are usually about timing the subsequent cycles of an oscillation to see how well things are damped. Then there are such checks as measuring the stick force needed to pull different levels of g and so on. Without trying to cover a year long course in a paragraph, the bottom line (in those days) was that you carried out a lot of academic test techniques, analysed the results and thus decided if the aircraft met the book of requirements.

The emphasis is different today and closer to the way you need to look at things. Test pilots are now taught to fly the aircraft as it would be flown in its role and, based on their experience of that role, decide if they are satisfied with the handling. If they are then that is that. Time is not wasted on getting lots of data to prove the handling is suitable. This is the same approach that you need to use when checking whether the handling of a type meets your needs. The difference in your case is that if you don't find it satisfactory that is the end of the matter. You do not have to give reasons or prove why it is unsatisfactory, unlike a test pilot who will be required to gather quantitative (numerical) data to back up his initial qualitative (subjective) assessment by doing relevant handling tests on the lines I mentioned earlier.

I think there is a big message for you here as you plan your test flight evaluation – namely that doing academic stability and control tests will not get you a better answer to the question 'Does it meet my needs?' You either like it or you don't and you do not have to justify your opinion to anybody else. Fly the aircraft as you intend to use it (just like the modern test pilot) and make up your mind whether it is satisfactory for you.

I hope this has convinced you that you do not need the training of a test pilot to evaluate an aircraft for your purposes but just need to use a similar mental approach. After all, a busy mum with a house full of kids does not need to know anything about the design and development of cars to decide whether the one in the showroom suits her purpose. She has a list of what she wants, such as power steering, a boot with a low sill height, easily cleaned interior and a seating configuration she can easily change. Thus in no time at all she can tell whether it meets her needs. I know there is less to consider when choosing a car compared to an aeroplane but the essence of the process is similar because you are answering the same question. 'Does it meet my needs?'

Performance issues hardly need any comment from me. The type will carry enough weight, go far enough and go fast enough to meet your needs or it will not. Similarly takeoff and landing distances will either match your needs or they will not.

Now to what your flight test should include. You certainly need to do some takeoffs and landings from the sort of site that you normally use for your flying. A poor view over the nose (or any other approach handling quirk) becomes much more apparent when you are faced with some tall trees on short finals into a strip, as opposed to when you are approaching a large airfield. For obvious reasons you should include an approach in a strong crosswind. When doing this, whether you favour a wing down or crab technique, make sure the aircraft does not object to your usual way of flying such an approach. If you are a wing down person, check at a safe height that the aircraft is happy with a more exaggerated slip than you would reckon to use on short finals.

I am sure some people may feel that I go on too much about the stall and flying slowly close to the stall. However, even if that applies to you, you still need to check the characteristics of the aircraft in the stall and during some low speed manoeuvring. In the event you are not confident to fly such manoeuvres in your current aeroplane, then you need help to build your confidence before evaluating them on a strange type. If this is not easy to arrange, then I suggest you need to ask the vendor if they are happy to watch you make a mess of flying the aircraft at low speed and in the stall. If they don't like the idea of that, you will have to make your mind up whether this is because the aircraft in question is a handful or whether they are simply not used to such 'instructional' issues. At the very least they should be happy to demonstrate to you that the low speed handling is benign.

I have two good friends who bought themselves aeroplanes and then crashed them. Both crashes were due to low speed handling issues. Neither pilot was what anybody would call inexperienced. One, an airline pilot, rang me up from his hospital bed to tell me the news and said, "You were right. I should have practised slow tight turns as you advised". Both survived their accidents only because there was no fire so I do have my reasons when I bang on about these slow flying matters.

As I said earlier, it is important to be honest with yourself about the evaluation of your potential purchase. If you realise that your own slow

413

flying and stalling abilities could be improved, then you might even consider spending some of your box of cash or credit on more instruction rather than buying whatever you had in mind.

Oh dear, perhaps I am showing my age. I fully accept that aviation and indeed the human race in general would be nowhere near where it is today without the arrogance of the young and inexperienced. Therefore if the colour and shape represent your heart's desire then perhaps you should just go ahead and buy it even if you risk learning a lesson the hard way later.

16. Being your own test pilot

You have built your own aeroplane – should you also test fly it yourself? 20 years ago the CAA took me to court and fined me for breaking one of their regulations. As we are all aware, it was no defence that I genuinely did not know of the rule. I am sure that the rules are considerably more complex today than they were in my day so the scope for breaking the law must be much greater now. However, what has all this got to do with building your own aeroplane and acting as your own test pilot on its first flight? The answer is that I want you to be quite clear that I know nothing about the regulations covering the activity I am going to write about here. You must look elsewhere for that advice.

I simply intend to discuss the test flying of a homebuilt aeroplane from the standpoint of ensuring the greatest possible safety for the first flight. If you feel that not discussing any relevant regulations makes this a pointless academic exercise, I disagree because if you get the flying wrong you could die, whereas if you get the regulations wrong you may get fined.

There are four things that need to be taken into consideration when judging whether any test flight is likely to be safe: the pilot, the aeroplane, the operating site and the plan. Please read nothing into the order in which I have listed them because, given the right (or wrong) circumstances, any one of them could be entirely to blame for an accident. I propose to consider these four risk factors in turn since it is simply not realistic to insist on perfection when we live in the real world where time and money are limited.

Let us start with the pilot. He or she will ideally be in current flying practice, be very experienced in general including some experience of the class of aircraft to be tested and preferably be a qualified test pilot to boot. I can hear you saying that there is not much chance of a home builder fitting this description so is the discussion over before we start? Not in my opinion.

If somebody has invested endless time, money and craftsmanship in building their own aeroplane then it has to be totally understandable that they would like to be the first person to fly it. Having the satisfaction of doing that successfully must be about as good as aviation life gets. Recognising that the builder is unlikely to have the ideal pilot background described above, let us re-examine that background and see if there is a basis for relaxing the spec. First consider the phrase 'be in current flying practice'. Make no mistake, there are no ifs or buts about this and the less you measure up to the other ideal pilot characteristics, the more important it is that you are in practice. Spending money on improving your current flying practice is unlikely to run up much of a bill compared to the value of the work and materials that have gone into your aircraft, which at the moment is still in one piece.

While we can certainly theoretically analyse each of the risk factors in turn, once we try and come up with a judgement of the overall risk, it is clear the factors interact with each other – take currency as an example. Currency should not be just about getting any old hours in during the couple of weeks before your test flight, rather it should be seen as an opportunity to practise the sort of flying you will be doing (or may be forced to do) on that first test flight – which means visual circuits, glide approaches and practise forced landings. Do not underestimate the value of using a type that is as close as practical to the sort you will test. If the aircraft you will test is a tail-dragger with an open cockpit then I would suggest doing your currency build-up in a tricycle with a cabin is not taking your preparation seriously. The other two factors that interact with the currency flying are the site and the plan.

If the test site will be grass, then it should be grass for the build-up. If the first flight will be from tarmac, then you should practise from tarmac. Similarly, if the test plan includes high speed taxying leading to a hop and immediate re-land, then you should also practise these. If you feel I am back to recommending perfection and so being over the top about this preparation, then just remember that you are not a qualified and experienced test pilot and therefore we have already moved a long way from the ideal pilot described above.

Now let us consider how good a pilot you are. Piloting involves so many different skills that it is pointless to say somebody is a good or bad pilot without discussing specifics. If this test flight is properly planned, it will use only a few of the many skills that exist in the overall activity of flying so let us consider which ones are important in this case. Top of the list must be good stick and rudder skills and the accurate judgement of attitude and flight path on the approach. If you are still at the stage of not knowing how a landing is going to work out until it has all happened, then this might be the time to appreciate your limitations and decide it is not sensible to act as your own test pilot after all. That is a call only you, or somebody who flies with you a lot, can make.

This brings me to the issue of pilot confidence. If you seriously doubt your ability to do what will be needed, then that is another show stopper. Please note I am not talking about being a little more nervous than usual, keyed up or even a tad apprehensive, because such feelings are only natural before a first flight (unless you are grossly overconfident to the point of being dangerous). However, those feelings must be totally under control and not in any way running away with you. Your reaction to them should make you super concentrate on accurately and carefully executing the plan, rather than induce a red mist where you abandon all logical processes and decide to just open the throttle and go for it.

Before going further, let us consider three other risk factors. These are the aircraft, the operating site and the plan. Is the aircraft just another example of a widely-built design in common use or is it essentially a near one-off? If the former, it is much more reasonable for a less experienced pilot to do the testing. The handling qualities of the type will be well known and there is nothing (except some money) to prevent the test pilot from getting prior experience of the type in an example that is known to be fully airworthy and reliable.

Such preparation is a common sense risk reducer and the cost is just part of the price you should be quite prepared to pay for the satisfaction of being the first to fly your own version of the aircraft. Clearly such a check-out on type leaves you much better placed to appreciate things that might turn out to be different on your aircraft and help you to identify and cope with problems on your test flight.

On the other hand, if your aircraft is a very rare and little used type, then you need serious help in coming to your decision as to whether it is sensible to be your own test pilot. You should have discussions with an experienced test pilot who is familiar with the class of aircraft you are building well before it is finished. Waiting until the last minute to arrange such a meeting is hardly likely to impress that person with how seriously you are taking your preparations. Such a mentor might also need time to establish from their contacts the probable handling characteristics of the type. For example, not all kit aircraft are stable in the pitch axis.

If you have never flown an unstable aircraft it is not easy to know how you might react to such handling. It is not too difficult to cope with a moderate degree of pitch instability but it can be a bit off-putting the first time you experience it. For example, it means that you cannot let go of the longitudinal control. While you can trim out gross forces, you cannot completely trim the aircraft which can lead some people to overcontrol.

I have said it before but it deserves repeating here. If you want to check your own natural aptitude to control the attitude of an unstable, light and sensitive aircraft, then you can do no better than pay for a trip in an R22 helicopter. Please note I am specifically talking attitude control both in the cruise and at lower speeds. If you decide to do this, make sure your instructor knows what you want out of the sortie and that the purpose of your flight is not a typical chopper familiarisation.

With regard to the operating site for the first flight, then without doubt the single most important aspect is size. The very last thing it is sensible to do is to fly a new aeroplane from a near limiting size of strip. I am sure the reasons for that are self-evident but if they are not, may I suggest you should definitely not be flying this trip. In my view, the more doubt there is about how this aeroplane will handle and perform, then the more important it is to have an ideal site. My own preference would be a nice hard runway that is into wind and long enough to land on again straight after unstick. The ability to build up with fast taxying and then progress to a hop along the runway before committing to a circuit has to be the biggest risk-reducing factor bar none you can have for any first flight.

I know grass is nicer for slow landing tail-draggers because it calms any tendency to ground loop but the problem is that it is seldom devoid of bumps. Being bumped into the air just before you want to lift off is not good news on a first flight. It negates your planned caution on the first takeoff, where you intend to do everything very carefully and gradually without any sudden or large control inputs. A few knots of wind can be very nice to keep down groundspeeds but I am sure you would not attempt to do your first takeoff in a crosswind or on a gusty day.

The interaction between the various risk factors is obvious. The less that is known about the aircraft type and the less experienced the pilot, the more it becomes extremely important to balance that with an ideal operating site and weather. Equally, a more experienced test pilot might accept some reduction on the operating site or weather criteria. That leaves the plan as the final risk factor to consider. You will note we have already discussed some aspects of this, for example the operating site and that hop before a circuit.

However, the thing that really makes the overall plan easy to get right is that you do not need to decide it by yourself. Discussing it with people who have an appropriate background in this sort of exercise is a must. You may be short of flying experience but this need not affect the quality of the plan. Again, if you don't see the need for talking to others, then I would query your attitude and suggest that perhaps you should not be doing this test flight.

Having reduced the risks as much as practicable, let us assume you get safely airborne. The aim now is to settle down and do whatever is necessary to help you carry out a safe approach and landing. Whether to do a stall would be one of the things discussed with your mentor. It could be that instead of doing a stall your plan includes flying a dummy approach at height. If so, this should be some five knots slower than you intend to fly in the circuit and you should make longitudinal and roll control inputs that are rather bigger and just a little more abrupt than you would normally use. This will give you the confidence that the aircraft will fly safely when handled normally on speed and close to the ground.

If you really want to do this first flight so much that you can taste it, then good luck with deciding whether you should. It will not be an easy decision to make but I hope that I have given you some food for thought that will help you make the right decision.

17. The PPL syllabus

One day my publisher, Ian Seager, asked me what changes I would make to the PPL syllabus if it were down to me. After some thought I decided my answer was nothing. However, if he had put the question to me 25 years earlier, I would have seen it as an opportunity for a good old rant about such matters as spinning, basic aerobatics and formation flying. Since none of these are in the PPL syllabus today what has caused me to change my views?

For a start, I now have much more knowledge of the general aviation scene and of what the PPL is about than I did then. At that time I had just reached the mandatory retirement age from my job as an industry test pilot and rather naïvely assumed that the whole world learned the basics of flying in broadly the same way as I had been taught by the RAF. Today I realise that is not true and I will try and justify both my 'nothing' response and some changes to the overall GA flying training and licensing system that I think could be worthwhile.

The present PPL syllabus represents a course of instruction and experience that is aimed at enabling an individual to be competent to carry out a fairly limited range of flying activities. Indeed, there are many similarities between a new PPL holder and someone who has just passed their driving test as they are both beginners, one at flying aeroplanes and the other at driving on the road.

When they are first issued both are really licences to learn. I know that is not an original phrase but it expresses exactly what I feel about them. I view the ways people are trained and tested for these licences as sound because they are based on the experience of good professional minds over many years. Accordingly I see no need to tamper with the process of granting either licence but I would certainly change what happens later in the case of the PPL holder.

Consider a pilot walking out to fly an aircraft six months after getting their licence. Whether they realise it or not, their every move will be dictated by flight safety issues as they consider the weather and do their external checks. Once strapped in, they will be concentrating on internal checks, ATC matters and later the takeoff checks. Let nobody doubt that the process of getting a PPL involves a very high level of safety indoctrination. While it is true that flying is inherently risky and the need to take care is common sense, nevertheless the present PPL syllabus does a good job of teaching the basics of safe aviation.

At this stage one is tempted to consider what a new driver has in mind as they get in their car six months after passing their test. However, this book is about flying not driving so I won't go down that route. In any event, driving is carried out by such a huge proportion of the population that the whole topic of post licence competency and any further training is so political that the deaths of up to ten people a day in the UK is nothing like enough reason to take action.

How different is the world of piloting. I believe pilots as a group are more thoughtful about their hobby or occupation and therefore more open to suggestion than many other groups which is perhaps one reason why you are reading this.

One issue that comes up over and over again on the internet is the relative merits of civil and military pilots and by implication the training systems that produced them. It is clear that there are experienced GA and civil trained airline pilots who view military pilots as something between legalised hooligans and ego-driven idiots who should never be allowed anywhere near a flight deck after they leave the military. These same people also have no doubt that, if they themselves were allowed access to high performance military aircraft, they would do a better professional job than the squadron pilots. Military pilots in their turn have difficulty understanding how anybody can be licensed as a pilot if they have not had full spin training and so on ad nauseam.

I was not born yesterday and I do realise that some posters to websites are wind-up merchants while others are engaging in banter but I suspect that still leaves a number who genuinely hold these views. However, there is no point in any simple comparison of the military and civil flying training systems (or of their graduates) because they are very different schemes with totally different objectives. The cost of one is measured in tens of thousands of pounds while the other is measured in millions.

Let us be honest, assuming they can pass a medical, there is no reason why anyone who is determined and able to spend enough time and money should not get a PPL because the task is not that difficult. On the other hand, the operational military pilot is required to think and work under pressure in the air to a level that happens to be beyond the capabilities of most people.

The military system is therefore geared to fail students after only a few extra-to-syllabus trips and as soon as there is doubt that they can continue to progress at a specified rate to an eventual operational standard. Furthermore, the sheer cost of flying military aircraft means it is necessary to restrict advanced training to those students who show real flair for the job. In this context the RAF ground-based aptitude and selection testing scheme, developed over many years, has shown itself to be a good predictor of those likely to reach military wings standards

Returning to the PPL syllabus, I would leave it alone but I would certainly rename it the Basic PPL (BPPL) and introduce a new Advanced PPL (APPL). To be awarded an APPL, I propose the pilot should reach higher standards in what I call 'pure flying and handling skills' beyond those currently needed for the PPL. Since the boundary between pure and applied flying is necessarily rather imprecise, what I have in mind is probably best indicated by specific examples. While all are drawn from exercises that are standard for military trainees, I have restricted their depth to what I feel is appropriate for the private pilot.

Spinning, formation flying and aerobatics would be my core items of such an APPL although I am not proposing these activities should be taken beyond the initial stages. For example, I would limit spinning to the ability to enter and recover from a standard four turn erect spin on a type having normal spin behaviour and certainly not require prolonged or inverted spinning or indeed any spinning on an aircraft type where the manual calls for unusual entry or recovery techniques.

The value of such training in spinning lies in developing the pilot's confidence to handle flying in general and is a necessary prerequisite to advanced stalling. It is not about turning them into spinning experts. Once a pilot is able to handle a standard, clean configuration, idle power spin of four turns, advanced stall training becomes acceptable. This should include deliberate stalling from a variety of attitudes and configurations all aimed at spin avoidance and not as part of advanced spin entry manoeuvres. The merit of being able to handle a basic spin is that it gives the pilot a real chance of recognising things at the incipient stage and so avoid a full blown inadvertent spin – just as the advanced stall training is aimed at reducing the likelihood of future inadvertent stalling.

My requirement for formation flying would be at the level of briefing and leading a pair clear of cloud. It would include flying in the echelon (port and starboard) and line astern positions. Manoeuvres would be limited to normal turns up to 30 degrees of bank plus sustained climbs and descents. Takeoffs or landings would be carried out in stream not close formation. The maximum formation size for acting as a wingman would be leader plus two. I would not see formating in cloud as a necessary part of the APPL syllabus as I would be reluctant to prevent somebody converting a BPPL into an APPL because they had no experience of instrument flying. My APPL holder would just be more experienced and safer at basic aircraft handling than somebody who only had a BPPL.

Such basic formation skills would enhance the general satisfaction of being a pilot and in some circumstances they might just offer a chance that the individual could be led to a safe landing by an experienced pilot. Without some prior experience of the basics of formation, trying to benefit from a shepherd might easily become counterproductive. An appreciation of what is involved in formation flying might also reduce DIY attempts between untrained friends that can so easily result in tears.

On the aerobatic front, I would limit the mandatory manoeuvres to the loop and barrel roll. I am sure that most people who master these are likely to want to go on to try their hand at inverted flight, a slow roll or even a stall turn and why not? However, I would not make them mandatory for the APPL because, while the loop and barrel roll can be flown quite gently and without experiencing any negative g, the same cannot be said for inverted flight and slow rolls. It would be a shame to exclude people from holding an APPL just because they found negative g was not for them. The benefit of being able to do a loop and barrel roll lies in the general satisfaction and enjoyment category rather than any specific value but is that not what private flying is all about?

If there were a debate about an advanced syllabus, people would have differing ideas as to what should be included. Therefore it might be wise to decide first whether the notion of an advanced 'handling' licence has any merit before getting bogged down in too much detail. However, for an advanced licence to be a worthwhile ambition for the private pilot, it would have to represent a reasonable step beyond the basic licence.

I conclude that the existence of an APPL syllabus would open the door to safer flying inside the normal PPL world and would reduce the worrying percentage of GA accidents where the pilot is said to have 'lost control'.

Acknowledgements

p 12 *John Farley Collection*

p 25 *John Farley Collection*

p 26 *Copyright unknown, via John Farley*

p 27 *Copyright unknown, via John Farley*

p 35 *Copyright unknown, via John Farley*

p 53 *© Crown Copyright/MOD. Reproduced with the permission of the Controller of Her Majesty's Stationery Office*

p 56 *© Crown Copyright/MOD. Reproduced with the permission of the Controller of Her Majesty's Stationery Office*

p 58 *© Crown Copyright/MOD. Reproduced with the permission of the Controller of Her Majesty's Stationery Office*

p 59 *Copyright unknown, via John Farley*

p 61 *Source unknown, via John Farley*

p 63 *Copyright unknown, via John Farley*

p 65 *Copyright unknown, via John Farley*

p 66 *© Crown Copyright/MOD. Reproduced with the permission of the Controller of Her Majesty's Stationery Office*

p 68 *© Crown Copyright/MOD. Reproduced with the permission of the Controller of Her Majesty's Stationery Office*

p 71 *© Crown Copyright/MOD. Reproduced with the permission of the Controller of Her Majesty's Stationery Office*

p 75 *© Crown Copyright/MOD. Reproduced with the permission of the Controller of Her Majesty's Stationery Office*

p 79 *Copyright unknown, via John Farley*

p 81 *Copyright unknown, via John Farley*

p 82 *Copyright unknown, via John Farley*

p 83 *BAE SYSTEMS*

p 89 *BAE SYSTEMS*

p 98 *BAE SYSTEMS*

p 100 *BAE SYSTEMS*

p 102 *BAE SYSTEMS*

p 105 *BAE SYSTEMS*

p 106 *BAE SYSTEMS*

p 107 *BAE SYSTEMS*

p 117 *BAE SYSTEMS*

p 122 *BAE SYSTEMS*

p 123 *BAE SYSTEMS*

p 144 *Copyright QinetiQ*

p 145 *Copyright QinetiQ*

p 146 *Copyright unknown, via John Farley*

p 146 *(Short SC1) © Crown Copyright/MOD. Reproduced with the permission of the Controller of Her Majesty's Stationery Office*

p 147 *Science Museum/SSPL*

p 149 *Copyright QinetiQ*

p 152 *Copyright Jamie Hunter/Aviacom*

p 163 *Copyright QinetiQ*

p 174 *Copyright unknown, John Farley Collection*

p 177 *BAE SYSTEMS*

p 178 *BAE SYSTEMS*

p 179 *BAE SYSTEMS*

p 181 *John Farley Collection*

p 182 *John Farley Collection*

p 184 *John Farley Collection*

p 186 *John Farley Collection*

p 190 *John Farley Collection*

p 194 *John Farley Collection*

p 195 (top) *US Navy*

p 195 *John Farley*

p 197 *BAE SYSTEMS*

p 199 *John Farley Collection*

p 200 *John Farley Collection*

p 207 *John Farley Collection*

p 210 *BAE SYSTEMS*

p 215 *BAE SYSTEMS*

p 217 *BAE SYSTEMS*

p 220 *BAE SYSTEMS*

p 223 *BAE SYSTEMS*

p 229 *BAE SYSTEMS*

p 230 *BAE SYSTEMS*

p 231 *BAE SYSTEMS*

p 235 *Copyright unknown, via Farley Collection*

p 237 *BAE SYSTEMS*

p 247 *BAE SYSTEMS*

p 284 *BAE SYSTEMS*

p 284 *BAE SYSTEMS*

p 284 (fig 4) *BAE SYSTEMS*

p 285 (fig 5) *BAE SYSTEMS*

p285 © *Crown Copyright/MOD. Reproduced with the permission of the Controller of Her Majesty's Stationery Office*

p 330 *McDonnell Douglas/Boeing*

p 334 *Courtesy Farnborough Air Sciences Trust*

p 336 *AgustaWestland*

p 337 *Courtesy of Aircraft Design Centre, Cranfield University*

We have made every effort to trace the copyright holders of photographs and welcome contact from any interested parties

The Earl of Kimberley's obituary reproduced by permission of The Daily Telegraph

Index

Acronyms

AAR	Air to Air Refuelling
ADD	Airstream Direction Detector
ADI	Attitude and Direction Indicator
AFB	Air Force Base
AGARD	Advisory Group on Aerospace Research and Development
agl	Above ground level
Alpha	Angle of Attack
AMD	Awareness of Mortal Danger
AMRAAM	Advanced Medium Range Air to Air Missile

AOA	Angle of Attack
APPL	Advanced Private Pilots' License (JFF suggestion)
APU	Auxiliary Power Unit
AR	Aspect Ratio
ARB	Air Registration Board
ASDL	Aeronautical Systems Designers Limited
ASI	Airspeed Indicator
ATC	Air Traffic Control
AUW	All Up Weight
BAe	British Aerospace
BEA	British European Airways
BIS	Board of Inspection and Survey
BLEU	Blind Landing Experimental Unit
BPPL	Basic Private Pilots' License (JFF suggestion)
BWB	Blended Wing Body
CAA	Civil Aviation Authority
CAFU	Civil Aviation Flying Unit
Capt	Captain
CAT	Clear Air Turbulence
Cdr	Commander
CDTC	Controlled Descent Through Cloud
CFS	Central Flying School
CG	Centre of Gravity
CIA	Central Intelligence Agency
C of A	Certificate of Airworthiness

CO	Commanding Officer
COD	Concentration Observation and Distance
Col	Colonel
CT	Continuation Training
CTP	Chief Test Pilot
CV	Curriculum Vitae
Demo	Demonstration
DERA	Defence and Evaluation Research Agency
DH	Digital Harrier
DIY	Do it Yourself
EAP	Experimental Aircraft Prototype
ECG	Electro Cardiogram
EFS	Enhanced Flight Screener
EPNER	Ecole du Personnel Navigant d'Essais et de Reception
ETPS	Empire Tests Pilots' School
FAA	Federal Aviation Agency
FBW	Fly by Wire
Fg Off	Flying Officer
FIR	Flight Information Region
Flt Lt	Flight Lieutenant
FOD	Foreign Object Damage
FSD	Full Scale Development
FTS	Flying Training School

G	Gravitational force
GA	General Aviation
GCA	Ground Controlled Approach
HAS	Hardened Aircraft Shelter
HMS	Her Majesty's Ship
HNC	Higher National Certificate
HOTAS	Hands On Throttle And Stick
hp	Horsepower
HPT	High Pressure Turbine
HRH	His Royal Highness
HSA	Hawker Siddeley Aviation
HUD	Head Up Display
IAF	Israeli Air Force
IAI	Israeli Aircraft Industries
IAM	Institute of Aviation Medicine
IAS	Indicated Air Speed
IFPCS	Integrated Flight and Propulsion Control System
IFR	Instrument Flight Rules
IGV	Inlet Guide Vane
ILS	Instrument Landing System
IM	Independent Monitor
IMC	Instrument Meteorological Conditions
IMN	Indicated Mach Number
IR	Instrument Rating
ISA	International Standard Atmosphere

JP	Jet Provost
JP	Junior Pilot
JSF	Joint Strike Fighter
LAE	Licensed Aircraft Engineer
L&D	Lateral and Directional
L/D	Lift over Drag
LE	Leading Edge
LSO	Landing Safety Officer
Lt	Lieutenant
Lt Cdr	Lieutenant Commander
Lt Col	Lieutenant Colonel
MACH	The speed of an aircraft relative to the local speed of sound
MAG	Marine Air Group
MD	Managing Director
MFD	Multifunction Display
MOD	Ministry of Defence
MOD(PE)	Ministry of Defence (Procurement Executive)
MOT	Ministry of Transport
NASA	National Aeronautics and Space Administration
NATC	Naval Air Test Centre
NATO	North Atlantic Treaty Organisation
NAVAIR	Naval Air Systems Command
NCO	Non-Commissioned Officer

NGTE	National Gas Turbine Establishment
NOTAM	Notice to Airmen
NPE	Navy Preliminary Evaluation
OFMC	Old Flying Machine Company
OR	Operational Requirement
OTT	Over the Top
Pax	Patuxent River
PIO	Pilot Induced Oscillation
PJB	Partially Jet-borne
PPL	Private Pilots' License
PR	Public Relations
PRO	Public Relations Officer
R/T	Radio-Telephony
RADA	Royal Academy of Dramatic Arts
RAE	Royal Aircraft Establishment
RAF	Royal Air Force
R&D	Research and Development
RHS	Right Hand Seat
RN	Royal Navy
rpm	Revolutions Per Minute
RRE	Royal Radar Establishment
RW	Runway
SBAC	Society of British Aerospace Companies
SCH	Simplified Combined Harness

SHAR	Sea Harrier
SL	Slow Landing
SME	Structural and Mechanical Engineering
SP	Stagnation Point
Sqn Ldr	Squadron Leader
SST	Supersonic Transport
STO	Short Takeoff
STOVL	Short Takeoff and Vertical Landing
SUV	Sport Utility Vehicle
TAS	True Air Speed
TD	Technology Demonstrator
TLC	Tender Loving Care
TOD	Takeoff Director
TRC	Translational Rate Control
TRG	Training
UAs	Unusual Attitudes
UFCP	Up Front Control Panel
UFO	Unidentified Flying Object
USAF	United States Air Force
USMC	United States Marine Corps
USN	United States Navy
USSR	Union of Soviet Socialist Republics
VAAC	Vectored thrust Aircraft Advanced Control
VG	Variable Gain

435

VG	Vortex Generator
VL	Vertical Landing
VMC	Visual Meteorological Conditions
VSI	Vertical Speed Indicator
VSTOL	Vertical and/or Short Takeoff and Landing
VTO	Vertical Takeoff
Wg Cdr	Wing Commander
WWII	World War Two
WWIII	World War Three